STAR WARS®

ROLEPLAYING GAME

CORUSCANT AND THE CORE WORLDS

CRAIG R. CAREY, CHRIS DOYLE, JASON FRY,
PAUL SUDLOW, JOHN TERRA, DANIEL WALLACE

DESIGNERS
CRAIG R. CAREY, CHRIS DOYLE, JASON FRY,
PAUL SUDLOW, JOHN TERRA, DANIEL WALLACE

DEVELOPERS
CHARLES RYAN, RODNEY THOMPSON

EDITORS
BRIAN CAMPBELL, RAY VALLESE, VAL VALLESE

MANAGING EDITOR
PENNY WILLIAMS

DESIGN MANAGER
CHRISTOPHER PERKINS

ART DIRECTOR
SEAN GLENN, ROBERT RAPER

GRAPHIC DESIGNER
ABIGAIL FEIN, LAURA KERBYSON, CHRIS HANIS

CARTOGRAPHER
TODD GAMBLE

GRAPHIC PRODUCTION SPECIALIST
ANGELIKA LOKOTZ

COVER ARTIST
TOMMY LEE EDWARDS

INTERIOR ARTISTS
ANTHONY WATERS, DANIEL GELON, DARREL
RICHE, SCOTT FISCHER, JON FOSTER, MARC
SASSO, MATT HATTON, RK POST, TOMMY LEE
EDWARDS, VINOD RAMS, LUCASFILM LTD.

CATEGORY MANAGER
ANTHONY VALTERRA

DIRECTOR OF RPG R&D
BILL SLAVICSEK

VICE PRESIDENT OF PUBLISHING
MARY KIRCHOFF

PROJECT MANAGER
MARTIN DURHAM

PRODUCTION MANAGER
CHAS DELONG

LUCAS LICENSING EDITOR
MICHELLE VUCKOVICH

LUCAS LICENSING ART EDITOR
IAIN MORRIS

2 CREDITS

References used for this product include *The Essential Guide to Planets and Moons* by Daniel Wallace (published by The Ballantine Publishing Group); *Star Wars Gamer* Magazine (published by Wizards of the Coast, Inc.); and the "Orbital Shipyard: Duro Delta Twelve" web enhancement by Rob Lazzaretti and Owen K.C. Stephens (originally presented on www.wizards.com/starwars).

U.S., CANADA, ASIA, PACIFIC, & LATIN AMERICA	EUROPEAN HEADQUARTERS
Wizards of the Coast, Inc.	Wizards of the Coast, Belgium
P.O. Box 707	P.B. 2031
Renton WA 98057–0707	2600 Berchem
Questions? 1–800–324–6496	Belgium
	+32–70–23–32–77

Based on the *Star Wars Roleplaying Game* by Andy Collins, Bill Slavicsek, and JD Wiker, utilizing mechanics developed for the new DUNGEONS & DRAGONS® game by Jonathan Tweet, Monte Cook, Skip Williams, Richard Baker, and Peter Adkison.

First Printing: January 2003   620–17663–001–EN
9 8 7 6 5 4 3 2 1

www.wizards.com   **www.starwars.com**

NEW GM CHARACTERS

NEW SPECIES

NEW FEATS

NEW EQUIPMENT

NEW VEHICLES

NEW STARSHIPS

NEW PRESTIGE CLASS

NEW CREATURES

NEW DROIDS

3

CONTENTS
C

Introduction: The Bright Center of Your Campaign

We're talking about Coruscant, the metropolitan city-planet that has anchored the Star Wars galaxy for more than twenty-five thousand years. Combining the sophistication of New York City, the politics of Washington D.C., the history of Rome, the high technology of Tokyo, and the wild dangers of the Amazon, Coruscant is full-to-bursting with an overwhelming amount of everything. The galaxy holds countless worlds, but there is nothing like Coruscant in all of civilized space.

Something for Everyone

This book contains essential information about Coruscant and other major planets throughout the Galactic Core. Players who need a specific planet of origin for their heroes or who wish to know more about the history, people, customs, and noteworthy locations of a specific world in the Galactic Core have ready access to this information.

The sections titled For the GM contain adventure seeds and game statistics to help Gamemasters stage encounters and build lavish, planet-based campaigns set on Coruscant and the other Core Worlds covered in this book. These sections also describe new alien species, creatures, droids, and feats that GMs can introduce into their games. If you are a player, do not read these sections, since doing so might spoil some of the surprises your GM has planned for future adventures.

A World for Heroes

More than a trillion citizens call Coruscant home. Having all the heroes in a campaign hail from Coruscant isn't unusual—it should almost be expected. Even if the heroes are visiting the capital for the first time, Coruscant offers unique opportunities for members of any heroic class.

The fringer, by definition, hails from somewhere other than the Galactic Core. A fringer might be drawn to Coruscant by wanderlust, curiosity, or a need to join the rest of galactic civilization. A fringer might find work as a freelancer or simply follow the lead of someone else in the adventuring party. Unscrupulous Coruscanti might try to dupe credulous-looking fringers, but savvy fringer heroes can often turn the tables on smug Core-worlders who perceive them as dim-witted yokels.

The noble is in her element on Coruscant. Whether she is a native or visiting the planet for political or business reasons, a noble can find plenty of opportunities to make new contacts, call in favors, or engage in diplomatic ventures. The noble keeps one finger on the pulse of the planet and knows where the heroes might find action and adventure on Coruscant.

The scoundrel, like the noble, is at home on Coruscant. The city's seedy underbelly is a playground for smugglers and thieves, while con artists and gamblers can find easy pickings kilometers above ground in the gleaming skyscraper penthouses of the decadent and well-to-do.

A scout seems better suited for roaming the galactic frontier, but a resourceful scout can find a lifetime of work in the Core. A scout might attract the attention of employers who desire a professional explorer to reconnoiter Coruscant's sublevels, to unearth secrets and treasures of the city-planet's ancient past, or to track down an escaped beast.

A soldier could find himself in the government's uniformed service during one of the three major eras of play, as a member of the Republic Judicial Department, the vast Imperial Military, or the New Republic Army and Navy. Underworld overlords periodically draft soldiers of fortune for shady yet lucrative ventures, and even legitimate Coruscanti business interests sometimes hire military specialists and mercenaries to pull off difficult jobs.

There's no shortage of work for a tech specialist on Coruscant. The planet is the most industrialized world in the galaxy, and its computer systems are unequaled. A particularly talented tech specialist might find work repairing ancient bits of technology for a billionaire collector or slicing into the Imperial Information Center, and powerful Coruscanti patrons are always looking for "tech talent."

No matter what the era, Coruscant serves as an interesting destination for a Force adept. During the Old Republic, a Force adept's lack of Jedi training could draw the curiosity of the Jedi Council, which might try to reeducate the odd maverick. During the Empire's rule, Force adepts are more likely to escape notice on Imperial Center than Jedi, although a careless Force-user will almost certainly be approached by Palpatine's agents for "routine questioning." Force adepts during the time of the New Republic might come to Coruscant to learn more about Luke Skywalker's Jedi training program or learn secrets of the Force from stolen Jedi and Sith holocrons.

The Jedi guardian and the Jedi consular are at home on Coruscant during the Rise of the Empire era. They know the city, its institutions, and the key locations surrounding the Jedi Temple. After Emperor Palpatine takes the throne, survivors of the Jedi Purge flee Coruscant to avoid the Emperor's dark side Jedi-hunters. Jedi guardians and Jedi consulars will not become common again until Luke Skywalker institutes his Jedi academy seven years after the Battle of Endor.

A Campaign on Coruscant

The opportunities for adventure on Coruscant are boundless, regardless of the era of play. No matter how far back in history one goes, Corsucant has been a sprawling cityscape inhabited by politicians, greedy business consortiums, and people from every walk of life. Even the intrusion of the Yuuzhan Vong cannot destroy all that defines Coruscant. That said, here are some points a GM should consider when using Coruscant during the three major eras of play.

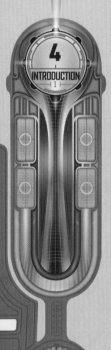

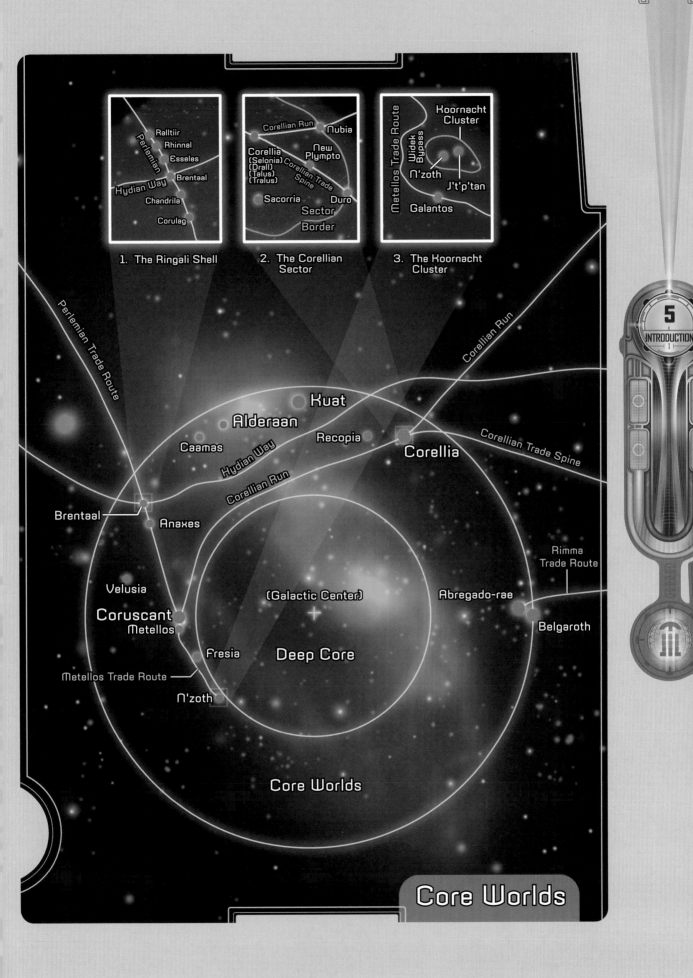

1. The Ringali Shell

Ralltiir
Rhinnal
Perlemian
Esseles
Hydian Way
Brentaal
Chandrila
Corulag

2. The Corellian Sector

Corellian Run
Nubia
Corellia (Selonia) (Drall) (Talus) (Tralus)
New Plympto
Corellian Trade Spine
Sacorria
Duro
Sector Border

3. The Koornacht Cluster

Metellos Trade Route
Koornacht Cluster
Widek Bypass
N'zoth
J't'p'tan
Galantos

Perlemian Trade Route

Corellian Run

Kuat

Alderaan

Caamas

Recopia

Hydian Way

Corellia

Corellian Trade Spine

Corellian Run

Brentaal

Anaxes

Rimma Trade Route

Velusia

(Galactic Center)

Abregado-rae

Coruscant
Metellos

Belgaroth

Fresia

Deep Core

Metellos Trade Route

N'zoth

Core Worlds

Core Worlds

Rise of the Empire Era

During the Rise of the Empire era, Coruscant is very cosmopolitan. Despite the growing corruption of the Senate, the "capital planet" is still enjoying a golden age. The Jedi maintain a strong presence on Coruscant, and local criminal syndicates keep a low profile. Alien species enjoy all the rights and privileges of the indigenous Human population, and the planet remains largely untouched by the widespread problems of the galaxy at large—even during the rise of Count Dooku's Confederacy of Independent Systems.

Rebellion Era

Following the Clone Wars, the Empire takes control of Coruscant. The Rebellion era marks a significant change in the culture of Coruscant. Aliens who were once welcomed are now persecuted and denied the basic rights of citizenship. Entrepreneurs and smugglers must contend with tediously restrictive customs and immigration policies, and nobles must ensure that their spoken words echo the teachings and philosophies of the New Order. The Jedi are gone—wiped out during the Purge or forced to flee to backwater worlds. Many Imperial citizens, however, consider "Imperial Center" glorious and regard Palpatine as a demigod. Members of the Rebel Alliance consider a trip to Coruscant a bold—if not foolhardy—venture at best and a death sentence at worst.

The New Jedi Order Era

In the years leading up to the New Jedi Order era, the New Republic establishes a fragile government on Coruscant despite the Empire's efforts to recapture the planet. The Yuuzhan Vong invasion of the galaxy twenty-one years after the Battle of Endor effectively turns Coruscant into a "fortress world," as Chief of State Borsk Fey'lya diverts military resources to protect the seat of government. Fey'lya's efforts fail, and two years into the war the Yuuzhan Vong capture the galactic capital. Immediately they begin transforming the planet into their mythical homeworld of Yuuzhan'tar by turning the cities into jungles. Heroes on Coruscant after its occupation will discover a bizarrely altered landscape and plenty of opportunities to strike at the enemy in guerrilla-style raids.

Coruscant and Beyond

Of course, most heroes won't be content to remain on the "capital planet" for long. Adventures will lead them to other destinations in the urbane Galactic Core, but Coruscant might be their home base. A quick visit to Corellia could lead to shady dealings in the scrapyards on Belgaroth, from there to a firefight in the streets of Esseles, and after that to a villain's stronghold on Ralltiir.

Enjoy this passport to the Core, playground of the nobles, where a mix of intellect and arrogance can get you far . . . maybe farther than a sneer and a blaster pistol.

Coruscant

Planet Type: Terrestrial
Climate: Temperate
Terrain: Urban cityscape
Atmosphere: Breathable
Gravity: Standard
Diameter: 12,240 km
Length of Day: 24 standard hours
Length of Year: 368 standard days
Sentient Species: Human, many alien species
Languages: Basic
Population: 1 trillion
Species Mix: 68% Human, 32% other
Government: Republic or dictatorship (depending on era)
Major Exports: None
Major Imports: Foodstuffs, medicinal goods
System/Star: Coruscant

Planets	Type	Moons
Revisse	Molten rock	0
Platoril	Barren rock	0
Vandor–1	Barren rock	0
Vandor–2	Barren rock	0
Vandor–3	Terrestrial	0
Coruscant	Terrestrial	4
Muscave	Gas giant	21
Stentat	Gas giant	23
Improcco	Ice ball	1
The Covey	Asteroid field	—
Nabatu	Barren rock	0
Ulabos	Frozen rock	0
Obo Rin	Comet cluster	—

Description

"An incandescent organ of life, visibly vibrating with the pulses of billions." That's legendary Chancellor Signet Mezzileen speaking of Coruscant, the planet he ruled for over seventy years and praised as "the galaxy's biggest little neighborhood." Contrast that with poet Adder Ain-la's famous denunciation of the Republic capital: "A dead metal shell of a world, Coruscant is soulless beyond salvation, so cold and empty its frozen carcass must be reheated with solar mirrors."

Neither commentary is right or wrong. Coruscant is the type of world that can be both spectacular and frightening, where indigents are sheltered in the shadow of restaurants selling food at ten thousand credits per plate. One thing it will never be is predictable—or dull.

From space, "the jewel of the Core Worlds" can almost be mistaken for an artificial construct. Where other worlds have forests, grasslands, and oceans, Coruscant has factories, skyscrapers, and aquifers. Every scrap of surface area, except for the tiny polar ice caps, has been smothered by a dense layer of urbanization. In many places, this layer is covered by another layer, then another and another, creating canyons that plunge vertically for kilometers. Even the Manarai mountain range, surely the planet's most distinctive feature in eons past, is now a mere swelling in the omnipresent cityscape, dusted in snow.

Monument Plaza is a bowl-shaped arena built around one of the lesser Manarai mountaintops. The place where the bare rock of the summit projects up through the center of the arena floor is one of the planet's most popular tourist attractions.

Orbital traffic encloses the planet like electrons around a nucleus, delivering food and supplies, ambassadors and tourists. Magnetic guidance lines organize atmospheric traffic into rows on a rigid grid. Landing platforms hovering among the traffic lanes accommodate the few private starships that are permitted to break orbit. Airbuses and air taxis ferry Coruscant's citizens, while cargo transfer passes through freight tunnels underground. Pipelines suck water from the polar ice caps and store it in reservoirs, which sometimes do double duty as aesthetic attractions for the locals—as in the so-called "Western Sea."

Many expanses of Coruscant, particularly those in the western hemisphere, are churning industrial powerhouses, sparsely populated but constantly generating energy and finished goods. Most of the planet's population is concentrated around the equator and in Imperial City—a metropolis the size of a continent and distinguished from the surrounding conurbation by its sheer height. The lowest levels of Imperial City (formerly known as Republic City) have not seen daylight in tens of thousands of years. Descending to ground level is like climbing into the depths of a murk-cave on Af'El—and nearly as dangerous. Haywire droids, carnivorous fungi, and mutated troglodytes run rampant in this terrifying shadow world.

But it's possible, and even expected, for Coruscanti to live their entire lives kilometers removed from the unpleasantness of the depths. Everything they need is a short walk or a flitter ride away, and the politicians for whom Coruscant is a second home have made sure the planet is never lacking in luxury.

History

For as long as there have been records, Coruscant has been the heart of the civilized galaxy. Whether the

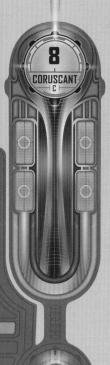

Human species originated on Coruscant remains a mystery. Many Humans believe this is the case—if only to bolster their Humanocentric political agendas. One of the planet's oldest recorded tales is the lyrical epic *Dha Werda Verda*, which recounts a clash between the Taungs and the Battalions of Zhell. A volcanic eruption is said to have buried the Zhell in fire and ash and inspired the Taungs to become menacing "Warriors of the Shadow." Like all legends, the details and date of *Dha Werda Verda* are unverifiable—geologists say the planet hasn't experienced volcanism in ages—but the tale of conquest says much about the culture of Coruscant.

Paleontologists believe most of Coruscant was already paved over by the time interstellar flight became common. Such rampant overpopulation forced the inhabitants to develop the first atmosphere scrubbers, hydroponic farms, delivery pipelines, and recycling plants. Rather than burying unrecyclable garbage, they developed cannons that shot waste canisters into orbit, where waiting scows towed them out-system.

The widespread dissemination of hyperdrive technology accelerated Coruscant's ultradevelopment. The planet found itself at the confluence of a number of lengthy hyperroutes—including those later named the Martial Cross, the Shawken Spur, the Koros Trunk Line, the Metellos Trade Route, the Perlemian Trade Route, and the Corellian Run. Despite its proximity to the unnavigable Deep Core, it became a nexus of trade, commerce, and exploration. Other Core Worlds, such as Corellia and Duro, became key players in the burgeoning Republic, but few argued that Coruscant deserved its honored station as seat of the galactic government.

Millennia passed and the Republic grew, but Coruscant was much the same—only *thicker*. Advanced architectural technology allowed new buildings to be built atop old ones without risk of structural collapse. As enterprise climbed higher and higher, the lowest levels were abandoned to disrepair and claimed by low-income contract workers and squatters. The most spectacular new constructions were concentrated in the eastern hemisphere north of the Manarais, in a district that was coming to be known as Republic City.

As Republic City expanded horizontally and vertically, iconic structures sprang up to reflect the glory of the star-spanning civilization. The Presidential Palace was a showpiece residence for the supreme chancellor, while Senate Hall was a cavernous political arena with benches of polished stone. The Republic's chancellors ran the gamut from the hawkish to the incompetent to the truly inspiring. There were internal crises—revolutions, scandals, coup attempts—but the ship of state sailed on through plentiful waters for centuries.

There were external threats as well. Discovery of new alien cultures sometimes led to conflicts in which Coruscant itself was a battleground, as was the case during first contact with the Duinuogwuin. Coruscant was nearly captured by the Sith Empire during the Great Hyperspace War, and a thousand years later the planet was again ravaged by Sith disciple Ulic Qel-Droma and the masked warriors of Mandalore.

Landmarks changed as history moved on. The Galactic Senate Chamber, with its floating delegate platforms, replaced Senate Hall. The Jedi Temple was erected as the seat of Jedi leadership shifted from Ossus to Coruscant. The new Republic Executive Building accommodated governmental overflow from the Presidential Palace.

The capital planet knew absolute peace for generations, but the atmosphere of contentment gave root to idle corruption. By the time of Supreme Chancellor Valorum's election, few on Coruscant held romantic notions of their government's ability to serve the common good. The invasion of Naboo proved that weak leadership led to chaos, and Senator Palpatine was elected in a landslide. But even Palpatine couldn't prevent Count Dooku's separatists from threatening the integrity of the Republic that had stood for a thousand generations. War was now inevitable, and the Clone Wars did what no enemy could ever have hoped to accomplish. The Republic fell, supplanted by an Empire created in Palpatine's image.

Emperor Palpatine did much more to Coruscant than renaming it Imperial Center (and applying the associated labels Imperial City and the Imperial Palace). He instituted the social concept of Human High Culture, which quickly spread to the other Core Worlds but which always held the most sway on Coruscant. As a consequence of the diminished status of non-Humans, the Empire established a walled-off Alien Protection Zone (unofficially known as the Invisible Sector or Invisec) in Imperial City to segregate "unclean" species that did not have slave permits from their owners.

The Human residents of Coruscant had more wealth than ever before, to such a degree that most never considered the price in personal freedom. Their charmed existence lasted until three years after the Emperor's death, when the New Republic captured the planet. Surprisingly few Coruscanti died during the battle, but the ensuing outbreak of the Krytos virus decimated the non-Human districts.

A few years into the New Republic's tenure, forces loyal to the resurrected Emperor seized the planet and devastated it through vicious infighting. At first, those envious of the privileged in Imperial City took pleasure in their discomfort, but as the misery increased, Coruscant became an object of pity. The New Republic soon recaptured the planet and poured billions of credits into relief efforts, but restoration could not bring back lost lives.

Coruscant returned to its former glory over the next fourteen years, at which point the Yuuzhan Vong arrived to menace the galaxy. Two years into their invasion, the aliens advanced into the Core far enough to strike at Coruscant. A massive naval attack, combined with the despicable tactic of forcing refugee vessels into the planet's energy shield, brought down Coruscant's defenses. Chief of State Borsk Fey'lya died in the invasion, and the cityscape suffered irreparable damage.

Yuuzhan Vong shapers began the task of transforming Coruscant into the image of Yuuzhan'tar, their long-vanished homeworld. Powerful dovin basals shifted the planet's orbit closer to its sun, raising the temperature and turning a cold world tropical. All four moons crumbled into rubble, forming a wide rainbow ring the survivors called the Bridge. Biological seeding spread across the cityscape until vegetation many meters thick covered all visible surface area.

People

Before the planet's transformation, visitors from pastoral worlds viewed Monument Plaza as the epitome of all that was wrong with Coruscant, equating the bare mountain-top with an animal placed in a zoo while its fellows are bulldozed into extinction. Native Coruscanti cared little for such criticisms. They knew they lived in the bright center of the universe—any nagging by outsiders could only be the result of jealousy.

Coruscanti are the most well educated people in the galaxy. For that reason, they can be highly controversial. While others respect their sophistication, they also view Coruscanti as insufferably arrogant. Native Coruscanti often act bored when traveling offworld, and they view visitors to their planet ("tourists," they call them, whether they are or not) with inborn insolence.

Humans were the most populous species on Coruscant prior to the Yuuzhan Vong, but aliens from every corner of the Rim and Core also made their homes in the city-planet. In terms of number of species, Coruscant had the greatest diversity of any world in the galaxy—though one would have never known it during the Rebellion era. Some non-Human Coruscanti have bitter memories of living in the city's forgotten sublevels or within the walled confines of the Alien Protection Zone.

Locations

Descriptions of several key locations follow.

Skyhooks

In the years prior to its capture by the Yuuzhan Vong, Coruscant had more tourist attractions than most star systems had within the totality of their borders. Orbital skyhooks were one of the sights that impressed visitors from more sedate Rim worlds. Skyhooks were tethered satellites in low geosynchronous orbits that featured waterfalls and manicured gardens in their bowl-shaped interiors underneath the arch of transparisteel domes. Visitors reached a skyhook by boarding a turbolift car on Coruscant's surface and riding all the way up the turbolift shaft found inside each orbital tether. Some skyhooks were more than a kilometer in diameter and were known as playgrounds for the rich. Both Emperor Palpatine and Black Sun's Prince Xizor had opulent personal skyhooks. Once the New Republic captured Coruscant three years after the Battle of Endor, the government grounded all skyhooks for safety reasons.

The Imperial Palace

The colossal pyramid of the Imperial Palace dominated the skyline of Imperial City, leaving lesser structures in its arrogant and indifferent shadow. Dazzling transparisteel crystals twinkled amid the unfathomable tons of gray-green rock that formed the palace exterior, and the interior courts were miniature masterworks featuring

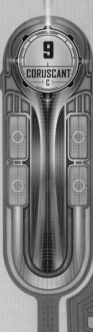

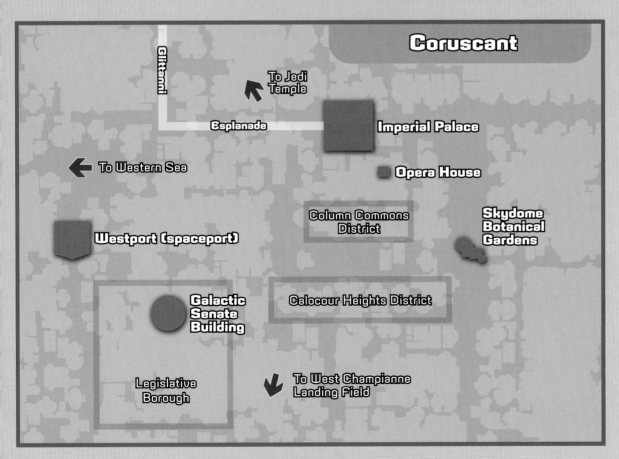

Coruscant

Glittani

To Jedi Temple

Esplanade

Imperial Palace

Opera House

To Western Sea

Column Commons District

Skydome Botanical Gardens

Westport (spaceport)

Galactic Senate Building

Calocour Heights District

Legislative Borough

To West Champianne Landing Field

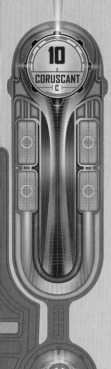

hanging gardens, marble pyramids, and zero-gravity fountains. The palace contained over twenty thousand chambers and over fifty connected structures, including a rumored treasure compartment built by the legendary "pirate general" Toleph-Sor.

The Grand Corridor served as the palace's main passageway, linking the Council Chamber with the assemblage auditorium. It was said that the Grand Corridor was so spacious it could accommodate an entire Star Destroyer beneath its vaulted ceiling. Twin rows of greenish-purple ch'hala trees lined the corridor's main walkway until the New Republic discovered their vibration-sensitive bark was part of an Imperial eavesdropping system. The residential areas of the palace, including the exclusive wood-paneled President's Guests floor, were reachable from the Grand Corridor, though the chief of state's quarters were located deep in the palace core with "windows" showing real-time holograms of the view outside. Emperor Palpatine's throne room sat near the palace roof so prismatic skylights could illuminate the raised pedestal where he sat.

Outlying areas of the palace included a full medical wing and the Mon Calamari Inglenook, a humid annex designed to resemble a coral reef with an enclosed pool circulating around the clear-walled rooms. The lowest floor of the palace contained the War Room, the Admiral's Office, and the Crypt, a computer slicing and decoding center. In the Coruscant bedrock beneath the military floor lay the Imperial Information Center, which contained everything from ancient hyperspace maps to the plans for the first Death Star. Despite the palace's celebrated history, much of the place is now gone forever. When the Yuuzhan Vong invaded Coruscant, Chief of State Borsk Fey'lya detonated a suicide bomb and took out 20,000 enemy warriors. A good chunk of the Imperial Palace went with them.

Glitannai Esplanade

Glitannai Esplanade was one of the most storied avenues in Imperial City, running along the broad-topped buildings of the Judicial Plaza. The ritziest shops and tastiest restaurants were found here, plying their wares to well-heeled tourists in the morning shadow of the Imperial Palace. The Imperial Fair (known as the Galactic Fair in other eras) was a traditional Coruscant celebration on Glitannai Esplanade incorporating dancing, acrobatics, shopping, technology exhibits, food pavilions, and a massive parade of military might. From the surrounding spires, thousands watched as the parade ended in the *Pliada di am Imperium*. There, at the base of the Imperial Palace, dignitaries would bestow blessings on the crowd from an open-air balcony.

The Galactic Senate Chamber

The Galactic Senate Chamber was another of Coruscant's striking edifices. Fronted by impressionistic statues, the chamber was built many levels above the site of the original Senate Hall in which Vodo Siosk-Baas and Exar Kun battled to the death. The Senate Rotunda contained 1,024 floating platforms, each belonging to a regional or sectorial Senator, forming a microcosm of the civilized galaxy. Directly behind each senatorial platform, delegates could retreat to a narrow slice of offices built to accommodate the environmental needs of each specific species.

Emperor Palpatine closed the Galactic Senate Chamber when he dissolved the Imperial Senate, and the New Republic convened its legislature in a newly constructed building called Senate Hall. Thirteen years after Endor, Senate Hall was damaged in a bombing, causing the New Republic to commission a new structure, the Grand Convocation Chamber. The original Galactic Senate Chamber came into the spotlight one final time when the Yuuzhan Vong used it as an aquatic habitat for their planet-shaping worldbrain.

The Jedi Temple

The foundations of the Jedi Temple were among the oldest on Coruscant. The Jedi Knights maintained a continual presence on the capital planet since before the birth of the Republic, but for many millennia, their primary base was on Ossus. After the fiery devastation of Ossus during the Sith War, the Senate approved funding for a greatly expanded Jedi Temple. Engineers expanded the existing foundation to create a massive edifice that could house tens of thousands of individuals.

Atop the blocky dormitory slab, five spires—one in the center and one at each corner—reached for the vault of Coruscant's crowded sky. The central spire held the most sacred Jedi holocrons. Three of the surrounding four towers were home to the Council of First Knowledge (home to Jedi scholars), the Council of Reconciliation (home to Jedi diplomats), and the Reassignment Council (home to Jedi "career counselors" who dealt with students not accepted as Padawan learners). The final tower held the famous Jedi Council Chamber, where the twelve members of the ruling Jedi Council convened.

From the outside, the Jedi Temple sometimes showed its age with flaking paint and cracks in the ferrocrete, but inside, the Jedi Order enjoyed state-of-the-art holographic equipment and military training gear. Jedi recordkeepers boasted that if they didn't have an item in their exhaustive Archive Library, then it didn't exist. After Palpatine's ascension to the Imperial throne, he closed the temple, but the ancient foundations were still in place at the time of the Yuuzhan Vong invasion.

The Western Sea

Coruscant locals who frequented the Western Sea could almost fool themselves into thinking they had traveled to a coastal resort on some tropical planet, even though the sea was merely an artificial aquifer. During the height of the Republic, the Western Sea hosted boat rentals and all-hours entertainment clubs on its shores, while "islands" (actually sand beds placed on top of rafts made from plasteel drums) floated lazily across the surface and catered to the very rich. Long-winged sea shrikes, imported from offworld, nested in the towers overlooking the reservoir and fed on schools of tiny, phosphorescent fish. During the Yuuzhan Vong invasion of Coruscant, the Western Sea was punctured by falling starships.

The aquifer drained out through the holes in its floor, flooding the lowest levels of the cityscape and drowning hundreds.

The Coruscant Opera House

The Coruscant Opera House was one of Imperial City's most ornate landmarks, bearing the elaborate design touches of indulgent pre-Republic architecture. From the Old Republic to the New, performances never ceased on the stage of the Opera House. Emperor Palpatine often attended premiere nights, sitting in a balcony that had formerly been reserved for Valorum family members for over five hundred years. The Coruscant Opera House accommodated an audience of two thousand in the traditional theater design, with an orchestra pit, tiered seating, and private balconies. In addition, a number of galleries were located directly underneath the floor, where those not wealthy enough to hold tickets for the main amphitheater could watch the performance via real-time hologram.

Skydome Botanical Gardens

Skydome Botanical Gardens attracted two types of visitors: bookish botanists and those who simply loved beautiful things. Skydome possessed some of the rarest forms of plant life in the galaxy, and public tours of the facility sold out months in advance. Of course, not all Skydome's collections were made available for public viewing. Two and a half tons of meat were needed every month to satiate the ravenous plants in the Carnivorous Flora exhibit, while the Poisonous Flora exhibit was off limits to anyone not wearing a biological hazard suit.

Westport

Westport was the starport most commonly associated with Imperial City. Though the city had other public spaceports—Eastport, Newport, and the West Championne landing field among them—the bustling aerodrome of Westport enjoyed a favorable location near the Imperial Palace and the Legislative Borough. Though the floating platforms seen throughout Imperial City may have looked attractive to a novice looking for a parking spot, they were usually reserved for Jedi or high-level government officials.

The Calocour Heights

The marketing district known as the Calocour Heights resembled a miniature Corporate Sector. Located south of the Imperial Palace, the Heights teemed with pushy survey-takers, free product samples floating on repulsorlift carts, and flashing, musical billboards. The Heights was also home to the galaxy's most cutthroat marketing and communications agencies, including SchaumAssoc and NullComm. A person seeking leading-edge gadgets would do well to visit the Heights, though the price tag would probably make a miser faint.

Column Commons

The publishing district called Column Commons fell between the Imperial Palace and the Calocour Heights. This mid-level district featured large, open areas interspersed with fat columns that supported the "ceiling" levels of cityscape overhead. Hundreds of holodrama and newsnet publishers kept offices here, along with all the major news bureaus, including TriNebulon and Nova Network. The businesspeople of "the Commons" boasted that nothing escaped their notice, and they considered it their solemn obligation to pass along this information to the consumer through limited edition datatexts and pay-per-read newsnet articles. During the Rebellion era, Column Commons crawled with COMPNOR "truth officers" who ensured that everything published was in line with the tenets of the New Order.

The Southern Underground

As one moved away from Imperial City, the cityscape grew seedier, but it didn't get truly dangerous until one moved down. Deep in the shadow levels where sunlight never reached, the destitute and the desperate scratched out a passable living. The Southern Underground district contained a hemispherical shopping center stuffed with run-down stores and impromptu barter stalls. The Crystal Jewel was perhaps the most infamous of the cantinas near the Underground, boasting on its sign "If the customers don't kill you, the drinks will." Anyone who visited the Southern Underground quickly learned to keep one hand on his credit pouch and the other hand on his blaster.

The Invisible Sector

If possible, the Invisible Sector—called Invisec by the locals and the Alien Protection Zone by Imperial apologists—was even more dangerous than the Southern Underground. Emperor Palpatine relocated all the more obvious non-Human species to Invisec several years into his reign, walling off the new ghetto with impassable ferrocrete barriers. Blaster-toting stormtroopers patrolled the borders, making sure that anyone passing in or out had proper documentation.

It goes without saying that aliens hated Invisec, and any Human visiting the district would attract unfriendly glares at best or a vibroblade to the ribs at worst. The district was a breeding ground for every sort of illegal activity from forgery to black marketeering to bare-knuckled pit fighting. Since Imperial officers seldom ventured inside the walls to see what the aliens were doing, Invisec became a sanctuary for guerrilla-style resistance against Imperial rule. The Alien Combine was one of several anti-Imperial, anti-Human groups that sprang up in Invisec, though one of their number—a Bothan pilot named Asyr Sei'lar—helped Rogue Squadron agents topple Ysanne Isard three years after the Battle of Endor.

Garbage Pits

Five thousand garbage pits dotted the bowels of Coruscant's cityscape, visible from the highest levels due to the necessity of providing an unobstructed field of fire for their waste-disposal cannons. These obligatory eyesores were two kilometers wide and three kilometers

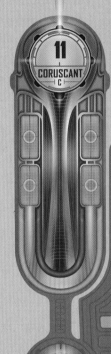

deep, covered with four convex accelerator shields stacked vertically. Hundreds of 10-meter-diameter holes perforated each shield. Every five seconds, the automated cannon sitting in the watery sewage at the base of the pit would fire a spray of canisters through the holes in the accelerator shields, where tractor fields would boost the canisters into a safe orbit high above Coruscant. Substances that could be recycled were often dumped into the pits to be digested by wet, coiling throngs of hundred-meter-long garbage worms.

Orbital Mirrors

Far above the surface of Coruscant, hundreds of Orbital Solar Energy Transfer Satellites (OSETS) act as miniature suns. Moving in synch with the planet's rotation, they deploy their broad mirrors to catch sunlight and reflect it down upon the northern and southern latitudes. Without the OSETS mirrors to heat Coruscant's air currents, WeatherNet would be unable to control the seasons, and those living near polar climes would have to pay twice as much to heat their buildings.

Each OSETS mirror consists of a small crew module and two silvery, reflective panels, hundreds of meters on a side but less than a millimeter thick. The crew module can accommodate up to six technicians, but forces them to share a single sleeping chamber. During the Rebellion era, the cramped quarters and mind-numbing boredom of OSETS duty ("riding the mirror," as it was known in technician slang) inspired the Imperial Navy to assign ineffectual officers to "command" the satellites as punishment. Since OSETS mirrors were usually controlled from WeatherNet stations on the ground, these officers weren't even allowed the dignity of directing their path through space.

If OSETS mirrors are cupped into a tight concave configuration, the diffused sunlight can become a concentrated, superheated beam. On two occasions the New Republic used orbital mirrors as makeshift weapons—once to melt a groundside building during the invasion of Coruscant, and again to overwhelm the invisibility cloak of the Shadow Academy.

WeatherNet

The Weather Control Network, or WeatherNet, modulates the seasons on Coruscant. Ages ago, the planet's rampant urbanization started to play havoc with seasonal climate changes, and WeatherNet originally began as an attempt to control the destructive "microclimes" that conjured thunderstorms inside city-canyons and tornadoes above factory thermals. An excerpt from WeatherNet's ambitious mission statement read "The rain may never fall until after sundown, and by eight the morning fog must disappear." Though the government said that's how conditions are on Coruscant, lifelong residents know that WeatherNet is unable to iron out every climatic anomaly. In addition to regulating precipitation, WeatherNet guides the passing of Coruscant's seasons by circulating air currents and tweaking the atmosphere's concentrations of nitrogen, oxygen, and carbon dioxide through Atmospheric Reclamation Complex Project (ARCP) substations.

Any deviations from scheduled weather patterns are announced well in advance on the public Holonet.

WeatherNet's control building, crowned with a thicket of vanes and balloon tethers, is located in the Boribos Prefecture north of Imperial City. The redundant nature of WeatherNet's equipment makes it virtually impossible to knock the system offline. For all the effort that goes into regulating Coruscant's environment, the irony of WeatherNet is that so many of the planet's citizens spend their lives indoors.

After the Yuuzhan Vong takeover of Coruscant, most of WeatherNet is smashed and unusable. However, the seeding of vegetation all across the planet has supplanted WeatherNet's original function, employing natural biochemical processes to freshen the planet's atmosphere and maintain a consistent (and newly tropical) temperature.

The Polar Ice Caps

When recycling and importing could no longer slack the thirst of Coruscant's citizenry, government officials opened the polar ice caps to private water utilities. Both the north and south pole are fringed with capacious pipelines that run toward the populous equator like the spokes of a wheel. Every year the circular ice sheets get a little smaller, a fact that worries the operators of the various polar resorts. Coruscanti who want to climb glaciers, go turbo-skiing, or simply experience the foreign sensation of snow can book vacations at these resorts, which bear names such as the Moonlight Crystal Lodge and the Iceflake Inn.

The poles have no accommodations for starships, and sensor monitoring of the polar orbital corridors is lax. Ships that want to "sneak" into Imperial City often have greater success if they approach from the poles. During the New Republic's invasion of Coruscant, a small strike team first secured the north pole before troop carriers landed the main ground force. After the Yuuzhan Vong's takeover of the capital planet, alien engineers shifted Coruscant's orbit closer to its sun. The polar ice caps melted completely, and tangled greenery took root in the formerly barren environments.

Xizor's Castle

The average citizens of Coruscant gazed at Prince Xizor's castle with a mix of envy and awe, amazed to see what sort of house was suitable for a trillionaire. Xizor, a Falleen of royal blood, started construction on his castle during the latter decades of the Republic, using a fraction of his fortune as head of Xizor Transport Systems to raze the historic Farfalla skyscraper east of the Presidential Palace and build a new tower from the subfoundations up. Following the Clone Wars, Xizor cultivated a close relationship with Emperor Palpatine, and his castle grew in magnificence. It remained one of Imperial City's splendors until its destruction shortly before the Battle of Endor.

What the public never knew was that Xizor also led the Black Sun crime syndicate. The Falleen prince's illegal operations necessitated top-of-the-line castle security systems. Holocameras and armed guards watched over the

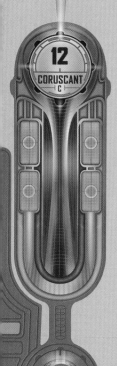

castle's ballrooms, combat chambers, meditation gardens, landing pads, guest suites, and treasure vaults. Xizor's vaults held wonders both real and intangible, including the only known copy of the Perlemian Charter and datafiles stuffed with dirt on Coruscant's political elite.

Despite the millions spent on security, Xizor's castle proved surprisingly vulnerable to internal sabotage—after infiltrating the structure, Lando Calrissian collapsed it by dropping a thermal detonator down the trash chute. The Imperial government claimed the disaster had been planned all along as part of a new construction project, then built a new Imperial Security Operations building in its place. During the New Republic's rule, the tower served as the Coruscant headquarters of the Bothan Spynet. It was rumored that the Bothans had successfully recreated Xizor's entire library of blackmail datafiles.

Petrax Historic Quarter

One of the oldest continually inhabited areas of the planet is the Petrax Quarter, a grouping of unremarkable skyscrapers slightly north of Imperial City. Archaeologists believe that Coruscant's vertical architecture started here and spread out across the rest of the planet. Though none of the ancient structures are still extant—the modern towers stand atop hundreds of meters of packed rubble—urban archaeologists have drilled deep into the ground for core samples, recovering artifacts such as cups, styluses, engraved glass fragments, and lightsaber handles.

The modern residents of the Petrax Quarter tend to be middle-income Humans employed in the service and manufacturing industries. The district does little to promote its historic status, though treasure seekers can sometimes find odd relics scattered amid the sublevels.

After the arrival of a Yuuzhan Vong occupation force on Coruscant, the bottom levels of the Petrax Quarter became the headquarters for a homegrown resistance movement of shopkeepers turned guerrilla fighters.

Galactic Museum

The Galactic Museum sits in the heart of Imperial City, just one kilometer south of the Imperial Palace. For over 12,000 years it has been the galaxy's premier repository for artifacts worth preserving. The museum's exhibit wings—each of which can take days to explore—include Annals of the Republic, The History of Hyperdrive, Flora and Fauna, Planetary Cultures, Masterpieces of Expression, and The Jedi Order.

The artifacts held by the Galactic Museum number well into the billions. Less than 1% are displayed in the actual museum; millions of other relics are stored in an archive building in Coruscant's Coco district. The bulk of the museum's holdings (the archival, less tourist-friendly items) are contained in massive underground vaults on the frozen moon that orbits Improcco. Since all three sites are a tempting target for thieves, museum security is top-notch. Anyone who visits the Galactic Museum has his image captured by security cameras, making it an unwelcome destination for anyone in trouble with the authorities.

During the Rebellion era, Emperor Palpatine sealed off the Jedi wing, and the Annals of the Republic hall was renamed "The New Order: The Glories of the Next Thousand Generations." Few artifacts were destroyed, however, and the New Republic government quickly restored the Galactic Museum to its original state. It remains to be seen how many of the museum's relics will survive the Yuuzhan Vong occupation.

Monument Plaza

For countless generations the bowl of Monument Plaza has encircled the summit of Umate, one of the highest peaks in the Manarai mountain range. Every day, thousands of curious visitors stand in the shadow of the protruding granite lump. Tourists flock to Monument Plaza with a sense of unsettled curiosity, scarcely believing that this is the only spot in the cityscape where one can touch true rock.

The surrounding mall is more interesting than the peak itself. Designed in the epic architectural style of the Hasennan period, it resembles a sports arena with the summit of Umate sitting at the center of the playing field. Heroic statues and colorful banners decorate the grounds, while restaurants and souvenir shops are built into the plaza walls. Chipping flakes of rock from the peak is, of course, forbidden, and such vandalism is prevented by the members of a local religious sect. Calling themselves the Flames of Umate, the robe-wearing disciples meditate while touching the rock in an effort to

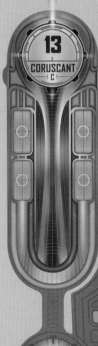

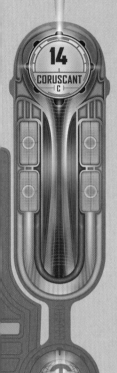

commune with the "world-spirit" in Coruscant's molten core. Admission to Monument Plaza is free, and it is open at all hours.

Grand Reception Hall

Located near the historic Petrax district, the Grand Reception Hall is the oldest continuously operated government building on Coruscant. Built during the time of the Old Republic, the building lies relatively close to the surface of the planet. Modern skyscrapers stretch up for kilometers on every side. Only a small window of sky can be seen through the Grand Reception Hall's open-air ceiling, and the shadows are so deep that aircars descending "the well" have to switch on their running lights.

The Grand Reception Hall is a rectangular stone structure more than a kilometer in length. The main floor features a landing pad for shuttles and aircars, which drop straight down through the open roof. Thousands of glassed-in balconies overlook the main floor, each one decorated with the banner of a Republic member world or star sector. Throughout the centuries of the ancient Republic, the Supreme Chancellor greeted arriving foreign dignitaries in the Grand Reception Hall and treated them to parties and shows. Later administrations put more value on preserving the Grand Reception Hall than actually using it, but the New Republic reversed that trend in a calculated move to tie its government to the glories of history. Four years after the Battle of Endor, Princess Leia Organa welcomed Prince Isolder of Hapes in a special ceremony held inside the Grand Reception Hall.

During the Yuuzhan Vong occupation, the former Grand Reception Hall is a gruesome sight. The alien invaders have disposed of unworthy prisoners and robotic abominations by throwing them, alive and screaming, down the shaft of "the well." The historic Grand Reception Hall is buried in heaps of corpses and droid parts.

The Kallarak Amphitheater

The legendary Kallarak Amphitheater has attracted the finest talent in the galaxy, from glamorous holo-actress Neile Janna to rowdy glimmik singer Boles Roor. The venue seats 1,000,000 spectators, and most nights there isn't an empty seat in the house.

The acoustics of Kallarak aren't particularly good; the arena thrives on the twin strengths of its reputation and its voluminous capacity. The sunken stage is surrounded on all sides by concentric rings of Sittana-marble benches, each higher than the last to create an unbroken line of sight from any seat. Nevertheless, the patron with ticket #999,999 isn't going to see much more than moving dots, and is advised to purchase a disposable holo-viewer for close-up views of the stage. A ticket to a Kallarak show can cost as much as 1,500 credits, but stealthy cheats often sneak past the observation droids during the arrival rush. The Kallarak's outer wall contains thirty-four low-powered lasers that shoot straight up and pierce the exosphere—a dramatic way to advertise the evening's concert, but one that has garnered scorn from generations of orbital pilots.

After the Yuuzhan Vong's capture of Coruscant, an unidentified impact weapon annihilates the Kallarak Amphitheater and leaves a kilometers-deep crater in its place. This gaping hollow, overgrown with Yuuzhan Vong-seeded mosses and vines, becomes a repository for biomachines that birthed thousands of bloodthirsty umrachs.

The University of Coruscant

Coruscant's oldest learning institution was founded by Chancellor Fillorean and Borz'Mat'oh of the Star Dragons following the peaceful resolution of the Duinuogwuin Contention. Though not the most prestigious university in the galaxy, it attracts some of the Republic's brightest minds who fall in love with the idea of studying and teaching on cosmopolitan Coruscant.

The university is actually a collection of buildings scattered throughout the Fobosi district; students must catch air taxis to make it to their classes on time. The main campus, however, is a self-contained blocky tower incorporating student housing, administrative offices, a few of the original lecture halls, and chalcedony statues of Fillorean and Borz'Mat'oh. The dean of the institution bears the traditional title of *Cadaeda*.

Under the New Order, the Empire passed a bylaw forbidding non-Humans from applying to the university and expelling those aliens who were already studying there. Young Human males filled the vacancies, many of them former members of COMPNOR's Sub-Adult Group youth brigades. These bullying ideologues, many of them washouts from the Empire's military academies, pursued careers in the Imperial government with single-minded zeal. For nearly two decades, the University of Coruscant's reputation suffered as other schools derided it as a "bureaucrat factory."

After the New Republic's liberation of the capital planet, the University of Coruscant again welcomes underclassmen of all species. The school has not completely shed its Imperial image, however, and resentment remains high among non-Human students.

Coruscant Livestock Exchange and Exhibition

Every year throughout the Rise of the Empire and Rebellion eras, the Grand Symposium in Imperial City plays host to the Coruscant Livestock Exchange and Exhibition. This four-week animal fair and open market is a place where visitors can buy virtually any variety of pet, beast of burden, or guard creature. The cavernous space of the Symposium's main hall becomes an anarchical checkerboard of stalls, pens, cages, and tanks. Conversation is nearly impossible over the roars of caged narglatches and the booming voices of the auctioneers. Lining the walls of the main hall are reinforced doors leading to private chambers, where particularly sensitive animals or "special acquisitions" (creatures exported illegally from their homeworlds) are exhibited for customers who present the proper credentials.

The dealers who work the Livestock Exchange range from upstanding to downright criminal; the worst try to pass off eopies as rare Grizmallt nerfs by gluing on false racks of antlers. Newcomers are encouraged to patronize the Anx and Amaran dealers. The fin-headed Anx offer a limited selection but are scrupulously honest, while the short, vulpine Amarans are notorious hagglers but can be counted on to have the rare animal that no one else can find.

The government of Coruscant always struggles with the Livestock Exchange. They value the money it brings in to the local economy, but hate the risk of stray beasts wandering off and populating the city sublevels with their feral offspring. After the bludgeoning death of a Calocour Heights businessperson was traced back to a veermok that had escaped from the Livestock Exchange, the event organizers have started hiring adventurer teams whenever animals go missing. In the case of the largest and fiercest animal escapees, sometimes the adventurer team goes missing, too.

Royal Icqui Aquaria
Public aquariums can be found all over Coruscant—in the seedier regions, they double as feeding tanks—but the Royal Icqui Aquaria is the most renowned. It encompasses several square kilometers at the summit of a megablock in the Hirkenglade Prefecture, and draws water for its exhibits directly from the Deodurn polar pipeline.

Millions of aquatic creatures live in the Royal Icqui tanks, from microscopic flecks of Baraboo biomold to ribbonlike seasnakes from Riome. The boiling waters of the Inner Orbit exhibit contain creatures that evolved in molten seas and volcanic vents on dozens of hellish worlds, while the ice-frosted tanks in the polar wing house both nimble Rhinnalian fireheads and sluggish Lurrian rimebats. The Aquaria's largest living animal is a 20-meter-long opee sea killer from Naboo, but the facility's interactive learning annex features a stuffed Mon Calamari whaladon, the skeleton of a Geonosian hydra, and a huge tooth that allegedly came from a Naboo sando aqua monster.

Admission to the Royal Icqui Aquaria is 10 credits per person. Many who couldn't care less about marine biology use the facilities as a neutral meeting ground. The Aquaria has plenty of side passages for quiet conversation, and the number of tourists makes it difficult for any faction to set up an ambush.

After the Yuuzhan Vong invasion in the New Jedi Order era, starving Coruscant survivors break into the Royal Icqui Aquaria to poach the sea life for their dinner tables.

The Holographic Zoo of Extinct Animals
Many planets have menageries, but the Holographic Zoo of Extinct Animals is perhaps the only institution in the galaxy dedicated to the preservation of life forms long gone. Rather than displaying stuffed carcasses in frozen poses, the zoo employs holographic projection banks to show extinct creatures hunting, feeding, and fighting in their natural environments. The most popular holo-dioramas include the mammoth krabbex of Mon Calamari, the snow falcons of Rhinnal, and the mantabog of Malastare (an airborne, blanket-shaped constrictor).

During the latter years of the Old Republic, the Holographic Zoo of Extinct animals was considered a showy but chic destination among Coruscant's elite. A change in ownership following the Clone Wars, however, resulted in a pumped-up, sensationalist approach to attract a broader, bottom-line crowd. The enhancements were both garish and silly, including blinking stars set into the ceiling and an unseen narrator who boomed, "*You will experience forgotten wonders from a long time ago and far, far away!*" The strategy didn't work, and visitors to the Holographic Zoo during the time of the New Republic will find a half-empty facility littered with discarded food wrappers.

Dexter's Diner
As longtime customer Slyther Bushforb used to say, "If you want juicy conversation and a hot cup of ardees, come to Dexter's Diner. If you want a *good* cup of ardees, try Biscuit Baron."

Dexter's Diner is one of those puzzling institutions common to the seedier quarters of Coruscant—beloved by the locals but unnoticed by everyone else. Located in a lower-income Coco Town neighborhood near the Senate district, the grease-speckled restaurant attracts a steady clientele of itinerant freighter pilots and dock workers, as well as an oddball assortment of regulars. The food is oily and unhealthy, but also cheap and filling (and is misleadingly advertised as "the best eats in the Coco Town streets"). Fried nerfsteak, pickled gartro eggs, and Dexter's mysterious ground-meat "sliders" are a few specialties of the house. Dexter's Diner is decorated in the early Med'soto style, with bright lights, chrome accents, and tile floors. The restaurant never closes and does a brisk business in the middle of the night as clubgoers return from the entertainment districts.

Decades before the Battle of Naboo, the diner bore the name Didi's Café after its owner, Didi Oddo. A short-statured Human who counted Qui-Gon Jinn among his friends, Oddo doubled as an informant, slipping information regarding local criminal activity to the Jedi Order. After Palpatine's election to supreme chancellor, Didi made his daughter a partner in the business and rechristened the property Didi and Astri's Café. A few years later, the two of them sold their investment to a Besilisk entrepreneur named Dexter Jettster. Visitors to Dexter's Diner were likely to encounter head server Hermione Bagwa or WA-7, an antique server droid. Throughout most of the Rebellion era, an aging Hermione owned and operated Dexter's Diner following her boss's rumored retirement.

Zlato's Place
A quiet restaurant and lounge in the middle of a residential megablock, Zlato's Place is staffed exclusively by Toydarians. It specializes in Toydarian dishes such as its signature *terratta*—seasoned strips of terk hide smothered in oil and groat milk. The walls are decorated with Toydarian confederacy banners and paintings of the Calcified Lichens. Yet despite the name, the decor, and the cuisine, Zlato's isn't run by a Toydarian at all.

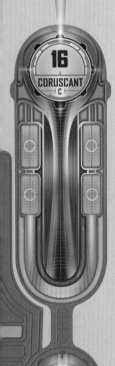

Zlato's Place is owned by Jeseej, a multitentacled Sljee. Though his restaurant is always half empty, Jeseej operates it as a loss-leading front company for his forgery business. Like all Sljees, Jeseej can't see. He does, however, employ two sharp-eyed, nimble-fingered Squibs who can duplicate a Coruscant ID in less than an hour. Jeseej also runs a side business in fortune-telling; his sensitivity to the Force makes him a capable soothsayer. Though he makes no guarantees as to the preciseness of his readings, Jeseej's underworld clients are known to plan major operations around his premonitions.

Anyone who wishes to take advantage of Jeseej's services has to present the proper password to the Toydarian maitre d', then select the correct entree (determined by a second, numeric password) from a special menu furnished by the waiter. At the conclusion of the meal, the maitre d' escorts the interested party through the kitchen and into Jeseej's tiny receiving room.

The Outlander

The neon-lit Outlander is characteristic of the night clubs found in the lower-level entertainment districts of Coruscant. Eschewing dignity for dazzle, the Outlander welcomes everyone's credits and traffics in high-risk vice. Young thrill-seekers and slumming nobles pack its dance floor every evening, sampling the ready menu of alcohol, death sticks (see page xx), and spice. Vidscreens built into the walls broadcast all manner of galactic sporting events from nuna-ball to illegal Podracing, and gambling is encouraged at the droid-staffed sports book.

The proprietors of the Outlander are a secretive band of Columi, but the true owner is local crime kingpin Volven Roxe. The Shistavanen spice lord owns several nearby nightclubs, competing for control of the entertainment district with rival club owners Quetemoor, Beuga Odell, and the Hutt bosses of Coruscant's undercity. Like the others, Volven Roxe made most of his profit not from the club itself but from the sale of illegal stimulants. Gorgeous clubgoers—secretly on Roxe's payroll—mingle through the Outlander's crowd, proffering spice and pleasures of the flesh. If they notice an outside dealer trying to cut his own sale, they sic the bouncers on him. The Outlander's bouncers are mute bruisers who throw undesirables into the puddle-spotted alley out back, usually after breaking a bone or two.

Weapons are freely allowed inside the Outlander and violence is common. Rumor has it that a vampiric Anzat frequents the club, observing her victims over several nights and attacking when she has determined a pattern. Several bodies, brains missing from their skulls, have been discovered in the entertainment district's dark corridors, but so far no one has been able to substantiate the Anzati story with hard evidence.

Gartro Rookery

The building known as the "gartro rookery" is an abandoned Nebula Consumables warehouse in Coruscant's spaceport district. When Nebula vacated the premises, it left behind thousands of tons of expired denta beans, which attracted flocks of green-skinned, dragonlike gartros. Inside the warehouse, countless gartros roost on the ceiling beams and the tops of cargo boxes, while the air seethes with flying gartro currents, flowing in loops and circles to the keening sound of a feeding cry. The warehouse floor is buried beneath a centimeters-thick layer of guano.

The Lost Ones gang uses the gartro rookery as an initiation for new members. One of the Lost Ones throws a power cell into the center of the room, then orders the rookie to bring it back. Once the new recruit has found it and is headed back out, the others slam the door shut and lock him in the warehouse overnight. If the initiate is still alive in the morning—and if he still has the power cell—the others welcome him as a full member.

The Ice Crypts

The ancient Coruscant legend recounted in *Dha Werda Verda* tells of a battle between the Taungs and the Battalions of Zhell that ended when a gush of volcanic ash smothered the Zhell army. More than twenty-five thousand years later, few archaeological artifacts of this pre-Republic incident survive. One of them is the Ice Crypts.

Located beneath the Hasamadhi warehouse district near the south pole, the Ice Crypts is a network of frozen caves bored into a glacial layer several hundred meters underground. Long, meandering side passages lead to thirteen chambers, each containing the mummified remains of what are believed to be Zhell war chieftains. Archaeologists theorize that these tombs contain the leaders of the thirteen Zhell nations, who retreated to the Ice Crypts after their loss to the Taungs and buried themselves alive. Entombed with their weapons, armor, and battle trophies, the bodies of the Zhell lords remained undiscovered for millennia.

The Ice Crypts is maintained by the government of Coruscant and is open to the public during the Rise of the Empire era. During the Rebellion era, the Empire restricted access to the Crypts in order to suppress knowledge of pre-Imperial glories. It isn't known whether the Crypts survived the Yuuzhan Vong's bioforming.

Temperatures are always kept below freezing to prevent the Ice Crypts' ceilings from dripping, and repulsor barriers keep the exhibits free from tourist contamination. Curators who pace the empty tunnels at night swear they can hear the echoes of the dead, whispering the mysterious words "*korah mahtah . . .*"

East Minor and Trophill Gardens

East Minor is a genteel residential and cultural borough located in the mid-southern hemisphere thousands of kilometers around the planet from Imperial City. This is a gathering place for poets, musicians, and artists, many of whom live with wealthy benefactors willing to put them up in their servants' quarters. East Minor's clubs and cafes are treated as stages for impromptu artistic performances, most of them chest-thumpingly pretentious and bitterly critical of the status quo. During the

Rebellion era, East Minor is a fruitful place for Alliance agents to find local contacts sympathetic to their ideals.

The Trophill Gardens, East Minor's most popular tourist attraction, draws visitors from every part of Coruscant. Contained within a high-walled circular plaza, the gardens sprawl over an area the size of a small town. Although not as exotic as Imperial City's Skydome Botanical Gardens, Trophill can fool sightseers into thinking they're strolling on some pastoral planet—if they don't glance up and see the rushing streams of skycars overhead. The most popular sights in the Trophill Gardens are the Green Mazes, artificial labyrinths of hedge and bramble. The Green Mazes are so difficult to navigate that visitors are given special comlinks at the start of the path. Eventually, more than half have to call the maze managers for pickup by airspeeder.

The Factory District

Not every megablock on Coruscant is filled with people; many regions in the hemisphere opposite Imperial City house only droids and a few organic overseers. This is the factory district, where goods are manufactured for export and for local consumption. Despite the sheer tonnage of the factory district's annual output, Coruscant's trillion citizens are far from self-sufficient.

The Grungeon block encompasses twenty square kilometers and is one of several areas in the factory district that has gone completely idle. Originally a production center for Serv-O-Droid, Huvicko, and Nebula Manufacturing, the block fell on hard times when its three clients cut output during an economic recession. The owner of the Grungeon block, unable to attract new businesses, allowed stratts and other vermin to overrun the stamping plants that once hummed with industry. Some of the Grungeon plants later came back on line. It's unclear whether this was due to vandalism or circuit decay, but these live factories are filled with unsafe, unsupervised, malfunctioning machinery. Anyone who enters risks losing a hand . . . or a head.

During the Rise of the Empire era, the Sith Lord Darth Sidious maintained a secret hangar in the factory district for use by his apprentice, Darth Tyranus. During the Rebellion era, Alliance agents used the district's low profile in a similar fashion to hide the existence of Coruscant-based resistance cells. After the Yuuzhan Vong's bioforming of the planet, the factory district becomes a largely vegetation-free "desert," rarely visited by the Yuuzhan Vong themselves but crawling with deadly predators.

PCBU

The Police Cruiser Backup Unit (PCBU) is a floating, droid-piloted vehicle used to chase and apprehend lawbreakers in Coruscant's vertical city. It was developed in the waning years of the Old Republic in response to a string of police officer murders in a seedy precinct known as the Crimson Corridor. The droid pilot sits in a transparisteel bubble (the PCBU can be operated by an organic operator in the same seat), and a backup autopilot takes control if the primary pilot is disabled. Scanners,

spotlights, sirens, and sensor jammers are arranged along the vehicle's equator.

Police Cruiser Backup Unit

Class: Speeder [Air]	Crew: 1 droid (Skilled +4)
Size: Large (5 m long)	Initiative: +3 (–1 size, +4 crew)
Passengers: 0	Maneuver: +3 (–1 size, +4 crew)
Cargo Capacity: 10 kg	Defense: 14 (–1 size, +5 armor)
Cost: 16,000 (new), 8,000 (used)	Shield Points: 0
	Hull Points: 20 (DR 5)
Availability: Licensed	Atmospheric Speed: 4 squares/ action (250 km/h)
Era: Rise of the Empire	Altitude: 4 km

* This vehicle provides full cover to its pilot.

Weapon: Two swivel laser cannons; **Fire Arc:** Turret; **Attack Bonus:** +7 (–1 size, +4 crew, +4 fire control); **Damage:** 5d8; **Range Increment:** 200 m.

Coruscant Survival Kit

Coruscant is not as civilized or as welcoming as it may appear. Those traveling to the "bright center of the universe" should be as prepared as those planning a trip to the Outer Rim. Anyone announcing a trip to Coruscant is approached by dealers selling survival kits for 250 credits or more (plus the value of the credit stick included in the kit). Anyone arriving on Coruscant is besieged by similar dealers, but the cost is doubled. Either way, a survival kit is generally a wise investment. Typical contents include the following items.

A credit stick containing a prepaid amount in Republic or Imperial currency, depending on the era.

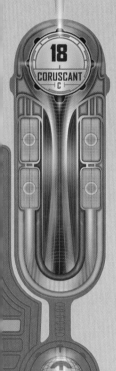

Life on Coruscant can be extremely expensive. If the survival kit is purchased offworld, the credit stick might be stolen or worthless.

Maps of all major areas and sections of the planet.

A breather and protective goggles for trips to Coruscant's polluted sectors.

A glow rod for forays into Coruscant's lower depths.

A small "stinger" hold-out blaster with a five-shot capacity. This item is illegal during the Rebellion era.

A small datapad for accessing and storing information from public data terminals.

A reliable comlink with multifrequency capabilities.

Racing Wings

Garbage pit races are one of the dangerous diversions cooked up by the fringers in Coruscant's lowest levels. Using homemade parawings, racers swoop into one of the planet's garbage pits, avoid canisters of tractor-boosted trash being rocketed into orbit, and retrieve a shining scale from one of the hundred-meter-long worms living in the soupy froth at the base of the pit. The racing wings are lightweight contraptions of metal and leather that fasten around the arms and torso. Small fuel cylinders feed maneuvering jets on the wings, and an optical cup over the eye scrolls data on fuel levels and structural integrity. Racing wings are not designed to support a Human on their own; instead, they rely on the pit's tractor fields to provide lift in the same way that a flying creature catches a thermal. Buzzing sensors in both palms alert the racer when he approaches a tractor field.

Racing Wing

Class: Speeder [Air]	Crew: 1 (Expert +6)
Size: Large (5m)	Initiative: +5 (–1 size, +6 crew)
Passengers: 0	Maneuver: +5 (–1 size, +6 crew)
Cargo Capacity: 0 kg	Defense: 9 (–1 size)
Cost: 4,000 (new), 2,000 (used)	Shield Points: 0
	Hull Points: 8 (DR 2)
Availability: Prevalent	Atmospheric Speed: 1 square/action (60 km/h)
Era:Rise of the Empire	Altitude: 250 m

* This vehicle provides one-fourth cover to its pilot.

Hot Rod Airspeeder (typical)

Most citizens of Coruscant don't own personal transports—the taxes on such vehicles are excessive, and there's no place to park them anyway. But rich thrill-seekers among the political and business classes use their money to buy expensive, customized hot rod airspeeders with flashy exteriors and military-grade repulsorlift hardware beneath their chassises. Nobles who take their hot rods out for a high-speed spin can escape prosecution for speeding violations by greasing the palms of friends in high places.

Senator Simon Greyshade of the Vorzyd sector was one of many Coruscant legislators with a passion for high-performance aircars. Around the time of the Clone Wars, Greyshade's pride and joy was a bright yellow, open-topped aircar built for a driver and a single passenger. Two massive turbojets fed thrust ducts at the rear of the

vehicle, propelling the aircar at speeds in excess of 700 kilometers per hour. An inertial compensator—a device typically found only on starships—negated the physiological effects of breakneck maneuvering, while two miniature tractor units helped keep the driver and the passenger glued to their seats. In an incident that left Greyshade afire with rage, Padawan learner Anakin Skywalker "borrowed" the senator's aircar to pursue fugitive assassin Zam Wesell.

Hot Rod Airspeeder

Class: Speeder [Air]	Crew: 1 (Skilled +4)
Size: Huge (6.23m)	Initiative: +2 (–2 size, +4 crew)
Passengers: 1	Maneuver: +2 (–2 size, +4 crew)
Cargo Capacity: 0 kg	Defense: 8 (–2 size)
Cost: 55,000 (new), 22,000 (used)	Shield Points: 0
	Hull Points: 20 (DR 5)
Availability: Prevalent	Atmospheric Speed: 12 squares/action (720 km/h)
Era:Rise of the Empire	Altitude: 5 km

* This vehicle provides one-half cover to its pilot.

Death Stick

Death sticks are a uniquely Coruscant problem—developed in Coco Town's illegal pharmaceutical labs, their popularity has resulted in thousands of deaths and millions of addicts in communities from Imperial City to East Minor. Users experience a temporary explosion of bliss when they administer a death stick dosage, neither noticing nor caring that the dose is simultaneously killing them.

There are two forms of death sticks, though both are derived from treated Ixetal cilona extract and sold in clear tubes. Liquid sticks contain colorful Ixetal cilona fluid which must be imbibed or injected. Hard sticks contain dried granules of the drug, which are crushed, then smoked or inhaled. Slythmongers, the street term for death stick dealers, sell their wares to slumming nobles in the entertainment district and desperate indigents in the Southern Underground. Each dosage only increases the user's craving for more, a fact that has made some slythmongers wealthier than the senators and businessbeings with whom they do business.

A character who samples a death stick, either intentionally or accidentally, must make a Will save (DC 16). If it fails, the character loses 3 points of Dexterity, loses 3 points of Intelligence, and is struck by the exhilarated (but delusional) sensation that he or she has found a pipeline to great wisdom. The effects persist for 1d2 hours. As the effects of the drug wear off, the character must make a Fortitude save (DC 20) or be considered addicted, automatically suffering a 1-point loss of Constitution. The character now will want to sample more death sticks, and each subsequent dose requires an initial Will save and ending Fortitude save.

A character who wishes to break the addiction (restoring lost Constitution points) can seek treatment in a rehab medcenter at a cost of 2,500–3,500 credits. At the Gamemaster's discretion, other characters may attempt to repair the damage using the Treat Injury skill or the Force skill Heal Another.

Spot-On Locator

On a world with Coruscant's level of urbanization, one can get hopelessly lost after walking less than a kilometer from one's starting point. For this reason, both tourists and natives make judicial use of spot-on locators, tiny navigational devices weighing less than an ounce that can easily fit into the palm of a hand. A typical spot-on locator is almost all screen—a user inputs an address directly onto the display, which then links with orbital satellites to provide an interactive map showing the best route and the destination's district, megablock, block, subblock, level, and unit number.

Obtaining spot-ons is almost ridiculously easy. Many big companies distribute customized versions for free at the spaceports, which work excellently provided the user doesn't mind watching an interactive sales pitch for Tanallay Suites or constantly hearing how many kilometers it is to the nearest Biscuit Baron. Rebel agents and smugglers were often known for slicing into individual spot-ons to provide on-the-fly coordinates to a secret rendezvous, or to direct an unsuspecting enemy into an ambush. Officially, the government of Coruscant encourages people to be discreet in their use of spot-ons—the presence of the devices will identify the users as newcomers to an area, tagging them for possible exploitation by observant con artists.

Spot-on Locator
Cost: 50 credits
Weight: —

Suppressor Riot Rifle

The security forces of Coruscant deal with crowds every day. On the rare occasions when crowds turn into mobs, security officers need something to subdue rioters in a hurry. Enter the Merr-Sonn R-88 Suppressor riot rifle, a nonlethal pacification device that combines the precise targeting of a blaster weapon with the broad area of effect of a stun grenade. The weapons were popular among Coruscant's stormtrooper forces during the Galactic Civil War, but also saw use during the Old and New Republics in times of urban unrest.

The Suppressor rifle has two cylindrical tanks clipped underneath its barrel, each filled with Brix-C stun fluid. A squeeze of the trigger fires the Brix-C in a compressed stream, which diffuses into an aerosol rain at a range of up to 100 meters. Targets are knocked unconscious by both skin absorption of the spray droplets and inhalation of the Brix-C aerosol cloud. If an R-88 Suppressor rifle is fired into a crowd, all characters within 4 meters of the point of impact must make a Reflex save (DC 16) to avoid the droplets. Characters who fail must make a Fortitude save (DC 20) or fall unconscious for 2d6 minutes. The Brix-C aerosol cloud extends out to 8 meters away from the point of impact (the Gamemaster may wish to adjust this to account for any prevailing wind). Any characters in the aerosol cloud (including those who already made successful saves to resist the contact droplets) must make a Fortitude save (DC 12) upon inhaling the mist. Those who fail fall unconscious for 2d6−1 minutes.

Of course, breath masks and full-body coverings can protect characters from either of the R-88 Suppressor's negative effects. People wearing *both* breath masks and full-body coverings (such as stormtroopers) are unaffected by Brix-C spray. Aliens with natural body armor may be immune to the stun effects of the Brix-C contact droplets at the Gamemaster's discretion. An R-88 Suppressor riot rifle carries enough stun fluid for ten firings.

Merr-Sonn R-88 Suppressor Riot Rifle
Cost: 2,000 credits
Damage: Special (see text)
Critical: n/a
Range Increment: 10 m
Weight: 3.5 kg
Stun Fort DC: 18
Type: See description
Size: Medium-size
Group: Blaster rifles

For the GM

The adventure hooks and supporting characters described in this section are meant for GMs only. If you're a player, stop reading now.

Adventures

Coruscant is a source of limitless excitement. The following adventure seeds are split into two sections to capture the dichotomy of upper-crust luxury and cutthroat poverty that makes up life in the galaxy's capital.

High Society

These adventures will take the heroes through Coruscant's influential political, business, and entertainment spheres.

A Night at the Opera

The new opera *Herald of the King's Decline* is premiering at the Coruscant Opera House. Rumors have swirled that an assassin will use the event to eliminate a high-profile target, and the heroes are enlisted by Republic or Imperial Security (or hired by fearful patrons) to apprehend the unseen killer. Uncovering the assassin is an open-ended mystery. Is a sniper hiding in the stage rigging? Does a cast member have a bomb? Does the caterer have an affinity for poisons? Is an orchestra player's instrument modified to fire a toxic dart? Depending on the importance of the target, there may be multiple plots occurring simultaneously. The heroes can stake out the Opera House from the audience or backstage, or they can go undercover as members of the cast or the orchestra. This is one adventure in which musical talent and performance skills can prove especially valuable.

Panic in the Plaza

Reina March and the anarchists of Edge-9 plan to sabotage the Imperial Fair. During the traditional military parade down Glitannai Esplanade, they plan to commandeer one of the armored vehicles and steer it through the crowd, sowing chaos and death. The heroes

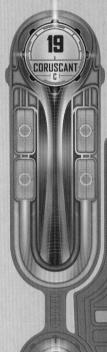

19
CORUSCANT
C

may be hired to stop the attack, or they could be enjoying the fair when the attack begins. As they circulate through costumed dancers and half-intoxicated spectators, a piece of heavy equipment (an AT-AT or a juggernaut, for example, depending on the era) wheels out of formation and triggers widespread panic as it threatens to crush fleeing onlookers. However, the parade mayhem is merely a noisy distraction. Reina March's true plan is to storm the Imperial Palace observation balcony overlooking the parade and assassinate the high-level politicians sitting there.

Murder at the Heights

A young female employee of the SchaumAssoc ad agency in the Calocour Heights has been murdered. The Jedi Council or a friend who knew the deceased asks the heroes to investigate her death. In the glitzy, fast-paced Heights district, the heroes discover that several other murders have already taken place, and all the victims had one thing in common: exposure to bafforr pollen. Select members of SchaumAssoc's marketing team had been given miniature bafforr cuttings as product samples from the Skydome Botanical Gardens. Armed with this data, heroes may be able to stop the killer before he strikes again.

What the Gamemaster knows, and the players may not, is that the killer is Ocka Dwei, a disguised Yuuzhan Vong scout. He has discovered the toxic effect bafforr pollen has on Yuuzhan Vong vonduun crab armor and is determined to eliminate what he perceives to be a dread biological weapon. The heroes' defeat of Ocka Dwei prevents any report from reaching Dwei's distant Yuuzhan Vong commanders, but due to the constraints of the era, the heroes won't realize the enormity of what they have accomplished.

Unhooked Skyhook

Disaster! A skyhook belonging to retired industrialist Archa Sabis has come loose from its moorings. Normally, the giant satellites attach to Coruscant's surface with slender tethers that double as turbolift shafts, but this tether ripped free. The skyhook is moving toward Imperial City, dragging its free-swinging tether through busy plazas and into residential spires. Can the heroes stop it?

Already, Coruscant security interceptors have scrambled and plan to shoot down the skyhook inside an hour, despite the massive civilian casualties that would result from a crash. But bold heroes can bypass the skyhook's protective energy field if they burn their way inside the dangling tether and ride the turbolift car up to the top. Inside the skyhook, the mad cyborg Archa Sabis will attack anyone who touches the piloting controls.

The Price of Fame

The heroes' past exploits have made them minor celebrities, and fame is a commodity to be exploited in the Column Commons publishing district. The disreputable Veritas Press has released the datatext *Neverending Valor: The Unauthorized Guide to the Galaxy's Newest Heroes* for the low price of only 7 credits. The heroes may be flattered at first, but the outrageous lies printed in the datatext should quickly drive them to disgust. Veritas Press tries to deflect the heroes' inquiries, and rival publishers will offer them lucrative contracts to get "the real story" (possibly resulting in a boost to the characters' Reputation bonuses). A recurring enemy from the heroes' past then arrives on Coruscant, gunning for revenge because of his unflattering portrayal in *Neverending Valor*.

A Capital Dogfight

The heroes, being skilled pilots (or at least mistaken for skilled pilots) are recruited to provide air cover for an ambassadorial procession from Alsakan. If the heroes have no military affiliation, they may be hired as freelancers for promised "easy money," but heroes with no piloting skills may choose to sit this one out. The Alsakan delegates are scheduled to take a ceremonial march down Glitannai Esplanade, then meet with Coruscant officials in the open-air Listoni Plaza. The air escort is mostly for show, but security officials believe that Alsakan dissidents may make an attempt on the ambassador's life.

The type of ships provided to the heroes will vary based on the era. They will be expected to take orders from the commander of the air escort, who will be Air Marshal Cargelogh during Imperial rule. All seems quiet at first, but as the procession winds its way down the street below, a motley starfighter squadron appears from the direction of the setting sun. When the heroes investigate, the newcomers open fire.

A chase through the vertical city-canyons ensues, with the hostile starfighters attacking the heroes and ignoring the Alsakan delegation. In truth, the enemy pilots don't know anything about the delegates. Their job is to provide cover for a fat, slow-moving freighter loaded with loot from a just-finished heist at the Galactic Museum.

Always a Bigger Fish

At the Royal Icqui Aquaria, the heroes are waiting to meet with a Rebel agent, an underworld employer, or some other contact befitting the heroes' motivations. What they don't realize is that their enemies (who could include Imperial Intelligence, a notorious bounty hunter, or an unpaid loan shark and his knee-breakers) have set up the meeting as an ambush.

When the trap is sprung, the heroes will have little choice but to fight. The Royal Icqui Aquaria building sprawls across several square kilometers, but thanks to the bad guys sealing off the blast doors, most corridors are dead ends. The majority of the exhibits, however, are meandering channels of water instead of self-contained tanks. Characters who don't mind getting their feet wet can elude their pursuers by swimming with the fishes. Some channels are filled with stone eels, krakanas, pierceskimmers, and other predatory horrors. Aquatic aliens will fare better than terrestrial characters, but no matter what their makeup, the heroes will have to fight off attacks from multiple corners.

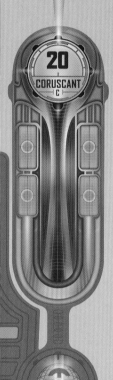

If the heroes reach the chamber nearest the exit, they'll notice a sealed tank containing the Icqui Aquaria's proudest acquisition—a 20-meter-long opee sea killer from Naboo. The room is perfect for a dramatic, final standoff—and if a misplaced blaster bolt should shatter the tank, the combatants will be joined by thousands of gallons of seawater and a hungry, snapping opee.

Something in the Water

The anarchists of Edge-9 have begun a new campaign of destruction. Dozens of public buildings, from utility stations to police offices, have been destroyed despite increased security all over Coruscant. Somehow, the Edge-9 gang is bypassing building defenses and delivering explosives into the heart of supposedly secure complexes.

Everyone on Coruscant wants to stop the anarchists. Whether they're hired by the government, the Jedi, or local crime syndicates, the heroes soon discover that every location that has been hit to date was supplied with water from the same pipeline network. The Edge-9 bombers have cut an airlock into a water pipeline near Coruscant's north pole and are riding through the pipes in nimble, single-person pods.

If the heroes take out the Edge-9 north pole encampment, two bombers escape. One of them shouts, "The Senate building will soon be a crater filled with cinders!" Then the two bombers plunge into the pipeline in pods. Can the heroes stop them by using the anarchists' own pods, chasing the bombers through a water-filled pipe at hundreds of kilometers per hour?

Lost and Lost

Shasheva Astopone, a deep-cover Rebel agent, has lost her ring. More than just a pretty bauble, Astopone's ring contains a datadot with reams of intelligence on Imperial operations. While crossing the Western Sea on a public ferry, she mistakenly believed a stormtrooper squad was searching for her, and she dropped the ring overboard. (During other eras of play, Shasheva Astopone's background can be adjusted accordingly, or she could be turned into a crime lord's courier if the heroes have mercenary motivations.)

The Empire isn't looking for the sunken ring, but that doesn't mean it will be easy to find. The heroes have to dive to the bottom of the reservoir and sweep the smooth, artificial floor meter by meter. Diving in the Western Sea is prohibited, which means the heroes must be careful not to attract Imperial attention.

The mindless droids known as scum-scrubbers converge on any heroes who stay near the bottom, delivering painful shocks with their scouring lasers. If a scum-scrubber reaches the ring first, the droid "swallows" it. Significant damage inflicted upon any one of the droids may cause it to explode. If this happens, the explosion blasts a hole in the floor, and the resulting whirlpool sucks the ring, the droids, and the heroes into the low-level city foundations supporting the bottom of the sea.

21
CORUSCANT
C

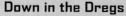

Down in the Dregs

The following undercity adventures will give the heroes a chance to see how the "other half" lives.

Deeper and Deeper

An underworld contact claims to have figured out a "foolproof" way of robbing the Imperial Palace. Depending on the era, he may be looking either to steal the Death Star plans from the Imperial Information Center or to loot a legendary "lost" treasure compartment built centuries ago by the pirate general Toleph-Sor.

A tunnel through Coruscant bedrock (that didn't exist a week ago) allows the heroes to infiltrate the palace from below. But the palace's security systems are top of the line, and even the lowliest worker is capable of raising a buildingwide alarm. Even worse is the surprising news that the heroes' access tunnel is the product of a burrowing, 30-meter-long taozin. The sound of intruders scratching through her hollow attracts the hungry beast's attention at the worst possible moment.

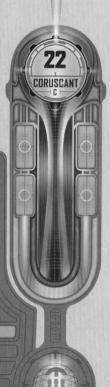

Every Droid Has Its Day

Archa Sabis, the mad cyborg industrialist (see Unhooked Skyhook, above), has appeared on a vid broadcast waxing grandiosely about a Great Droid Revolution, a short-lived mechanized uprising that occurred on Coruscant more than four millennia in the past. As his speech is punctuated by the whir of stirring servos, it becomes clear that Sabis wishes to bring about a Second Droid Revolution. Hundreds of droids—from sewer scrubbers to automated PCBUs—attack the nearest organics at the conclusion of the speech. Sabis has erased their inhibition safeguards with a viral program. A forty-story-tall construction droid is hungrily devouring a city block where the heroes' ship is berthed. Unknown to anyone, Archa Sabis is broadcasting from a control center in the bowels of the mammoth construction droid. If the heroes storm the towerlike automaton, they can force a confrontation.

A Whole New World

In this adventure in The New Jedi Order era, the Yuuzhan Vong have captured Coruscant. The bioshaping of the city-planet into the image of Yuuzhan'tar is well under way. From the air, Coruscant resembles a mountainous jungle, and the shapes of its towers are still apparent beneath a blanket of moss. The heroes might try to escape Coruscant, or they could be part of an infiltration team making life difficult for the Yuuzhan Vong occupation army. From the planet's undercity, desperate survivors strike back at the Yuuzhan Vong through sabotage. The heroes can use buried corridors to pop up near enemy surface encampments, plant explosives, and disappear before the fireworks begin. Obvious Yuuzhan Vong targets include warrior barracks, shaper damuteks (laboratories), and shrines in which prisoners are sacrificed to the Yuuzhan Vong gods. Master Shaper Gengi Tung does not sit idly by while his forces are threatened. He keeps two umrachs with him at all times, and he has ordered hundreds of them to fan out and hunt down the heroes' hidden base. Gengi Tung will make every effort to

capture one of the saboteurs alive and force him to turn traitor through brainwashing.

Mayhem at 2,000 Meters

Beuga Odell, the crime madam of Coruscant's undercity, wants to hire the heroes for a bit of high-stakes mischief. She wishes to steal one of the floating landing platforms found throughout Imperial City and use it as an arena. If the heroes are dyed-in-the-wool good guys, consider setting them up as undercover agents trying to infiltrate Odell's organization. Success in this mission will earn Odell's trust.

The heroes must locate a vulnerable platform somewhere in the city, deactivate the tractor system that holds it in place (but not the repulsor system), and tow it away with a ship big enough to handle that much mass (a space transport or capital ship). Coruscant's security patrols, meanwhile, will be very interested if a landing platform suddenly goes missing.

Once she has it, Beuga Odell sets up her landing platform in the air above Coruscant's unpopulated factory district on the planet's far side. Offering a 10,000-credit prize per contest, she pits drivers in wheeled vehicles against each other in a high-altitude demolition derby. The heroes have a chance to win big . . . but vehicles that come up short are shoved rudely over the side, often with their drivers still inside.

Love, Ortolan Style

Sleta Suke, the daughter of Orto's ambassador to Coruscant, is getting married. The Ortolan embassy is hosting an elaborate engagement party in the Grand Reception Hall, attended by scores of pachydermoid Ortolans visiting from their homeworld. The heroes are providing event security for what appears to be an easy way to score a few credits.

The party is splendidly catered, featuring hundreds of pastries, fruits, jellies, and sauces. Ortolans love to eat, and soon everyone is shoveling down the food, with the notable exception of the bride-to-be. Before long Ortolans are dropping like flies, victims of virulent food poisoning. (Any heroes who sampled the food will be similarly incapacitated.)

Into this scene, a knot of toughs from the Lost Ones gang springs up through the floor grates. Their leader, the Ortolan known as Trunks Bibo, moves to abduct Sleta Suke. The Lost Ones try to incapacitate, not kill, any remaining defenders. If the heroes try to protect Sleta Suke, she turns on them, because she secretly wants to run away with Trunks Bibo.

If Trunks gets the girl, the Ortolan ambassador offers to pay the heroes to get his daughter back. But is it wise to oppose Coruscant's toughest street gang, and is it right to stand in the way of true love?

Late Shift at Dex's

Dex's Diner, the popular eatery in Coruscant's Coco district, is being squeezed by a local crime syndicate. Beuga Odell recently sent her thugs to pay a "social call" on owner Dexter Jettster; after he tossed them onto the street, they vowed to come back and put the diner out of business for good.

Dexter Jettster doesn't know when Odell's goons will return, so he's looking for muscle to head them off when they do. Dex has contacts within the Jedi Order and may contact the heroes that way; if not, he's looking for promising fighters from any walk of life to work in his diner and keep their eyes open for trouble. For several days the heroes work from midnight to dawn, serving food to the stream of drunken revelers filing out of the all-hours nightclubs. Colorful distractions liven up the graveyard shift, including a customer who habitually skips out his bill and an illegal drag race, organized by outlaw racer Zip Beeline in the street outside.

Eventually Odell's henchmen return, armed with metal pipes and vibroblades. If the heroes drive them off they'll return the next day, but the second attack is merely a cover for the arsonists sneaking around back. Saving Dexter's Diner from burning down will turn the heroes into local celebrities and earn them free lunches for life.

Powerhouse

The Grungeon block of Coruscant's factory district has been idle for years. Now the crime lord Beuga Odell wants to quietly reactivate four of the forgotten factories, then use them to manufacture illegal equipment under the noses of the Coruscant customs office. All four factories are still drawing power, and their machinery has gone haywire. Odell sends the heroes to each plant with orders to locate and reset the master circuit breakers. A big payoff will motivate those heroes who possess questionable motivations, and more noble heroes might accept Odell's offer as part of a more elaborate plan to infiltrate Coruscant's underworld.

Factory One is a durasteel foundry. The temperature inside the firebrick walls is blisteringly hot. The old work crew, a squad of circuit-scrambled ASP Series labor droids, will throw boiling metal at passersby.

Factory Two is a carbon-freezing facility. Molten carbonite gushes through trenches, and ceiling vents spew jets of supercooled chemicals.

Factory Three boasts several malfunctioning metal-shredders. Giant toothed wheels rip apart durasteel beams, spraying shrapnel in every direction.

Factory Four was once an armaments plant. Amid empty casings from proton torpedoes are numerous vials of high explosives, which will detonate if jostled.

If the heroes reset all four power grids, they will inadvertently reactivate the Grungeon master security system. Floating sentry droids will fire at anyone who moves.

Unearthing Evil

With tens of thousands of years of civilization, Coruscant has one of the richest archaeological records in the galaxy. The problem is, no one can reach it beneath all the buildings. Fortunately for archaeologists, a construction droid has just razed a five-hundred-story skyscraper in Coruscant's historic Petrax Quarter. Beneath the building's ancient foundation, scientists believe they have located the legendary Cell of Imu,

which belonged to the Jedi eccentric Humat more than nineteen thousand years ago.

Humat was known for collecting odd and arcane devices, many of which had sinister applications. To prevent thieves from raiding his artifacts, he equipped the storage chamber with dozens of deadly traps. If one of the heroes is a Jedi or an expert thief, the group may be called in by the archaeologists to penetrate the innermost chamber. If no one in the party fits these qualifications, the heroes may be summoned simply because of their all-around skills in getting out of tight situations.

The Cell of Imu is a dusty catacomb riddled with booby traps. Past the trapdoors, tripwires, and ceiling spikes are the dried corpses of long-extinct animals, animated through dark side magic and ready to attack. The center-piece of Humat's collection is a milky-white talisman known as the soul stealer, which will take over any character in the room who fails a Fortitude save (DC 20). Possessed heroes become Gamemaster characters for 5 minutes and will try to kill anyone they see. Can the heroes survive the traps and retrieve the soul stealer? And once the foul talisman tries to take possession of their bodies, will they wish they hadn't tried?

Troglodyte Terror

The Veritas Press publishing company is missing an employee. Elbee Bribb, a manuscript courier, vanished while making a simple delivery. Coruscant officials are too preoccupied to investigate the disappearance, and Veritas is looking for trackers willing to take on a corporate job.

The search will begin at the Veritas offices in the Column Commons district, but the heroes will eventually trace Bribb to the spice lord Volven Roxe's crime den in the worst part of the undercity. The gangsters won't take kindly to snoops, but discreet heroes may learn that Bribb is no longer there. After selling Roxe the contents of his courier satchel (an unpublished exposé of Coruscant's spice trade), Bribb was snatched by mutated Cthons from the deepest sublevels.

Volven Roxe may help the heroes wipe out the Cthons if he can be convinced that they are a threat to his turf. When the heroes eventually reach Bribb, they find him locked in a Cthon fattening cage—but they can't afford to drop their guard. The ordeal has so terrified Bribb that he will refuse to leave his cage. The heroes must drag the courier back against his will, with his bulk slowing them down and making them vulnerable to Cthon counterattacks.

Stratt Catchers

Five years ago, a repulsortruck carrying a shipment of juvenile stratts overturned near Coruscant's entertainment district and spilled its cargo. The drunken repulsortruck driver, one Arne Marson, covered up the incident and hoped it would go away. Now full-grown stratts have begun poaching nightclub patrons, leaving their chewed skeletons behind to be discovered by the morning janitors.

The government of Coruscant hires the heroes, offering a substantial bounty for each dead stratt they produce.

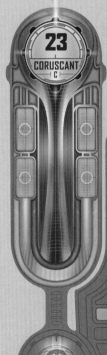

CALDER BRYA DR

Tracking the nocturnal stratts through the sublevels will be a good workout for a scout character, and a cornered stratt is a match for any soldier.

Meanwhile, a wealthy nightclub owner has hired her own team to eliminate the stratts to protect her regular clientele from future attacks. As soon as the heroes have successfully killed a stratt, her thugs ambush them and attempt to claim the carcass for themselves. The nightclub owner is paying three times the government rate for dead stratts—if the heroes discover this fact (and get rid of their competitors), they can make a lot more money by switching benefactors.

Allies and Antagonists

Following are several characters the heroes can interact with during their time on Coruscant. The characters are designed to be integrated into an existing Coruscant-based campaign with little difficulty. Most characters can appear in any era, and those few that are era-specific, such as Major Potiphar Migg, can be tweaked as necessary to create a customs inspector or a New Republic bureaucrat.

Calder Brya

A young, good-looking noble with a blue-blood pedigree and a million credits in his bank account, Calder Brya is the kind of rich socialite people love to hate. After they meet him, however, even his worst critics walk away singing his praises. Calder Brya possesses a natural gift for connecting with people and has a disarming, self-deprecating sense of humor. Trim and fit, Brya is not much of a combatant but plays a mean game of shockball. He has connections within the highest levels of Coruscant society and is a good friend for any group of heroes to have.

Calder Brya: Male Human Noble 5; Init +1; Defense 15 (+1 Dex, +4 class); Spd 10 m; VP/WP 22/10; Atk +3 melee (1d3, punch) or +4 ranged (3d4, sporting blaster); SQ bonus class skill (Gather Information), coordinate +1, favor +2, inspire confidence, resource access; SV Fort +1, Ref +4, Will +4; SZ M; FP 1; DSP 0; Rep +5; Str 10, Dex 12, Con 10, Int 13, Wis 10, Cha 14. Challenge Code C.

Equipment: Comlink, code cylinder, personal jewelry, credit stick, private aircar, sporting blaster.

Skills: Appraise +7, Computer Use +5, Diplomacy +10, Entertain (drama) +8, Gamble +4, Gather Information +10, Knowledge (business) +8, Knowledge (Coruscant) +8, Knowledge (politics) +7, Read/Write Basic, Read/Write Huttese, Read/Write Ryl, Sense Motive +4, Speak Basic, Speak Huttese, Speak Rodese, Speak Ryl.

Feats: Fame, Persuasive, Trustworthy, Weapon Group Proficiencies (blaster pistols, simple weapons).

Trey Duna

Mayor of Imperial City, Trey Duna has held his position for decades throughout the shifting rules of Republic, Empire, and New Republic. As a youth Duna wanted to be an inventor, and he never lost the spirit of innovation once he decided on a career in politics. Duna scrapped the stereotype that the mayor's office was merely a puppet of the Senate and fought for laws improving the lives of the locals. Despite his impressive work ethic, Mayor Duna has never gone after Quetemoor, Beuga Odell, or any of the other criminal syndicates—he just tries to minimize the damage their operations inflict upon innocents. Though he is well liked by most, some citizens consider him a coward for his repeated failure to stand up to organized crime. A round-faced, smiling man, Trey Duna can often be found digging into a grilled mercury-fish fillet at one of Coruscant's finest restaurants. The heroes will undoubtedly be aware of this public figure, and will probably encounter him only if he seeks them out based on their reputations.

Trey Duna: Male Human Diplomat 11/Noble 3; Init +0; Defense 14 (+4 class); Spd 10 m; VP/WP 10/9; Atk +7/+2 melee (1d3, punch) or +7/+2 ranged (3d4, hold-out blaster); SQ bonus class skill (Bluff), favor +2, inspire confidence, resource access; SV Fort +5, Ref +5, Will +14; SZ M; FP 0; DSP 0; Rep +6; Str 10, Dex 10, Con 9, Int 16, Wis 12, Cha 17. Challenge Code D.

Equipment: Hold-out blaster, code cylinder, datapad, multiple comlinks, 1,500 credits, chauffeured luxury aircar.

Skills: Appraise +10, Bluff +17, Computer Use +10, Diplomacy +21, Gather Information +15, Intimidate +15, Knowledge (Coruscant) +13, Knowledge (bureaucracy)

+18, Knowledge (politics) +18, Profession (mayor) +17, Read/Write Basic, Search +8, Sense Motive +13, Speak Basic, Speak Bothese, Speak Durese, Speak High Galactic, Speak Huttese, Speak Old Corellian.

Feats: Combat Expertise, Great Fortitude, Headstrong, Influence, Iron Will, Persuasive, Sharp-Eyed, Trustworthy, Weapon Group Proficiencies (blaster pistols, simple weapons).

Shasheva Astopone

Shasheva Astopone is well known in blue-blood circles as the heir to the Astopone exporting fortune. A raven-haired woman with exotic features and an appreciation of fine art, she is one of the most generous sponsors of the Galactic Museum, the Skydome Botanical Gardens, and other cultural institutions. What her rich friends don't know is that Shasheva Astopone is secretly an agent for the Rebel Alliance.

Originally recruited by Bail Organa, she has used her wealth to fund local intelligence cells and her exporting business to smuggle goods (and people) onto and away from Coruscant. Astopone also leverages her social power to arrange dinners with Imperial admirals and moffs. The intelligence she uncovers is stored in a tiny datadot, which she typically hides inside her firegem ring until she can hand it off to a Rebel field contact. Though Astopone has spent years in the service of the Alliance, she still has nightmares that one day Imperial Intelligence agents will burst into her penthouse apartment carrying orders for her arrest. Heroes with Rebel affiliations may be instructed to make contact with Astopone at the Coruscant Opera House, where she can be found in a private box at every premiere.

Shasheva Astopone: Female Human Noble 5; Init +1; Defense 15 (+1 Dex, +4 class); Spd 10 m; VP/WP 15/10; Atk +3 melee (1d3, punch) or +4 ranged; SQ bonus class skill (Bluff), coordinate +1, favor +2, inspire confidence, resource access; SV Fort +1, Ref +4, Will +7; SZ M; FP 0; DSP 0; Rep +2; Str 10, Dex 12, Con 10, Int 11, Wis 12, Cha 15. Challenge Code C.

Equipment: ID card, encrypted credit stick, firegem ring containing hidden datadot.

Skills: Appraise +3, Bluff +9, Computer Use +8, Diplomacy +10, Disguise +8, Gather Information +7, Knowledge (business) +6, Knowledge (Coruscant) +8, Read/Write Basic, Sense Motive +9, Speak Basic.

Feats: Iron Will, Persuasive, Trustworthy, Weapon Group Proficiencies (blaster pistols, simple weapons).

Major Potiphar Migg

Major Migg of the Imperial Security Bureau is a tall, haughty man with smooth brown skin and milky white eyes, which burn with twin red pinpoints from his cybernetic ocular implants. An enthusiastic supporter of Emperor Palpatine's New Order, Migg supervises a cadre of ISB field agents tasked with the vague job of "verifying the loyalty" of all citizens in Imperial City. One day Migg might show up at Westport insisting on random customs inspections; the next day he might be seen at the Galactic

Museum, demanding the name of an artist whose paintings fail to sufficiently convey the glory of Palpatine. Heroes can run afoul of Migg for no practical reason at all, including walking on the wrong side of the skywalk. Migg's secret dream is to become a member of the Imperial Court, and has been networking with the lesser courtesans in the hopes that one of them will put in a good word for him. A sure way to get on Migg's good side is to obtain an invitation for him to the monthly Imperial Ball.

Major Potiphar Migg: Male Human Soldier 5/Noble 2; Init +5 (+1 Dex, +4 Improved Initiative); Defense 17 (+1 Dex, +6 class); Spd 10 m; VP/WP 38/12; Atk +6/+1 melee (1d3, punch) or +7/+2 ranged (3d6, blaster pistol); SQ bonus class skill (Gather Information), favor +1, inspire confidence, ocular implants; SV Fort +7, Ref +4, Will +6; SZ M; FP 0; DSP 0; Rep +2; Str 10, Dex 12, Con 12, Int 12, Wis 10, Cha 14. Challenge Code D.

Equipment: Blaster pistol, encrypted ISB code cylinder, comlink.

Skills: Appraise +6, Computer Use +8, Diplomacy +9, Disguise +9, Gather Information +9, Hide +4, Intimidate +9, Knowledge (bureaucracy) +9, Move Silently +4, Read/Write Basic, Sense Motive +1, Speak Basic, Speak High Galactic, Spot +2.

Feats: Armor Proficiency (light), Combat Reflexes, Great Fortitude, Improved Initiative, Iron Will, Point Blank Shot, Stealthy, Track, Weapon Group Proficiencies (blaster pistols, blaster rifles, heavy weapons, simple weapons, vibro weapons).

Ocular Implants: Major Migg's ocular implants give him a +2 bonus on all Spot checks.

Quetemoor

Quetemoor, a pallid, lantern-jawed Human, heads a Mugaari crime family that holds sway over much of Imperial City's underworld. Properly known as Quetemoor the Sub-Elder, he shares power with his older sister Quetemoor the Elder, his father Quetemoor the Venerable, and his nephew Quetemoor the Younger, as well as family members from other lineages. Though he has worked out a peace with Prince Xizor's overarching Black Sun syndicate, Quetemoor constantly battles his smaller rivals for a bigger piece of the underworld action, reserving a special hatred for the crime lord Beuga Odell. Heroes will meet the powerful Quetemoor only after working their way through his legions of underlings. Though Quetemoor can be brutally sadistic to his enemies, he has a robust sense of humor and a booming laugh. Freelance employees who amuse Quetemoor will be placed on his list of "grimacers" and receive plum assignments from his majordomo.

Quetemoor: Male Mugaari Noble 2/Soldier 4/Crime Lord 8; Init +3 (−1 Dex, +4 Improved Initiative); Defense 18 (−1 Dex, +9 class); Spd 10 m; VP/WP 71/14; Atk +12/+7 melee (1d3+3, punch) or +8/+3 ranged (3d6, blaster pistol); SQ bonus class skill (Bluff), contacts (3), exceptional minions, favor +1, inspire confidence, inspire

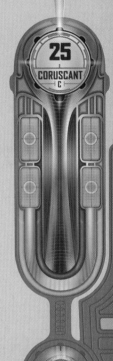

fear –4, resource access; SV Fort +8, Ref +6, Will +12; SZ M; FP 2; DSP 6; Rep +11; Str 16, Dex 9, Con 14, Int 11, Wis 14, Cha 12. Challenge Code F.

  Equipment: Blaster pistol, Mugaari genealogy bracelet, customized bulk transport (*Cold Front*).

  Skills: Appraise +5, Bluff +13, Diplomacy +11, Gather Information +9, Knowledge (alien species) +12, Knowledge (Coruscant) +12, Knowledge (streetwise) +11, Pilot +5, Read/Write Basic, Read/Write Mugaar, Sense Motive +10, Speak Basic, Speak Mugaar, Speak Huttese.

  Feats: Heroic Surge, Improved Initiative, Infamy, Persuasive, Quick Draw, Sharp-Eyed, Spacer, Starship Operation (space transport), Weapon Group Proficiencies (blaster pistols, blaster rifles, heavy weapons, simple weapons, vibro weapons).

New Species: Mugaari

Heavy-browed, lantern-jawed aliens with skin the color of slate, the Mugaari were the original masters of the Javin sector. Though they have learned to live with Humans over the past few centuries, they still harbor resentment over their culture's decline and do not make friends with outsiders easily.

Mugaari Commoner: Init –1; Defense 9 (–1 Dex); Spd 10 m; VP/WP 0/12; Atk +1 melee (1d3+1, punch) or –1 ranged; SV Fort +1, Ref –1, Will +1; SZ M; FP 0; DSP 0; Rep +0; Str 12; Dex 8, Con 12, Int 8, Wis 12, Cha 8.

  Equipment: Variety of personal belongings.

  Skills: Craft (any one) +1 or Knowledge (any one) +1, Profession (any one) +1, Read/Write Basic, Read/Write Mugaar, Speak Mugaar, Speak Basic.

  Species Features: +2 Str, –2 Dex, +2 Con, –2 Int, –2 Cha.

  Automatic Languages: Mugaar and Basic.

Beuga Odell

Beuga Odell, the crime boss of Imperial City, is a heavyset Human female in her seventh or eighth decade of life. Surveillance holographs make her look like a sweet-natured old woman, but anyone familiar with the Coruscant underworld knows she is deadly serious about dominating the gambling, smuggling, and narcotic trades. Odell has butted heads with the Quetemoor crime family for decades, dating back to Quetemoor the Venerable's days as head Mugaari. Her organization is now as large as Quetemoor's, but both gangs are dwarfed by the galaxy-spanning specter of Black Sun. Beuga Odell takes comfort in the fact that Black Sun is too large to take an active interest in her operations, and she keeps Black Sun envoy Mal Coramma at bay with regular bribes. She would dearly love to wipe out the much smaller organization of "the wolfman" Volven Roxe, but fears that doing so will trigger a gang war. Heroes can find Odell in her private block of seats at major concerts in the Kallarak Amphitheater, and she maintains a number of secret hideouts in the sparsely populated Factory District.

Beuga Odell: Female Human Scoundrel 4/Noble 2/Crime Lord 5; Init –1; Defense 16 (–1 Dex, +7 class); Spd 10 m; VP/WP 29/9; Atk +5/+0 melee (1d3–1, punch) or +5/+0 ranged (3d6, blaster pistol); SQ bonus class skill (Bluff), contacts (2), favor +1, illicit barter, inspire confidence, inspire fear –2, lucky (1/day), minions, precise attack +1, resource access; SV Fort +1, Ref +8, Will +11; SZ M; FP 1; DSP 6; Rep +12; Str 8, Dex 8, Con 9, Int 15, Wis 13, Cha 16. Challenge Code E.

  Equipment: Blaster pistol, armored luxury hovervan.

  Skills: Appraise +11, Bluff +19, Computer Use +5, Diplomacy +17, Forgery +12, Gather Information +17, Intimidate +16, Knowledge (Coruscant) +12, Knowledge (politics) +15, Knowledge (streetwise) +12, Profession (crime lord) +13, Read/Write Basic, Sense Motive +11, Sleight of Hand +2, Speak Basic, Speak Huttese, Speak Mugaar.

  Feats: Combat Expertise, Fame, Infamy, Iron Will, Persuasive, Skill Emphasis (Profession [crime lord]), Weapon Group Proficiencies (blaster pistols, simple weapons).

Volven Roxe

Volven Roxe is a preening, narcissistic Shistavanen who makes a living as Coruscant's top spice lord. Unlike other crime bosses, who have their fingers in gambling rackets and weapons smuggling, Roxe limits his dominion to the import and sale of andris, ryll, glitterstim, and lumni-spice. Roxe also owns several nightclubs, including the Outlander, which has made him a target for rival gangsters who periodically try to put "the wolfman" in his place. Heroes who make a scene in the Outlander may find themselves dragged before Roxe for personal chastisement. Though he makes it a point to never sample the spice he traffics, Roxe is addicted to an unrelated narcotic known as Drovian zwil. Volven Roxe rarely appears in public but can be identified by his red-and-black striped fur (which is unusual for Shistavanen)

Volven Roxe: Male Shistavanen Scoundrel 7; Init +6 (+2 Dex, +4 Improved Initiative); Defense 17 (+2 Dex, +5 class); Spd 10 m; VP/WP 27/10; Atk +5 melee (1d3, punch) or +7 ranged (3d8, heavy blaster pistol); SQ illicit barter, low-light vision, lucky (2/day), precise attack +1, xenophobia; SV Fort +2, Ref +7, Will +3; SZ M; FP 2; DSP 4; Rep +2; Str 10, Dex 15, Con 10, Int 11, Wis 12, Cha 13. Challenge Code D.

  Equipment: Heavy blaster pistol, comlink, engraved zwil container.

  Skills: Appraise +10, Bluff +11, Escape Artist +10, Gather Information +10, Hide +10, Knowledge (business) +10, Knowledge (Coruscant) +8, Move Silently +10, Read/Write Shistavanen, Sleight of Hand +10, Speak Basic, Speak Huttese, Speak Mugaar, Speak Shistavanen.

  Feats: Alertness, Dodge, Heroic Surge, Improved Initiative, Mobility, Skill Emphasis (Gather Information), Spring Attack, Weapon Group Proficiencies (blaster pistols, simple weapons).

Mal Coramma

Within the snake pit that is Coruscant's criminal underworld, the Black Sun syndicate rules all. The blue-skinned

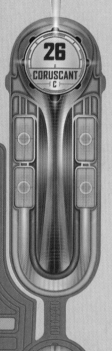

Chagrian known as Mal Coramma is Black Sun's envoy to the lesser crime cabals, responsible for keeping Quetemoor, Beuga Odell, and the others from overstepping their limited boundaries. A fastidious perfectionist, Coramma is known for his cultured Coruscanti accent and his meticulously polished horns. Like many Chagrians, he believes that the mythical god-king Aram Acheron will one day burst forth from Champala's sacred Logue Rock, leading loyal Chagrians to victory against their enemies.

When Black Sun's leader, Prince Xizor, died prior to the Battle of Endor, Mal Coramma allied himself with Xizor's niece Savan. She failed to preserve Black Sun after the Battle of Endor, and Coramma went underground, staying far away from resurgent mobs such as Quetemoor's. Three years later, after the New Republic's capture of Coruscant, Mal Coramma hooked up with some of his former associates and helped restore Black Sun to its former glory.

Mal Coramma: Male Chagrian Scoundrel 1/Noble 4; Init +0; Defense 13 (+3 class); Spd 10 m; VP/WP 15/11; Atk +3 melee (1d3, punch) or +3 ranged (3d6, blaster pistol); SQ amphibious, bonus class skill (Gather Information), coordinate +1, favor +2, illicit barter, inspire confidence, low-light vision, radiation resistance, resource access; SV Fort +1, Ref +4, Will +8; SZ M; FP 0; DSP 1; Rep +2; Str 10, Dex 10, Con 11, Int 15, Wis 15, Cha 12. Challenge Code C.

Equipment: Blaster pistol, encrypted comlink, Black Sun documentation guaranteeing safe passage among Coruscant's crime families.

Skills: Appraise +10, Computer Use +9, Diplomacy +9, Gather Information +7, Knowledge (business) +10, Knowledge (Coruscant) +10, Knowledge (history) +8, Knowledge (politics) +9, Knowledge (streetwise) +10, Read/Write Basic, Read/Write Chagri, Sense Motive +4, Speak Basic, Speak Chagri, Speak Huttese.

Feats: Iron Will, Persuasive, Weapon Group Proficiencies (blaster pistols, simple weapons).

Mazumoda

His employers call him "the big bug," but Mazumoda doesn't care. He has made a comfortable living as a freelance thug-for-hire, a profession where his frightening appearance is a considerable asset. Mazumoda is a Worrite, a half-crustacean, half-insectoid species from an unknown part of the galaxy. As tall as a Wookiee, he is protected by a knobby, segmented carapace the color of dried blood. Two small manipulator arms are kept close to his body, while two crushing arms end in gigantic claws. In a fight, Mazumoda swings his claws like wrecking balls; if he catches someone between his pincers, he can easily snip off a limb. His face is a mass of sensory feelers, and his four eyes swivel at the end of long stalks.

Mazumoda has been an underworld fixture for years. Beuga Odell and Quetemoor have long tried to add him to their permanent payrolls, but he prefers to remain unattached. Crime bosses retain him as a bodyguard and enforcer, while bookies such as Tuchap sometimes hire "the big bug" to intimidate their nonpaying clients. If the heroes see Mazumoda heading their way, they'd better start running.

Mazumoda: Male Worrite Thug 6/Soldier 4; Init –1; Defense 18 (–1 Dex, +4 class, +5 natural); DR 7; Spd 8 m; VP/WP 40/17; Atk +14/+9 melee (1d8+4/crit 19–20, claw) or +9/+4 ranged; SV Fort +12, Ref +2, Will +3; SZ M; FP 2; DSP 1; Rep +2; Str 18, Dex 8, Con 17, Int 8, Wis 10, Cha 11. Challenge Code D.

Equipment: None.

Skills: Climb +10, Intimidate +9, Profession (thug) +6, Speak Basic, Speak Huttese, Speak Mugaar, Speak Rodian.

Feats: Armor Proficiencies (light, medium), Athletic, Blind-Fight, Cleave, Great Cleave, Improved Critical (claw), Power Attack, Weapon Group Proficiencies (blaster pistols, blaster rifles, simple weapons, vibro weapons).

Archa Sabis

Once one of the wealthiest men on Coruscant, Archa Sabis bought his way into high society with a fortune made from energy shield generators. He lost his status as a social player when a nonlethal form of Knowt's disease claimed his right arm, his torso, and half his face. Cyborg parts replaced the obvious losses, and a computer interface band was also required to supplement the damaged parts of his brain. After his shallow "friends" abandoned him, Archa Sabis retired from public life, preferring to brood aboard his luxury skyhook. By the time the heroes encounter him, a computer virus has infected his brain and driven him thoroughly insane.

Archa Sabis: Male Human Noble 10/Expert 7; Init +6 (+2 Dex, +4 Improved Initiative); Defense 23 (+2 Dex, +6 class, +5 natural cyborg parts); Spd 10 m; VP/WP 45/10; Atk +15/+10/+5 melee (1d4+3, punch) or +15/+10/+5

ARCHA SABIS

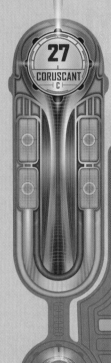

melee (1d8, laser scalpel) or +14/+9/+4 ranged (3d6, blaster pistol); SQ bonus class skill (Gather Information), coordinate +2, favor +3, inspire confidence, resource access; SV Fort +5, Ref +9, Will +11; SZ M; FP 0; DSP 0; Rep +6; Str 16, Dex 14, Con 10, Int 12, Wis 9, Cha 11. Challenge Code F.

Equipment: Datapad, laser scalpel, blaster pistol.

Skills: Appraise +4, Astrogate +5, Computer Use +12, Craft (computers) +18, Craft (electronic devices) +12, Demolitions +6, Diplomacy +8, Disable Device +4, Gather Information +6, Knowledge (Coruscant) +8, Knowledge (engineering) +10, Knowledge (physics) +14, Knowledge (technology) +16, Pilot +6, Profession (shield engineer) +13, Read/Write Basic, Read/Write Binary, Read/Write Durese, Repair +13, Search +3, Sense Motive +1, Speak Basic, Speak Durese, Treat Injury +7.

Feats: Blind-Fight, Dodge, Gearhead, Heroic Surge, Improved Initiative, Influence, Martial Arts, Mobility, Sharp-eyed, Skill Emphasis (Profession [shield engineer]), Weapon Group Proficiencies (blaster pistols, simple weapons).

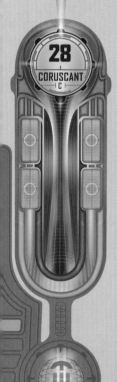

Jeseej

One of the few Sljees on Coruscant, Jeseej is easily mistaken for a bizarre animal or some form of motile plant. He looks like a short gray table topped with tentacles and bulbs, moving on a set of squat, stumpy legs. Like all Sljees, Jeseej lacks visual organs and interacts with the world through hearing and touch. For years, he has owned Zlato's Place, a Toydarian restaurant and lounge. He operates a secret forgery business out of the back room. Underworld clients have recently started hiring Jeseej as a fortune-teller, after finding he has an uncanny prescience concerning future events. Jeseej operates with paramount secrecy to avoid attracting the attention of Coruscant security. His employees, including two top Squib forgers and a dozen Toydarian restaurant workers, are unswervingly loyal to their boss. Although known for his forgeries, Jeseej is versed in all manner of underworld intrigue and happily will provide information to beings with fat credit purses.

Jeseej: Male Sljee Expert 8/Force Adept 2; Init –2; Defense 13 (–2 Dex, +1 size, +4 class); Spd 4 m; VP/WP 7/10; Atk +7/+2 melee (1d2–1, tentacle slap) or +6/+1 ranged; SQ blindness, scent; SV Fort +6, Ref +2, Will +14; SZ S; FP 2; DSP 0; Rep +2; Str 8, Dex 6, Con 10, Int 15, Wis 16, Cha 10. Challenge Code C.

Equipment: None.

Skills: Appraise +12, Craft (electronic devices) +11, Diplomacy +4, Forgery +16, Gather Information +12, Hide +2, Intimidate +5, Knowledge (biology) +15, Knowledge (Coruscant) +15, Profession (restaurateur) +16, Repair +12, Speak Basic, Speak Sljee.

Force Skills: Enhance Senses +6, Farseeing +5.

Feats: Force-Sensitive, Great Fortitude, Iron Will, Skill Emphasis (Forgery, Knowledge [Coruscant], Profession [restaurateur]), Trustworthy.

Force Feats: Alter, Sense.

Special Qualities: See Sljee Commoner, below.

New Species: Sljee

A Sljee is easily mistaken for a bizarre animal or some form of motile plant. It looks like a short gray table topped with tentacles and bulbs, moving on a set of squat, stumpy legs. Sljees lack visual organs and interact with the world through hearing and touch.

Sljee Commoner: Init –2; Defense 9; Spd 4 m; VP/WP 0/10; Atk –1 melee (1d2–1, tentacle slap) or –2 ranged; SQ blindness, scent; Fort +1, Ref –1, Will +0; SZ S; FP 0; DSP 0; Rep +0; Str 8, Dex 6, Con 10, Int 12, Wis 14, Cha 10. Challenge Code A.

Equipment: Variety of personal belongings.

Skills: Knowledge (any one) +2, Profession (any one) +2, Speak Sljee.

Special Qualities: Blindness—The Sljee are blind and rely on scent and hearing to interact with their environment. Away from their homeworld, they can be overwhelmed by the strange smells of alien beings. When encountering a new alien species for the first time, a Sljee suffers a –8 penalty on all Listen, Sense Motive, and Spot checks. After five encounters, the Sljee no longer suffers the penalty.

Scent—Sljees can identify familiar odors just as Humans recognize familiar sights. Sljees can detect other beings within 100 meters by sense of smell.

Species Features: –2 Str, –4 Dex, +2 Int, +4 Wis.

Automatic Language: Sljee. Sljee characters do not automatically speak or read/write Basic.

Nibber Swoo

This high-strung Rybet is a professional cabbie, licensed by the government to operate his air taxi outside the designated traffic lanes. In his red, open-topped Barkhetta he zooms through the city canyons, launching into a spittle-flying fury if a cargo hauler cuts him off or if Coruscant Security stops him for a speeding violation. Swoo has an uncanny knack of pulling up just when someone needs a ride, though he charges double if he's asked to elude blaster-toting pursuers.

Nibber Swoo's cousin works for a funeral house, where he operates an organic disintegrator. Various underworld figures pay him to dispose of bodies after hours, and Nibber is a reliable source of secondhand rumors concerning criminal activities.

Nibber Swoo: Male Rybet Expert 3/Scoundrel 1; Init +2; Defense 14 (+2 Dex, +1 size, +1 class); Spd 6 m, swim 6 m; VP/WP 6/10; Atk +2 melee (1d2–1, punch) or +5 ranged (3d4, hold-out blaster); SQ amphibious, illicit barter; SV Fort +1, Ref +7, Will +4; SZ S; FP 0; DSP 0; Rep +0; Str 8, Dex 14, Con 10, Int 10, Wis 13, Cha 10. Challenge Code B.

Equipment: Hold-out blaster pistol, Coruscant taxi license, six-seater Barkhetta aircar.

Skills: Appraise +4, Astrogate +4, Bluff +6, Gather Information +6, Hide +6, Knowledge (Coruscant) +5, Knowledge (streetwise) +6, Pilot +13, Profession (cab driver) +6, Read/Write Basic, Read/Write Rybese, Repair +6, Speak Basic, Speak Rybese.

Feats: Lightning Reflexes, Run, Skill Emphasis (Pilot, Repair), Spacer, Weapon Group Proficiencies (blaster pistols, simple weapons)

Special Qualities: *Bonus Feat*—Male Rybets receive the bonus feat Spacer.

Lieutenant Ia

Cops and cabbies are the only people permitted to deviate from Coruscant's midair traffic streams, and Coruscant Security's Lieutenant Ia is there to ticket anyone who violates skylane protocol. Piloting an armored swoop built to operate at high altitudes, she monitors aircar traffic, assists accident victims, and keeps one eye open for nighttime vandals or skyscraper suicide-jumpers. Lieutenant Ia stays in constant contact with Security Dispatch via her helmet comlink; though she is armed with only a blaster pistol, if faced with a serious threat she can summon a flotilla of PCBUs in minutes. Ia is a middle-aged, white-haired woman who speaks in a husky monotone. She takes her job very seriously, and considers air taxi pilot Nibber Swoo her professional nemesis. The manic Rybet and the no-nonsense security officer are perpetually at loggerheads concerning Swoo's "interpretations" of skylane regulations. Wayward heroes stopped by Lieutenant Ia must be on their best behavior, lest they land in the police lockup.

Lieutenant Ia: Female Human Soldier 4; Init +6 (+2 Dex, +4 Improved Initiative); Defense 16 (+2 Dex, +4 class); Spd 10 m; VP/WP 22/11; Atk +4 melee (1d3, punch) or +6 ranged (3d6, blaster pistol); SV Fort +4, Ref +5, Will +1; SZ M; FP 0; DSP 0; Rep +1; Str 10, Dex 14, Con 11, Int 15, Wis 11, Cha 10. Challenge Code C.

Equipment: Blaster pistol, Coruscant Security ID, flight helmet with secure-channel comlink, wrist binders, armored security swoop #CS-117.

Skills: Computer Use +9, Intimidate +7, Knowledge (Coruscant) +9, Knowledge (politics) +9, Pilot +9, Profession (Coruscant security officer) +7, Read/Write Basic, Repair +3, Search +3, Speak Basic, Spot +2.

Feats: Armor Proficiencies (light, medium), Combat Expertise, Dodge, Improved Initiative, Lightning Reflexes, Quick Draw, Weapon Group Proficiencies (blaster pistols, blaster rifles, heavy weapons, simple weapons, vibro weapons).

Zip Beeline

"Zip Beeline" is a pseudonym created by this spunky Drall when he first entered the professional speeder racing circuit. After fans started screaming for him as he crossed the finish line, Beeline legally assumed the name as his own. But his promising career ended in ignominy when he triggered a multispeeder pileup during a championship race on Boonta. He retired in disgrace to Coruscant, where he found a new life as a ringer in the capital city's illegal Podraces, speeder relays, garbage pit races, and swoop rallies. A self-described speed demon, Beeline is an honest competitor who won't sabotage his fellow pilots. He has a taste for Corellian lum, however, and always posts his worst times the day after a drinking binge.

Beeline usually pilots customized swoops and speeders specially designed for his small size. At any competition involving speed, Zip Beeline is sure to be a top competitor. Heroes who can best him in a race could win a fortune from the gambling receipts.

Zip Beeline: Male Drall Fringer 5; Init +2; Defense 18 (+2 Dex, +1 size, +5 class); Spd 6 m; VP/WP 20/10; Atk +3 melee (1d2–1, punch) or +6 ranged; SQ barter, bonus class skill (Read/Write Basic, Repair), jury-rig +2, survival +2; SV Fort +4, Ref +5, Will +2; SZ S; FP 0; DSP 0; Rep +4; Str 8, Dex 15, Con 10, Int 10, Wis 12, Cha 12. Challenge Code C.

Equipment: Comlink, flask of Corellian lum, customized Podracer, customized swoop, customized landspeeder.

Skills: Hide +6, Knowledge (Corellia) +6, Knowledge (Drall) +8, Knowledge (engineering) +8, Knowledge (technology) +8, Listen +3, Pilot +13, Read/Write Basic, Read/Write Drallish, Repair +3, Ride +6, Speak Basic, Speak Drallish, Spot +3, Survival +3.

Feats: Alertness, Fame, Skill Emphasis (Pilot), Weapon Group Proficiencies (primitive weapons, simple weapons).

Dexter Jettster

A four-armed Besalisk, Dexter Jettster is the owner of Dex's Diner in Coruscant's Coco district. Jettster has lived a frantic life, holding jobs as an animal hunter, an Outer Rim scout, a bartender, a gunrunner, and an

DEXTER JETTSTER

expeditionary oil prospector. During one oil-harvesting stint on remote Subterrel, Jettster worked alongside a number of cloned miners created by the Kaminoans. His unique knowledge of Kaminoan habits would come in handy years later, after Jettster made a fresh start on Coruscant as a restaurateur. His old friend Obi-Wan Kenobi brought him a poisoned Kaminoan saberdart, and Jettster's identification of the artifact touched off a chain of events that led to the start of the Clone Wars.

Dexter Jettster: Male Besalisk Scoundrel 6; Init +3 (–1 Dex, +4 Improved Initiative); Defense 13 (–1 Dex, +4 class); Spd 10 m; VP/WP 36/14; Atk +6 melee (1d3+2, punch) or +6 melee (1d4+2, knife) or +3 ranged (3d8, heavy blaster pistol); SQ +2 species bonus to cold-weather Survival checks, illicit barter, lucky 2/day, precise attack +1; SV Fort +4, Ref +4, Will +3; SZ M; FP 3; DSP 2; Rep +1; Str 14, Dex 9, Con 14, Int 13, Wis 12, Cha 13. Challenge Code D.

   Equipment: Butcher's knife, heavy blaster (under counter), Coruscant diner.

   Skills: Appraise +9, Bluff +6, Climb +4, Computer Use +4, Diplomacy +6, Gather Information +12, Knowledge (business) +5, Knowledge (spacer lore) +9, Knowledge (streetwise) +9, Pilot +6, Profession (cook) +4, Profession (merchant) +10, Read/Write Besalisk, Repair +6, Search +5, Sense Motive +5, Speak Basic, Speak Besalisk, Speak Huttese, Spot +5, Swim +6.

   Feats: Improved Initiative, Skill Emphasis (Appraise, Diplomacy, Gather Information), Trustworthy, Weapon Group Proficiencies (blaster pistols, simple weapons).

WA-7

WA-7 is an antique server droid obtained by Dexter Jettster during his time as a miner on Subterrel; in fact, Jettster's acquisition of WA-7 is one of the reasons he eventually chose to go into the restaurant business. Nicknamed "Flo" for the Aurebesh lettering imprinted on her chassis, WA-7 glides through Dex's Diner on a gyroscopically stable unipod wheel. She competes with the Human head server, Hermione Bagwa, to see who can score the biggest tips.

WA-7: Wheeled server droid, Diplomat 2; Init +0; Defense 10; Spd 10 m; VP/WP 0/10; Atk +1 melee (1d4, hand) or +1 ranged; SQ amenable quirk (+4 equipment bonus on Diplomacy checks, –5 penalty on Intimidate checks); SV Fort +0, Ref +0, Will +4; SZ M; FP 0; DSP 0; Rep +1; Str 10, Dex 10, Con 10, Int 14, Wis 12, Cha 13. Challenge Code A.

   Equipment: Order transmitter, repulsor stabilizer, vocabulator.

   Skills: Appraise +6, Bluff +6, Computer Use +5, Diplomacy +5, Gather Information +6, Intimidate –3, Knowledge (Coruscant) +7, Profession (server) +6, Search +4, Sense Motive +6.

   Unspent Skill Points: 0.

   Feats: Ambidexterity, Sharp-Eyed, Weapon Group Proficiencies (blaster pistols, simple weapons).

   Cost: 2,500 credits.

Anniha Nega

One of the top bounty hunter/assassins operating out of Coruscant, this Human male in his early twenties has built a top-notch reputation despite his relative youth. Though none of his employers know it, Anniha Nega hasn't accomplished many of the tasks described on his falsified Bounty Hunters' Guild kill list. But Nega has an almost primal talent for tracking, and he believes that soon his legitimate kills will far outnumber his imaginary ones. So far he has had no shortage of work. Everyone on Coruscant seems to be hiring—including criminal kingpins such as Volven Roxe and Quetemoor as well as politicians in the Senate district. To preserve the mystery of his identity, Anniha Nega wears a full-body suit of Ithullian war armor beneath a woven desert poncho. Heroes can contact Nega for a job if they write up their request and place it beneath a particular paving stone in Monument Plaza, but they had best hope that Nega never comes after them.

Anniha Nega: Male Human Soldier 7/Bounty Hunter 3; Init +6 (+2 Dex, +4 Improved Initiative); Defense 20 (+2 Dex, +8 class); Spd 10 m; VP/WP 48/10; Atk +12/+7 melee (1d4+2, combat gloves) or +12/+7 melee (1d3+2, punch) or +12/+7 melee (2d8+2, force pike) or +12/+7 ranged (3d8/19–20, blaster carbine) or +12/+7 ranged (3d6, ion pistol); SQ sneak attack +1d6, target bonus +2; SV Fort +7, Ref +6, Will +5; SZ M; FP 1; DSP 2; Rep +7; Str 14, Dex 15, Con 10, Int 10, Wis 12, Cha 11. Challenge Code E.

   Equipment: Blaster carbine, ion pistol, force pike, tracking device, Ithullian war armor, Z-95 Headhunter (*Flare*).

   Skills: Astrogate +4, Demolitions +3, Disguise +6, Gather Information +8, Intimidate +5, Move Silently +7, Pilot +8, Read/Write Basic, Search +6, Sense Motive +9, Speak Basic, Spot +6, Survival +4.

   Feats: Ambidexterity, Armor Proficiency (light), Dodge, Fame, Heroic Surge, Improved Initiative, Point Blank Shot, Sharp-Eyed, Starship Operation (starfighter), Track, Weapon Group Proficiencies (blaster pistols, blaster rifles, heavy weapons, simple weapons, vibro weapons).

Trunks Bibo

The leader of the Lost Ones street gang is a lanky Ortolan who decorates his blue fur with geometric tattoos of purple, red, and green. Bibo shows disdain for the rich, the police, and rival street gangs, and some say he even hates his subordinates in the Lost Ones. Until he became smitten with the daughter of Orto's ambassador to Coruscant, Trunks Bibo took pleasure in only three things: theft, vandalism, and torturing new gang initiates. The Lost Ones' gartro rookery hazing ritual, devised by Bibo, is notorious in the underworld for its needless cruelty.

   Like most Ortolans, Bibo loves food. Living the desperate life of a Lost One has caused him to miss many a meal, and his tattooed fur now hangs from his frame in loose folds. Those seeking an audience with Bibo are advised to bring a basket of edibles, for a full stomach can greatly improve his humor.

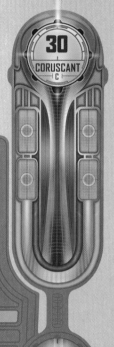

Trunks Bibo: Male Ortolan Fringer 5; Init +0; Defense 16 (+1 size, +5 class); Spd 6 m; VP/WP 29/12; Atk +4 melee (1d2+1, punch) or +3 ranged (3d4, hold-out blaster); SQ barter, bonus class skills (Intimidate, Move Silently), forager, intestinal fortitude, jury-rig +2, keen smell, survival +2; SV Fort +5, Ref +3, Will +2; SZ S; FP 0; DSP 0; Rep +1; Str 12, Dex 10, Con 12, Int 10, Wis 13, Cha 13. Challenge Code C.

Equipment: Hold-out blaster, Lost Ones medallion of rank (an aircar grill ornament).

Skills: Climb +5, Hide +8, Intimidate +9, Knowledge (Coruscant) +8, Knowledge (streetwise) +8, Listen +4, Move Silently +4, Read/Write Ortolan, Search +3, Speak Basic, Speak Ortolan, Spot +5, Survival +7.

Feats: Stealthy, Track, Weapon Group Proficiencies (blaster pistols, primitive weapons, simple weapons).

Special Qualities: *Intestinal Fortitude*—Ortolans can eat and digest a wide range of foods. They receive a +2 species bonus on Fortitude saves to resist ingested poison.

Forager—Ortolans receive a +4 species bonus on Survival checks when foraging for food.

Keen Smell—Ortolans have a keen sense of smell. An Ortolan with the Track feat receives a +4 species bonus to track a subject within 2 kilometers of the Ortolan's current location.

Murble and Fierce

Murble is a pathetic sight in Coruscant's undercity. A slight, bearded man with a pallid face and dark purple patches under his eyes, he shuffles through the bazaars of the Southern Underground, leading his trained bursa Fierce on a chain. For the price of a credit, Murble will put on a makeshift animal show on the street corner, ordering Fierce to stand on one foot and balance a ball on her snout. Despite her name, Fierce is shy around crowds and will only turn vicious if Murble's life is threatened. Her ribs poke through her filthy, matted coat, and a cloud of floater fleas perpetually surrounds her.

Murble: Male Human Fringer 3; Init +0; Defense 14 (+4 class); Spd 10 m; VP/WP 19/9; Atk +2 melee (1d3, punch) or +2 melee (2d6, vibroblade) or +2 ranged; SQ barter, bonus class skill (Entertain), jury-rig +2; SV Fort +2, Ref +2, Will +2; SZ M; FP 1; DSP 0; Rep +0; Str 10, Dex 10, Con 9, Int 11, Wis 13, Cha 9. Challenge Code C.

Equipment: Vibroblade, leash and muzzle for bursa, bursa training equipment.

Skills: Disguise +4, Entertain (comedy) +4, Entertain (storytelling) +1, Handle Animal +7, Hide +3, Jump +3, Knowledge (streetwise) +5, Read/Write Basic, Ride +8, Speak Basic, Spot +5, Survival +7.

Feats: Animal Affinity, Mimic, Run, Weapon Group Proficiencies (primitive weapons, simple weapons, vibro weapons).

Fierce: Female bursa, swamp predator 2; Init −1; Defense 13 (−1 Dex, −1 size, +5 natural); Spd 8 m; VP/WP 8/11; Atk +4 melee (2d6+2, bite) or +4 melee (2d4+2, 2 claws) or +1 ranged; SQ camouflage (swamp environments only); SV Fort +3, Ref +4, Will +1; SZ L;

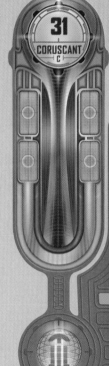

Face/Reach 2 m by 4 m/2m; Rep +0; Str 14, Dex 8, Con 11, Int 6, Wis 13, Cha 11. Challenge Code A.

Skills: Climb +9, Intimidate +5, Jump +7.

Feats: Track.

Note: Fierce's statistics reflect her age and poor physical condition and are not representative of healthy Naboo bursas.

Lexia Ginorra

Padawan Ginorra studied under the best instructors in the Jedi Temple, but she abandoned the Order after she was abducted by a criminal syndicate on Kamparas. Fearing for her life, and convinced in a moment of panic that the morality of the Jedi Code was a hindrance that could kill her, Ginorra slaughtered her kidnappers in an explosion of rage, then disappeared into the jungles of Kamparas. Though Ginorra was a mere Padawan (and thus could not be counted among the Lost Twenty), the Jedi Council and her former master made every effort to find her, without success. Years later, she reappeared on Coruscant, leading a corps of undercity vigilantes in a bloody crusade against crime. Though not a conscious follower of the dark side, Ginorra slipped farther and farther from the Jedi path every time she executed a petty thief or a glitterstim dealer. Volven Roxe, Quetemoor, and other crime lords placed bounties on the mysterious vigilante they superstitiously called "the Sith."

Lexia Ginorra: Female Human Jedi Guardian 5/Dark Side Marauder 3; Init +7 (+3 Dex, +4 Improved Intitiative); Defense 20 (+3 Dex, +7 class); Spd 10 m; VP/WP 47/12; Atk +10/+5 melee (3d8+1/19–20, lightsaber) or +9/+4 melee (1d3+1, punch) or +11/+6 ranged (3d8, heavy blaster pistol) or +11/+6 ranged (3d8/19–20, blaster rifle); SQ deflect (attack −4, defense +1), increase lightsaber damage +1d8, tainted; SV Fort +8, Ref +9, Will +6; SZ M; FP 3; DSP 7; Rep +3; Str 13, Dex 16, Con 12, Int 10, Wis 12, Cha 13. Challenge Code D.

Equipment: Lightsaber*, blaster rifle, heavy blaster pistol.

*Lexia Ginorra has constructed her own lightsaber.

Skills: Craft (lightsaber) +8, Hide +5, Intimidate +7, Knowledge (Jedi lore) +4, Move Silently +5, Read/Write Basic, Speak Basic, Tumble +6.

Force Skills: Affect Mind +6, Battlemind +7, Drain Energy +3, Enhance Ability +5, Fear +5, Force Defense +7, Force Grip +4, Force Lightning +2, Force Stealth +4, Force Strike +2, Heal Another −3, Move Object +4.

Feats: Armor Proficiency (light), Combat Reflexes, Exotic Weapon Proficiency (lightsaber), Force-Sensitive, Improved Initiative, Power Attack, Stealthy, Weapon Group Proficiencies (blaster pistols, blaster rifles, primitive weapons, simple weapons, vibro weapons).

Force Feats: Alter, Burst of Speed, Control, Hatred, Rage, Sense.

Zesi Phinx

Even older than the ancient cityscape through which she hunts, Zesi Phinx is an Anzat killer who haunts the shadows of Coruscant's entertainment district. She resembles

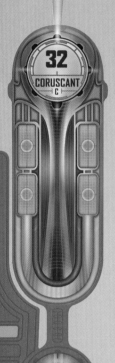

a slim Human female in her late twenties, evidencing none of the puffiness around the nose found on most Anzati. She still possesses nasal proboscises, however, and feeds on sentient beings at least twice per month. Those who encounter Zesi Phinx when she isn't hungry will find her a personable yet mysterious figure, telling oblique tales of the great schism between darkness and light and Coruscant's long-forgotten glories. If the evidence is to be believed, Phinx has survived on the capital planet for millennia and is responsible for murders numbering in the hundreds of thousands. Zesi Phinx spends her nights observing the decadence at the Outlander club, and any heroes who visit that establishment may find themselves stalked by a vampiric killer older than the Republic itself.

Zesi Phinx: Female Anzati Scoundrel 8/Force Adept 4; Init +2; Defense 19 (+2 Dex, +7 class); Spd 10 m; VP/WP 52/12; Atk +12/+7 melee (1d4+3, punch) or +11/+6 ranged; SQ hypnotism, illicit barter, lucky 2/day, precise attack +1, proboscises; SV Fort +5, Ref +10, Will +7; SZ M; FP 6; DSP 9; Rep +0; Str 17, Dex 14, Con 12, Int 15, Wis 13, Cha 11. Challenge Code F.

Equipment: None.

Skills: Disguise +10, Hide +15, Knowledge (alien species) +11, Knowledge (Coruscant) +8, Knowledge (history) +11, Knowledge (streetwise) +10, Listen +9, Move Silently +4, Read/Write Anzati, Speak Anzati, Speak Basic, Speak Huttese, Speak Old Galactic Standard, Spot +8, Survival +3.

Force Skills: Affect Mind +10, Drain Energy +5, Empathy +11, Enhance Ability +11, Enhance Senses +6, Force Stealth +4, Move Object +4, See Force +13, Telepathy +5.

Feats: Alertness, Blind-Fight, Force-Sensitive, Heroic Surge, Low Profile, Martial Arts, Power Attack, Skill Emphasis (Hide, Knowledge [alien species]), Stealthy, Track, Weapon Group Proficiencies (blaster pistols, simple weapons).

Force Feats: Alter, Control, Sense.

Ra-Zyrth

Five thousand years ago, this mutated Massassi warrior served in Sith Lord Naga Sadow's invasion force during the Great Hyperspace War. Before the Sith invasion, Naga Sadow summoned his top commanders, including Ra-Zyrth, and used dark side alchemy to transform them into muscular monstrosities. (A millennium later, Exar Kun would use a similar technique to create the Massassi Night Beast on Yavin 4.) Ra-Zyrth and his fellows slept in suspended animation capsules until Naga Sadow's assault on Coruscant, at which point the capsules were fired into Coruscant's cityscape.

After that, the stories are vague. Some say Ra-Zyrth awoke immediately and fought Coruscant's Jedi defenders to the death. Others say his capsule is still intact in some forgotten corner of the undercity, waiting for someone to accidentally activate it and unleash Ra-Zyrth upon the modern world.

Ra-Zyrth: Male Mutated Sith (Massassi) Thug 5/Soldier 3; Init +6 (+2 Dex, +4 Improved Initiative); Defense 21 (+2 Dex, +3 class, +6 natural); DR 5; Spd 10 m; VP/WP 35/23; Atk +13/+8 melee (1d8+5, sword) or +10/+5 ranged (3d4, Sith lanvarok); SQ warrior culture, natural armor; SV Fort +12, Ref +4, Will +1; SZ M; FP 0; DSP 0; Rep +2; Str 20, Dex 14, Con 20, Int 8, Wis 8, Cha 6. Challenge Code C.

Equipment: Massassi insignia of rank, Sith lanvarok, sword.

Skills: Climb +12, Intimidate +4, Jump +10, Listen +1, Speak Sith, Spot +1, Swim +7.

Feats: Armor Proficiency (light), Athletic, Cleave, Exotic Weapon Proficiency (Sith lanvarok), Great Cleave, Improved Initiative, Power Attack, Toughness, Weapon Group Proficiency (simple weapons).

Special Qualities: *Warrior Culture*—Massassi are trained from birth to be ruthless, efficient soldiers for the glory of the Sith empire. This violent upbringing gives Massassi a +2 species bonus on Intimidate, Listen, and Spot checks.

Natural Armor—Due to Naga Sadow's alchemical manipulations, Ra-Zyrth has gained an armored hide that grants a +6 bonus to Defense and damage reduction 5.

Reina March

Head lieutenant in the anarchist organization Edge-9, Reina March believes in her cause with the fervor of youth. Edge-9 has called for the dismantling of Coruscant's government and the abolishment of its noble upper class. Though many of their motives seem noble, March and the others have turned to violence to get their point across. Reina March is an excellent hand-to-hand combatant who favors inconspicuous black clothing. She keeps her brown hair cut short and wears a perpetual scowl.

Reina March: Female Human Scoundrel 10; Init +3; Defense 19 (+3 Dex, +6 class); Spd 10 m; VP/WP 36/10; Atk +7/+2 melee (2d4/19–20, punch) or +7/+2 melee (2d6, vibroblade) or +10/+5 ranged (3d8, heavy blaster pistol); SQ illicit barter, lucky 2/day, precise attack +2; SV Fort +3, Ref +10, Will +3; SZ M; FP 0; DSP 0; Rep +2; Str 10, Dex 16, Con 10, Int 12, Wis 10, Cha 12. Challenge Code E.

Equipment: Encoded comlink, frequency jammer, vibroblade, heavy blaster pistol.

Skills: Astrogate +5, Bluff +9, Climb +4, Computer Use +4, Demolitions +8, Disable Device +6, Disguise +10, Escape Artist +6, Gather Information +9, Hide +11, Intimidate +5, Knowledge (Coruscant) +11, Knowledge (politics) +16, Listen +11, Move Silently +7, Pilot +8, Read/Write Basic, Repair +6, Search +6, Speak Basic, Spot +10, Tumble +7.

Feats: Alertness, Dodge, Heroic Surge, Improved Martial Arts, Martial Arts, Point Blank Shot, Skill Emphasis (Hide, Knowledge [politics]), Weapon Group Proficiencies (blaster pistols, simple weapons, vibro weapons).

Senator Canny Mandary Bertar

A Mrlssi Senator from the world of Mrlsst in the Tapani sector, Canny Mandary Bertar loves the game of politics more than she loves her own people. Senator Bertar is chair of the Senate Dispensation Committee, which oversees special government grants to freelancers such as shipping licenses, bounty hunting permits, and the loan of Republic cruisers for important missions. She came to Coruscant a few years prior to the Battle of Naboo and held on to her Senate seat throughout the Clone Wars and Palpatine's establishment of a New Order. Though Bertar hated the resulting antialien sentiment, she didn't join the Rebel Alliance for fear of hurting her career. The Senator is no fan of Palpatine's, however, and knows when to look the other way.

Canny Mandary Bertar: Female Mrlssi Noble 9; Init +4 (+4 Improved Initiative); Defense 16 (+1 size, +5 class); Spd 6 m; VP/WP 39/9; Atk +7/+2 melee (1d3, claw) or +7/+2 ranged; SQ bonus class skill (Bluff), coordinate +2, favor +3, inspire confidence, resource access; SV Fort +2, Ref +4, Will +10; SZ S; FP 4; DSP 1; Rep +8; Str 10, Dex 10, Con 9, Int 15, Wis 15, Cha 15. Challenge Code D.

  Equipment: Code cylinder, encrypted datapad, electrum-plated cigarra case.

  Skills: Appraise +7, Bluff +12, Computer Use +10, Diplomacy +14, Entertain (storytelling) +8, Hide +4, Knowledge (Coruscant) +12, Knowledge (Mrlsst) +10, Knowledge (politics) +14, Profession (senator) +14, Read/Write Basic, Read/Write Mrlssese, Ride +3, Search +4, Sense Motive +14, Speak Basic, Speak Mrlssese, Spot +10.

  Feats: Combat Expertise, Fame, Improved Initiative, Influence, Iron Will, Sharp-Eyed, Weapon Group Proficiencies (blaster pistols, simple weapons).

Air Marshal Cargeloch

This old-guard Imperial officer loves the New Order so much it is said he sleeps in his uniform. New Imperial Navy recruits have nightmares of Cargeloch crinkling the leather on his black flight gloves before he slaps them across the face for incompetence in the TIE simulators. Cargeloch is a lean, gray-haired TIE ace who holds the dual duty of instructing at the naval base and leading the wing of Imperial starfighters assigned to defend the airspace around the Imperial Palace. He earned his rank by blasting a rebellious city to rubble with only four TIE bombers.

Air Marshal Cargeloch: Male Human Soldier 7/Noble 1/Officer 3; Init +5 (+1 Dex, +4 Improved Initiative); Defense 19 (+1 Dex, +8 class); Spd 10 m; VP/WP 60/12; Atk +10/+5 melee (1d3+1, punch) or +10/+5 (3d6, blaster pistol); SQ bonus class skill (Gather Information), favor +1, leadership, requisition supplies; SV Fort +8, Ref +8, Will +8; SZ M; FP 2; DSP 6; Rep +8; Str 13, Dex 13, Con 12, Int 15, Wis 11, Cha 13. Challenge Code E.

  Equipment: Blaster pistol, code cylinder, TIE fighter (*Valkyrie*).

  Skills: Astrogate +15, Computer Use +8, Diplomacy +8, Gather Information +8, Intimidate +11, Knowledge (Coruscant) +13, Knowledge (tactics) +15, Pilot +17, Read/Write Basic, Repair +15, Speak Basic.

  Feats: Armor Proficiency (light), Fame, Heroic Surge, Improved Initiative, Iron Will, Lightning Reflexes, Point Blank Shot, Spacer, Starship Dodge (starfighter), Starship Operation (starfighter), Weapon Group Proficiencies (blaster pistols, blaster rifles, heavy weapons, simple weapons, vibro weapons).

Ocka Dwei

No one in the galaxy knows Ocka Dwei's real name, nor does anyone suspect his mission. Ocka Dwei is an advance scout for the Yuuzhan Vong. He is trying to gather information about this infidel realm to prepare for the day when the Supreme Overlord approves a full military invasion. On the surface, Dwei appears to be a tall man in his mid-twenties with dark hair and a pudgy face. This is a disguise created by Dwei's ooglith masquer. His true appearance is that of a proud, tattooed Yuuzhan Vong warrior. Ocka Dwei speaks flawless Basic and is an expert on Coruscant customs. *Note:* The GM should take care to leave Ocka Dwei's true identity ambiguous. The galaxy will not learn of the Yuuzhan Vong until the events of *Vector Prime*.

If Ocka Dwei's threat level is too low for the player group, the GM may wish to make him the head of a small Yuuzhan Vong infiltration team.

Ocka Dwei: Male Yuuzhan Vong Scout 11; Init +1; Defense 18 (+1 Dex, +7 class); Spd 10 m; VP/WP 72/14; Atk +10/+5 melee (1d3+2, punch) or +10/+5 melee (1d6+2, coufee) or +9/+4 ranged (2d6, thud bug); SQ biotechnology, evasion, extreme effort, Force absence, heart +2, skill mastery (Bluff, Spot), technophobia, trailblazing, uncanny dodge (can't be flanked, Dex bonus to Defense); SV Fort +7, Ref +6, Will +4; SZ M; FP 0; DSP 2; Rep +3; Str 14, Dex 12, Con 14, Int 13, Wis 8, Cha 10. Challenge Code E.

  Equipment: Coufee, 20 thud bugs, 4 blorash jellies, ooglith masquer, 2 villips, tizowyrm.

  Skills: Bluff +7, Climb +5, Computer Use +5, Disguise +11, Hide +10, Jump +5, Knowledge (Coruscant) +5, Knowledge (Yuuzhan Vong) +9, Listen +7, Move Silently +6, Read/Write Basic, Read/Write Yuuzhan Vong, Ride +5, Search +8, Speak Basic, Speak Yuuzhan Vong, Spot +4, Survival +11.

  Feats: Combat Expertise, Endurance, Exotic Weapon Proficiency (thud bug launcher), Heroic Surge, Power Attack, Skill Emphasis (Survival), Weapon Group Proficiency (simple weapons).

Tuchap

A jovial, smiling Farghul, Tuchap's mood can turn ice-cold when he feels someone has let him down. Because Tuchap makes his living as a race bookie and information broker in Coruscant's seedy undercity, many people have let him down—delinquents, snitches, and racers who refused to take a fall. This overweight felinoid has soft golden fur and sneezes uncontrollably in the presence of cigarra smoke. Under the right circumstances, Tuchap can be a useful (but still dangerous) ally.

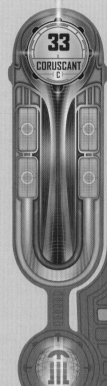

Tuchap: Male Farghul Scoundrel 5; Init +1; Defense 15 (+1 Dex, +4 class); Spd 10 m; VP/WP 19/9; Atk +2 melee (1d3–1, punch) or +4 ranged (3d6, blaster pistol); SQ illicit barter, lucky 1/day, precise attack +1, prehensile tail; SV Fort +0, Ref +5, Will +2; SZ M; FP 0; DSP 2; Rep +1; Str 8, Dex 12, Con 9, Int 14, Wis 10, Cha 12. Challenge Code C.

Equipment: Datapad with racing results, encoded comlink, bag of ryll spice, concealed blaster pistol.

Skills: Appraise +7, Bluff +11, Computer Use +6, Disguise +5, Forgery +6, Gamble +6, Gather Information +7, Hide +7, Intimidate +3, Knowledge (Coruscant) +7, Knowledge (streetwise) +8, Listen +6, Move Silently +3, Profession (bookie) +8, Read/Write Basic, Read/Write Farghul, Search +6, Speak Basic, Speak Farghul, Speak Huttese, Speak Rodese, Spot +7.

Feats: Combat Expertise, Headstrong, Skill Emphasis (Bluff), Stealthy, Weapon Group Proficiencies (blaster pistols, simple weapons).

Master Shaper Gengi Tung

Gengi Tung is secretly amazed at the position in which he now finds himself. As a young adept, he never dreamed he would one day ascend to master. Even after he was entrusted with the bioshaping of Imperial City, a small part of him kept thinking, "There must be some mistake." It follows that he will do anything in his power to keep from being humiliated in his new role, often over-compensating by accompanying his warriors on field missions. Tung wears a tentacled headdress the color of dried blood and has replaced his teeth with needle-sharp animal quills. He is always accompanied by Toi and Tixo, his pet umrachs.

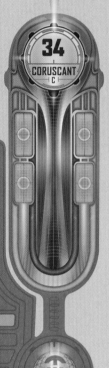

post
UMRACH

Gengi Tung: Male Yuuzhan Vong Expert 10/Noble 8; Init +5 (+1 Dex, +4 Improved Initiative); Defense 17 (+1 Dex, +6 class); Spd 10 m; VP/WP 34/10; Atk +13/+8/+3 melee (1d3, punch) or +13/+8/+3 melee (1d6, tsaisi) or +14/+9/+4 ranged; SQ biotechnology, bonus class skill (Intimidate), coordinate +2, favor +3, Force absence, inspire confidence, resource access, technophobia; SV Fort +5, Ref +8, Will +14; SZ M; FP 0; DSP 8; Rep +5; Str 10, Dex 12, Con 10, Int 17, Wis 12, Cha 15. Challenge Code F.

Equipment: Tsaisi, ceremonial headdress, ooglith masquer, 2 villips, tizowyrm, 2 pet umrachs.

Skills: Appraise +10, Bluff +6, Craft (control organism) +24, Craft (prosthetic organism) +24, Craft (space transport organism) +16, Craft (starfighter organism) +16, Craft (weapon organism) +21, Diplomacy +12, Gather Information +4, Handle Animal +16, Intimidate +10, Knowledge (biology) +20, Knowledge (Yuuzhan Vong) +11, Read/Write Yuuzhan Vong, Search +10, Sense Motive +8, Speak Yuuzhan Vong, Spot +6, Survival +4, Treat Injury +14.

Feats: Combat Expertise, Exotic Weapon Proficiencies (amphistaff, tsaisi), Improved Initiative, Sharp-Eyed, Skill Emphasis (Craft [control organism], Treat Injury), Trustworthy, Weapon Group Proficiency (simple weapons).

New Creature: Umrach

Introduced into Coruscant's ecosystem by Yuuzhan Vong biomachines, the umrach is a hulking reptile whose face is a seething mass of razor-tipped tentacles. When hunting, the umrach sprints forward on two powerful legs and seizes its prey with prehensile forepaws, lowering its head to deliver a messy killing strike with its mouth-spears. Since their arrival on Coruscant, umrachs have become a nightmare for those residents still trying to survive in the city's underlevels.

Umrach: Jungle predator 9; Init +6 (+2 Dex, +4 Improved Initiative); Defense 21 (+2 Dex, –1 size, +10 natural); Spd 16 m; VP/WP 60/15; Atk +14/+9 melee (2d8+5, mouth-tentacle "bite") or +14/+5 melee (1d4+5, slam) or +14/+5 melee (1d4+5, tail slam) or +11/+6 ranged; SQ blindsight 30 m, constrict 1d4+5, Force absence; SV Fort +9, Ref +9, Will +4; SZ L; Face/Reach 4 m by 4 m/4 m; Rep +0; Str 20, Dex 15, Con 15, Int 4, Wis 13, Cha 7. Challenge Code F.

Skills: Hide +5, Intimidate +3, Jump +10, Listen +4, Move Silently +8, Spot +5, Survival +5.

Feats: Blind-Fight, Improved Initiative, Track.

Special Qualities: *Constrict*—If an umrach successfully grapples an opponent, it can constrict for 1d4+5 points of damage and attempt a bite attack in the same round.

New Creature: Gartro

Gartros resemble miniature dragons, with batlike wings, spike-studded tails, and long reptilian jaws filled with needle teeth. Most Coruscanti consider them nuisances for their tendency to congregate in vast, shrieking flocks, but a coalition of gartro-lovers has been petitioning the government to recognize the creatures as a protected species. Gartros are omnivorous and will rarely attack anything larger than a grain-fly, unless they feel threatened by an incursion into their home territory.

Gartro: Airborne scavenger 2; Init +6 (+2 Dex, +4 Improved Initiative); Defense 13 (+2 Dex, +1 size); Spd 4 m, fly 20 m (good); VP/WP 10/8; Atk +0 melee (1d4–1, bite) or +5 ranged; SQ low-light vision; SV Fort +2, Ref +2, Will +1; SZ S; Face/Reach 2 m by 2 m/2 m; Rep +0; Str 8, Dex 14, Con 8, Int 3, Wis 13, Cha 7. Challenge Code A.

   Skills: Listen +5, Spot +6, Survival +4.
   Feats: Flyby Attack.

New Creature: Cthon

Mothers scare their children with stories of Cthons, stringy-haired, eyeless monsters with skin the color of a fish's belly. Cthons are found only in the blackest sublevels of Coruscant. Biologists believe they are related to Coruscanti ogres, but Cthons are distinguished by the flaps of skin covering their eye sockets and their flat, skull-like noses. Cthons scavenge for dead vermin and rotting meat, but hunt larger prey when food is scarce. They have been known to set traps using electroshock nets, and they will happily engage in cannibalism if their trap ensnares a fellow Cthon.

Cthon: Subterranean scavenger 6; Init –1; Defense 14 (–1 Dex, –1 size, +5 natural); Spd 10 m; VP/WP 26/16; Atk +10 melee (1d4+6, slam) or +3 ranged; SQ blindsight 10 m; SV Fort +8, Ref +1, Will +2; SZ L; Face/Reach 2 m by 2 m/4 m; Rep +0; Str 24, Dex 9, Con 16, Int 3, Wis 11, Cha 2. Challenge Code C.

   Skills: Hide +5, Listen +8, Move Silently +5, Survival +4.
   Feats: Blind-Fight, Power Attack, Track.

New Creature: Stratt

Cuddly balls of fur at birth, stratts quickly grow into voracious, musclebound carnivores measuring nearly two meters from snout to tail. Enough stratts have escaped from black-market pet shops over the years to create a stable population in Coruscant's darkest sublevels. Stratts only prowl at night, when their jet-black fur helps hide them from their nervous prey.

Stratt: Urban predator 4; Init +3; Defense 13 (+3 Dex); Spd 16 m; VP/WP 25/14; Atk +8 melee (2d4+4, 2 claws) or +8 melee (1d8+4, bite) or +7 ranged; SQ camouflage; SV Fort +6, Ref +7, Will +1; SZ M; Face/Reach 2 m by 2 m/2 m; Rep +0; Str 18, Dex 16, Con 14, Int 4, Wis 11, Cha 8. Challenge Code B.

   Skills: Climb +8, Hide +8, Jump +8, Move Silently +8.
   Feats: Power Attack, Track.
   Special Qualities: *Camouflage*—The dark fur of stratts allows them to blend in with the shadows. They gain a +8 circumstance bonus on Hide checks in dimly lit environments or at night.

New Droid: Construction Droid

Coruscanti like to brag that their construction droids are the biggest droids in the galaxy. They are certainly among the most complex. These shambling, forty-story behemoths tear down old buildings and excrete gleaming, finished structures. The atomic incinerators in their innards can break down almost any material. Normally, construction droids travel at a slug's pace, but one programmed to raze buildings indiscriminately could charge forward like a rancor, consuming everything in its path.

Construction Droid: Walking construction droid, Expert 10; Init –5; Defense 30 (–5 Dex, –8 size, +3 class, +30 natural); Spd 10 m; VP/WP 0/160; Atk +14 melee (10d6+15, 2 heavy shovel arms) or +14/+9 melee (10d6+30, battering ram) or +14/+9 melee (8d6, implosion wrecking balls) or +14/+9 melee (3d8+4, plasma cutters) or +14/+9 melee (4d6, explosive electrical claws) or –6/–11 ranged; SV Fort +8, Ref –1, Will +7; SZ C; Face/Reach 10 m by 10 m/20 m; Rep +2; Str 40, Dex 1, Con 20, Int 4, Wis 11, Cha 8. Challenge Code F.

   Equipment: Heavy shovel arms, battering ram, implosion wrecking balls, plasma cutters, explosive electrical claws.
   Skills: Balance –3, Computer Use –1, Demolitions +5, Disable Device +6, Hide –21, Knowledge (Coruscant) +13, Repair +15, Speak Binary.
   Unspent Skill Points: 0.
   Feats: Ambidexterity, Cautious, Endurance, Gearhead, Skill Emphasis (Knowledge [Coruscant], Repair), Steady.
   Cost: 900,000 credits.

Labor Droid: ASP Series

ASP Series labor droids are common throughout the galaxy. They perform a variety of simple tasks, including maintenance, repair, sanitation, delivery, and simple hard labor. Cheap and effective, they are designed as "entry-level" droids for first-time buyers. Many ASP owners modify the droids heavily instead of actually replacing them.

ASPs are built for strength and sturdiness, not intelligence. Since the main virtue of the ASP is versatility, it's programmed with only the most basic functions—leaving the owner to instruct the droid in its specific duties.

ASP Series: Walking labor droid, Expert 1; Init +0; Defense 10 (+0 class); Spd 6 m; VP/WP 0/12; Atk +4 melee (1d6+4, claw) or +0 ranged; SV Fort +3, Ref +0, Will +1; SZ M; Face/Reach 2 m by 2 m/2 m; Rep +0; Str 18, Dex 10, Con 12, Int 6, Wis 8, Cha 10. Challenge Code A.

   Equipment: None.
   Skills: Speak Basic.
   Unspent Skill Points: 15.
   Feats: Ambidexterity, Great Fortitude, Weapon Group Proficiencies (blaster pistols, simple weapons).
   Cost: 1,000 credits.

Abregado-rae

Planet Type: Terrestrial
Climate: Temperate
Terrain: Hills, rivers/lakes
Atmosphere: Breathable
Gravity: Standard
Diameter: 12,000 km
Length of Day: 23 standard hours
Length of Year: 349 standard days
Sentient Species: Gados
Languages: Basic
Population: 40 million
Species Mix: 60% Gados, 36% Human, 4% other
Government: Repressive bureaucracy
Major Exports: Technology
Major Imports: Foodstuffs
System/Star: Abregado/Anza

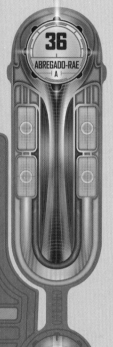

Planets	Type	Moons
Abregado-dai	Molten rock	0
Abregado-san	Barren rock	0
Abregado-rae	Terrestrial	1
Abregado-fus	Gas giant	9
Abregado-taki	Frozen rock	0

Description

Abregado-rae hardly seems like a Core World, and plenty of Core citizens would love to deny the planet that coveted title. Though the rough-and-tumble smugglers' planet has no interest in Human High Culture or the Coruscanti opera, the locals aren't about to surrender their status as residents of the Core. If nothing else, they relish the irritation it engenders on "snooty" worlds such as Corulag.

Abregado-rae's continents are low, rolling swells of land. The ground never reaches an elevation where a hill can be considered a mountain. Much of the planet's fresh water is locked in channels beneath the crust, where it bubbles to the surface in volcanolike "gushers." Water flows out in radial patterns to form webs of rivers cutting through the surface limestone.

The planet's ecology is surprisingly sparse, supporting less than 5 percent of the biodiversity found on worlds such as Ithor. Livestock dies within one generation for reasons unknown, requiring the residents to import most of their meat. On all Abregado-rae, one can count the number of large-sized, indigenous animal species on two (Human) hands.

History

Abregado-rae's position at the head of the Rimma Trade Route indicates its age. First scouted by the Republic over ten thousand years ago, the planet remained uncolonized for millennia. The trailblazers that ventured into the unexplored galactic southern quadrant gravitated toward the Tapani sector instead. Three thousand years before the Battle of Yavin, explorers had blazed and mapped the full length of the Rimma, but the planet still hadn't become much of a metropolis. Later, when most "official" Rim traffic left from Tapani, Abregado-rae became a jumping-off point of choice for smugglers and pirates.

The native Gados welcomed offworlders and turned a proverbial blind eye to all but the most heinous crimes. Abregado-rae entered a relative golden age of piracy that lasted through the early years of the New Republic. When the Tundei regime usurped the planet's nominal government, legalities swiftly changed. Within a few days of the usurpation, armed constables stood guard on every street corner. Abregado-rae instantly lost its outlaw image as "a pocket of the Rim in the heart of the Core."

The Tundei spent millions to modernize the planet's sole spaceport and erect manufacturing plants in the countryside. Smuggling continued as usual, but illegal business took place under the table. As the Tundei leaders flexed their newfound power, they persecuted lawbreakers to a sickening extreme, torturing those who were even suspected of armed violence or trafficking contraband. Ironically, the law-and-order-or-else climate created more smuggling opportunities, such as when the Tundei cut off all supply shipments to a colony of dissidents in the southern hills. Despite this, most smugglers decided the payoff wasn't worth the risk. Over the next few years, Abregado-rae saw less and less traffic as outlaws bypassed the planet in favor of free markets. The Tundei regime utterly failed in its efforts to attract legitimate outside investment.

During Grand Admiral Thrawn's campaign, Imperial forces seized a region of space bordering Abregado-rae. It appeared as though Thrawn might capture the world and advance on Coruscant with a twin-pincer tactic through the galactic northern and southern quadrants. His offensive collapsed at Bilbringi. Over the next decade, the New Republic, embarrassed by the excessive judicial zeal of its member world, tried to get the Tundei regime to repeal its sentences of amputation or execution for anyone caught "endangering the peace"—a crime that was very loosely defined. All such attempts failed.

More recently, the Yuuzhan Vong drove tens of thousands of refugees to Abregado-rae, overloading the spaceport and causing the Tundei to lose its grip on the populace. Observers say the planet is now ripe for revolution.

People

Most people are unfamiliar with the Gados species, except for those who remember the Alsakan Circo-Menagerie from their childhoods. Leaping Tee, a Gados family of tumblers and acrobats, still performs with the Alsakan show at sold-out venues across the galaxy.

Not all Gados are as agile as the members of the Tee family, but compared to most species, their bodies are impossibly supple. Their skeletons are composed of small knots of bone connected by ligaments and muscle. Gados seem to be wound up like springs, and they are capable of prodigious leaps. (As part of this, all Gados characters have the Acrobatic feat; see below.)

The Gados are an extremely adaptable people. Since Abregado-rae's first colonization, they have welcomed offworlders with open arms. The accepting nature of the planet's natives cemented Abregado-rae's reputation as a smuggler's haven—until the unfortunate rise of the Tundei regime. Basic has all but replaced the ancient Gados tongue as the official language. If the species' adaptability has a downside, it is that the Gados have almost no sense of species history. There is no Gados cuisine, no Gados art, and no Gados culture. Almost everything in a modern Abregado-rae city has been imported from somewhere else. The feeling that they lost their heritage long ago induces a deep melancholy in many Gados.

Visitors are certain to cross paths with another local lifeform while on the planet: Moochers. They typically have to run a gauntlet of the pawing, half-sized aliens upon arrival at the spaceport. Locals who don't keep their food stores locked up may find them raided down to the last crumb by bands of the hungry creatures. Restaurateurs shoo away Moochers on sight to prevent them from plucking food right off the customers' plates. Outsiders may be inclined to think of them as mindless panhandlers, but Moochers are actually semisentient animals, perfectly capable of understanding simple commands and performing basic tasks.

Wild Moochers, rarely encountered by city dwellers, live in caves beneath Abregado-rae's rounded hills. They can move on four feet as easily as two and manipulate objects with their tails. Most city residents hate Moochers and wish they'd go back to the countryside, but in truth, the spaceport Moochers are the outcasts. For reasons poorly understood, Moochers who don't measure up to some esoteric standard of fitness are expelled from their home warrens to scratch out a living among the Humans and Gados.

The Moocher language is based on gestures, with the occasional bark or whistle thrown in for emphasis. These gestures have led many spacers to think of Moochers as desperate and fidgety. In truth, they simply have a lot to

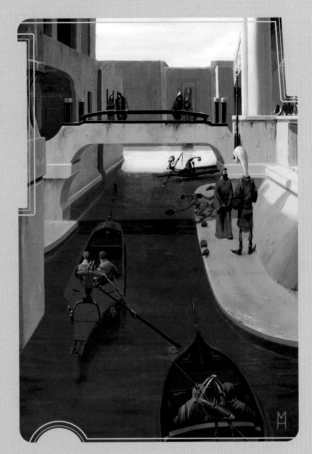

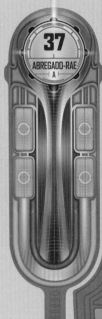

say—and may be looking for the companionship they lost after exile from their dens.

Locations

Descriptions of two key locations follow.

Abregado-rae Spaceport

Abregado-rae Spaceport lacks a catchy name, but that's one of the tradeoffs the Gados made when they opened their doors to the galaxy. Over the centuries, the community's original Gados name has fallen out of use. Its earliest buildings have been relegated to a canal district known as the Old Patch.

The Old Patch is situated around the Spaceport Gusher, which pumps millions of liters of water to the surface every day. The canals branching away from the Gusher are thick with floatboats carrying passenger and freight traffic. Pedestrians must walk along narrow bridges and sidewalks. The LoBue Cantina can be found on the outskirts of this borough, where veteran smugglers gather to swap tales and make connections for their next assignment. Away from the Old Patch, the modern spaceport district is identical with those found throughout the Outer Rim—the same cantinas, the same gambling dens, and the same discount sleeping bunks. The Tundei regime has tried to "modernize" the Abregado-rae Spaceport, but beneath the fresh paint, the city is remarkably seedy.

Map labels:

Abregado-rae Spaceport

Abregado-rae Spaceport →

← Landing Pad

The Old Patch

LoBue Cantina

Southern Hills

Wild Moocher Den

Dissident Stronghold

Ocean

Gilt Gushers

Out in the country, the curious can investigate the Gilt Gushers, a string of tributary fountains that supposedly reach deep into the planet's crust, where they tap a vein of raw electrum. According to rumor, the electrum flakes sometimes bubble to the surface, and when they do, they can make a prospector rich. No one ever seems to be able to locate the right gusher at the right moment, but not for lack of trying. Cavernous Moocher dens lie somewhere deep beneath the ground, but few people in town admit to having seen one.

Gados Floatboat

The canals running through the Old Patch district of Abregado-rae are navigated by floatboats: amphibious vehicles that travel on repulsorlifts when they leave the canals for dry land. Floatboats are brightly painted red, yellow, or green and are often used as taxis. A ride in a floatboat typically costs 5 or 10 credits. A floatboat occupies an area 10 squares long by 2 squares wide.

Gados Floatboat

Class: Speeder [Ground]	Crew: 1 (Skilled +4)
Size: Huge (10 m long)	Initiative: +2 (–2 size, +4 crew)
Passengers: 15	Maneuver: +2 (–2 size, +4 crew)
Cargo Capacity: 50 tons	Defense: 8 (–2 size)
Cost: 13,000 (new), 4,000 (used)	Shield Points: 0
	Hull Points: 20 (DR 5)
Availability: Prevalent	Atmospheric Speed: 1square/ action (50 km/h)
Era: All	Altitude: 0.5 km

* This vehicle provides full cover to its pilot.

   Weapon: Laser cannon (security models only); **Fire Arc:** Front; **Attack Bonus:** +6 (–2 size, +4 crew, +4 fire control); **Damage:** 4d8; **Range Increment:** 20 m.

For the GM

The adventure hooks and supporting characters described in this section are meant for GMs only. If you're a player, stop reading now.

Adventures

Feel free to use or adapt the following adventure hooks for your home campaign.

Mercy Mission

The Tundei regime has cut off all supply lines to a group of dissidents hiding in the southern hills. The leader of the dissidents offers to pay handsomely for a simple cargo of food. Heroes with noble hearts may determine that helping the victims of Tundei oppression is the simply the right thing to do. A Gados transparisteel maker in the Abregado-rae Spaceport named Trarr has connections with the local underground. He's willing to supply a speederload of surplus war rations. (In the Rise of the Empire era or the Rebellion era, the GM can substitute a powerful local crime lord in place of the Tundei regime.) Can the characters get the food to the dissidents before they starve?

To avoid detection, the safest course of action is to offload the cargo into a rented floatboat and navigate down the canals to the southern hills. Tundei constables are vigilant, however, and a boat cruise can easily turn into a police chase and high-speed shootout. Worse, the traitorous Trarr is concealing his Tundei affiliations. After establishing his false motives, he attempts to track the heroes to find the dissidents' secret stronghold. His thugs shoot to kill. The nonviolent dissidents may prove useless in a firefight.

Extermination!

A colony of wild Moochers has been raiding food stores and attacking those who venture into their caverns. Rumor has it that the Moochers have been driven mad by Veizen fever. If something isn't done soon, the contagion could spread across the planet. Should the heroes block off the Moochers' subterranean tunnels, or should they exterminate the entire Moocher den to contain the pestilence?

Any course of action is perilous, especially considering that the hundreds of maddened Moochers are likely to attack anything they see. The infected Moochers fight to the death to protect their queen, who tries to kill anyone who has dared harm her offspring.

Topple the Tundei

Shelov, head of the vicious Tundei Tribunal, is one of the most tempting targets for assassination on Abregado-rae. A number of offworld Gados colonies have posted a bounty on this sadistic bureaucrat's head. Shelov keeps an office in the Tundei administrative headquarters, a fortress protected by sentries, guard animals, and security countermeasures—but even a tyrant gets out once in a while. The heroes may learn of Shelov's regular sabacc games at the LoBue Cantina and of the light escort that regularly accompanies him.

If the heroes try to seize and keep Shelov, they quickly discover two facts: Shelov is a formidable combatant in his own right, and his Tundei cronies consider him expendable in a firefight.

Allies and Antagonists

The following supporting characters are designed for use in your campaign.

Trarr

Trarr appears to be a kindly transparisteel maker in the Old Patch district of Abregado-rae, but the wily Gados leads a double life. In addition to his legitimate business, he works as a forger, and the Tundei regime has recently enlisted him as a spy. His skin has turned yellow with age, but the Gados is still as flexible as he was in his youth.

Trarr: Male Gados Scoundrel 6; Init +2; Defense 16 (+2 Dex, +4 class); Spd 12 m; VP/WP 18/8; Atk +4 melee (1d3, punch) or +6 ranged (3d6, blaster pistol); SQ illicit barter, lucky 2/day, precise attack +1; SV Fort +1, Ref +7, Will +1; SZ M; FP 1; DSP 1; Rep +1; Str 11, Dex 14, Con 8, Int 10, Wis 9, Cha 12. Challenge Code D.

Equipment: Expensive tailored clothing, pouch containing 800 credits and a membership ID in the Transparisteel Makers' Guild, concealed blaster pistol.

Skills: Appraise +5, Bluff +11, Craft (tools) +9, Disguise +5, Forgery +8, Gather Information +7, Intimidate +3, Jump +2, Knowledge (alien species) +4, Knowledge (politics) +9, Listen +7, Profession (transparisteel maker) +8, Read/Write Basic, Repair +5, Speak Basic.

Feats: Acrobatic, Dodge, Persuasive, Quickness, Skill Emphasis (Bluff), Track, Weapon Group Proficiencies (blaster pistols, simple weapons).

Shelov

A tenth-generation resident of Abregado-rae, the Herglic known as Shelov believes he knows what's best for his planet. Working with other Abregado-rae natives from many different species, he helped found the Tundei regime that seized control of the planet several years after the Battle of Endor. Shelov earned a position as head of the Tundei Tribunal, where he meted out tortures to political dissidents and other lawbreakers. Like many Herglics, Shelov is an avid gambler. He is easily recognized by the black ring-tattoos circling the blow hole on his massive cetacean head.

Shelov: Male Herglic Diplomat 10/Soldier 6; Init +3 (−1 Dex, +4 Improved Initiative); Defense 16 (−1 Dex, −1 size, +6 class, +2 natural); Spd 8 m; VP/WP 50/15; Atk +12/+7 melee (1d4+2, punch) or +9/+4/−1 ranged (3d6, blaster pistol); SQ gambling addiction; SV Fort +11, Ref +4, Will +11; SZ L; FP 2; DSP 1; Rep +5; Str 14, Dex 8, Con 12, Int 12, Wis 10, Cha 12. Challenge Code E.

Equipment: Blaster pistol.

Skills: Bluff +12, Climb +4, Computer Use +9, Diplomacy +12, Gamble +9, Gather Information +9, Hide −5, Intimidate +10, Knowledge (alien species) +13, Knowledge (politics) +15, Read/Write Herglese, Repair +5, Sense Motive +10, Speak Basic, Speak Herglese, Speak Rodese, Swim +4.

Feats: Armor Proficiency (light), Athletic, Endurance, Great Fortitude, Heroic Surge, Improved Initiative, Iron Will, Persuasive, Power Attack, Run, Skill Emphasis (Gamble), Toughness, Weapon Group Proficiencies (blaster pistols, simple weapons).

New Species: Gados

As a rule, the Gados are an agreeable lot. Most are friendly toward strangers and tolerant of odd quirks. Their limberness and agility help make up for their fragile physiques. Gados aliens can somersault almost indefinitely, rolling rapidly into a room to surprise their foes.

Their internal organs are laid out in long ribbons running the length of their bodies. For this reason, every part of a Gados's body is a critical part—a blaster bolt in the foot is as life-threatening as a shot to the chest. A Gados who has to amputate any part of his body will almost certainly die.

Gados Commoner: Init +2; Defense 12 (+2 Dex); Spd 12 m; VP/WP 0/8; Atk +0 melee (1d3, unarmed) or +2 ranged; SQ species traits; SV Fort −1, Ref +2, Will −1; SZ M; FP 0; DSP 0; Rep +0; Str 10, Dex 14, Con 8, Int 10, Wis 8, Cha 10. Challenge Code A.

Equipment: Variety of personal belongings.

Skills: Craft (any one) +2 or Knowledge (any one) +2, Jump +2, Profession (any one) +1, Read/Write Basic, Speak Basic, Tumble +4.

Feats: Acrobatic (bonus feat).

Species Traits: +4 Dex, −2 Con, −2 Wis.

Automatic Language: Basic.

New Species: Moocher

Semisentient scavengers, Moochers are usually encountered begging for handouts in the Abregado-rae Spaceport. Wild Moochers seldom stray from their subterranean nests of five thousand to ten thousand individuals, all birthed by a single queen who is far more intelligent than any of her children. For unknown reasons, the queen sometimes expels members of her den into the outside world. The hive's outcasts and their descendants are the filthy specimens encountered near the landing pads. Moochers can perceive their surroundings in total darkness by sensing an energy field around them, but they cannot perceive anything farther away than 80 meters.

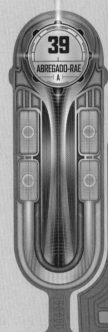

Moocher Commoner: Init +1; Defense 12 (+1 Dex, +1 size); Spd 10 m; VP/WP 0/8; Atk +1 melee (1d3, bite) or +2 ranged; SQ blindsight 80 m, prehensile tail; SV Fort −1, Ref +1, Will +0; SZ S; FP 0; DSP 0; Rep +1; Str 8, Dex 12, Con 8, Int 6, Wis 10, Cha 6. Challenge Code A.

   Equipment: Spare change, rags.

   Skills: Listen +1, Spot +1, Survival +2.

   Special Qualities: *Prehensile tail*—A Moocher can use its tail to lift up to a medium load, leaving its hands free to do other things. This negates the check penalty associated with medium loads, but the Moocher's speed is reduced to 2 meters. A Moocher's tail can also support up to twice the weight of a heavy load when firmly wrapped around an object that can support at least that much weight. A Moocher never incurs attacks of opportunity when making trip attacks with its tail.

   Species Traits: −2 Str, +2 Dex, −2 Con, −4 Int, −4 Cha.

Queen Moocher

Head breeder of the largest Moocher colony in the southern hills, the Queen Moocher protects her progeny with a mother's ferocity. Like all queens, she is larger and far more intelligent than the average Moocher. She has ruled her colony for thirteen Moocher generations, ever since she suffocated the former queen, who had become sterile in her advancing years.

Queen Moocher: Female Moocher Fringer 12; Init +5 (+1 Dex, +4 Improved Initiative); Defense 19 (+1 Dex, +8 class); Spd 10 m; VP/WP 48/7; Atk +8/+3 melee (1d3−1, punch) or +10/+5 ranged; SQ barter, blindsight 80 m, jury-rig +6, prehensile tail, survival +4; SV Fort +5, Ref +7, Will +4; SZ M; FP 1; DSP 0; Rep +0; Str 8, Dex 13, Con 7, Int 11, Wis 11, Cha 9. Challenge Code D.

   Equipment: None.

   Skills: Climb +10, Handle Animal +8, Hide +11, Knowledge (alien species) +8, Knowledge (tactics) +10, Listen +10, Move Silently +3, Read/Write Basic, Search +6, Speak Basic, Spot +10, Survival +10, Swim +7.

   Feats: Endurance, Heroic Surge, Improved Initiative, Low Profile, Quickness, Run, Stealthy, Weapon Group Proficiencies (primitive weapons, simple weapons).

40
ABREGADO-RAE
A

Alderaan

Planet Type: Terrestrial
Climate: Temperate
Terrain: Forests, plains
Atmosphere: Breathable
Gravity: Standard
Diameter: 12,500 km
Length of Day: 24 standard hours
Length of Year: 364 standard days
Sentient Species: Human
Languages: Basic
Population: 2 billion
Species Mix: 100% Human
Government: Representative democracy
Major Exports: Wine, art, luxury goods
Major Imports: Manufactured goods, electronics
System/Star: Alderaan/Alderaan

Planets	Type	Moons
Raisa	Searing rock	0
Alderaan	Terrestrial	0
Delaya	Terrestrial	0
Avirandel	Barren rock	1
Avishan	Frigid rock	0

Description

Alderaan is a world of lush grasslands, mysterious and intriguing alien ruins, halls of learning, and gentle climates. It's a utopian paradise where people build their cities in harmony with nature. The planet has no large oceans, but it does have a single ice-rimmed polar sea. The rest of the planet's surface water is composed of thousands of lakes and connecting waterways.

The Alderaan system is home to more than eight thousand subspecies of grass and even more species of wildflowers. Its flora includes a dizzying array of spices, herbs, and grains.

As for its fauna, two species stand out and are widely known throughout the galaxy. The first is the thrantas, huge airborne animals that resemble manta rays. Thrantas ride the gentle breezes of Alderaan, bearing passengers strapped to their backs. The second is the nerfs, herd animals whose meat is exceptionally delicious and sought all over the galaxy. Both species exist on other worlds, but in greatly reduced numbers.

In the later years of the Rebellion era, when sentients speak of the worst tragedies that have ever occurred in the galaxy, Alderaan is always foremost on everyone's lips. The Empire ruthlessly shattered this peaceful, idyllic utopia when it tested the Death Star's planet-killing beam. The destruction of Alderaan was an atrocity that will be long remembered and mourned by anyone who loves justice, beauty, and peace.

History

The first Human colonists arrived on Alderaan thousands of years before the Battle of Yavin. Human settlers discovered ancient ruins of alien origin—a clear sign that they were not the first species to colonize Alderaan. Explorers and scholars speculated as to how this pre-Human species, which they called the Killiks, could die out on such a peaceful, tranquil planet with no scars of war. Did the aliens abandon the planet? If so, why? Did disease wipe them out? Although the mystery was a great one, its importance to the Human settlers was overshadowed by the planet's beauty and perfect environment for colonization.

Presented with paradise, the settlers decided not to pave the planet with ferrocrete—one Coruscant was enough for the galaxy! Instead, they constructed cities in canyon crevasses, beneath the ice of polar seas, or on platforms on the shores of the larger Alderaan lakes. As Alderaan grew and prospered, it quickly gained the reputation of a world where gentle sentients prized art, culture, and education. Alderaan attracted many poets, artists, philosophers, and educators. Alderaan University served as the heart of the planet's educational and cultural dominance.

Although the planet's government had always been a democracy, a royal family eventually rose. House Organa ruled from Aldera, the planet's capital. Approximately twenty-five hundred years after the Human colonization of Alderaan, the system incorporated itself into the Old Republic and participated enthusiastically in its politics. The High Council of Alderaan became the legislative body controlling the planet's government, while the High Court of Alderaan assumed its formal role as a royal house that presided over the High Council.

In the aftermath of the Clone Wars, and under the leadership of Bail Organa, the natives of Alderaan adopted pacifism as a worldwide way of life. The planet's remaining superweapons of mass destruction were placed aboard a huge armory ship named *Another Chance*. The automated vessel was programmed to perpetually jump through hyperspace unless called back by the Council of Elders.

As Senator Palpatine began instituting his New Order, Alderaan backed the parties opposing his rule. Bail Organa, who also represented Alderaan in the Old Republic Senate, worked behind the scenes to foil the schemes of the new Emperor. Since Alderaan was a world known for pacifism, one with no standing army, the emerging Empire didn't see the need to occupy it. Enough planets required a heavy Imperial hand that Alderaan could be left alone for the time being.

Although they didn't act militarily, Alderaan's people quietly did what they could to foil the Empire's schemes. For instance, a tip from Bail Organa saved future Rebel leader Mon Mothma from Imperial capture. She managed to escape the Emperor's clutches with minutes to spare. Organa gave up his seat on the Senate and returned to Alderaan to attempt to talk his people out of their pacifism. His adopted daughter, Princess Leia Organa, embraced her father's call to arms and began running secret errands for the Rebels. But before Alderaan could mobilize its forces and join the Rebellion, a cosmic tragedy struck. The Empire had perfected a terrible new weapon of almost incomprehensible destruction: the Death Star. This colossal space station, the size of a small moon, was meant to be not only a symbol of the Empire's power and technological might but also a means of keeping Imperial worlds in line. Grand Moff Tarkin ordered that Alderaan would be the first test of the Death Star's weaponry. In a single, searing blast, all the beauty, culture, and majesty that was Alderaan vanished in a heartbeat. All that remains is an asteroid field appropriately called the Graveyard.

If any good came of the tragedy, it was this: Rather than making other worlds fear the Empire and fall into line, the destruction of Alderaan created anger and outrage across the galaxy. Species that were indecisive about joining the Rebels flocked to their cause. Rather than shattering the Rebels' will, the destruction of Alderaan actually spurred the Rebellion.

People

The average Alderaanian is an educated and cultured pacifist, a sentient capable of appreciating the finer things in life, both material and spiritual. When some people hear the word "pacifist," however, they picture

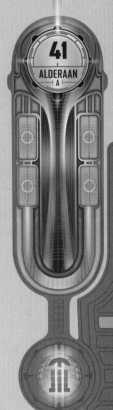

a physically weak person, someone who is afraid to fight and never loses his temper. Alderaanians are pacifists, but they are hardly passive. Although peace-loving, most Alderaanians possess a formidable inner strength. They refuse to fight not because they are unable, but because they choose a nobler path. Beings who understand the difference greatly respect and admire Alderaanians.

Poets and artists thrive on Alderaan. The planet's beauty moves the pens and hearts of the poets, while the vast grasslands serve as canvases of "grass paintings." These paintings, each measuring up to dozens of kilometers square, are completely visible only when observed from the vantage of flying observation boats. Another fine art that Alderaan is justly famous for is cuisine. Its vast variety of spices and herbs allow chefs to experiment and come up with some of the finest dishes in the galaxy. Steamed Alderaanian spiced wine is a favorite beverage of many epicures, both natives and offworlders.

About sixty thousand people survived the destruction of Alderaan because they were out of the system when tragedy struck. It is hoped that this remnant can keep alive—and possibly restore—the harmonious vision of a utopian world of high culture and peace. Most of the refugees have resettled on New Alderaan, a world chosen especially for them. While the survivors are certain to make New Alderaan into something truly special, most observers privately agree that there will never be another planet like Alderaan again.

Locations

Due to its pacifistic nature, Alderaan is hardly the world for rough-and-tumble spacefarers to visit for hair-raising adventures, barroom fights, and shoot-outs with bounty hunters. If anything, Alderaan's locales serve to nourish the mind and spirit—and perhaps impart wisdom and knowledge.

Crevasse City

Alderaan has several cities built into canyons and crevasses. The first and largest of these is called (fittingly enough) Crevasse City. Due to its locale, Crevasse City has no spaceport. Public transportation carries passengers between Crevasse City and Aldera, and the latter's spaceport handles all space traffic.

Crevasse City is a full-sized facility with all the amenities a traveler could want: restaurants, hotels, places of business, bars, and leisure facilities. The older buildings tend to be closer to the surface, with future expansion going downward, deeper into the crevasse. The deepest areas of the crevasse contain cavern complexes left untouched. These beautiful places feature crystal formations, underground lakes, and even hot springs.

Because of its location, Crevasse City gets fewer hours of sunlight than a city built on the surface would. The uppermost reaches of the city never get more than 6 hours of daylight at a time. As a result, the place depends heavily on artificial lighting. The natives have raised illumination to an art form, creating lights of all shapes and

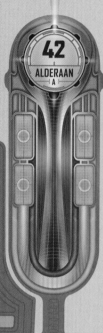
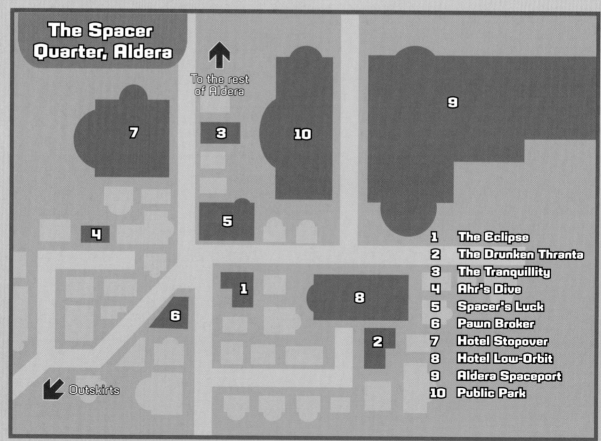

The Spacer Quarter, Aldera

↑ To the rest of Aldera

↙ Outskirts

1 The Eclipse
2 The Drunken Thranta
3 The Tranquillity
4 Ahr's Dive
5 Spacer's Luck
6 Pawn Broker
7 Hotel Stopover
8 Hotel Low-Orbit
9 Aldera Spaceport
10 Public Park

sizes. Some lights are out in the open, while others are cunningly built into the architecture. In fact, lights have become such a fact of life for Crevasse City that different colored lights take on different significance. White represents death and mourning, while blue means happiness and contentment. Green is the color of love, silver of prosperity, and orange of warning.

Crevasse City also boasts some of the best hotels and inns on the planet. The weary traveler can find everything from outlandish, sprawling luxury hotels to humble, cozy inns.

For all its beauty and comfort, Crevasse City has industry as well. Isolated in a far section of the city are a series of mines and geothermal power plants. Digging mines into the crevasse spares the surface from typical mine scarring. The ore quality is by no means the best anyone can find, but the metals extracted are fine enough.

Aldera

Aldera, the capital city of Alderaan, features the Royal Palace and Alderaan University. Its excellent spaceport has full facilities and accommodations. Spaceports traditionally tend to attract the "seedier element." While that's true on Alderaan, seediness is relative. The seedier element in Alderaan's spaceport would be considered downright respectable in, say, Mos Eisley on Tatooine.

Aside from the spaceport, Aldera has a fine collection of museums, schools, concert halls, parks, hotels, and gourmet restaurants. Tourists and traders are welcome, provided they respect local laws. Even in the most dangerous sections of the city, the Aldera Peace Force keeps order, using nonlethal methods of subduing and restraining what few malcontents manage to find their way to Alderaan. Unless the crimes are of a violent nature, the offenders are usually confined to their ships for the duration of their stay, or in some cases, escorted out of the system.

The Spacer Quarter is a section of Aldera devoted to offworlders and the services they require. Among the bars located here are the Eclipse, the Drunken Thranta, the Tranquility, and Ahr's Dive. The Spacer Quarter also has several good hotels, a gambling hall called Spacer's Luck, and a pawnbroker of local renown.

The keystone of Alderaan's educational power is Alderaan University, founded early in Alderaan's millennia-spanning history. From almost the beginning of Alderaan's society, its people knew that the acquisition, storage, and dissemination of knowledge were high priorities at the university.

The Aldera Universal Medcenter is a marvel of medical technology. This complex of a dozen buildings has the most up-to-date facilities for treating injuries and diseases for almost every known species. It is said that medical miracles are routine at Aldera Universal. Medical advancement and compassion go hand in hand at this facility. No one is turned away due to lack of money.

Besides healing, Aldera Universal also teaches. The facility includes a medical school and a medical droid research and development facility. For a fee, those seeking medical knowledge may take classes and training.

When it comes to perfection in food, few locales in the galaxy can beat the Epicurium, Aldera's ultimate cooking school. Sentients from all over the galaxy come to the Epicurium to learn its many schools of cooking. The Epicurium's library banks contain a staggering amount of recipes of every conceivable kind. Adjacent to the Epicurium is Latli's, a gourmet restaurant of great renown. Many graduates of the Epicurium end up working a term or two at Latli's. The restaurant is a favored spot for the wealthy, the cultured, and those who wish to impress friends and clients.

The Killik Mounds

The Killiks are the Humans' predecessors on Alderaan. Not much is known of them or their fate. The only surviving remnant of that civilization is the Killik Mounds: large, empty, petrified dirt mounds that once served as Killik dwellings. The greatest concentration of Killik Mounds can be found in the region called the Castle Lands, a favorite place for philosophers to sit and ponder existence. Inquisitive scholars have launched many expeditions to the Killik Mounds. Sometimes, adventurous types who desire a bit of light work for some pocket change hire themselves out as security for archaeological expeditions.

The Graveyard

After the destruction of Alderaan by the first Death Star, all that is left of the planet is an asteroid field called the Graveyard. The remains of Alderaan's moon, a large hemisphere of pitted rock, orbits at the Graveyard's sunward edge. Stories, legends, and rumors have sprung up around it—tales of ghost ships, intact ruins, hidden wealth, and mysterious Jedi artifacts. For instance, after the Battle of Yavin, some rumors suggested the Royal Palace actually survived the destruction of Alderaan. This was eventually found to be a story planted by the Empire to lure Princess Leia and her allies to the Graveyard and capture them.

Many Alderaanians who were offplanet, and thus survived the planet's destruction, adopted a new ritual called "the Returning" to cope with their loss. Part of the ritual involves Returnees purchasing a small memorial capsule and filling it with personal gifts and tokens for the friends and family lost on Alderaan. The capsule is jettisoned into orbit as the Returnee makes a remembrance speech.

Some Alderaanian exiles spend time patrolling the Graveyard, watching for scavengers. These exiles call themselves Custodians and consider the patrols a sacred trust. Many Custodians feel that every Alderaanian exile should dedicate a month each year to patrolling the asteroid field as a gesture of respect and loss. Not every exile feels this way, and large portions of the Graveyard often remain unguarded.

For the GM

The adventure hooks and supporting characters described in this section are meant for GMs only. If you're a player, stop reading now.

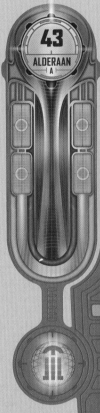

Adventures

Although Alderaan is a peaceful world, events often transpire behind the scenes that run counter to the world's philosophies. Nobody's perfect, and apparently, no place is either.

Codename: Restoration

This adventure can be played only after Alderaan is destroyed—preferably while the Empire is still around. An upper-middle-class Alderaanian family, one whose members were offworld when the planet was destroyed, hires the heroes' ship for a charter trip. The family wishes to visit the Graveyard and perform the ritual of the Returning. However, when the heroes' ship arrives at the Graveyard, the vessel's sensors pick up an energy surge from deep in the asteroid belt.

The beacon is part of an installation built centuries ago and placed 200 kilometers underground on one of the larger asteroids. An Alderaanian team of visionaries constructed this secret installation to plan for any possible future and christened it Restoration. A series of durable vaults contain what could possibly be the future survival of Alderaan: thousands of vials of cataloged genetic material, one vial for each species of Alderaanian flora and fauna. The visionaries reasoned that if a great calamity hit the planet and an entire species was wiped out in a war or ecological disaster, the species could be restored through cloning of the stored genetic material.

Shock waves from Alderaan's destruction caused the vault complex's beacon system to automatically activate. The Empire detected the signal after decoding the transmissions of a routine sensor probe that passed through the system several days before the heroes arrived. The Empire is sending an Imperial naval force to check out the sensor anomaly. The heroes must explore the complex, discover what's there, beat back the Imperials, and somehow get the genetic material into Rebel hands. The Alliance has numerous contacts with Alderaanian survivors who would know how best to handle the matter. But if the heroes do not act quickly, the Empire may destroy (or exploit) what it cannot recover.

The Alderaan-Belgaroth Run

This adventure takes place sometime during the Rebellion era but before the destruction of Alderaan. Tor Aramatha, a devoted pacifist and influential member of Alderaan's government, requires the heroes' help and arranges a meeting. Although it scarcely seems believable, some sort of weapons trade is going on in the Alderaan system. Aramatha wishes the matter to be handled discreetly. He prefers that reliable, altruistic offworlders deal with this, since it most likely involves outworlders setting up an arms trade network, with Alderaan as one of the stops.

Lorac Nonnaihr is the guilty culprit. He runs his smuggling operation from the Spacer Quarter of Aldera. Would-be customers deal with his proxies, never directly with him. Customers put in an order, pay up front, and pick up their weapons in the Belgaroth system. While the Rebellion might find this arrangement equitable,

Aramatha would be horrified by the thought of a merchant of death exploiting Aldera's peaceful surroundings. Can the heroes dig past the proxies and find the truth behind the Alderaan–Belgaroth run? What will they do with the information if and when they get it?

Allies and Antagonists

Not everyone on Alderaan is high-minded, peaceful, and altruistic. Even in the greatest societies, greed and corruption can thrive.

Lorac Nonnaihr

Lorac is proof that no society is perfect. Ironically, he thinks he's doing his world a good turn. Lorac is an arms dealer—a rarity in Alderaanian society. Each transaction he conducts carries an exacting condition: Each weapon he sells must never be used on his homeworld or, for that matter, anywhere in the Alderaan system. Sticking to the shadows, Lorac puts on a good front as a respectable merchant and businessman loved by all. Perhaps a sense of boredom or desire for a thrill motivates him. Whatever the reason, Lorac has a small but fanatically loyal staff of offworlders who enjoy a semipermanent stay on Alderaan. To maintain his anonymity, Lorac never deals directly with his own people. He uses a shadowcloak field (see below) to remain shrouded in darkness.

Lorac is a Human male in his early thirties at the time of Alderaan's destruction. He has green eyes, long blond hair, and a subtle regal bearing about himself, although he loves a good party.

Lorac Nonnaihr: Male Human Scoundrel 5/Noble 4; Init +2; Defense 17 (+2 Dex, +5 class); Spd 10 m; VP/WP 63/12; Atk +7/+2 melee (1d3+1, punch) or +8/+3 ranged (3d6, blaster pistol); SQ bonus class skill (Bluff), coordinate +1, favor +2, illicit barter, inspire confidence, lucky 1/day, precise attack +1, resource access; SV Fort +3, Ref +8, Will +9; SZ M; FP 4; DSP 1; Rep +1; Str 12, Dex 14, Con 12, Int 16, Wis 17, Cha 19. Challenge Code E.

Equipment: Blaster pistol, shadowcloak device (see sidebar), comlink, credit chip (500 credits), datapad, stylish clothing, hip flask filled with Alderaanian wine, expensive chrono.

Skills: Appraise +12, Bluff +16, Computer Use +10, Diplomacy +15, Disguise +11, Gamble +7, Gather Information +5, Hide +12, Intimidate +18, Knowledge (business) +7, Knowledge (engineering) +10, Listen +13, Pilot +3, Profession (businessman) +7, Read/Write Basic, Sense Motive +14, Speak Basic, Spot +10.

Feats: Dodge, Endurance, Headstrong, Low Profile, Mobility, Persuasive, Skill Emphasis (Disguise), Weapon Group Proficiencies (blaster pistols, simple weapons).

Shadowcloak

Sometimes, an individual wants to communicate with another person face to face without being identified. A shadowcloak grants a certain level of anonymity. The device's electrical field distorts the owner's voice so that

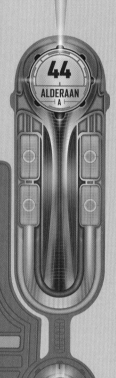

it's unrecognizable, even to any sort of voice reader. Furthermore, the device generates a static "black field" that lays a field of blackness over the wearer's entire body, rendering the subject featureless to all eyes and sensors. The device grants a +20 bonus on Disguise checks to maintain this facade of anonymity; seeing through the illusion requires a successful opposed Spot check. However, the subject cannot walk around after the device is activated without being identified—the field's flexibility is limited. The wearer typically sits down somewhere and activates the device, bringing up the shadowcloak field for a secret meeting. After 1 hour of use, the field must cool down and recharge for 4 hours due to the device's enormous power requirements.

Shadowcloak
Cost: 10,000 credits
Weight: 2 kg

Milessa Kand

Alderaan has many individuals whose love for the planet and its ecology distinguishes them from the general populace. Milessa Kand is one of these rare people. Although not part of the government, Milessa puts forward the message of pacifism and coexistence with all. Despite her equanimity, the Empire disturbs her greatly, since it is the biggest challenge to her philosophy. Therefore, Milessa aids Rebels or Rebel sympathizers whenever she can. She has decided that quiet aid to opponents of the Empire would do more good than taking up open arms against Imperial forces. She is a perfect resource for heroes who need to rest, recuperate, and heal.

Milessa has hazel eyes and brown hair that she wears in a single, very long braid. Her gentle demeanor is an island of tranquility amid a sea of trouble. She can remain calm through even the worst circumstances. Should the heroes meet and befriend her, they will find a steady, reliable ally who treasures all life. Milessa is in her mid-twenties at the time of Alderaan's demise.

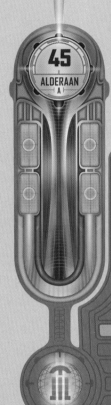

MILESSA KAND

Milessa Kand: Female Human Force Adept 6; Init +1; Defense 16 (+1 Dex, +5 class); Spd 10 m; VP/WP 30/10; Atk +4 melee (1d3, punch) or +4 melee (1d6/1d6, quarterstaff) or +5 ranged; SQ Force weapon +1d8; SV Fort +5, Ref +4, Will +10; SZ M; FP 10; DSP 0; Rep +1; Str 10, Dex 13, Con 10, Int 15, Wis 20, Cha 20. Challenge Code D.

Equipment: Quarterstaff, robes, medpac.

Skills: Balance +5, Computer Use +4, Diplomacy +7, Hide +7, Knowledge (Alderaan) +10, Knowledge (biology) +8, Move Silently +5, Read/Write Basic, Ride +3, Search +5, Sense Motive +8, Speak Basic, Survival +9, Swim +6, Treat Injury +9.

Force Skills: Force Stealth +9, Heal Another +10, Heal Self +6, Move Object +7, See Force +7.

Feats: Animal Affinity, Force-Sensitive, Great Fortitude, Nature Affinity, Run, Skill Emphasis (Heal Another), Track, Weapon Group Proficiencies (primitive weapons, simple weapons).

Force Feats: Alter, Control, Sense.

New Feat: Nature Affinity

You are especially in tune with natural surroundings. This mystical bond allows you to sense what the local environment contains.

Prerequisite: Force-Sensitive, Sense, Wis 15.

Benefit: By walking in a natural setting and meditating for a full minute, you can get a sense of what living organisms exist in the area. Under these conditions, characters with Nature Affinity can make a Wisdom check (DC 10) to detect the kinds of plant or animal lifeforms in a 200-meter-radius area. Living creatures that don't wish to be found can oppose the user's Wisdom check with a Hide check. Due to the amount of strain this ability puts on its wielder, the Nature Affinity feat can be used only once per hour.

Special: A character with Nature Affinity can get a "sense" of the environment's state of well-being by making a Wisdom check (DC 15). This information translates as an empathic result, such as "harmonious," "threatened," or "dying."

Christoph Jam

Considered slightly eccentric, the overly opinionated Christoph Jam has a network of spies and informants whose sole function is to send him information on violent or aggressive situations. Most occurrences that interest him involve injustice and terror, affecting victims who cannot defend themselves. Christoph takes this information and hires teams of "Rectifiers" to remedy each situation. Of course, Christoph prefers using groups much like the heroes.

As a nobleman, he has tried going into politics to bring about change, but he has been frustrated at how long it takes to get things done. Instead, he is the head of an Alderaan-based corporation called Descorp. Christoph's corporation specializes in restaurants and spice production. He uses some of his company's wealth to fund the Rectifiers, and he pays very well.

An impatient but fair man, Christoph despises seeing people pushed around or living in misery. Moreover, he is highly opinionated and used to having his way. This makes him the perfect contact for heroes looking to make a difference in the galaxy while earning a little money as well. It is not unusual for Christoph, after donning a cloak as a disguise, to wander through spaceport bars looking for deserving folk. This activity drives his bodyguards insane with frustration and worry.

Christoph is in his late fifties and stands 2.1 meters tall. He's solidly built and looks imposing. His blue-gray eyes pierce through insincerity and deception. Christoph's hair is brown and white, worn in a long braid down his back.

Christoph Jam: Male Human Noble 9; Init +1; Defense 16 (+1 Dex, +5 class); Spd 10 m; VP/WP 44/12; Atk +8/+3 melee (1d3+2, punch) or +7/+2 ranged; SQ bonus class skill (Bluff), coordinate +2, favor +3, inspire confidence, resource access; SV Fort +4, Ref +5, Will +12; SZ M; FP 5; DSP 0; Rep +5; Str 14, Dex 12, Con 12, Int 18, Wis 17, Cha 23. Challenge Code D.

Equipment: Walking stick, expensive clothes, comlink, datapad.

Skills: Appraise +10, Bluff +10, Computer Use +11, Craft (holoart) +12, Diplomacy +14, Gamble +8, Gather Information +12, Hide +6, Intimidate +19, Knowledge (Alderaan) +12, Knowledge (alien species) +12, Knowledge (business) +12, Knowledge (politics) +12, Listen +5, Read/Write Basic, Search +10, Sense Motive +14, Speak Basic, Speak Mon Calamarian, Speak Huttese, Speak Rodese, Speak Ryl, Spot +8.

Feats: Headstrong, Influence, Iron Will, Persuasive, Sharp-Eyed, Skill Emphasis (Intimidate), Trustworthy, Weapon Group Proficiencies (blaster pistols, simple weapons).

New Creature: Thranta

A thranta resembles a flying fish with large, finlike wings growing from its sides. Its head is shaped like that of a rodent, with a pointed nose and forward-set eyes. The skin of a thranta is smooth and cool to the touch, with a gray or blue tint. Thrantas have no legs or arms. An adult can grow to be over 8 meters long.

Thranta: Airborne herd animal 5; Init +9; Defense 16 (–2 size, +3 Dex, +5 natural); Spd fly 26 m (poor); VP/WP 48/50; Atk +7 melee (1d6+7, bite) or +7 melee (2d6+7, tail slam); SQ Low-light vision; SV Fort +11, Ref +4, Will +2; SZ H; Face/Reach 8 m by 8 m/2 m; Rep +0; Str 25, Dex 16, Con 25, Int 4, Wis 13, Cha 2. Challenge Code C.

Skills: Listen +6, Spot +11, Survival +2.

Feats: Improved Initiative (bonus feat).

Anaxes

Planet Type: Terrestrial
Climate: Temperate to arctic
Terrain: Plains, forests, mountains
Atmosphere: Breathable
Gravity: Standard
Diameter: 16,100 km
Length of Day: 26 standard hours
Length of Year: 352 standard days
Sentient Species: Human
Languages: Basic
Population: 512 million
Species Mix: 94% Human, 6% other
Government: Democracy
Major Exports: Some high-tech goods
Major Imports: Raw materials, consumer goods, processed foods
System/Star: Axum/Solis Axum

Planets	Type	Moons
Selgon	Searing rock	0
Grastes	Toxic rock	1
Axum	Terrestrial	2
Anaxes	Terrestrial	1
Urfon	Frozen rock	1
Phlors Rex	Gas giant	18
Phlors Regina	Gas giant	15
Ichium	Barren rock	0
Anaxes Station	Artificial	0

Description

Anaxes, the Defender of the Core, is a fortress world that has served as a seat of galactic power and naval prestige for millennia.

Although the Axum system has two heavily populated worlds and three inhabited moons, no one hearing its name thinks of megacorporations or industrial might. Instead, most Core Worlders think of security and tradition—a rock of military might upon which their region's safety rests.

The plots of most holodramas about the Planetary Security Forces, Republic Navy, and the Imperial Navy follow the same traditional arc: A young man rises from his sector military school to fleet camp, and then to his sector military academy. Thriving there, he catches the eye of his sector governor and wins admittance to the pinnacle of officer-training schools: the Naval Academy on Prefsbelt IV. (The academy's location is officially a secret, but all children from good Core families believe the holodramas.) By the time the credits roll, the triumphant hero stands on the

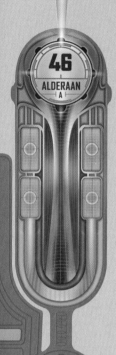

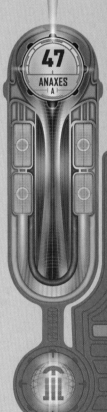

gleaming azure marble flagstones of the Grand Piazza of the Anaxes Citadel.

History

Humans have inhabited Anaxes for tens of thousands of years. In pre-Republic times, Anaxes's sister world Axum was the throneworld of the so-called Azure Imperium, which sprawled along what would become the Perlemian Trade Route. That empire was absorbed peacefully by Coruscant centuries before the founding of the Republic. Anaxes served as the chief shipyard and fortress of the Azure Imperium. As the Republic expanded, its location on the Perlemian (near the trade route's intersection with the Hydian Way) made it a logical place to concentrate warships guarding the Core Worlds. Seven centuries before Emperor Palpatine took power, the Republic built the massive Anaxes Citadel to further its navy's power and prestige.

Palpatine's New Order worked to break the cherished traditions of the Planetary Security Forces that formed the core of the Imperial Navy. Many career officers from "generational" families were cast aside in favor of devotees of the New Order. But the Empire also made sure the wellsprings of the Navy's tradition continued to flow. Anaxes became the command center of Imperial Center Oversector, known among spacers as "Sector Zero." (The sector includes all worlds whose XYZ galactic coordinates are positive and begin with a zero, from Coruscant—at 0,

0, 0—to Kiribi, nearly 5,000 light-years away in the Colonies at coordinates 099, 099, 011.) On maps of the galaxy, Sector Zero is a wedge encompassing about a third of a circle and hugging the Deep Core to the "southeast" of Coruscant. Spacers know that Imperial justice is swift and unyielding within this region. An infraction that earns a freighter jock a warning in the Inner Rim results in arrest in Sector Zero.

During the Rebellion era, Anaxes was the command center for Azure Hammer Command, whose Super Star Destroyer *Whelm* and fifty-seven other capital ships were tasked with defending Sector Zero against any threats. (A separate command, Azure Shield, protected the Azure sector and its neighbors.) Two full deepdock fleets were based in the Anaxes system, supplementing its shipyards until needed elsewhere in the Core. Until the Battle of Yavin, Azure Hammer Command and Anaxes Citadel—and ultimately, all forces in Sector Zero—answered to Grand Admiral Osvald Teshik. Anaxes changed hands a number of times as various Imperial factions struggled to succeed Palpatine, then passed into New Republic control when handed over by its last Imperial commandant, Osted Wermis.

People

The Anaxsi, as they're called, are model Core Worlders, drawing on millennia of almost unbroken peace and privilege. In most sectors, Anaxes would be an industrial powerhouse, but in its own star system, its output is dwarfed by Axum. That fact doesn't bother the Anaxsi, however. They draw on centuries of pride in their role as the defenders of the Core Worlds and the keepers of one of the galaxy's proudest military traditions.

The Anaxsi are hardly provincial folk (what's naval service without the lure of distant suns?), but few sons or daughters of the planet emigrate. Anaxsi social circles are closed to offworlders, with one significant exception: those who have proved themselves in naval service. The terraced hills above the Citadel are dotted with estates held by families that may not be Old Anaxsi, but whose names are synonymous with naval service. The manses of Holts and Ozzels stand beside those of Trommers and Jerjerrods, or just down the shady lanes from Wermises or Banjeers. Anyone sufficiently familiar with the aristocracy of the Empire would consider a map of the hills akin to a map of Imperial genealogy.

Locations

Descriptions of several key locations follow.

Anaxes Citadel

This massive complex of training schools, research labs, intelligence centers, offices, archives, and parade grounds is famous throughout the galaxy. It is the site where the Navy's highest honors are bestowed. One-third the size of the Imperial Palace, the Citadel is nearly as rich in tradition and intrigue. The center of its Grand Piazza sports a 40-meter band of brilliant azure flagstones flanked by walks of golden serpentine, which are in turn bordered by

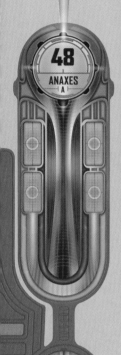

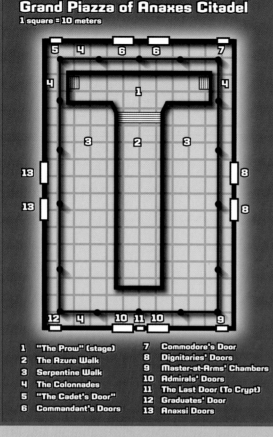

Grand Piazza of Anaxes Citadel
1 square = 10 meters

1	"The Prow" (stage)
2	The Azure Walk
3	Serpentine Walk
4	The Colonnades
5	"The Cadet's Door"
6	Commandant's Doors
7	Commodore's Door
8	Dignitaries' Doors
9	Master-at-Arms' Chambers
10	Admirals' Doors
11	The Last Door (To Crypt)
12	Graduates' Door
13	Anaxsi Doors

Pols Anaxes

Even the bustle is carefully orchestrated in graceful Pols Anaxes, the planet's largest city and civilian spaceport. Traffic-control officers shunt robohacks and speed-ertruck vehicles into underground highways that connect with the sublevels of the city's skyscrapers. There, one hack may unload lacquered greelwood for groundcoaches while another picks up frozen nerfsteaks for shipment out of the system. Aboveground, decorated float-coaches, groundlimos, and keffi teams bear the city's middle managers to their jobs along graceful, garden-lined boulevards. High above them, sleek airspeeders deliver Pols Anaxes's true power brokers to their office aeries.

Anaxes Groundcoach

Rich Anaxsi use archaic and graceful vehicles pulled by a quartet of keffis when traveling from their estates. Groundcoaches roll on large wooden wheels painted with shimmering lacquer, while the coaches themselves range from simple open-air platforms to climate-controlled cabins whose exteriors drip with bejeweled fixtures. A typical coach holds four to six passengers, with an exterior front seat for a driver and servant and a rear platform where two more servants perch.

Anaxes Groundcoach

Class: Wheeled [Ground]	Crew: 1 (Normal +2)
Size: Large (4.2 m long)	Initiative: +1 (–1 size, +2 crew)
Passengers: 4	Maneuver: +1 (–1 size, +2 crew)
Cargo Capacity: 200 kg	Defense: 9 (–1 size)
Cost: 42,000 (new), 28,000 (used)	Shield Points: 0
	Hull Points: 12 (DR 3)
Availability: Prevalent	Speed: 20 m
Era: All	

* This vehicle provides full cover to its passengers and one-quarter cover for the driver and servant.

Pols Anaxes Airspeeder

Local airspeeders, used by the elite who work in Pols Anaxes, come in a host of brilliant metallic hues and bright colors. For instance, the Citadel's official airspeeders are azure and gold. Airspeeder connoisseurs debate the merits of streamlined, unadorned older models versus the finned and ornamented craft that have become popular in recent years.

Pols Anaxes Airspeeder

Class: Airspeeder	Crew: 1 (Untrained +0)
Size: Large (3.6 m long)	Initiative: –1 (–1 size)
Passengers: 4	Maneuver: –1 (–1 size)
Cargo Capacity: 30 kg	Defense: 9 (–1 size)
Cost: 11,000 (new), 8,000 (used)	Shield Points: 0
	Hull Points: 18 (DR 5)
Availability: Prevalent	Atmospheric Speed: 9 squares/action (550 km/h)
Era: All	Altitude: 0.5 km

* This vehicle provides full cover to its pilot and passengers.

the soaring Colonnades. Junior officers can be seen at all hours gazing wistfully out at the blue-and-gold floor. Only those who have been personally decorated in the Piazza may set foot on the azure flagstones. No one below the rank of captain is permitted on the golden serpentine flooring. The Colonnades lead to a maze of corridors, offices, and conference rooms that extends for kilometers on all sides of the Piazza.

Sirpar Hills

These hills look down over the Great Plain of Anaxes and its Citadel. Scores of great houses sprawl among copses of purple-leafed sirpar trees and flowering gardens. The manses of Sirpar Hills belong to families with generations of naval service, Anaxsi of surpassing wealth and power, and high-ranking officers stationed at the Citadel. This last group must content itself with merely opulent houses low down in the Sirpar Hills. By ancient tradition, motorized ground vehicles are forbidden here. House servants tend coaches pulled by teams of shaggy, placid beasts called keffis. Sirpar Station, at the gated entrance to the hills, serves as a transfer point between coaches and speeders. Another tradition of the hills is that fleet orders must be written and delivered by hand. At all times, Citadel cadets can be seen disembarking from swoops at Sirpar Station or running through the hills, clutching their orders in their black gloves.

For the GM

The adventure hooks and supporting characters described in this section are meant for GMs only. If you're a player, stop reading now.

Adventures

Feel free to use or adapt the following adventure hooks for your home campaign.

At the Heart of the Citadel

Admiral Arhul Holt wants to defect to the Alliance. The Rebels know that luring away a scion of a legendary Navy family would be invaluable in recruiting other Imperial officers with a tradition of family service to the Navy.

Rebel operatives have managed to get a young Alliance slicer named Pash Galae appointed to Anaxes as a cadet. Pash promises he can bilk Anaxes's supercomputers into issuing phony orders that will get Holt safely offplanet—but only if he gets uninterrupted hours in one of the Citadel's info-labs. Besides keeping Galae safe, the heroes will have to find someone to play cadet, fetching Holt's phony orders and presenting them at the admiral's mansion. Do any of the heroes have the acting ability and raw nerve to successfully impersonate a cadet? And what will they do when they discover the Imperial agent awaiting them on the grounds of Holt's estate?

If the Gamemaster prefers to play in a time period other than the Rebellion era, Holt might be a Republic admiral defecting to a newly risen empire beyond the Rim, or a New Republic admiral who's had a change of heart and wants to join the Imperial Remnant.

The Needle in the Nerfsteaks

Being a smuggler on Anaxes isn't a life for the nervous. Renegade Anaxsi have hidden some contraband—perhaps sensitive military equipment or a stolen antique ground-coach—aboard one of the many freight barges leaving Pols Anaxes. They've hired the heroes to stay with the goods until they're safely out of the system. Imperial agents are on the hunt in the city and in space. If the players can reach orbit, they can dock with one of the superfreighters outbound from the Axum system. They can lose themselves and their prize in a vast cargo bay filled with countless frozen nerfsteaks. Of course, Imperial agents can board such freighters, and there's no shortage of capital ships to intercept a superfreighter during the sublight crawl to the approved jump zones beyond Anaxes Station. Even heroes can't hide forever.

Anaxes Masquerade

A New Republic senator sends the heroes to Anaxes to persuade a crafty Imperial Remnant officer to come out of retirement and help plan strike missions against the Yuuzhan Vong. When the heroes show up at General Jodd Zarfane's estate in Pols Anaxes, the general's aide escorts them into a spacious, octagonal study with multiple exits. Zarfane arrives soon thereafter to hear what the heroes have to say. With a successful Spot check (DC 25), heroes notice the absence of service droids, not to mention the empty trophy cases in Zarfane's study that once held exotic manufactured weapons. Zarfane claims his estate is in the midst of a security system upgrade, although no engineers or guards can be seen.

The real Zarfane is dead—eliminated by Yuuzhan Vong seeking to infiltrate Anaxes's military hierarchy. Impersonating Zarfane, his aide, and two close guards are four Yuuzhan Vong warriors wearing ooglith masquers. While "Zarfane" prods the heroes for information about the New Republic and gently turns down their best offer, the other three Yuuzhan Vong don their vonduun crab-shell armor, grab their weapons, and wait near the exits. If the heroes uncover the deception or act strangely, the three warriors burst into the room and attack. Meanwhile, "Zarfane" grabs a tsaisi and some razorbugs hidden inside the general's desk and joins in the fray.

Allies and Antagonists

The following supporting characters are designed for use in your campaign.

Pash Galae

Young and hyperconfident, Pash Galae grew up on cosmopolitan Utrost, just a few light-years from Coruscant. But while Galae learned his social graces, he concealed a growing hatred of the Empire and the corrupt institutions propping it up. Galae became an ace HoloNet slicer, dedicating himself to embarrassing any Imperial institution whose network he could infiltrate. At sixteen, he fled Utrost and joined the Alliance. The lanky Galae is brash, argumentative, and arrogant. His first inclination is to underestimate people, since he has a hard time believing other people can be trusted to do anything correctly.

Pash Galae: Male Human Scoundrel 4/Tech Specialist 6; Init +2; Defense 17 (+2 Dex, +5 class); Spd 10 m; VP/WP 27/9; Atk +6/+1 melee (1d3–1, punch or +9/+4 ranged (3d6, blaster pistol); SQ expert (Craft [electronic devices]), illicit barter, instant mastery (Search), lucky 1/day, precise attack +1, research, tech specialty (computer specialist +1); SV Fort +2, Ref +9, Will +5; SZ M; FP 0; DSP 0; Rep +2; Str 8, Dex 14, Con 9, Int 16, Wis 13, Cha 12. Challenge Code E.

Equipment: Modified computer, blaster pistol, master-craft security kit, comlink, datapad, naval cadet's uniform.

Skills: Bluff +17, Computer Use +22, Craft (electronic devices) +11, Disable Device +16, Disguise +8, Escape Artist +9, Forgery +10, Hide +15, Knowledge (streetwise) +8, Listen +5, Move Silently +15, Read/Write Basic, Read/Write Binary, Repair +12, Search +7, Sleight of Hand +4, Speak Basic, Speak Huttese, Speak Shyriiwook (understand only), Spot +5.

Feats: Alertness, Gearhead, Multishot, Point Blank Shot, Rapid Shot, Skill Emphasis (Bluff, Computer Use), Weapon Group Proficiencies (blaster pistols, simple weapons).

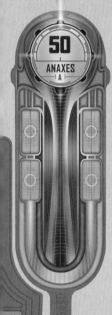

Arhul Holt

Holts have dwelled in the Sirpar Hills for nearly seven centuries, and the Holt Cross—awarded for dedication to duty—is one of Anaxes's highest honors. Arhul Holt, however, finds himself in a terrible position. He has served the Empire for nearly four decades since the day he took his first lap around the Colonnades as a cadet, but he no longer believes in its principles. The regal, silver-haired Holt has an effortless command of people and situations. He can be plain spoken or subtle, as events dictate.

Arhul Holt: Male Human Noble 6/Officer 10; Init +0; Defense 19 (+9 class); Spd 10 m; VP/WP 97/13; Atk +11/+6/+1 melee (1d3, punch) or +11/+6/+1 ranged (3d6, blaster pistol); SQ bonus class skill (Bluff), coordinate +1, favor +2, improved tactics, inspire confidence, leadership, requisition supplies, resource access, uncanny survival; SV Fort +8, Ref +8, Will +14; SZ M; FP 0; DSP 0; Rep +9; Str 11, Dex 10, Con 13, Int 14, Wis 14, Cha 16. Challenge Code G.

Equipment: Datapad, blaster pistol, Anaxes ground-coach, Azure Motorworks SirparSpeeder.

Skills: Astrogate +10, Bluff +19, Computer Use +8, Diplomacy +27, Gather Information +8, Intimidate +27, Knowledge (Anaxes) +17, Knowledge (politics) +16, Knowledge (tactics) +20, Move Silently +2, Pilot +10, Read/Write Basic, Ride +8, Search +4, Sense Motive +20, Speak Basic.

Feats: Influence, Iron Will, Persuasive, Sharp-Eyed, Skill Emphasis (Diplomacy, Gather Information, Intimidate), Spacer, Starship Operation (capital ship), Trustworthy, Weapon Group Proficiencies (blaster pistols, blaster rifles, simple weapons).

Hilas Bannock

A young member of Imperial Intelligence's Bureau of Operations, Bannock's obsession is ferreting out traitors. Born on the Outer Rim backwater of Yarnil, Bannock became a star of his local Sub-Adult Group, attracting the attention of COMPNOR (the Commission for the Preservation of the New Order) for his zeal in reporting seditious thought among Yarnil's farmers and merchants. Since joining Imperial Intelligence, he has targeted traitors in the Core Worlds and within those institutions traditionally seen as bulwarks of Imperial power. Bannock is a squat but powerful man with a trace of a Rim accent in his speech.

Hilas Bannock: Male Human Scoundrel 6; Init +2; Defense 16 (+2 Dex, +4 class); Spd 10 m; VP/WP 23/14; Atk +5 melee (stun DC 15, stun baton) or +5 melee (1d3+1, punch) or +6 ranged (3d4, hold-out blaster); SQ illicit barter, lucky 2/day, precise attack +1; SV Fort +4, Ref +7, Will +4; SZ M; FP 3; DSP 0; Rep +1; Str 12, Dex 14, Con 14, Int 13, Wis 14, Cha 10. Challenge Code D.

Equipment: Hold-out blaster, baton, comlink, datapad, mastercraft security kit, electrobinoculars.

Skills: Bluff +11, Computer Use +8, Demolitions +6, Disable Device +9, Disguise +8, Escape Artist +10, Forgery +8, Gather Information +11, Intimidate +6, Knowledge (tactics) +5, Listen +5, Move Silently +9, Read/Write Basic, Search +11, Sense Motive +4, Speak Basic.

Force Skills: Empathy +5.

Feats: Force-Sensitive, Heroic Surge, Persuasive, Sharp-Eyed, Skill Emphasis (Gather Information, Listen), Weapon Group Proficiencies (blaster pistols, simple weapons).

New Creature: Keffi

Keffis are the handsome riding beasts of Anaxes. These furry quadrupeds have three-toed feet with thick, horny nails—perfect for digging grasses and soft dirt, racing along beneath a trained rider, or hauling a groundcoach as part of a team. Keffis are relatively intelligent and docile, thanks to millennia of selective breeding. They come in a dizzying array of sizes and colors. Racing keffis have black, feltlike coats over lean muscles; parade keffis are stocky with long, golden fur. Two Anaxsi of even moderate social status can spend hours talking of keffis in perfect happiness.

Keffi: Domesticated herd animal 3; Init +3; Defense 16 (+3 Dex, +3 natural); Spd 20 m; VP/WP 13/14; Atk +2 melee (1d6+1, kick) or +2 (1d3+1, bite) or +4 ranged; SV Fort +5, Ref +4, Will +3; SZ M; Face/Reach 2 m by 2 m/2 m; Rep +0; Str 13, Dex 17, Con 14, Int 5, Wis 14, Cha 8. Challenge Code B.

Skills: Climb +2, Hide +4, Listen +8, Survival +8.

Feats: Endurance.

HILAS BANNOCK

Belgaroth

Planet Type: Terrestrial
Climate: Temperate
Terrain: Urban, desert (rocky)
Atmosphere: Breathable
Gravity: Standard
Diameter: 6,500 km
Length of Day: 20 standard hours
Length of Year: 300 standard days
Sentient Species: Human
Languages: Basic
Population: 10 million
Species Mix: 90% Human, 10% other
Government: Imperial
Major Exports: None
Major Imports: None
System/Star: Belgaroth/Matanya A and Matanya B

Planets	Type	Moons
Ember	Searing rock	0
Ash	Searing rock	0
—	Asteroid belt	—
Flotsam	Barren rock	0
Belgaroth	Terrestrial	2
Colossus	Gas giant	24

Description

Belgaroth is a small world on the edge of the Core Worlds region. Most of the planet consists of rocky, rugged, and inhospitable mountains, with an occasional hill, plain, or valley. The bodies of water that pass for oceans on Belgaroth are a pair of large seas of a murky mustard-brown color, a result of the heavy mineral sediment.

The world has one city, Belgar, and several large scrapyards. Anything pertaining to or from Belgaroth is called "Belgarian." Belgarians classify their seasons as "cold-wet," "mud," "heat and humidity," and "more rain"—travelers don't come to Belgaroth for the weather. If they can help it, respectable travelers don't come to Belgaroth at all.

The planet orbits a binary sun. Matanya A is an orange sun; Matanya B is a smaller yellow sun. Matanya B rises and sets first; Matanya A follows about 15 minutes later. During the Empire's heyday, Belgaroth's two moons, Tregan and Tyrel, served as targets for Imperial gunnery. The only other satellite of any note is a small orbiting repair yard that can barely accommodate an Imperial Star Destroyer.

Belgaroth is a perfect example of a small, inconsequential world that has been wrecked by the Empire for its own foul ends. The planet's lifeforms have evolved and adapted to suit the climate and terrain, including the recent ecological trauma inflicted by the Empire. Most of the local lifeforms easily digest harsh chemicals, refined metal slag, and toxic waste—common terrain on Belgaroth during the Rebellion era.

History

Six hundred years before the rise of the Empire, Belgaroth was discovered and colonized by a pair of freelance explorers. After naming the world, Belgar Overlord and Roth Skimm worked hard to turn it into a bustling way station and commerce point. Before they could truly execute their grander plans, they killed each other over a "friendly" game of cards, a harbinger of the difficult times the planet would face as its history unfolded.

Until the rise of the Empire, Belgaroth remained an insignificant way station with one pathetic city and a barely passable spaceport. When the Empire took power, the Naval Department decided it required an unimportant world on which to test new weaponry and conduct training maneuvers. Belgaroth was the lucky world chosen. The generally apathetic and transient population had even less to say about the Empire moving in than most worlds did. In fact, the Empire was a welcome presence to some, since it brought money, ships, and jobs. And while stormtroopers weren't easily bullied or swindled, the average Imperial technician, low-grade officer, or laborer was an easy target for the Belgarian criminal element.

Until the end of the Rebellion era, Belgaroth was routinely patrolled by a small flight of TIE fighters, reinforced by an occasional visit from a Star Destroyer. When the Empire finally collapsed, Belgaroth was practically forgotten. It could be said that Belgaroth was one of the last Imperial worlds to find out that the Empire was no more. This assertion is even more tragic when one realizes just how close to Coruscant Belgaroth truly is.

When the New Republic finally made contact with the system, it found an abandoned Imperial installation, a handful of broken-down TIE fighters, and a single decrepit city. The population is now just as satisfied with the governance of the New Republic as they were with Imperial rule.

People

The vast majority of Belgarians are Human descendants of the original settlers. Most of the rest are refugees, runaways, fugitives, and wanderers. The species mix varies

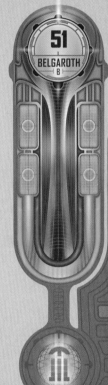

MH

two standard weeks. During these intervals, the system was crawling with TIEs, Star Destroyers, and other Imperial craft.

Locations

Belgaroth has little in the way of exotic places to visit. Even during the best of times, its purpose was unglamorous and straightforward. However, it's also true that adventures sometimes start in the most unlikely of places.

Upside

The Imperial dockyard that orbits Belgaroth is nicknamed "Upside." It was constructed a year after the Empire came to Belgaroth and lasted well into the time of the New Republic. The lieutenant in charge of the facility failed to blow up the dockyard during the Empire's evacuation—frankly, he couldn't be bothered. In the days of the New Republic, Upside is used to conduct routine repairs and maintenance on the few ships that pass through the system. Fortunately, it brings in enough cash to keep the economy moving, albeit sluggishly.

Belgar

Belgar is the planet's only city. It's a dreary collection of sediment-encrusted buildings, cheap bars, flophouses, and some scattered mercantiles. During the Rebellion era, the largest and best-looking buildings were the Imperial headquarters and barracks. In the time of the New Republic, the City Boss uses it as living quarters and administration. Six hangars, three warehouses, a control tower, two repair bays, and an electronics array building make up Belgar Spaceport. The sediment-filled rains make most of the buildings look rusted and muddy.

Xot's Megabar

This huge, three-story bar is barely on spaceport property. It is the only watering hole within easy walking distance from the port. Inevitably, anyone who lands at the spaceport winds up at Xot's if they want a half-decent drink or something to munch on. There's even a pair of low-slung buildings adjoining the bar where spacers can pay a few credits and flop for the night. Xot himself is a mystery. So far, patrons have seen over three dozen different species/gender combinations claiming to be Xot. No one's sure if Xot is simply a shapechanger or if the explanation is a lot more complicated, and no one seems in a hurry to find out. Belgaroth's criminal element frequents Xot's often, and they know everything that goes on in the local underworld.

The Scrapyard

Although Belgaroth has many junkyards, only one is definitively known as the Scrapyard. Covering an area of 900 square kilometers, the Scrapyard is the main depository for obsolete equipment, worn-out ship parts, expended weapons, burned-out droids, toxic waste, and the occasional victim of the local crime syndicate. Clouds of chemicals hang in the air. The soil oozes with poisons

from year to year, but a significant number of Rodians, Twi'leks, and Sullustans move through the system.

The typical Belgarian philosophy can be summed up in three words: "Fine by me." Belgarians don't expect much out of life, and thus are rarely disappointed. They simply cruise through the years, working toward financial security and safety as best as they can. To the average Belgarian, governments rise and fall, and occupying armies come and go. Nothing changes except the flags and bureaucracy. Belgarians could care less for politics, preferring instead to concentrate on the ongoing struggle for financial security, or even better, passage offplanet. In keeping with the Belgarian "live and let live" philosophy, not much in the way of government exists. Belgar has a City Boss, whose orders serve as suggestions. The best way to describe Belgaroth's government is "benevolent anarchy."

The Belgarians' mindset is reflected in their terminology. "ABH" (pronounced "ab") stands for "Anywhere But Here," the ultimate goal of all Belgarians. "Living at the Scrapyard" is a local euphemism for the recently deceased. "WYS" (pronounced "wiss") stands for "Whatever You Say," the central philosophy of every self-respecting Belgarian.

During the Rebellion era, a skeleton crew of Navy personnel remained stationed on Belgaroth. Naturally, when maneuvers or weapons testing occurred, the size of the garrison increased appropriately. As a rule, testing happened every three months for a period of

dumped here over the years. Heaps of junk are piled in mounds, some reaching 50 to 60 meters high. The Scrapyard has no watchman, since there's not much there to steal.

For the GM

The adventure hooks and supporting characters described in this section are meant for GMs only. If you're a player, stop reading now.

Adventures

Belgaroth may be a backwater world, but it's still a place where dangerous adventures unfold—especially when the Empire is testing weapons.

An Unexpected Stop

While the heroes are traveling through space, their ship's hyperdrive unit blows out. Their ship drops back into normal space in the Matanya binary system, where Belgaroth is located. Once insystem, the heroes witness four Imperial Star Destroyers firing on one of the planet's two moons. A flight of TIE fighters closes with the heroes' ship. A local commander informs them that all business is to be handled on the planet, and that they should follow the coordinates given in order to land. Any deviation will result in the ship being fired upon and boarded.

When the group lands at Belgar Spaceport, they can get their ship repaired. However, they notice a lot of Imperial types around, and secrecy seems to be the watchword. At Xot's bar, the heroes meet a Rebel spy who has been sent to ascertain exactly what the Empire is testing on the system's moons. If they decide to help, the mission requires some sneaking and observation, as well as some daring flying to get close enough to the Star Destroyers to take sensor readings. The Empire is testing firing mechanisms that will be used in a new super-weapon (possibly the Death Star itself). Naturally, the heroes can't know the exact name of the weapons platform, but even getting an inkling about a "secret weapon" can foreshadow future events.

A-Hunting We Will Go

While the heroes are planetside, the local criminal element approaches the group. Apparently, they have declared the heroes' ship to be in violation of local codes—although anyone who's astute may figure out the violations were just made up. To get their ship back, the group needs to run an errand for the syndicate. A local crime lord wants a Belgarian lifeform nicknamed "droid-breaker." Some offworlders with ferrous diets are willing to pay top credits for droidbreaker steaks. That means hunting the things down, and droidbreakers are lethal. The syndicate will release the heroes' ship back to them once they go to the vicinity of the Scrapyard, hunt down a wild droidbreaker, and bring its carcass back for steaks. (And no disintegrations!)

Let's Pick through Garbage!

The heroes' ship needs a redundant hyperdrive governor unit, a hard-to-find spare part. Belgaroth doesn't have cargo ships and traders knocking at the door every day, however. The yardmaster tells the heroes that the best place to get the part is in the Scrapyard, among the wreckage of the countless ships deposited there over the years. The place is huge, which means a lot of looking, and the local wildlife should present a few challenges. To add a further wrinkle, a group of smugglers are in the Scrapyard, burying some contraband until they can safely move it. When the heroes become witnesses, the smugglers try to eliminate them.

Allies and Antagonists

The following supporting character is designed for use in your campaign.

Lieutenant Brivyl Goss

"Imperial stormtroopers cannot be bribed or black-mailed. Belgarian officers make up for all of them."
— Belgarian proverb

The Empire puts forth an image of ruthlessly efficient stormtroopers and competent elite officers. In most cases, this image is accurate. Lt. Goss is the proverbial fly in the ointment. He's everything an Imperial naval officer shouldn't be. Goss got as far as he did through sheer dumb luck, managing to do at least passably well in each

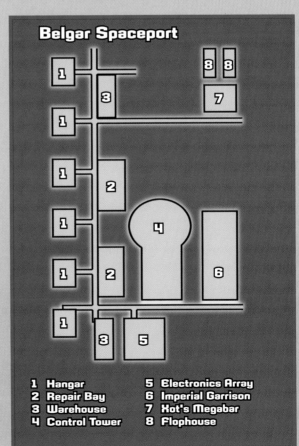

Belgar Spaceport

1	Hangar	5	Electronics Array
2	Repair Bay	6	Imperial Garrison
3	Warehouse	7	Xot's Megabar
4	Control Tower	8	Flophouse

assignment he was given. When the Empire moved in on Belgaroth and set up its base, it wanted a marginal military presence there to run things, an officer whom no one would miss, but one who would have Imperial authority if the need arose.

Goss was as marginal as an Imperial officer could be. He took command of the facility twelve years before the Battle of Yavin. Two years later, he received the order to destroy the orbital docks and evacuate. Goss couldn't be bothered to destroy the docks. Instead, he selected a few trusted junior officers and high-tailed it out of the system on a commandeered shuttle.

Lt. Goss is not a violent man. On the contrary, he avoids confrontation as much as possible. He is lazy, unkempt, and fickle, and he drinks too much. Frankly, he's an embarrassment to the Empire, and he is probably the only officer who doesn't mind being assigned to a nowhere backwater such as Belgaroth. On the plus side, he's the perfect connection for heroes who want information or gossip about the Empire (provided their credits are good).

Lieutenant Brivyl Goss: Male Human Soldier 4/Noble 1/Officer 2; Init +1; Defense 17 (+1 Dex, +6 class); Spd 10 m; VP/WP 33/10; Atk +6 melee (1d3+1, punch) or +6 ranged (3d6, blaster pistol); SQ bonus class skill (Gather Information), favor +1, leadership; SV Fort +6, Ref +5, Will +4; SZ M; FP 1; DSP 0; Rep +3; Str 12, Dex 13, Con 10, Int 10, Wis 9, Cha 13. Challenge Code D.

Equipment: Blaster pistol, comlink, datapad, uniform, rank insignia.

Skills: Bluff +5, Computer Use +5, Diplomacy +9, Gather Information +7, Knowledge (tactics) +5, Pilot +5, Read/Write Basic, Search +3, Sense Motive +8, Speak Basic, Treat Injury +2.

Feats: Armor Proficiencies (light, medium), Combat Reflexes, Dodge, Mobility, Point Blank Shot, Rapid Shot, Shot on the Run, Weapon Group Proficiencies (blaster pistols, blaster rifles, heavy weapons, simple weapons, vibro weapons).

New Creature: Droidbreaker

Of all the sentient lifeforms on Belgaroth, the one nicknamed "droidbreaker" has been the most successful in adapting to its new, polluted environment. Known as the swamphulk for generations, the creature managed to alter its chemistry within a single generation to thrive in its new environment.

Droidbreakers devour plasteel and refined metal as easily as they eat organic matter. They especially savor circuitry and wiring, and droids are among the better sources of these delicacies. Because the species has developed a sense for active power supplies, it can find functioning power packs from 200 meters away.

Droidbreakers stand 5 meters tall at the shoulder. Each has four stubby legs and a gray leathery hide. Beady black eyes are recessed into their skulls. Their heads are roughly

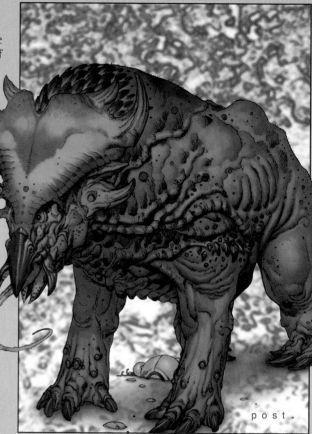

DROIDBREAKER

triangular, with an elongated proboscis made of bone. Their slimy, gray tongues are prehensile and tough. Droidbreakers use their sharp, tough proboscises to crack armor, metal plating, and natural hides. Species that ingest ferrous-based foods savor droidbreaker steaks as a delicacy. A single meal-sized steak fetches at least 200 credits.

Droidbreaker: Predator 5; Init +4 (+4 Improved Initiative); Def 21 (–1 size, +12 natural); Spd 12 m; VP/WP 34/15; Atk +9 melee (3d6+5, proboscis) or +4 ranged; SQ metal sense, energy sense, low-light vision, acid resistance 10, +6 species bonus on Fortitude saves against poison; SV Fort +6, Ref +4, Will +2; SZ L; Face/Reach 4 m by 2 m/4 m; Str 20, Dex 10, Con 15, Int 9, Wis 12, Cha 12. Challenge Code C.

Skills: Hide +2, Search +3, Spot +3, Survival +3.

Feats: Improved Initiative, Track.

Special Qualities: *Metal Sense*—Through a series of electromagnetic emissions, droidbreakers can track down sources of metal within 10 meters. Finding metal requires a Wisdom check (DC 10).

Energy Sense—Through those same emissions, droidbreakers can pinpoint the location of power outputs. A droidbreaker can make a Search check to locate an energy source in a 2-meter-by-2-meter area from up to 200 meters away.

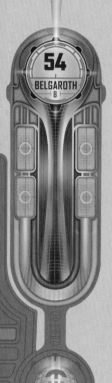

Brentaal

Planet Type: Terrestrial
Climate: Temperate
Terrain: Urban, ocean, mountains
Atmosphere: Breathable
Gravity: Standard
Diameter: 11,242 km
Length of Day: 23 standard hours
Length of Year: 342 standard days
Sentient Species: Human
Languages: Basic
Population: 65 billion
Species Mix: 88% Human, 12% other
Government: Guild
Major Exports: Trade goods, financial services
Major Imports: Trade goods, foodstuffs
System/Star: Brentaal/Brenta

Planets	Type	Moons
Sollace	Searing rock	0
Tremaal	Searing rock	1
Gastol	Gas giant	3
Brentaal	Terrestrial	2
Gumbus	Gas giant	16
Cavas	Gas giant	2
Javaal	Ice ball	0

Description

Brentaal is an arid world and a fairly young planet. A chain of highly salty seas separates its eight large continents. Numerous mountain chains raised by groundquakes and volcanic activity dominate its landmasses, though most of the volcanoes are now long dormant. Most settlements, packed into valleys and deltas, suffer from overcrowding. Many of Brentaal's commercial spaceports and storage facilities have been built upon the flattened tops of mountains, where real estate is cheaper.

The planet's weather is temperate and on the warm side throughout the world, except for the equatorial area, which features steaming seas and sweltering deserts, and the poles, where small ice caps provide some relief for vacationers seeking escape from the heat.

The original colonizers—who landed on Brentaal thousands of years ago—didn't think much of its indigenous flora and fauna, which consisted largely of ferns and large flying insects. Over generations, local species of plants and animals were supplanted in a series of ecological programs with those popular on other Core Worlds, including forests of various perennial plants and elaborate food chains of mammals and reptiles.

History

Located at a major hyperlane junction where the Perlemian Trade Route intersects with the Hydian Way, Brentaal has long been a primary trade world. Dominated by commercial starports and storage facilities, its noble houses and their trade guilds handle a huge volume of traffic flowing into the Core, out to the Corporate Sector Authority, throughout the Colonies, and beyond.

Most of Brentaal's commerce is controlled by the hundreds of noble families that dominate the various trade guilds. Nearly all of them engage in complicated battles both political and economic, although there is little difference between those two areas of influence on Brentaal. In the time of the Old Republic, foreigners could not legally invest in domestic trade guilds, but this tradition fell by the wayside as Imperial lackeys forced their way into the lucrative market.

For several thousand years, Brentaal served as the major jumping-off point from the settled Core Worlds into the unsettled Colonies, and it was the first stop for goods flowing back into the Republic. Aside from a few civil wars and clashes with the Trade Federation, Brentaal largely avoided military adventures during the Rise of the Empire era, due in part to its economic importance and in part to its impressive orbital defenses.

Affairs changed very little on Brentaal with the rise of the Empire. Not even the most draconian government could long survive without robust trade. However, Brentaal was not entirely able to escape the Galactic Civil War. As the New Republic fleet drove retreating Imperial forces back toward Corulag, the Brentaal system became a key battleground because of its strategic location. The planet itself was spared major damage in the Battle of Brentaal, but orbital shipping facilities were all but wiped out, plunging the economy into a recession from which it was still recovering in the time of the New Republic.

People

Despite its status as a major trade center, Brentaal is primarily a Human world. While significant alien settlements and enclaves are sprinkled among the trade bunkers and spaceports, their inhabitants are considered transient visitors. Only Brentaal-born Humans may claim citizenship. Genetically, Brentaalans are standard Humans, usually pale-skinned with blond or white hair.

Brentaal citizens are no-nonsense when it comes to business. Most are either involved either in commerce or in an ancillary industry. Below the merchant princes are millions of merchants, investors, and bureaucrats who

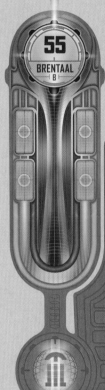

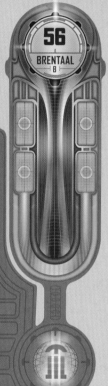

stoke the economic engines and keep them running. The citizens. equally dedicated to recreation, devise extreme sports and elaborate hobbies with which to entertain themselves during their downtime. Perhaps because of Brentaal's cosmopolitan nature, it also has well-regarded cuisine, which has developed over millennia of cross-pollination with other cultures.

Brentaal's reputation for commerce and shipping is legendary. This heritage has colored its culture and society. The traditional folk hero is the fearless spacefarer trailblazing new hyperspace routes for a merchant fleet. In reality, graft and bribes, though hardly legal, are commonplace "business strategies" on Brentaal.

Locations

The valleys and flatlands of Brentaal are dominated by commercial starports, warehouses and container storage facilities, trade markets for a variety of goods, financial markets, and industrial centers. The areas around the poles are dedicated to recreational pursuits, ranging from glacier climbing to ice ball stadiums.

The Trade Hall

Cormond, Brentaal's sprawling capital, runs along the narrow strip of salt flats between the Suporro Sea and the Gravaal mountain range. While the rest of Brentaal is dedicated to handling cargo, Cormond's Trade Hall is the mind that directs the hands of commerce. In its august halls, nobles and their guild representatives gather to make economic policy and manage investments. Merchants, diplomats, and nobles who wish to grease the palms of industry or make contacts in the guilds traffic here.

The Trade Hall features several stadium-sized trade floors, a variety of gardens and shopping areas, and thousands of office suites. It also has its own dedicated

spaceport. Commercial pilots must buy expensive landing permits to use it, but many do so to boost their insider status among the locals.

Alfex Cargo Stacks

Most of the cargo arriving on Brentaal is ultimately bound for somewhere else. Many storage facilities are devoted to sorting through shipments and loading cargo headed for the same destination into huge modular shipping containers, which are then lifted by shuttle to orbiting transports and then taken to their destination.

Alfex Cargo Stacks is one such complex, but one with a difference. It's also a front for Black Sun, one of the galaxy's most potent criminal syndicates. During the Rise of the Empire era and the Rebellion era, its ties extend throughout the Core. Buried deep within the company's maze of ship-sized cargo containers are a series of networked containers refitted to provide work and living quarters for the senior members of the syndicate's Brentaal headquarters. From this nexus, Black Sun manages its smuggling and market manipulation schemes, moving billions of tons of contraband through Brentaal spaceports.

The Favis Resort

The Favis Resort is an artificial island anchored in Brentaal's mild south polar sea. It is one of the playground resort communities where Brentaal's nobles and guild officers retire when the heat of the planet becomes oppressive in the southern hemisphere's summer months. Casinos, luxury hotels, and sports stadiums abound, as do yacht regattas and glacier-climbing expeditions. Because merchants never leave their work behind, Favis has become infamous as a site for corporate espionage.

HoloNet Relay Station

High in Brentaal's orbit, protected by a defense platform, is the primary HoloNet relay station for the sector. This station, composed of a small suite of offices and a huge transmission generator, picks up incoming military holographic transmissions and passes them on to other relay stations farther into the Core. The network is a strategic asset providing a vital link between Coruscant and military outposts and vessels operating along the Perlemian Trade Route. It is therefore guarded by whatever government is in power on Coruscant.

Cargo Container Loader

The 20-meter-long modular cargo containers used by many Brentaal shipping facilities are wrangled from site to site on the ground by specialized heavy-duty cargo skiffs. A cargo container loader drops down onto modules before lifting them up and into orbit.

The Travis Motors Starlifter is a loader used by Alfex Cargo Stacks. It is a hulking, angular craft with a flat bottom and long landing claws that descend from each of the four corners of the craft's undercarriage. A single cargo module fits flush beneath each landing claw, secured to the craft with a combination of physical and electromagnetic clamps. The ship has no room for passengers—the one-seat enclosed cockpit holds only one humanoid. A droid socket behind the cockpit allows a droid to pilot the craft if necessary. The Starlifters used by Alfex have been modified with two concealed blasters. Black Sun operatives typically use them only when facing imminent danger at their hidden headquarters.

Travis Motors Starlifter

Class: Speeder [Ground]	Crew: 1 (Normal +4)
Size: Gargantuan (16 m long)	Initiative: –2 (–4 size, +2 crew)
Passengers: 0	Maneuver: –2 (–4 size, +2 crew)
Cargo Capacity: 75 tons	Defense: 11 (–4 size, +5 armor)
Cost: 100,000 (new),	Shield Points: 0
7,000 (used)	Hull Points: 35 (DR 5)
Availability: Prevalent	Speed: 60 m
Era: All	

* This vehicle provides full cover to its pilot.

Weapon: Double blaster cannons (fire-linked); Fire Arc: Front; Attack Bonus: +0 (–4 size, +4 fire control); Damage: 4d8; Range Increment: 80 m.

For the GM

The adventure hooks and supporting characters described in this section are meant for GMs only. If you're a player, stop reading now.

Adventures

Brentaal is a vital, cosmopolitan organism where everything—from gundark pelts to house loyalties—is for sale.

Here are a few adventure ideas to bring the heroes into the thick of Brentaal intrigues.

HoloNet Down

The Alliance sends the heroes to Brentaal to disable (but not destroy) the HoloNet relay station as its fleet hits a nearby Imperial Navy installation. The Rebels hope the deed will disrupt Imperial distress calls sent to nearby fleets and bases. The heroes must sneak aboard the relay station to sabotage it, because it is too well protected by a nearby defense platform to make a direct frontal attack. Security aboard the station is tight, so the heroes must obtain security clearances, floor plans, and transportation to the station. Likely sources include station employees susceptible to bribery or coercion, Imperial computer nets, and local underworld and Rebel contacts. Once on board the station, they've got to dodge stormtroopers and Brentaal technicians as they plant their charges and slice into the databanks. The fun really starts when the station commander chooses to run a hull breach drill.

Stacked Deck

The heroes have been hired (or dispatched to Brentaal) to resupply a Rebel cell with weapons, spy gear, and a 500,000-credit bribe fund. Despite their iron-clad cover as merchants and a well-hidden secret hold, the heroes find their ship quarantined in Imperial customs by a Brentaal inspector named Surl who claims to detect traces of a deadly virus in the main hold. After the heroes regain access to their ship, they discover that the secret cache is missing.

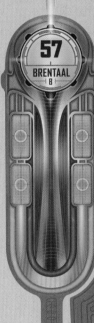

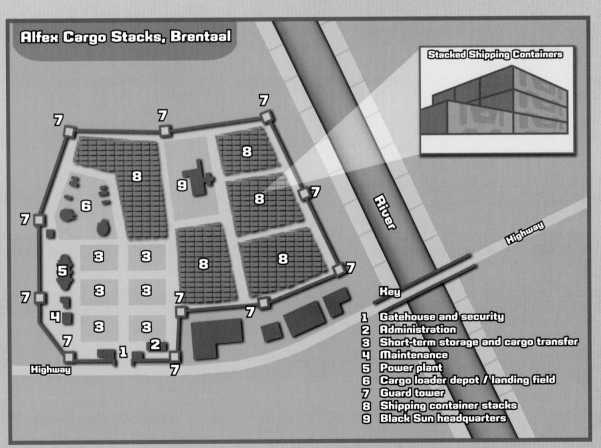

Alfex Cargo Stacks, Brentaal

Stacked Shipping Containers

Key
1. **Gatehouse and security**
2. **Administration**
3. **Short-term storage and cargo transfer**
4. **Maintenance**
5. **Power plant**
6. **Cargo loader depot / landing field**
7. **Guard tower**
8. **Shipping container stacks**
9. **Black Sun headquarters**

The Empire releases their ship with no comment. With backup from the Rebel cell, the heroes learn that Surl is an Imperial Security Bureau operative—but he hasn't reported the confiscation of the secret cache to Imperial authorities.

As the heroes investigate, Imperial forces begin to dog their every move. Although they may think so at first, Surl isn't responsible for sending the Imperials against them. That culprit is Dania, a traitorous member of the Rebel cell, with whom Surl plans to abscond with the credits. She's the one who told him to expect the heroes' ship, and she's been sending anonymous tips to the Imperial authorities. A final showdown at the Favis Resort goes from bad to worse when Dania lowers the boom on the heroes and Surl alike in a deadly ambush led by some house toughs. When ISB operatives show up gunning for their rogue agent, all hell breaks loose.

Sun Storm

A criminal organization that's no longer content to operate on the fringes of Brentaal commerce is making a move to muscle into the mainstream. Through blackmail and intimidation, they're taking over House Okeefe. The heroes are recruited to stop the hoods by an angry house noble named Barthos Okeefe. Tracking down the heavies making the actual move on House Okeefe isn't too tough, since they show up regularly to bully, threaten, and scheme with various house members. The characters should make considerable headway in recovering blackmail material, neutralizing thugs, and otherwise foiling the takeover attempt before they discover who their rivals are. They realize that they've actually picked a fight with the ruthless Black Sun syndicate—probably when it dispatches its troubleshooter, Fellion, to take care of them. They might deal with her, but there's worse on the way if they can't figure out how to distract the local chapter. Barthos suggests that a raid on the Alfex Cargo Stacks might do the trick.

Allies and Antagonists

The following supporting characters are designed for use in your campaign.

Surl

A ruddy, beefy man with a trim red beard and perpetual sweat stains beneath his arms, Surl is a mid-level customs agent working the capital's spaceports. He has the look of a dull-witted bureaucrat, but he's actually a corrupt Imperial Security Bureau operative who uses his position to cut a little extra for himself from time to time. He hasn't been caught yet, but he's getting more ambitious. Surl is a formidable foe with a head for developing spy networks. One of his agents is his lover Dania, a no-nonsense member of a local Rebel cell. By nature a mild-mannered person, Surl prefers to nurse grudges in secret rather than oppose someone outright.

Surl: Male Human Scoundrel 4/Soldier 2; Init +1; Defense 15 (+1 Dex, +4 class); Spd 10 m; VP/WP 30/12; Atk +6 melee (1d3+1, punch) or +6 ranged (3d8, heavy

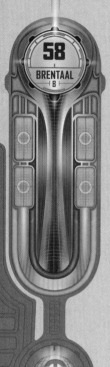

blaster pistol); SQ illicit barter, lucky 1/day, precise attack +1; SV Fort +5, Ref +5, Will +0; SZ M; FP 0; DSP 0; Rep +2; Str 12, Dex 13, Con 12, Int 14, Wis 9, Cha 16. Challenge Code D.

Equipment: Heavy blaster pistol, comlink, datapad.

Skills: Appraise +5, Bluff +14, Computer Use +4, Demolitions +5, Diplomacy +10, Forgery +8, Gather Information +9, Intimidate +10, Knowledge (Brentaal) +7, Knowledge (streetwise) +9, Listen +8, Move Silently +7, Profession (customs inspector) +3, Read/Write Basic, Repair +5, Search +6, Sense Motive +5, Speak Basic, Spot +4.

Feats: Alertness, Armor Proficiency (light), Heroic Surge, Persuasive, Sharp-Eyed, Skill Emphasis (Knowledge [streetwise], Sense Motive), Weapon Group Proficiencies (blaster pistols, simple weapons).

Barthos Okeefe

Lord Barthos, a member of the Okeefe merchant house, is a robust sixty-year-old man with close-cropped white hair. As the one-time director of the orbiting HoloNet relay station, he knows its many systems—as well as its security backdoors and weaknesses. Okeefe has retired to a penthouse in a north polar resort villa, where he alternates between being an outdoorsman and managing his house's financial accounts. Barthos has little love for the Empire, but he isn't convinced the Rebel Alliance is strong enough to replace it. If the heroes can convince him with their successes on Brentaal, they'll earn a wealthy and well-connected ally.

Barthos Okeefe: Male Human Noble 4; Init –1; Defense 12 (–1 Dex, +3 class); Spd 10 m; VP/WP 17/12; Atk +5 melee (1d3+2, punch) or +5 melee (1d4+2, knife) or +2 ranged (3d6, blaster pistol); SQ coordinate +1, favor +2, inspire confidence, bonus class skill (Survival), resource access; SV Fort +2, Ref +1, Will +5; SZ M; FP 0; DSP 0; Rep +2; Str 14, Dex 9, Con 12, Int 10, Wis 13, Cha 15. Challenge Code C.

Equipment: Blaster pistol, knife, comlink.

Skills: Appraise +4, Diplomacy +10, Gather Information +4, Knowledge (bureaucracy) +7, Profession (financier) +8, Read/Write Basic, Ride +2, Search +3, Sense Motive +5, Speak Basic, Spot +4, Survival +7.

Feats: Endurance, Quickness, Trustworthy, Weapon Group Proficiencies (blaster pistols, simple weapons).

Fellion

Fellion is a nondescript woman in her thirties. Nature has endowed her with a mousy and timid-looking demeanor, which in her case is extremely misleading. While Black Sun has plenty of thugs, thieves, and slicers, Fellion is one of its few secret enforcers on Brentaal—the woman who gets the call when a well-protected mark must disappear or die. Fellion was trained in a private militia in the Kathol Outback. She then drifted Coreward to seek her fortune with the Black Sun syndicate. She eschews battle armor and exotic toys, preferring to rely on her martial arts skills and an array of blaster weapons to get most jobs done.

Fellion: Female Human Soldier 7; Init +3; Defense 19 (+3 Dex, +6 class); Spd 10 m; VP/WP 43/11; Atk +10/+5 melee (1d4+3, punch) or +10/+5 ranged (3d6, blaster pistol) or +10/+5 ranged (3d8/19–20, blaster rifle) or +10/+5 ranged (3d6/stun DC 15, ion gun) or +10/+5 ranged (4d6+1, frag grenade); SV Fort +5, Ref +5, Will +2; SZ M; FP 0; DSP 0; Rep +2; Str 17, Dex 16, Con 11, Int 12, Wis 10, Cha 9. Challenge Code D.

   Equipment: Blaster pistol, ion gun pistol, blaster rifle, 5 frag grenades, comlink, macrobinoculars, medpac, security kit.

   Skills: Climb +7, Computer Use +7, Demolitions +5, Disable Device +4, Hide +8, Intimidate +3, Read/Write Basic, Search +6, Speak Basic, Speak Bothese, Survival +5, Treat Injury +2.

   Feats: Armor Proficiency (light), Far Shot, Martial Arts, Multishot, Point Blank Shot, Precise Shot, Rapid Shot, Run, Track, Weapon Group Proficiencies (blaster pistols, blaster rifles, heavy weapons, simple weapons, vibro weapons).

New Creature: Kundril

The kundril is an enormous, multisegmented flying insect—one of Brentaal's few surviving indigenous life-forms. It is long, slender, and flattened, with mean-looking mandibles at one end and a blunted hard wedge at the other, which it uses to lash out at enemies. Rows of delicate, translucent wings help the creature maneuver, but they do not keep it aloft. Internal bladders within each segment filled with lighter-than-air gases aid airborne locomotion. Because kundrils lack eyes, they hunt by sound.

   Several kinds of kundril exist. Most are seagoing creatures with exoskeletons in various shades of blue and green. From the air, they dip down into the waves to snatch up fish or seagoing mammals. There were once many land-based varieties as well, but most have died out or been hunted into extinction. Imperial kundrils, hulking monstrosities with thick hides that are colored red and flaked with gold, can still be found in isolated mountain canyons, particularly areas near active volcanoes. All kinds of kundrils mate and lay eggs on land, usually along rocky coastlines.

   Despite their fearsome aspect, kundrils usually hunt much smaller game than Humans, typically avoiding Medium-size or larger creatures (not to mention boats, airspeeders, and starships). If attacked or hounded, however, they are deadly foes.

Kundril: Airborne predator 6; Init +9 (+7 Dex, +2 species); Defense 19 (+7 Dex, –8 size, +10 natural); Spd 6 m, fly 60 m (poor); VP/WP 43/120; Atk +4/–1 melee (2d6+6, slam) or +4/–1 melee (4d8+6, bite) or +5/+0 ranged; SQ +2 species bonus on initiative checks; SV Fort +7, Ref +12, Will +0; SZ C; Face/Reach 10 m by 20 m/8 m; Str 22, Dex 24, Con 15, Int 4, Wis 6, Cha 6.

   Skills: Hide +0, Listen +9, Spot +5.

   Feats: Flyby Attack, Power Attack, Skill Emphasis (Spot).

Caamas

Planet Type: Terrestrial (see text)
Climate: Temperate to arctic
Terrain: Barren wasteland (rocky)
Atmosphere: Toxic
Gravity: Standard
Diameter: 15,540 km
Length of Day: 25 standard hours
Length of Year: 375 standard days
Sentient Species: Caamasi
Languages: Caamasi, Basic
Population: 250 (after Imperial orbital bombardment)
Species Mix: 80% Caamasi, 14% Ithorian, 6% other
Government: Representative democracy
Major Exports: None
Major Imports: Foodstuffs
System/Star: Cirius/Cirius

Planets	Type	Moons
Lis	Molten rock	0
Caamas	Toxic rock	0
Caamor	Frozen rock	1
Sirilla	Gas giant	17

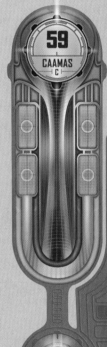

Description

Caamas was once a lush, temperate planet composed of three main landmasses. Rolling fields, steppes, stout hillocks, and dense forests teeming with life dominated the landscape. However, shortly after the Clone Wars, an unknown enemy attacked the planet. With the aid of operatives on the surface who disabled the planetary shields and then escaped, the enemy rained fiery destruction on the peaceful world. The ensuing firestorm decimated all vegetation and animals and wiped out most of the sentient Caamasi.

   Caamas became a barren, rocky wasteland. The destruction was complete, destabilizing the planet's ecosystem. Plants no longer released oxygen into the atmosphere. Any animals that survived the initial attack died a slow death of starvation and asphyxiation. Immense clouds of soot and smoke filled the atmosphere, radically altering the climate. The resulting atmosphere is toxic to most aliens, and a breath mask is now required for any sustained activity. Without vegetation, erosion runs rampant and dust storms commonly sweep the landscape. Even the oceans have become polluted from runoff.

History

Before its destruction, Caamas was home to the Caamasi, a pacifist society of scholars and nobles with high moral values. Some legends claim that the first Jedi Knights traveled to Caamas to learn how to use their powers ethically. Just after the Clone Wars, the planet was devastated by an unknown enemy.

   In truth, Palpatine secretly engineered the destruction of Caamas with assistance from Bothan operatives. The Caamasi were wise and free-thinking, clinging to the ideals of the Old Republic. Palpatine perceived them to be a threat to his domination and quickly removed them. The planet's destruction caused galaxywide outrage due to the extent of the attack. A few Caamasi survived and fled to refugee camps on Kerilt, Susevfi, and Alderaan. Of course, those on Alderaan died soon thereafter when that planet was destroyed as well.

Following the destruction, a splinter group of Caamasi resettled at a small outpost called Refuge City in the northern hemisphere of Caamas. These few Caamasi, with the help of the Ithorians, are researching methods to decontaminate the planet. Few other travelers have the need to come to this inhospitable world.

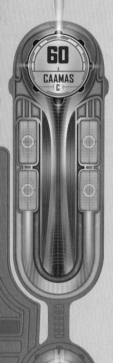

People

The name Caamasi, in many languages, translates to "friend from afar" or "stranger to be trusted." The Caamasi are artistic, wise, pacifistic, and free-thinking, possessing a strong sense of moral values. Most become scholars, diplomats, or merchants. They have a deep respect for others, even their enemies.

All Caamasi can create vivid telepathic memories called *memnii*, which can be shared with others of their species. Often, clans intermarry for the purposes of spreading these collective memories. *Memnii* can also be shared with Jedi who possess at least a rudimentary command of telepathy.

Caamasi have a few peculiar mannerisms. The first is the Caamasi bow, a full stoop used to acknowledge others. The bow is an important diplomatic proceeding. The second is a full body shrug, a side effect of the Caamasi's advanced perception and intuition. The shrug begins in the upper torso and spreads to the ends of the extremities.

Locations

Descriptions of several key locations follow.

Refuge City

Refuge City is located in the northern hemisphere of the planet, amid a ruined city. The "city" is a fabricated dome with a few outlying structures. A pair of landing pads provides little more than a patch of even terrain for a ship to put down. Alongside the main dome is a large power grid that supplies energy to the settlement via power cables strewn on the rocky ground. The city's main purpose is to provide a base of operations for scientists to research methods for establishing a natural ecology on the planet.

The interior of the main dome is lit by massive biolum globes, spheres of water containing phosphorescent plankton. An indoor garden at the center of the dome is tended by Ithorian ecologists. The garden provides oxygen, food, and plant materials for reclamation experiments. Living quarters for about three hundred encircle the garden on several levels. Living space is cramped, since most of the larger areas are used for recreation, research laboratories, and similar functions. No markets or cantinas are present, because the community shares all and has little need to cater to visitors.

About two hundred Caamasi live in the dome, along with several dozen Ithorian ecologists. A few Humans and members of other species are present, conducting private research or having been hired by the Caamasi. Refuge City is governed by Elek D'cel, a Caamasi diplomat who hopes to one day discover a way to decontaminate his homeworld.

Bothan Debris, Inc.

An immense crater is situated about 70 kilometers south of Refuge City. This geographical feature was caused by a meteor crash a few years after the destruction of Caamas. The Bothans, interested in financially aiding the Caamasi but still looking for a gain in the process, drafted a hundred-year lease for the crater area. For the sum of 50,000 credits a year, the Bothans use the crater as a dump. The funds go to Refuge City to support its decontamination efforts for the planet. Once a week, a bulk cruiser from Bothawui arrives to offload debris.

The dump is operated by a Bothan named Kursk Te'tell. A dozen of his Bothan assistants receive the debris, disassemble it for useful parts and cataloging, and stash it in the crater. The workers are stationed in a light cruiser hull that has no engines; its interior provides living space, offices, a galley, and a recreation area. Using vacuum suits, ASP droids, and cargo skiffs, they spend all day, every day, moving debris and filling out endless paperwork.

Kursk Te'tell is actually a member of the famed Bothan spynet, and Bothan Debris, Inc., is a front. He's stationed here in case anyone comes to Caamas to search for clues regarding the planet's devastation. Above all else, he is to report any suspicious behavior to his superiors, who will arrive within hours to assist.

Alien Jungle

An alien jungle about 15 kilometers in diameter is located on Caamas's smallest landmass in the southern hemisphere. It's the first reestablishment of vegetation since the devastation of the planet, and it's growing at the rate of approximately 1 kilometer a year. The twisted jungle is composed of low-growing shrubs; short, sticky trees with leathery leaves; and odd fungus. Most of the plants have deep roots and vines or tendrils. Research teams from Refuge City explore the jungle on a regular basis. They are determined to discover its origin and means of survival.

Unknown to all but a few Ithorians, the source of the jungle is hidden in its center. The jungle conceals the shattered remains of an Ithorian herdship that crashed under mysterious circumstances. The herdship, literally carrying a jungle inside it, has seeded Caamas with new strains of vegetation. Some of these strains have been able to colonize the harsh landscape, and they are almost flourishing due to the lack of competition. The jungle sprawls uninhibited in all directions. However, the pollution of the planet has brought a spiritual taint to this oasis—though only a Force-sensitive Ithorian priest would be likely to sense the presence of the dark side in its midst.

Ruined Jedi Temple

Ages ago, legends say, the first Jedi Knights arrived on Caamas to learn proper moral judgment. Since then, Jedi following their example established a temple on the planet for contemplation and learning. The temple lies in ruins, having suffered direct hits from Palpatine's firestorm attacks. Located in a moist lowland, it is gradually being encroached upon by hardy specimens from the alien jungle. Most of the Jedi lore in the temple has been destroyed, but a few underground chambers survived with little damage. Forgotten Jedi heirlooms (and the traps guarding them) could still be found.

Shield Generator Stations

Being a peaceful species, the Caamasi lacked any armies. Instead, they focused their attention on planetary defense, relying on a powerful shield generator. The planet had sixteen separate shield generator stations situated at equidistant locations on the equator. Each station was located deep underground, and each boasted a complex security system.

During the destruction of Caamas, Bothan operatives infiltrated the shield generator stations and sabotaged the power supply, crippling the shield. During the attack, most of the stations were destroyed, but at least one is mostly intact. Station number 14, although still hidden and inoperative, remains relatively unscathed. Even the workers at Bothan Debris, Inc., do not suspect it contains clues relating to the Bothan involvement, including an insane resident.

For the GM

The adventure hooks and supporting characters described in this section are meant for GMs only. If you're a player, stop reading now.

Adventures

Life is returning to the fragile ecosystem of Caamas. Opportunities for adventure are abundant as well.

Exploration

While at Refuge City on Caamas, the heroes are approached by Ish'tay, an Ithorian Force adept. The heroes could be on Caamas for ship repairs or on courier service to deliver a message or parcel to a Caamasi resident. Ish'tay would like to hire the heroes to explore part of the alien jungle. He is collecting soil and plant samples from the jungle to continue researching a means to reestablish growth on Caamas.

During the exploration, the heroes locate a piece of twisted metal, part of a starship. This leads to the discovery of an Ithorian herdship buried beneath the forest. Is the herdship the source of the alien jungle? What secrets are concealed in its hull? Why did it crash? By exploring the ship's interior, the heroes can discover answers to these questions. But what horrors lurk there? The heroes may encounter mutated beasts or carnivorous and poisonous plants—or even the influence of the dark side.

Verifying the Document

The Caamas Document, an Imperial file detailing the Bothans' involvement in the destruction of Caamas, has come into the possession of the New Republic. The heroes are sent to Caamas to verify its contents. They could be New Republic representatives or operatives sent by another faction (possibly a powerful crime lord) to recover the information. On arrival, the heroes can learn

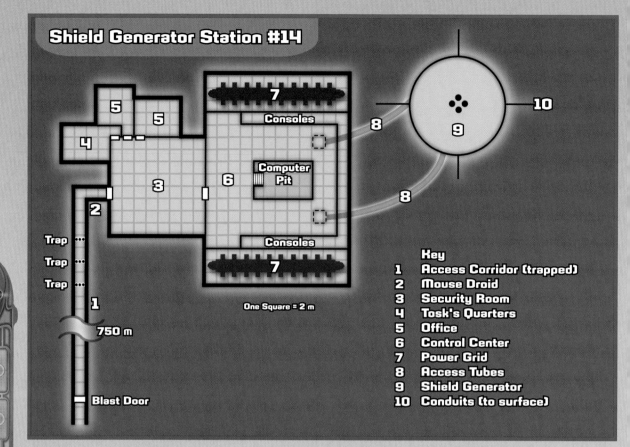

Shield Generator Station #14

Key
1. Access Corridor (trapped)
2. Mouse Droid
3. Security Room
4. Tosk's Quarters
5. Office
6. Control Center
7. Power Grid
8. Access Tubes
9. Shield Generator
10. Conduits (to surface)

One Square = 2 m

750 m

Blast Door

the locations of the sixteen shield generator stations and begin exploring one. They might even gain the attention of Kursk Te'tell and Bothan Debris, Inc. The Bothans attempt to thwart the exploration of the stations, using force if necessary. The mission then becomes a race against time to locate station number 14 and reach Tosk-tar'ilya, the insane Bothan operative, before the Bothans discover him.

The Missing Scientist

A research scientist from Refuge City is missing, and the heroes have been hired by Administrator Elek D'cel to locate him. All clues point toward a recent breakthrough in the decontamination of the planet. Elek D'cel suspects foul play, but who's responsible, and why? Is it a company seeking to profit from selling the discovery to the Caamasi? Is it an unknown enemy making sure that its efforts to destroy Caamas are not foiled? Maybe the scientist merely feigned his disappearance and is attempting to sell his discovery to the highest bidder. Whatever the answer, the beings responsible respond with deadly force to make sure that their secrets remain hidden.

Allies and Antagonists

The following supporting characters are designed for use in your campaign.

Ish'tay

Ish'tay is a tall, lanky Ithorian with ochre-colored skin. He wears a simple cloak and leans on a gnarled rosewood staff. He sports several neck piercings holding an odd assortment of metal rings. Ish'tay, as a deeply spiritual Ithorian, worships an aspect of the Force. His slow, deliberate manner of movement is enforced by his monotone voice (even though it's broadcast in stereophonic sound). The ecologist originally came to Caamas to study the alien jungle in the southern hemisphere. Now he has sensed a spiritual presence on the planet that thoroughly disturbs him.

Ish'tay: Male Ithorian Force Adept 5; Init –1; Defense 14 (–1 Dex, +5 class); Spd 10 m; VP/WP 31/12; Atk +3 melee (1d3, punch) or +3 melee (1d6/1d6, quarterstaff) or +2 ranged; SQ Force weapon +1d8; SV Fort +4, Ref +2, Will +8; SZ M; FP 3; DSP 0; Rep +1; Str 10, Dex 9, Con 12, Int 14, Wis 16, Cha 18. Challenge Code C.

   Equipment: Quarterstaff, medpac, 2 datapads, biolum torch, all-temperature cloak, survival kit, breath mask, neck rings.

   Skills: Handle Animal +12, Knowledge (biology) +10, Read/Write Basic, Read/Write Ithorese, Speak Basic, Speak Huttese, Speak Ithorese, Survival +15, Treat Injury +11.

   Force Skills: Empathy +13, Enhance Ability +9, Friendship +12, Heal Another +13.

62
CAAMAS
C

Feats: Force-Sensitive, Track, Two-Weapon Fighting, Weapon Group Proficiencies (primitive weapons, simple weapons).

Force Feats: Alter, Compassion, Control, Sense.

Tosk-tar'ilya

Tosk is a male Bothan with tan-white fur that's usually matted and dirty. His eyes are black and uncaring, and his left ear is torn from an old injury. He wears a dirty set of clothes and a tattered, stained cloak. He conceals four knives on his person and carries a huge pipe in one hand.

Tosk was an undercover operative assigned to sabotage shield generator station number 14. After disabling the security force with stun gas and securing the station, he accessed the main computers and witnessed the firestorms raining down upon the hapless planet. When he realized the atrocity he had unleashed upon an unsuspecting world, he ran into a small closet and locked himself inside.

That was decades ago. Tosk survived. He ekes out an existence in the ruins of the station's water purification system by hunting down vermin. Tosk is certifiably insane and often babbles in his native tongue at length. He is fond of sending reports to his supervisors via a broken comlink. Tosk has a nervous twitch that begins at his left eye and runs down his left arm. If he held a blaster, the twitches would cause him to fire it repeatedly.

Tosk-tar'ilya: Male Bothan Scout 8/Scoundrel 6; Init +5; Defense 22 (+5 Dex, +7 class); Spd 10 m; VP/WP 62/10; Atk +11/+6 melee (1d4+1, punch) or +11/+6 melee (1d4+1, knife) or +11/+6 melee (1d6+1, metal pipe) or +15/+10 ranged (3d4, hold-out blaster); SQ evasion, extreme effort, heart +1, illicit barter, lucky 2/day, precise attack +1, skill mastery (Computer Use), trailblazing, uncanny dodge (can't be flanked, Dex bonus to Defense); SV Fort +6, Ref +14, Will +7; SZ M; FP 0; DSP 0; Rep +1; Str 13, Dex 21, Con 10, Int 14, Wis 13, Cha 14. Challenge Code F.

Equipment: Four knives, metal pipe (club), comlink (broken), hold-out blaster (no power pack), dirty cloak, tool kit, security kit, field kit, breath mask.

Skills: Bluff +13, Computer Use +24, Disable Device +16, Disguise +19, Escape Artist +19, Forgery +19, Gather Information +13, Move Silently +16, Pilot +21, Read/Write Bothese, Repair +15, Speak Basic, Speak Bothese, Speak Huttese, Speak Rodese, Spot +3, Survival +7.

Feats: Cautious, Gearhead, Low Profile, Martial Arts, Nimble, Skill Emphasis (Computer Use, Pilot), Spacer, Starship Operation (space transport), Weapon Group

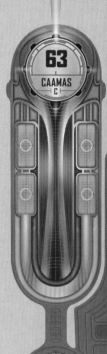

TOSK-TAR'ILYA

Proficiencies (blaster pistols, blaster rifles, simple weapons).

Elek D'cel

Elek D'cel is a typical Caamasi, with golden down and light purple feathers encircling his eyes. He is adorned in a shimmersilk noble's outfit and typically wears a full-length cloak. He always has a breath mask at hand, as he frequently leaves the shelter of Refuge City to take long, reflective walks outside. When nervous, he tends to twitch his nose and flex his fingers.

Elek was offplanet when Caamas was devastated. In typical Caamasi fashion, he doesn't cry for revenge. Instead, he focuses his efforts on searching for a means to reclaim his homeworld through decontamination. Elek is the founder of Refuge City and has been the administrator of the place since its inception. He manages all facets of the city's operations.

Elek D'cel: Male Caamasi Diplomat 6/Noble 3; Init +0; Defense 13 (+3 class); Spd 10 m; VP/WP 10/8; Atk +4 melee or +5 ranged; SQ memory sharing, gentle reputation, bonus class skill (Bluff), favor +2, inspire confidence, resource access; SV Fort +2, Ref +4, Will +13; SZ M; FP 1; DSP 0; Rep +3; Str 9, Dex 11, Con 8, Int 19, Wis 17, Cha 17. Challenge Code C.

Equipment: Noble's outfit, breath mask, all-temperature cloak, credit chip (800 credits), 2 datapads, recording rod.

Skills: Bluff +17, Computer Use +16, Diplomacy +19, Forgery +7, Gather Information +17, Intimidate +5, Knowledge (bureaucracy) +16, Knowledge (history) +16, Knowledge (politics) +16, Read/Write Basic, Read/Write Bothese, Read/Write Caamasi, Search +6, Sense Motive +20, Speak Basic, Speak Bothese, Speak Caamasi, Speak Ryl.

Feats: Iron Will, Persuasive, Sharp-Eyed, Skill Emphasis (Diplomacy, Sense Motive), Trustworthy, Weapon Group Proficiencies (blaster pistols, simple weapons).

Special Qualities: *Memory Sharing*—Caamasi are able to create strong, lasting memories and share them with others of their species using a kind of telepathy. Among the Caamasi, this is an automatic ability, requiring only time. Force-using characters can also receive *memnii* from Caamasi with a successful Telepathy check (DC 15). Sharing a memory requires as much time as the events remembered. Remembering specific details of the shared memories afterward requires a successful Intelligence check (DC 15).

Gentle Reputation—Caamasi have a reputation for tranquility and wisdom, allowing them to negotiate a peace treaty or a dinner bill with equal skill. As such, they have a +2 species bonus on Diplomacy checks.

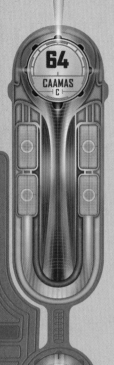

New Creature: Mutated Behemoth

Once a primary predator on Caamas, the mutated behemoth hibernates for years at a time. A few of these beasts were hibernating underground when Caamas was destroyed. As toxins seeped into the planet, the slumbering beasts became poisoned as well. Some survived, but their genetic material was altered, twisting them into mutated aberrations. Each creature is over 4 meters long, with long, shaggy fur falling out in patches, revealing a sturdy, scaly hide. It sports three pairs of legs, each ending in a clawed appendage. Its oblong head is set with bony ridges, and oversized incisors dominate a tooth-filled maw. It also has a short tail, which it uses for balance.

Mutated Behemoth: Predator 3; Init +2; Defense 19 (+2 Dex, –1 size, +8 natural); Spd 12 m; VP/WP 34/20; Atk +6 melee (2d6+4, bite) or +4 ranged; SQ low-light vision; SV Fort +6, Ref +5, Will –1; SZ L; Face/Reach 2 m by 4 m/2 m; Rep +0; Str 19, Dex 15, Con 17, Int 4, Wis 6, Cha 6. Challenge Code C.

  Skills: Balance +5, Climb +10, Intimidate +2.
  Feats: Power Attack, Toughness.

New Creature: Thornsniper Plant

The alien jungle contains numerous species of dangerous plants, and the thornsniper is a notable example. The thornsniper is a short, woody shrub with broad leaves dangling from its branches, which radiate off a thick trunk. The leaves are covered with thousands of thorns. The plant's extensive shallow root system extends up to 10 meters around the base of the plant. A thornsniper's roots can sense vibrations as light as those caused by a footfall, triggering the plant to release several volleys of thorns in the direction of the disturbance. For 5 rounds after it senses a victim, the plant fires thorns. Any creatures killed by the thorns decompose over the roots and nourish the plant.

Thornsniper: Scavenger 3; Init –5; Defense 9 (–5 Dex, +1 size, +3 natural); Spd 0 m; VP/WP 9/10; Atk +4 ranged (3d4, thorns); SQ camouflage, tremorsense; SV Fort +3, Ref –4, Will +0; SZ S; Face/Reach 2 m by 2 m/2 m; Rep +0; Str 10, Dex 1, Con 10, Int 2, Wis 8, Cha 1. Challenge Code A.

  Skills: Hide +5, Survival +5.
  Feats: Weapon Focus (thorns).
  Special Qualities: *Tremorsense*—A thornsniper is sensitive to vibrations in the ground and can automatically sense the location of anything within 20 meters that is in contact with the ground.

Chandrila

Planet Type: Terrestrial
Climate: Temperate
Terrain: Plains, forests
Atmosphere: Breathable
Gravity: Standard
Diameter: 13,500 km
Length of Day: 20 standard hours
Length of Year: 368 standard days
Sentient Species: Human
Languages: Basic
Population: 1.2 billion
Species Mix: 96% Human, 4% other
Government: Imperial governorship or democracy (depending on era)
Major Exports: Foodstuffs
Major Imports: High tech
System/Star: Chandrila

Planets	Type	Moons
Expora	Searing rock	0
Chandrila	Terrestrial	2
Lorora	Toxic rock	1
Quenus	Gas giant	3
Asimuse	Gas giant	9
Dolucar	Gas giant	12
Sissubo	Frozen rock	1

Description

Chandrila is one of the most pleasant and affluent of the Core Worlds—which helps explain why many people simply can't stand Chandrilans. It's not that their planet is ugly or unpleasant, or that its natives are ignorant or cruel. They have none of these disadvantages, and people are skeptical of a society that seemingly has no flaws.

Chandrila is an idyllic world of grassy plains and gentle, lapping seas. The inhabited areas of the planet's two continents have been kept free of urban pollution, and all citizens are educated from birth in methods of maintaining a balanced ecosystem. Most animal life is docile, posing little threat to Humans, and the climate is moderate year round. Chandrila followed much the same path as Alderaan in environmental and political development, but the planet was spared the miseries of the Clone Wars and the tumult of the Rebellion against the Empire. Given this last fact, some surviving Alderaanians may hate the Chandrilans more than they hate any other Core Worlders.

History

The Chandrila system is located in the Bormea sector of the Ringali Shell, which lies along the Perlemian Trade Route. Chandrila sits between Corulag and Brentaal, a bucolic oasis flanked by its more urbanized and victimized neighbors. The planet has been settled since the earliest years of the Republic's expansion into the galaxy, but it bears none of the martial or industrial scars found on worlds of comparable age. Over the course of twenty-five millennia, Chandrila has never been a major battleground, and its manufacturing needs have always been satisfied by importing offworld goods. By the time of the Great Sith War, the planet's economic engine was driven by hundreds of automated agrifarms that grew grains, beans, and produce for export throughout the Core Worlds.

Chandrila quickly developed a reputation for encouraging political candor, so it surprised no one when a Chandrilan senator, Mon Mothma, became one of the Emperor's most eloquent critics in the years following the Clone Wars. The senator's seditionist planning with fellow revolutionary Bail Organa caused her to be condemned as a traitor to the Empire. Mon Mothma went underground and formed the Rebel Alliance, allowing Canna Omonda to assume her seat as Chandrila's representative to the Senate.

Apparently Omonda hadn't learned from the fate of her predecessor—or perhaps the Chandrilan need for self-expression overruled the need for self-preservation—but she openly criticized the Emperor for his dissolution of the Imperial Senate. Palpatine's operatives executed Omonda for crimes against the Empire, and Imperial commerce regulators slapped stiff agricultural tariffs on the Bormea sector. Chandrila's economy went into a tailspin. Moff Seerdon exacerbated the situation when he blockaded the planet in retaliation for the unrelated Rebel theft of Imperial AT-PTs from Fest. Rogue Squadron helped break Seerdon's blockade, but the agricultural taxes remained. Despite economic troubles, Chandrila itself remained largely unscathed, a fact that struck some as unfair in light of the Imperial punishments meted out to similarly outspoken Core Worlds such as Ralltiir and Alderaan.

A second blockade struck Chandrila six months after the Battle of Endor, when Grand Vizier Sate Pestage dispatched seven Star Destroyers to cut off all traffic to and from the planet. Pestage's plan—to use Chandrila as a bargaining chip against the surging New Republic military—collapsed when Ysanne Isard took his place as head of the Empire. Chandrila kept a low profile until its liberation by New Republic forces shortly after the fall of Coruscant.

The new government suited Chandrila, and its citizens lent their voice to policy discussions under the leadership of their prodigal daughter, Mon Mothma. Not even the return of the reborn Emperor rattled the pastoral world. During Operation Shadow Hand, Chandrila served as a haven for wounded evacuees from war-torn Coruscant and other Core Worlds. In that same spirit, Chandrila has

opened its borders to thousands of displaced citizens since the onset of the Yuuzhan Vong invasion—and fortunately, it has not yet become a target of the alien aggressors. Because their world lacks significant military assets, Chandrilans hope they will make it through the war unharmed.

People

The population of Chandrila is overwhelmingly Human. It has remained at around 1.2 billion for thousands of years, largely due to a government policy requiring small families. In keeping with their respect for nature, Chandrilans maintain flower gardens, fish ponds, and insect hives at their homes, and they spend much of their free time looking after them.

Chandrilans have a direct voice in their planet's government and are encouraged to argue politics in the public rotundas found in every town square. Even under the rule of the dictatorial Empire, Imperial Governor Gerald Weizel chose not to disband the democratic Chandrilan House. The Chandrilans' emphasis on political education contributes to an image of them among others as "know-it-alls." Many view them as one might view the spoiled children of a rich parent—smart, but unfamiliar with hard work and sacrifice.

Besides Mon Mothma, several other Chandrilans have made names for themselves away from their birthworld. Admiral Drayson, head of the top-secret New Republic

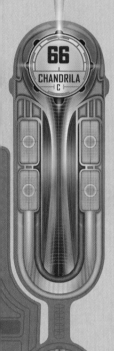
intelligence agency Alpha Blue, was once head of Chandrila's homeguard defense fleet. Sera Faleur, a native Chandrilan who became a social worker on Coruscant, married Rogue Squadron leader Gavin Darklighter after the defeat of the reborn Emperor.

Locations

Descriptions of several key locations follow.

Hanna

Hanna, Chandrila's capital, is one of only three cities on Chandrila with full starport facilities. (The others are Emita and Nayli.) Constructed on the rippling banks of the Silver Sea, Hanna is a mishmash of shops, businesses, private residences, and government offices with no definable "districts" other than a public plaza and debating rotunda at the city's heart. One of the most spectacular coral reefs this side of Spira is just offshore. In most years, Hanna does a brisk tourist business.

Brionelle Academy and the Imperial Garrison

Two martial establishments located to the north of the capital might seem out of place on peaceful Chandrila, but both speak to different aspects of the planet's heritage. The Brionelle Memorial Military Academy is a revered old-world establishment that has produced officers for the Chandrilan home defense fleet for generations. Not too far from the academy's moss-

covered stone walls is the Chandrilan Imperial garrison, constructed after the rise of the Empire. It was used by Imperial Governor Gerald Weizel as his base of operations. By the time of The New Jedi Order era, the garrison's electrified fence is deactivated and its phalanx of patrolling AT-ATs long gone, but it still serves as a stark reminder of the Empire's once-ubiquitous authority.

Hanna Wild Game Reserve

Bumping up against Hanna's outskirts is the Hanna Wild Game Reserve, the only place on the planet where one can openly carry a weapon. Chandrilans encourage controlled hunting within the reserve's borders to cull animal populations before the onset of Hanna's winter. From the air, the game reserve is a deep green blotch of primeval forest. It stands out against the white rooftops of Hanna and the boundless hectares of chestnut and golden agrifarms off to the west. Inside this restricted acreage, hunters can track cairnmogs and flying blackbacks across a rocky wilderness of sienta trees and gurgling whitewater creeks. Outside of the game reserve, hunting is forbidden. It's not unusual to see herds of squalls and other animals roaming aimlessly over unfenced fields and across thoroughfares.

Datadagger

Chandrilans, while maintaining a nonviolent society, nurse personal grudges just like the rest of the galaxy's citizens. A popular (though seldom discussed) weapon among the political class is the datadagger. A slim, 20-centimeter-long ivory cylinder with inlaid patterns of silver and gold, the datadagger seems to be precious art at first glance. Upon closer inspection, it is revealed as a code cylinder capable of interfacing with door locks, computer terminals, and datapads. Upon even closer inspection, one discovers that a narrow, needle-sharp blade extends from the center of the plug-in socket when the owner twists the hilt. The datadagger is a weapon of surprise typically employed for self-defense, but poisoned datadaggers are occasionally used in assassination attempts. The hidden blade is almost impossible to detect with a standard weapons scan. High-quality datadaggers and code cylinders are heirlooms handed down within families for generations. Not every diplomat carrying an ivory rod is necessarily the owner of a datadagger. The cylinder design is common on Chandrila, but the hidden blade is not.

Datadagger

Cost: 2,000 credits
Damage: 1d4
Critical: 20
Weight: 1 kg
Type: Piercing
Size: Small
Group: Exotic
  Special Qualities: The code cylinder allows access to restricted data via scomp link based on the owner's level of personal security clearance.

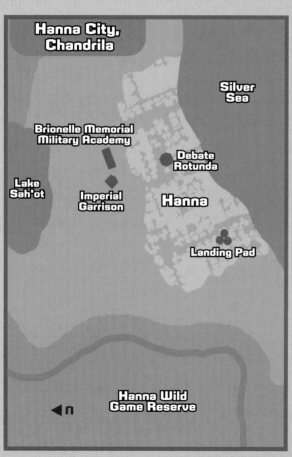

Hanna City, Chandrila

Silver Sea

Brionelle Memorial Military Academy

Debate Rotunda

Lake Sah'ot

Imperial Garrison

Hanna

Landing Pad

◄ n

Hanna Wild Game Reserve

For the GM

The adventure hooks and supporting characters described in this section are meant for GMs only. If you're a player, stop reading now.

Adventures

Feel free to use or adapt the following adventure hooks for your home campaign.

Poison Politics

Chandrila's capital, Hanna, is in the throes of a tumultuous election campaign, with Jovive Centi running for another term as governor. The heroes have been dispatched to oversee the process and to act as a deterrent if violence is threatened by either side. When Governor Centi appears at a public rally, a figure slips from the crowd and thrusts a poisoned datadagger at her, which her bodyguard Tristan Pex intercepts at the last instant. Stopping the would-be assassin before he melts into the crowd proves impossible.

The wily killer later makes an effort to implicate the heroes as accomplices by either planting the data-dagger on one of them or hiding it in a hero's possessions. Will an overzealous Chandrilan police force arrest the heroes and lock down their ship? Heroes who try to fight their way out may find themselves wanted throughout the Core. Meanwhile, the assassin's trail grows colder by the hour.

The assassin, a Malkite Poisoner known as Ratambo Gale, was actually hired to kill Tristan Pex, not the governor herself. With his mission accomplished and the police thrown off his path, he doesn't bother to go into hiding. That's good for the heroes, because finding Gale may be the only way for them to clear their names.

The Hunt Is On

A fugitive has been tracked by Chandrilan law enforcement to the Hanna Wild Game Reserve. The fugitive has a Z-95 Headhunter stashed away under a camouflage tarp next to a waterfall. Tracking a runaway through the rocky woods of the game reserve is a stiff challenge. Among the many obstacles are the reserve's terrain and roving herds of cairnmogs. Chandrilan wild-game hunters were recently recalled from the reserve by police order, but did the word get out to all of them? A few poorly equipped hunters might still be out there, firing their blaster rifles at any disturbance (including a hero, but especially an alien hero) in a clueless attempt to bag a trophy animal.

Vilthar's Goodbye

An assassin believed responsible for the destruction of a space transport carrying Cilyn Gara, a Corellian shipping magnate, has been sighted on Chandrila. The industrialist's daughter, Magda Gara, hires the heroes to find the assassin and return him to Corellia to face swift justice.

The Human assassin, Kodi Vilthar, plans to meet with his benefactor—a Human crime lord named Yustavan Dreezien. Dreezien is living large in Hanna. For years,

Dreezien has used Gara's company to transport illegal spice shipments. A few months ago, his relationship with the magnate soured, and Gara refused to transport any more of Dreezien's goods, so the crime lord had Gara killed. Dreezien plans to sway Gara's daughter toward his way of thinking—but not before eliminating Vilthar and tying up a loose end.

The heroes track Vilthar to Dreezian's secret spice plant in Hanna. They can either save Vilthar from the treacherous crime lord or let him perish. Use the high-level assassin's statistics in Chapter Fourteen of the *Star Wars Roleplaying Game* for Kodi Vilthar. For Yustavan Dreezien, use the high-level crime lord's statistics.

Allies and Antagonists

The following supporting characters are designed for use in your campaign.

Jovive Centi

A tall, dignified woman, Jovive Centi is the governor of Hanna and wields great influence in the Chandrilan House. When not in her office, she often strolls the streets of Hanna, chatting with citizens and joining in the impromptu discussions near the debating rotunda. She never appears in public without Tristan Pex, her administrative aide and bodyguard. (During the Rise of the Empire era, Mon Mothma's mother Tanis is governor of Hanna. Use the same stats as those for Jovive Centi.)

Jovive Centi: Female Human Diplomat 7; Init +0; Defense 12 (+2 class); Spd 10 m; VP/WP 0/10; Atk +2 melee (1d3–1, punch) or +3 ranged; SV Fort +2, Ref +2, Will +8; SZ M; FP 2; DSP 0; Rep +5; Str 9, Dex 10, Con 10, Int 15, Wis 12, Cha 14. Challenge Code B.

    Equipment: Comlink, datapad, Hanna code cylinders.

    Skills: Appraise +4, Bluff +8, Computer Use +4, Diplomacy +15, Gather Information +10, Intimidate +4, Knowledge (bureaucracy) +10, Knowledge (Chandrila) +10, Profession (governor) +10, Read/Write Basic, Read/Write Bothese, Search +7, Sense Motive +10, Speak Basic, Speak Bothese, Spot +6.

    Feats: Fame, Iron Will, Persuasive, Sharp-Eyed, Skill Emphasis (Diplomacy), Trustworthy.

Tristan Pex

A native Chandrilan, Tristan Pex spent a dozen years away from his homeworld before returning to accept a bodyguard position with Jovive Centi, the governor of Hanna. Only his closest friends know that Pex is trying to put behind him his recent career as a Benelex Guild bounty hunter. His former guild comrades are currently feuding with the notorious Malkite Poisoners. Pex hopes that he will be safe from Malkite reprisals on this well-protected Core World. Tristan Pex is a quiet man with a dark, angular face and a piercing stare.

Tristan Pex: Male Human Soldier 7/Bounty Hunter 4; Init +6 (+2 Dex, +4 Improved Initiative); Defense 20 (+2 Dex, +8 class); Spd 10 m; VP/WP 76/12;

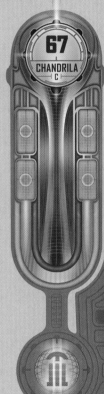

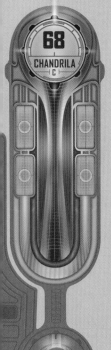

RATAMBO GALE

Atk +12/+7/+2 melee (2d4+1/19–20, punch) or +13/+8/+3 ranged (3d6, blaster pistol); SQ sneak attack +2d6, target bonus +2; SV Fort +8, Ref +6, Will +4; SZ M; FP 3; DSP 0; Rep +8; Str 12, Dex 14, Con 12, Int 12, Wis 10, Cha 10. Challenge Code E.

Equipment: Comlink, macrobinoculars, wrist binders, blaster pistol.

Skills: Climb +3, Disguise +5, Gather Information +10, Hide +4, Intimidate +5, Knowledge (streetwise) +6, Listen +8, Move Silently +7, Pilot +4, Read/Write Basic, Search +5, Sense Motive +10, Speak Basic, Speak Huttese, Spot +7, Treat Injury +6.

Feats: Armor Proficiency (light), Dodge, Fame, Improved Initiative, Improved Martial Arts, Martial Arts, Mobility, Point Blank Shot, Spring Attack, Track, Weapon Group Proficiencies (blaster pistols, blaster rifles, heavy weapons, simple weapons, vibro weapons).

Ratambo Gale

The Malkite Poisoners are a secretive sect devoted to the art of killing. Ratambo Gale has been with the sect for more than forty years and is an expert on Chandrila operations. In all that time, encompassing scores of Chandrilan assassinations, he has never been caught. Silver-haired and wiry, he has a variety of costumes he can change into at a moment's notice. His devotion to the arts of his guild has instilled in him a kind of quiet fanaticism. If one of his poisons fails, he can fly into a crazed fury.

Ratambo Gale: Male Human Scoundrel 5/Soldier 9; Init +3 (–1 Dex, +4 Improved Initiative); Defense 18 (–1 Dex, +9 class); Spd 10 m; VP/WP 70/11; Atk +12/+7/+2 melee (2d4/19-20, punch) or +12/+7/+2 melee (2d6, vibroblade) or +12/+7/+2 melee (1d4, datadagger) or +11/+6/+1 ranged (3d4, hold-out blaster); SQ illicit barter, lucky 1/day, precise attack +1; SV Fort +7, Ref +6, Will +5; SZ M; FP 1; DSP 3; Rep +3; Str 11, Dex 9, Con 11, Int 15, Wis 12, Cha 12. Challenge Code F.

Equipment: Comlink, disguise kit, listening device, datadagger, vibroblade, hold-out blaster.

Skills: Bluff +11, Computer Use +6, Disguise +10, Escape Artist +8, Forgery +8, Gather Information +10, Hide +15, Knowledge (Chandrila) +13, Knowledge (street-wise) +16, Listen +7, Move Silently +8, Pilot +7, Read/Write Basic, Search +4, Sense Motive +3, Sleight of Hand +11, Speak Basic, Speak Bothese, Speak Huttese, Spot +9.

Feats: Blind-Fight, Combat Reflexes, Heroic Surge, Improved Initiative, Improved Martial Arts, Martial Arts, Point Blank Shot, Quick Draw, Quickness, Run, Sharp-Eyed, Skill Emphasis (Hide), Track, Weapon Group Proficiencies (blaster pistols, blaster rifles, simple weapons).

New Creature: Squall

A cute, furry, floppy-eared mammal, the squall is loved by millions—but hated by offworlders who do business on Chandrila. Squalls hop through the streets and around landing pads in packs, getting underfoot and raiding edible stores left unguarded. It is against the law to kill or capture a squall, but a careful captain who smuggles the animals offworld as live cargo can often sell them as pets (or food) for a hefty profit.

Squall: Herd animal 2; Init +4; Defense 16 (+4 Dex, +2 size); Spd 10 m, burrow 2 m; VP/WP 3/5; Atk –1 melee (1d3, bite); SQ keen senses; SV Fort +3, Ref +4, Will –1; SZ T; Face/Reach 1 m by 1 m/1 m; Str 2, Dex 18, Con 10, Int 4, Wis 9, Cha 10. Challenge Code A.

Skills: Hide +15, Listen +5, Spot +3.

New Creature: Cairnmog

A hoofed lizard covered with bony spikes used in dominance displays, the cairnmog inhabits the rocky hills within the borders of the Hanna Wild Game Reserve. Cairnmogs typically hibernate during the winter. If a female lays a clutch of eggs in the fall, both she and her mate will give up their den to their incubating young, remaining outside to freeze or starve. Although not carnivorous, the cairnmog can trample with its hooves or gore with its spikes if it feels threatened.

Cairnmog: Herd animal 4; Init +2; Defense 19 (+2 Dex, –1 size, +8 natural); DR 5; Spd 18 m; VP/WP 24/14; Atk +5 melee (1d8+4, kick) or +5 melee (1d6+4, gore); SQ trample 1d8+4; SV Fort +6, Ref +3, Will +1; SZ L; Face/Reach 2 m by 4 m/4 m; Rep +0; Str 18, Dex 14, Con 14, Int 4, Wis 10, Cha 6. Challenge Code B.

Skills: Spot +6, Survival +10.

Feats: Skill Emphasis (Survival).

Corellia

Planet Type: Terrestrial
Climate: Temperate
Terrain: Hills, forests, plains
Atmosphere: Breathable
Gravity: Standard
Diameter: 11,000 km
Length of Day: 25 standard hours
Length of Year: 329 standard days
Sentient Species: Human
Languages: Basic
Population: 3 billion
Species Mix: 60% Human, 20% Selonian, 20% Drall
Government: New Republic governorship
Major Exports: Alcohol, starships, agricultural goods
Major Imports: Luxury items, raw materials, weaponry
System/Star: Corellia/Corell

Planets	Type	Moons
Corellia	Terrestrial	0
Drall	Terrestrial	0
Talus	Terrestrial	0
Tralus	Terrestrial	0
Centerpoint	Artificial	0
Selonia	Terrestrial	0
Crollia	Barren rock	0
Soronia	Frozen rock	0

Description

Possibly one of the most famous planets in the galaxy, Corellia is nearly synonymous with space travel. To some, Corellia is also synonymous with piracy and troublemakers. In any event, there is little doubt that Corellia has produced some truly outstanding heroes, colorful personalities, and skilled pilots and will continue to do so for a long time to come.

Corellia is a world of rolling hills, dense forests, lush fields, and vast seas. Although the planet is classified as an industrial world, its spaceyards are located in orbit around the planet, thereby sparing the environment and making this old world surprisingly pristine. The majority of the population lives on farms or in small towns on Corellia's three large continents. Naturally, Corellia has interesting lifeforms as well. The Corellian grass snake and Corellian sand panther are two of the most noteworthy species. The latter is quite vicious and widely feared.

Many details about Corellia set it apart from other worlds in the galaxy. One of these is the fact that the Corellian system has not one but five terrestrial planets. Usually, when a spacebound power colonizes planets in its system, the colony must use terraforming—a process that demands time and great expense—to make the world hospitable. Since Corellia never needed to do this, the time, resources, and money colonists saved was invested into researching technology to build ships better and in greater numbers. Having a home system with four "extra" planets was a tremendous advantage for Corellia.

The five terrestrial planets in the Corellian system are Corellia, Selonia, Drall, Talus, and Tralus. Collectively, they are called the Five Brothers. Centerpoint Station, an ancient device that some believe was responsible for transporting all five planets through hyperspace to their present orbits, lies equidistant between Talus and Tralus.

The system is policed by the Corellian Defense Force (CDF) and the Corellian Security Force, also known as CorSec. The Corellian Defense Force is an armed forces service that guards the entire Corellian sector. CorSec is the main law enforcement agency on Corellia. The CDF is run like a military unit, while CorSec resembles a police force.

History

Since before recorded history began on Corellia, there has always been a Corellian people: a mix of Humans, Drall, and Selonians. Some say the Corellians invented the hyperdrive, while others say the Corellians picked it up from a wandering alien species. Whatever the truth, the booming Corellian civilization became one of the founding members of the Galactic Republic.

Once the Corellians had access to the hyperdrive, their first galactic scouts went out to explore. Corellian ships used two well-traveled hyperspace paths when exploring: the Perlemian Trade Route and the Corellian Run. The two routes formed the boundaries of the Slice, a wedge-shaped area of space that ran from the Core out to the Outer Rim. The Corellian Treaty was later drawn up to delineate areas of exploration and colonization. Most early Republic exploration occurred within the Slice; the two trade routes acted as its borders. Although there were many exceptions, the Slice was the only widely settled area until about three thousand years before the Battle of Yavin.

Corellia was a member in good standing of the Old Republic. As the planet continued to prosper, it also expanded its influence into neighboring space. This expansion resulted in the acquisition and colonization of several dozen star systems, collectively known as the Corellian sector. The Corellian system is considered the most important; other systems in the sector are known as the Outliers.

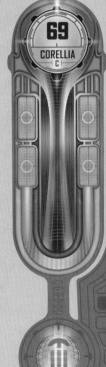

VR

sympathetic to the Diktat: the Public Safety Service. Eventually, the Diktat lost power completely and was replaced by a New Republic governor-general. The Corellian economy still has not fully recovered from its past ill fortune.

Fourteen years after the Battle of Endor, Thrackan Sal-Solo, cousin to Rebel hero Han Solo, attempted to proclaim himself the new Diktat and create a new independent Corellian sector. Thrackan was thwarted by the Solo family and apprehended, ending his dreams of conquest and power.

During the Yuuzhan Vong crisis, the New Republic hopes to lure the Yuuzhan Vong into attacking the Corellian system, but numerous groups oppose the New Republic's plan to turn the sector into a battleground.

Corellia continued to prosper over the millennia, gaining a reputation for building excellent ships, giving the galaxy excellent pilots, and harboring notorious smugglers. In the waning days of the Old Republic, Moff Fliry Vorru governed the Corellian sector, allowing smugglers free rein. When Palpatine took over and created the Empire, an underworld kingpin named Prince Xizor betrayed Vorru to the new Emperor. Vorru was sent to the spice mines of Kessel; the pilots of Rogue Squadron freed him three years after the Battle of Endor.

A second Corellian Treaty was signed a little less than two years before the Battle of Yavin. Whereas the ancient Corellian Treaty established the Slice and its trade routes—which indirectly established the borders of the Old Republic in its infancy—the new Corellian Treaty unified the three largest revolutionary groups opposing the Empire. The new unified party was formally called the Alliance to Restore the Republic, though it was commonly known as the Rebel Alliance. Among its most famous supporters were Bail Organa of Alderaan, Mon Mothma of Chandrila, and Senator Garm Bel Iblis of Corellia.

The Empire kept tight control of the Corellian sector during the Rebellion era. Corellia was ruled by a "Diktat," the title given to the Corellian chief of state. The Corellian Engineering Corporation's shipyards became a great strategic asset to the Empire. After the Battle of Endor, the Empire increased the system's defenses even more. As the war against the Rebel Alliance intensified, the Corellian system became increasingly isolated. Trade fell off and corporations left the restrictive system for freer and more lucrative markets. The Diktat, which at this point was little more than a mouthpiece for the Empire, gradually lost power to the Triad of Sacorria (see the entry on Sacorria for more details).

Around the time when the Empire collapsed and the New Republic rose to power, the Corellian Diktat dissolved CorSec and created a new police order more

People

The term "Corellians" is typically reserved for the Human natives of Corellia, although the planet's native population includes plenty of Drall and Selonians as well. Throughout Corellia's long, storied history, the three species have had high and low points of harmony and cooperation. During the days of the Empire, the three species were forced to work together and cooperate unconditionally. The main system language is Basic, although the language known as Old Corellian still exists among smugglers and pirates.

Family loyalty is valued highly among Corellians, regardless of their species. There are many traditions and important occasions to observe, covering everything from family get-togethers to the proper protocol when a Corellian Force-user ascends to the status of Jedi Master. Some sociologists find it unusual that a people who have given birth to so many amoral pirates and smugglers also revere family ties with such devotion.

As a people, Corellians tend to be risk takers: independent, pragmatic, almost habitually reckless, and daring. An old saying cites them as having "rocket fuel for blood." Corellians typically have great instincts and reflexes, making them excellent pilots and explorers. They are a dynamic people who sometimes hide their intensity under a veneer of disinterest and self-centeredness. Corellians are also known as great tinkerers, innovators who adapt and customize their ships' systems to suit their individual tastes. It is precisely this sort of experimentation that has made Corellian shipyards the birthplace of many innovations.

Some Corellians who serve in the military wear red piping on the sides of their trousers. This red stripe, called the Bloodstripe, distinguishes them as performers of heroic acts.

Corellians not only play hard but also drink hard, as is evidenced by a plethora of types of alcohol and mixed drinks. Many are the spacefarers who have sampled Corellian whiskey, Corellian rum, Corellian double brandy, the Corellian Twister, or Corellian spiced ale. Despite the vast types and quantities of alcohol available, the average Corellian doesn't seem easily impaired by alcohol. Some guess that either Corellians are extremely adept at holding their liquor, or they merely produce the potables and sell them to other worlds, drinking only moderately themselves. Nastier individuals believe that Corellia wants to get the entire galaxy drunk, and then rob it blind.

Locations

Descriptions of several key locations follow.

Coronet

Coronet is the capital city of Corellia. A large city teeming with Humans, Drall, and Selonians, Coronet is located on the coast of the southernmost continent. Its starport is second to none, a hardly surprising fact considering Corellia's spacefaring heritage. The city's Selonian population dwells in tunnels built under the city. Most offworlders end up at Coronet. Its infrastructure includes a subway system, monorails, and a maddening series of streets and boulevards that twist and turn every which way. It is sometimes said that the roads were simply the paved-over tracks of drunken Corellian grass snakes.

As the capital, Coronet is a heavily patrolled city. The city hosts the Diktat's complex, which is always well guarded, and boasts CorSec's main headquarters as well. Despite the heightened security, however, there are still many troublemakers and much rowdiness. Most of the craziness is confined to the area known as Blue Sector, or the Wild Sector.

Blue Sector, so named because Blue Sky Boulevard is the main road leading into it, is a place where offworlders congregate. As a result, CorSec tends to be lenient when it comes to minor infractions committed in this area. Blue Sector hosts a high proportion of bars, flophouses, pawn shops, brothels, tattoo parlors and other body-altering businesses, casinos, and fences.

Despite the presence of CorSec, Blue Sector has a shockingly high proportion of violent crime. To the normal observer, walking through Blue Sector is no different from walking through any other part of Coronet. However, many dark deeds happen behind the scenes, and plenty of "troublemakers" disappear there, never to be seen again. This is especially true at The Pit, a large junkyard that lies at the outskirts of Blue Sector. The talk around the area is that more "organic drop-offs" are buried at The Pit than is junk of a manufactured nature.

Treasure Ship Row is a large, open-air bazaar located just inside Blue Sector. It's a lively, garish place where a shrewd customer can find just about anything his or her heart desires. Thanks to its location, most native Corellians can easily access it without going too deep into Blue Sector. Treasure Ship Row is also an excellent place to make a few smuggler contacts or sell hot merchandise with no questions asked.

Although the city is known mostly as either the capital or a center of rowdiness, Coronet has its cultural side as well. Corellians have a colorful history in space, and several museums are dedicated to exhibiting that heritage. The Corellian Space Museum is the best known of these facilities, with artifacts dating back to the beginning of Corellian history. It even has a genuine copy of the original Corellian Treaty, thousands of years old.

The Corellian Stock Exchange located in Coronet is host to an army of traders in commodities, stocks, and anything else requiring legal investment. The dealing and trading can get as cutthroat and intense as any transaction in the garish and less "refined" Treasure Ship Row.

Numerous trade guilds and unions have their headquarters in Coronet. During times of labor negotiations or strikes, people are advised to walk and speak carefully. Tensions rise, and sometimes cooler heads don't prevail.

The Gold Beaches

Boasting fine golden sand, the Gold Beaches are an ideal choice for relaxation and swimming. Located between Coronet and Tyrena, the area is a well-known tourist spot. Along a strip of about 80 kilometers, the Gold Beaches offer numerous hotels, restaurants, resorts, and casinos, and even a few amusement parks. Unlike the typical spaceport hotels, bars, and casinos, these places are well patrolled, safe locales that tend not to attract the usual scum and villainy that frequents such places. They have a reputation for being clean and trouble-free. That's not to say that nothing interesting ever happens on the Gold Beaches. Smooth, less violent characters such as con artists and classier gamblers haunt the Gold Beaches. Some come to find an easy mark, others to gamble, and still others to woo a wealthy, naive individual.

Thanks to Corellia's ocean currents, the water remains a constant 21° C, with waves ideal for surfing and general frolicking. Numerous grottos and sheltered coves bracket both ends of the beach, serving as locales for private and romantic rendezvous. Like the rest of Corellia, the Gold Beaches are a place with something for everyone. Whether it's a vacation with the family, a romantic getaway, a plush resort, or some high-class mischief you're after, the Gold Beaches have it all.

The closest city is Tyrena, which has its own spaceport and handles the vast majority of beachbound offworlders. A grav-train line runs between Tyrena and the Gold Beaches.

CEC Shipyards

The Corellian Engineering Corporation is one of the largest starship construction firms in the galaxy. The company produces fast, durable, heavily armed commercial vehicles that are easily modified. Although the CEC builds the Republic cruiser, it is better known for its line of civilian freighters. Among the more notable ship classes are the Corellian Corvette, the YT-1210 freighter, and the YT-1300 transport. Han Solo's *Millennium Falcon* is a modified YT-1300.

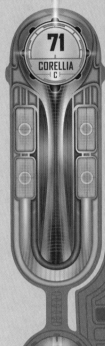

The CEC shipyards are in orbit around Corellia. While not as extensive or planet-encircling as the Kuat Drive Yards, they are still impressively huge. By putting the yards in orbit, the Corellians have kept the surface of their planet unmarred by massive manufacturing complexes. The corporate headquarters of CEC is located in Coronet.

Corellians not only know how to fly ships well but also know how to design and build them. Such adept space jockeys are easily recruited by CEC.

Corellians are fiercely proud of their ships, and they do not tolerate hints of sabotage, industrial espionage, or general vandalism. Shipbuilders are all too aware of how stiff competition is, and they know the underhanded means that are sometimes used to bring down a competitor. Thus, CorSec and the CDF patrol the yards with special vigilance. They tend to shoot first and ask questions of the charred remains later.

Groola's Place

Located in the city of Tyrena, Groola's Place is a large underground complex devoted to the fine arts of carousing, gambling, drinking, and plotting. Groola is a Hutt who claims to be different from his corrupt brethren. Although most of the clients are skeptical, Groola has so far shown some very uncharacteristic patience and consideration. Groola's is one of the better places to go for an underworld contact, hot gossip, leads on a smuggling job, or a decent shot of Corellian whiskey. There's a saying in Tyrena: "Sit in Groola's long enough, and every-

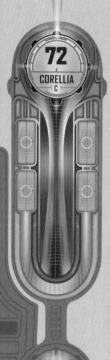

Groola's Place

Storage

Bar Level

1	Stairs to surface
2	Lift tubes to lower levels
3	Bar
4	ID check and security door
5	Droid check
6	Booths
7	Band stage
8	Groola's private booth
9	Slot machines

Bar
Restaurant
Casino
Games & Amusements
Private Halls
Groola's Den

One Square = 4 Meters

one in the sector will pass through it eventually." Although that's a bit of an exaggeration, it's not too far off. Lately, Groola's has been experimenting with package-deal excursions to the Gold Beaches. Many people are baffled by this new business tactic, wondering if Groola is trying to go legit or if this is the prelude to another big scam.

For the GM

The adventure hooks and supporting characters described in this section are meant for GMs only. If you're a player, stop reading now.

Adventures

Corellia's dynamic atmosphere makes it a place where interesting things are always happening. The trick in adventuring on Corellia is to strike a balance between insanity and bravery. Sometimes finding out where the balance lies is half the fun.

Such a Deal!

This adventure is best for a beginning group of heroes. Spring it on your heroes when they end up visiting Groola's Place. Groola himself meets the heroes and tells them that he has noticed the group. He's intrigued by the fact that they haven't been here before.

The Hutt tells the heroes that he wants to help them establish a presence and reputation in the Corellian system. To see how reliable they are, Groola gives them a simple mission: smuggling a shipment of a particularly expensive and exclusive batch of Corellian ale to Tatooine. Once they get to Tatooine, they should make contact with Groola's agents at Mos Eisley. Groola offers them 4,000 credits: 1,000 up front and 3,000 when they return to Corellia.

Yes, there is a shipment of ale, but it's not the "good stuff." Groola was aware that some outsystem pirates were planning on intercepting his goods, so he's taken precautions and found some stooges. Groola is using the characters as a decoy. The actual shipment is traveling by a different route, in the custody of one of Groola's more experienced and reliable smugglers.

The plot thickens when pirates intercept the heroes' ship, believing (as the heroes do) that it is carrying the good ale. The pirates may be beaten back, or they may abscond with the cargo.

If the heroes lose the cargo, they may as well not bother going back to Groola—he has no further use for them. If they go back to him after delivering the cargo intact, Groola pays them the remainder of the money and uses them later in genuine jobs.

The Wreck of *Boolarg*

Sometimes adventure falls out of the sky—literally. As the heroes are wandering through any rural area of Corellia—preferably a forest, empty beach, or secluded plain—a lifepod screaming out of the sky manages to make a last-second soft landing about 50 meters away from the stunned heroes. Gaber Rollobad, a Sullustan trader, staggers out, shaken, agitated, and badly injured. If calmed down, Gaber explains his situation. He's a trader with a YT-1210 light freighter, *Boolarg*. As he was jumping into the Corellian system, the old ship's power plant overloaded and started a fire. Gaber was barely able to maneuver *Boolarg* close to Corellia's orbit before losing power altogether. He crawled into a lifepod and jettisoned himself free of the stricken vessel. Although it's clear that Gaber needs medical attention, he begs the heroes to go to his ship and salvage whatever they can. Gaber promises them one-third of the salvage value, although he can be haggled up to forty percent with a bit of diplomacy or illicit bartering.

Gaber is a rotten liar. The Imperial Star Destroyer *Shrike* was on patrol just outside the Corellian system. It ordered *Boolarg* to stand down and prepare to be boarded for cargo inspection. Since he was smuggling a cache of illegal weaponry in a secret compartment, the foolish Sullustan actually tried to outrun the Star Destroyer and its wing of TIE fighters. Gaber managed to get into Corellia's orbit before the TIEs shot up the ship. The rest of the story is true. Gaber got into a lifepod and ejected. Heroes who play along might find themselves in trouble with the Empire very quickly.

Unfriendly Competition

A representative of the Corellian Engineering Corporation contacts the heroes. It seems that for the past few months, CEC has been having trouble getting new blood. Three promising young Corellians that were supposed to be recruited into CEC have vanished. Each one was last seen in or around the area of the Skids, a rather bad section of Tyrena. The CEC wants some freelance people of good character and reliability to nose around and find out what's going on. Pay is negotiable, depending on the heroes and how experienced they are.

Kuat Drive Yards is behind the disappearances. KDY is a direct competitor of CEC, and it's been upping the stakes recently when recruiting talented people. Of late, KDY has been scouting prospects on Corellia, right under the nose of CEC. Of the three missing Corellians, one actually went voluntarily, one has been coerced through threats of harm to her family, and the last one has been "detained." He is being browbeaten into cooperation, but so far he has held out. To make matters worse, KDY has hired some nasty thugs to run interference for the four KDY agents who engineer the abductions. All the disappearances happened near a dive called Norbet's Nest. The Nest actually is used as an informal meeting point and headquarters for the KDY team.

If the heroes pull off this mission spectacularly, CEC rewards them with a brand-new freighter in addition to the promised fee. Naturally, if accused, KDY takes no responsibility for what happened. Instead, it assigns some vague blame to a merchant guild that allegedly acted on its own. KDY's corporate heads insist they knew nothing of the "aggressive recruiting methods" of the renegade guild.

Allies and Antagonists

Corellia produces interesting, colorful characters. Regardless of the era, a handful of heroes and scoundrels from Corellia make their mark on the galaxy.

Eryk Kroogar

After Han Solo's exploits on Yavin, Hoth, and Endor became common knowledge, younger Corellians were further inspired to make their own marks. One such Corellian is Eryk Kroogar, also known as Talonscar (thanks to a run-in with a Corellian sand panther). In Talonscar's mind, the best way to emulate Han Solo is by following the path that he took, so the younger man plunged into the seedier aspect of Corellia and became a pirate and smuggler.

Eryk is a tall, thin young man in his early twenties. He has dark hair and a goatee, along with that jaunty, self-confident air so common to Corellians. He has a scar on the base of his throat where the envenomed talon of a Corellian sand panther grazed him. He managed to resist the poison's effects and battle the panther to a draw. Although he strives to be a hero, Eryk enjoys the shadier aspects of life, at least for now. If presented with a clearcut moral choice of helping a good cause or turning his back and saving his own skin, he will certainly do the right thing, just like his hero Han Solo did at the Battle of Yavin.

Eryk's biggest goal at present is getting his own ship. For now, he's been hiring himself out as a freelance pilot and smuggler. He'll jump at the opportunity to make enough credits to get his own vessel at long last, which may mean taking an assignment that's far too risky.

Eryk Kroogar: Male Human Scoundrel 6; Init +2; Defense 16 (+2 Dex, +4 class); Spd 10 m; VP/WP 43/14; Atk +5 melee (1d3+1, punch) or +6 ranged (3d6, blaster pistol); SQ illicit barter, lucky 2/day, precise attack +1; SV Fort +4, Ref +7, Will +2; SZ M; FP 2; DSP 0; Rep +1; Str 12, Dex 14, Con 14, Int 12, Wis 10, Cha 14. Challenge Code D.

   Equipment: Blaster pistol, comlink, credit chip (500 credits).

   Skills: Appraise +4, Astrogate +8, Bluff +5, Computer Use +8, Diplomacy +4, Escape Artist +4, Gather Information +5, Hide +6, Intimidate +4, Knowledge (Corellia) +6, Listen +5, Move Silently +5, Pilot +12, Read/Write Basic, Read/Write Huttese, Read/Write Old Corellian, Repair +6, Search +5, Sense Motive +2, Speak Basic, Speak Huttese, Speak Old Corellian, Speak Shyriiwook (understand only), Spot +4, Survival +4, Treat Injury +4.

   Feats: Cautious, Gearhead, Heroic Surge, Skill Emphasis (Pilot), Spacer, Starship Operation (space transport), Weapon Group Proficiencies (blaster pistols, simple weapons).

Gilflyn

Sensing how Corellia seems to be a breeding ground for resourceful, good-hearted types, one man has decided to

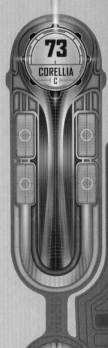

try to cut the supply off at the source. Gilflyn is a corrupt Jedi and a self-professed hero hunter. Shortly after the establishment of the New Republic, Gilflyn concluded that the light side had grown far stronger than the dark side, tipping the balance of the Force. With so many "good guys" running around, Gilflyn sees it as his duty to cull them from the galaxy. In his mind, if he can kill another Luke Skywalker, Leia Organa, Han Solo, or Lando Calrissian before he or she gets too strong and popular, it will serve the dark side better and hopefully restore some semblance of balance to the Force.

Gilflyn stands 1.75 meters tall and is in his late twenties. His head is completely shaved, including his eyebrows, and his eyes are a piercing cold blue. The man radiates menace. In fact, Gilflyn is slightly psychotic, but he's an excellent tactician and very adept at using the Force. He is obsessed with the Sith. More than anything else, he wishes that he could be the one pupil the Dark Lord of the Sith takes on. In fact, he is so enamored of the Sith that many beings' last mistake is thinking that he is one. This gives Gilflyn an edge in combat.

This Dark Jedi's agenda is a simple one: Lurk where there seems to be a high concentration of up-and-coming galactic movers and shakers, then strike them down while they are inexperienced and barely aware of their own power and limitations. Who knows how many new heroes the galaxy will be without, thanks to Gilflyn's self-appointed and highly predatory mission?

Gilflyn: Male Human Jedi Guardian 8; Init +10 (+6 Dex, +4 Improved Initiative); Defense 22 (+6 Dex, +6 class); Spd 10 m; VP/WP 86/14; Atk +14/+9 melee (3d8+3/19–20, lightsaber) or +11/+6 melee (1d3+3, punch) or +14/+9 ranged (3d6, blaster pistol); SQ deflect (attack –4, defense +1, extend defense and attack), increase lightsaber damage +1d8; SV Fort +8, Ref +12, Will +6; SZ M; FP 10; DSP 12; Rep +2; Str 16, Dex 22, Con 14, Int 16, Wis 15, Cha 17. Challenge Code E.

Equipment: Lightsaber, blaster pistol, comlink, credit chip (400 credits), black clothing with cloak and cowl, YZ-775 Corellian space transport (*Mutilator*).

Skills: Computer Use +4, Hide +8, Intimidate +10, Knowledge (Corellia) +7, Knowledge (Jedi lore) +7, Knowledge (Sith lore) +5, Knowledge (tactics) +8, Move Silently +7, Pilot +10, Read/Write Basic, Read/Write Huttese, Search +5, Sense Motive +5, Speak Basic, Speak Huttese, Speak Shyriiwook (understand only), Spot +6, Survival +5.

Force Skills: Battlemind +6, Enhance Ability +7, Fear +5, Force Defense +6, Force Grip +6, Force Stealth +7, Move Object +7, See Force +6.

Feats: Ambidexterity, Cleave, Combat Reflexes, Exotic Weapon Proficiency (lightsaber), Force-Sensitive, Improved Initiative, Power Attack, Weapon Finesse (Lightsaber), Weapon Group Proficiencies (blaster pistols, simple weapons)

Force Feats: Alter, Control, Force Mastery, Sense.

Groola

When a Hutt says that he is not like his people, is he telling the truth, or is he simply perpetrating a fraud typical of his species? That's the question many beings ask after dealing with Groola, who insists that he's not a typical representative of the Hutts. He arrived on Corellia five years before the Battle of Yavin and reopened an old, closed-down bar. Renamed Groola's Place, it's now a large underground complex. Some locals speculate that Groola won it in a game of chance somewhere offplanet.

Groola's Place is located in the city of Tyrena, near the spaceport. It's well known for its decent drinks, mostly honest games of chance, useful contacts, and general good times. Although showy displays of violence are frowned upon, the occasional bar fight or blaster casualty is accepted as part of business.

Groola's law is simple: The victor gets the victim's spoils. Dead bodies are discreetly disposed of for a small fee.

It should come as no surprise that Groola is much more like a typical Hutt than he insists. Groola is no idiot, and he realizes the stigma and reputation that his species has carried to the stars. Although less arrogant and maliciously greedy than the average Hutt, Groola is a Hutt through and through, with loads of underworld contacts, a nasty, brutish temper, and the mind of an

GROOLA THE HUTT

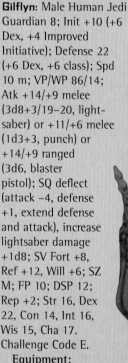

opportunist. However, doing business with Groola can be quite profitable, because the jobs he lines up for his favorites always pay well. Groola generously rewards those who succeed. Those who fail him wind up dead. Fortunately for the Hutt, he covers his tracks well.

Groola: Hutt Scoundrel 4/Noble 2/Crime Lord 7; Init +3 (−1 Dex, +4 Improved Initiative); Defense 16 (−1 Dex, −1 size, +8 class); Spd 2 m; VP/WP 100/22; Atk +12/+7 melee (1d4+6, punch) or +5/+0 ranged; SQ bonus class skill (Bluff), can't be knocked prone, contacts (3), favor +1, Force resistance (+6 species bonus on Will saves against Force skills and Force feats.), illicit barter, inspire confidence, inspire fear −4, lucky 1/day, minions, precise attack +1, resource access; SV Fort +9, Ref +9, Will +12; SZ L; FP 5; DSP 5; Rep +12; Str 22, Dex 8, Con 22, Int 12, Wis 14, Cha 16. Challenge Code F.

   Equipment: Comlink, datapad.

   Skills: Appraise +7, Bluff +19, Diplomacy +12, Forgery +6, Gamble +12, Gather Information +15, Hide −5, Intimidate +14, Knowledge (Corellia) +8, Knowledge (Nal Hutta) +8, Knowledge (streetwise) +10, Listen +7, Profession (bartender) +8, Read/Write Basic, Read/Write Huttese, Search +7, Sense Motive +16, Speak Basic, Speak Huttese.

   Feats: Headstrong, Improved Initiative, Infamy, Influence, Persuasive, Sharp-Eyed, Skill Emphasis (Bluff), Weapon Group Proficiencies (blaster pistols, simple weapons).

New Creature: Spukamas

The Corellians' favorite (and most frustrating) pet is the spukamas, or Corellian housecat. All spukami are black with gold eyes and are the size of an average cat. They are unusually intelligent and fiercely loyal, though they conceal these traits behind a typical feline attitude of detached indifference.

A spukamas gets into everything. It especially enjoys chewing holes in various kinds of plasteel, flimsiplast, and even soft metal. However, the feline does this only when bored, so smart owners do their best to keep the cat occupied. Many pilots enjoy having a spukamas on their ship to keep away small, unwanted vermin, which may stow away in cargo or gain entrance when a hatch is left open.

Many owners train their spukami to follow certain commands, and the cats obey them two times out of three. In general, however, the spukamas is a solitary, territorial, and jealous animal. Woe to any pet owner who tries to keep more than one, since the cats will fight each other in the nastiest way possible until one runs off, never to be seen again.

Spukamas: Predator 2; Init +9 (+5 Dex, +4 Improved Initiative); Defense 17 (+5 Dex, +2 size); Spd 12 m; VP/WP 10/5; Atk +1 (1d3−3, claw) or +1 (1d4−3, bite) or +9 ranged; SV Fort +3, Ref +8, Will +2; SZ T; Face/Reach 1 m by 1 m/1 m; Rep +0; Str 4, Dex 20, Con 10, Int 4, Wis 14, Cha 16. Challenge Code A.

   Skills: Jump +2, Listen +7, Spot +4, Survival +4.

   Feats: Improved Initiative, Run, Track.

Corulag

Planet Type: Terrestrial
Climate: Temperate
Terrain: Urban, oceans, forests
Atmosphere: Breathable
Gravity: Standard
Diameter: 12,749 km
Length of Day: 25 standard hours
Length of Year: 371 standard days
Sentient Species: Human
Languages: Basic
Population: 1.5 billion
Species Mix: 98% Human, 2% other
Government: Imperial Governor/House of Citizens
Major Exports: Raw materials, foodstuffs
Major Imports: High tech, luxury goods
System/Star: Corulus

Planets	Type	Moons
Solag	Searing rock	0
Biolag	Gas giant	7
Garulag	Gas giant	15
Corulag	Terrestrial	3

Description

Thanks to its pleasant climate and ideal location, Corulag was one of the first worlds settled in the Bormea sector. The planet features a varied climate—ice caps at the poles, tropics at the equator, and the usual range of more

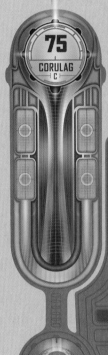

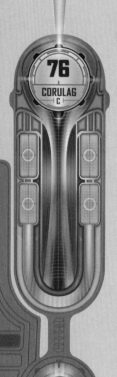

moderate climes between them. Three rather smallish continents—Resoria, North Kallis, and South Kallis—are all located in the southern hemisphere, and all share the same cycle of seasons.

The landmasses, at least in the undeveloped areas, are covered in forests of sturdy bamboo. Corulag bamboo grows fast and thick, and it is all but impassable except on foot or in special bulldozer craft equipped to fell the tall stalks as they move. On this world, herbivores and carnivores alike are small and limber, allowing them to thrive in the impenetrable growth.

History

Corulag was settled by Human Coruscanti colonists thousands of years ago. It was long a favored world in the Old Republic, partly because of its heritage, but chiefly because its primary export was bureaucrats. While the Republic Senate and its many supporting bodies spent their days mired in endless debate, Corulag's interests seldom languished. A cadre of loyal bureaucrats guided favorable legislation and treaties through the shoals of the legal system. The situation only improved with the rise of Chancellor Palpatine, with whom Corulag's leaders allied themselves.

When Palpatine pronounced himself Emperor, Corulag received rewards for its early loyalty, including key appointments in Imperial government, the privilege of retaining its senator as its Imperial governor, and the sponsorship of a new Imperial military academy second only to the Raithal campus. When not advising the Emperor, the sector moff made his home in Curamelle, Corulag's capital city. Life for Corulag's citizens changed little with the rise of the Empire, though there was less political dissent than in the past.

Corulag fared less well after the fall of the Empire. While the planet was spared direct assault during the New Republic's first drive toward Coruscant, it became a major battleground when a renewed Imperial offensive drove New Republic forces off Coruscant. Curamelle and other cities suffered the brunt of the damage, along with military installations, but lesser communities also suffered.

Recovery was slow in the aftermath of the Galactic Civil War. Few in the New Republic Senate were eager to come to the aid of a world so closely tied with Palpatine's New Order. Corulag's bureaucratic cadres lost much of the influence they once wielded.

People

The vast majority of Corulag's citizens are Humans of varying races, though a few alien communities thrive in North Kallistan enclaves. Many Humans are descended from Coruscanti colonial stock—and are fiercely proud of it. The system's society is homogenous and cosmopolitan. Its people are wealthy and productive, basking in the knowledge that their success as a society is entirely due to their superior abilities and culture. Unlike many other Human-dominated worlds, Corulag culture is devoid of provincial values and patriotism centered on the homeworld. All loyalties are directed toward Coruscant. Law and order are valued commodities on Corulag (except perhaps in Crullov City). Naturally, all notions of natural superiority were severely shaken with the defeat of the Empire and the battles that destroyed several of Corulag's urban centers. Corulag remains a prominent Core World, but culturally, its people are ill prepared to face a universe in which they do not play a central role. They are adrift and dispirited, receptive to any charismatic leader who can appeal to their wounded pride.

Locations

As one would expect, Corulag's architecture is heavily influenced by that of Coruscant. Its cities consist of sweeping, towering skyscrapers. Even its less developed areas bear the marks of Coruscanti designers, particularly those eager to set their creations amid natural environments entirely lacking on their urban homeworld.

Imperial Academy

The Corulag branch of the elite Imperial Academy located in Curamelle is second only to the primary campus on Raithal. Corulag Academy prepares the most talented young Imperial citizens for military service. Most of its qualified students come from the Core; a smaller number are accepted from other regions. A decent number of students from Corulag itself enter the Academy. As a result, many senior Imperial officers are natives of the planet.

Whether a hero prefers to deal over or under the table, the Imperial Academy is a rich source of intelligence and contacts. High-ranking Imperial officers lecture its cadets in closed classes, revealing tactics they're sure to use against the Rebel Alliance in future encounters. Sympathizers with much to offer the Alliance dabble with defection, needing perhaps only a little push to cross over into full rebellion.

Sienar Advanced Research Division

Nestled in a series of lush, rolling hills a few kilometers north of Curamelle's outermost suburbs, Sienar Fleet Systems's Advanced Research Division is a sprawling installation of labs and manufacturing plants. Sienar's R&D department on Corulag develops and tests new propulsion and fire-control systems. Since it poses a natural target for Rebel spies, Sienar's campus has tight security. A wing of Curamelle-based TIE fighters enforces airspace restrictions. Few get onto the grounds without Sienar knowing about it.

Residents in the area, primarily the students at nearby Dammon University, occasionally spy starfighters streaking through the sky bearing unusual pods and test configurations or hear strange rumblings in the woods beyond Sienar's perimeter fence. Occasionally, a foolish scholar details such encounters via pirate student-run stations on the galaxywide newsnet—only to disappear soon thereafter.

Abersaith Aviary

The Abersaith Aviary—an exotic bird preserve located in an enclosed canyon—is one of Corulag's primary tourist attractions. The immense Abersaith Canyon is kilometers wide in spots and two dozen kilometers long. The aviary is home to some twenty million species of birds culled from a variety of worlds. Many are kept in specific artificial ecosystems separated by weak repulsor fields. The top of the canyon is sealed by enormous canopies of transparisteel. Visitors are free to hike down the sides of the canyon, wander through its lush gardens, and tour its various crannies in rented skiffs. The aviary is not only a popular trysting place for lovers but also a favored rendezvous for spies and scoundrels engaging in corporate espionage.

Crullov City

The culture that passes for Corulag's underworld is centered in Crullov City on the eastern seaboard of Resoria. The city was originally an industrial center dedicated to manufacturing starship power plants, until most of its factories collapsed in a groundquake a hundred years ago. The disaster flooded the streets and left smoking ruins to a depth of 6 meters. Many buildings still stand, but few beings living there can claim honest careers. Squatters, refugees, and smugglers putter through flooded streets in boats and hovercraft, usually on their way to gang hide-outs hidden in the ruins or the bamboo groves that grow thick around the outskirts. So far, the Corulag government suffers Crullov City's existence, largely thanks to some strategic blackmail. If the dark rumors prove to be true—that a Hutt runs Crullov City's criminal enterprises—Corulag's citizens will almost certainly demand its destruction. Even after the fall of the Empire, they don't care for being enthralled by alien entities of any sort.

TIE/Ad Defender Prototype

The Advanced x7 was one of the last TIE prototypes developed by Sienar Fleet Systems before the fall of Palpatine's Empire. Decades of experience and advances in TIE technology influenced its design and construction. Like the TIE avenger, the defender starfighter was a radical departure from previous TIE designs in both appearance and performance.

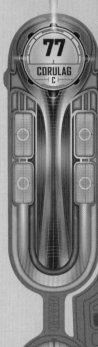

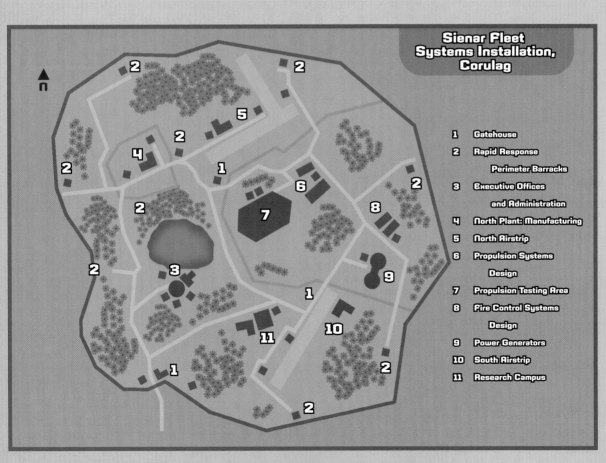

Sienar Fleet Systems Installation, Corulag

↑
n

1 Gatehouse
2 Rapid Response
    Perimeter Barracks
3 Executive Offices
    and Administration
4 North Plant: Manufacturing
5 North Airstrip
6 Propulsion Systems
    Design
7 Propulsion Testing Area
8 Fire Control Systems
    Design
9 Power Generators
10 South Airstrip
11 Research Campus

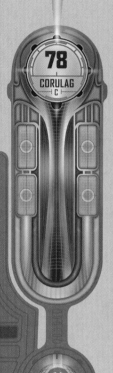

The defender features three solar collectors dispersed evenly around the cockpit pod. The new wing design greatly boosts the energy feed to the power plants, allowing the ion engines to achieve speeds previously possible only in the lighter interceptor. Triple arrays of maneuvering jets mounted on the three solar panels greatly enhance maneuverability. Unlike most other TIEs, the defender is equipped with a hyperdrive.

This particular prototype serves as a test bed for the new drive system and primary weapon targeting system. It lacks other key systems that will make their way into the final defender design, including a hyperdrive, ion cannons, and missile launchers.

Sienar Fleet Systems TIE/Ad x7 Prototype

Class: Starfighter	Crew: 1 (Skilled +4)
Size: Diminutive (9.2 m long)	Initiative: +8 (+4 size, +4 crew)
Hyperdrive: ×1	Maneuver: +8 (+4 size, +4 crew)
Passengers: None	Defense: 24 (+4 size, +10 armor)
Cargo Capacity: 85 kg	Shield Points: 0
Consumables: 2 days	Hull Points: 90 (DR 5)
Cost: Prototype not available for sale	
Maximum Speed in Space: Ramming (10 squares/action)	
Atmospheric Speed: 1,200 km/h (20 squares/action)	

Weapon: Laser cannons (4 fire-linked); Fire Arc: Front; Attack Bonus: +12 (+4, +4 crew, +4 fire control); Damage: 6d10×2; Range Modifiers: PB +0, S −2, M −4, L −6.

For the GM

The adventure hooks and supporting characters described in this section are meant for GMs only. If you're a player, stop reading now.

Adventures

Feel free to use or adapt the following adventure hooks for your home campaign.

Strike Breakers

The Orbital Transports Union has gone on strike while protesting new berthing taxes, effectively stalling the planetary economy. Governor Zafiel Snopps (or Senator Snopps, depending on the era) arranges for a gang of thugs from Crullov City to break the strike—by force, if necessary. After a few bloody encounters, union leaders respond by hiring the heroes to intervene on their behalf.

If the characters choose to confront the thugs directly, they must descend into the underground of Crullov City as they track down the gangs' leaders. They might choose to use political methods as well—delving into the backroom dealings of Curamelle, getting dirt on politicians and Snopps, and creating political pressure to force them to back off the union and settle.

Mob boss Reni Wajetta is one source for inside information on Curamelle's movers and shakers. He might share his knowledge in exchange for other favors, such as snatching an especially rare bird from the Abersaith Aviary for a wealthy client or helping to ensure that his "clean" son Kurlo, currently enrolled in Dammon University, passes a coming exam he needs to graduate.

Escaping the Birdcage

Haris Causus, a leading researcher and lecturer at the Imperial Academy, has indicated through back channels that he wants to defect to the Rebel Alliance. The heroes are assigned the task of extracting him. Because of his value to the Empire, the few excursions permitted him are tightly managed and rigorously guarded. When he does move about, four bored bodyguards accompany him.

The characters have a chance to make a brief first contact with Causus at a ritzy banquet being held at the Imperial Academy. If they can get themselves invited, they might outfox his cagey keepers. The best option for snatching him might be a day trip he and his fellow researchers are taking to Abersaith Aviary. The park offers plenty of potential sites for ambushes and escape routes. The millions of alien birds secured in their delicate ecosystems could cause quite a diversion should the shielding separating predators from their prey fail. Neither Causus nor his bodyguards know that they are monitored and tailed at all times by a team of skilled Imperial agents led by Colonel Hadis Ato. The Imperial agents are expert snipers with orders to kill Causus rather than let him be seized by enemy forces.

TIE Acquisition

Sienar Fleet Systems is testing a new hyperdrive-equipped TIE defender prototype on Corulag. Whether the heroes work for the Rebellion or some other faction, they're asked to steal it. They must first obtain access codes to the plant. The Alliance can supply some of these, but the rest must be sifted out through a little corporate espionage at Sienar's planetary headquarters.

After some challenges, the heroes get what they need and infiltrate the orbital platform where the test run is to begin. Everything goes smoothly until they discover that Sienar has changed its plans and is testing a different subsystem with a different prototype—one lacking a hyperdrive unit! (Hopefully, the heroes learn this before getting into the craft with the expectation of flying it out of the system.) With some quick thinking, they might be able to find a hiding place for the TIE defender in a nearby asteroid field until a Rebel transport can arrive to pick it up—if the heroes can avoid both ice rocks and Imperial pursuers long enough.

Allies and Antagonists

The following supporting characters are designed for use in your campaign.

Colonel Hadis Ato

Ato is a fair-haired man in his late thirties, fit but otherwise unremarkable in appearance. He was born and raised on Corulag, and he was in the first class of cadets to pass through the Corulag Academy. After graduation, he entered the Imperial Army and spent several tours in the Outer Rim, honing his skills as a sniper and bodyguard for Imperial VIPs. He transferred back to Corulag two years ago and has since served as an undercover agent tailing and protecting valued scientists and engineers. Ato is level headed and cautious in the hunt, never taking a shot before spending time to aim.

Colonel Hadis Ato: Male Human Soldier 6/Noble 1/Officer 2; Init +3; Defense 20 (+3 Dex, +7 class); Spd 10 m; VP/WP 51/10; Atk +8/+3 melee (1d3+1, punch) or +10/+5 ranged (3d8/19–20, blaster carbine); SQ bonus class skill (Spot), favor +1, leadership; SV Fort +7, Ref +10, Will +6; SZ M; FP 0; DSP 0; Rep +7; Str 13, Dex 16, Con 10, Int 12, Wis 11, Cha 14. Challenge Code E.

Equipment: Blaster carbine, comlink.

Skills: Computer Use +6, Demolitions +7, Diplomacy +11, Gather Information +8, Intimidate +8, Knowledge (tactics) +7, Listen +2, Read/Write Basic, Search +9, Sense Motive +11, Speak Basic, Speak Rodese, Spot +4, Treat Injury +3.

Feats: Armor Proficiencies (light, medium), Dodge, Fame, Far Shot, Lightning Reflexes, Mobility, Point Blank Shot, Sharp-Eyed, Shot on the Run, Weapon Group Proficiencies (blaster pistols, blaster rifles, heavy weapons, simple weapons, vibro weapons).

Reni Wajetta

Reni is one of Crullov City's many blackmailers of the rich and famous. He's loaded with inside information on Corulag's ruling elite and plenty of owed favors. This slender, effeminate, sharp-dressed man surrounds himself with beautiful women, objets d' art, and fast speeders. His easygoing manner only serves to hide his brutal ambition, and he is ruthless in pressing an advantage. Reni grew up in Crullov City. Although he would dearly love to move to nicer digs, his career demands his presence in the watery city.

Reni Wajetta: Male Human Scoundrel 4; Init +2; Defense 15 (+2 Dex, +3 class); Spd 10 m; VP/WP 18/16; Atk +3 melee (1d3, punch) or +5 ranged (3d6, blaster pistol); SQ illicit barter, lucky 1/day, precise attack +1; SV Fort +4, Ref +6, Will +1; SZ M; FP 0; DSP 0; Rep +1; Str 10, Dex 14, Con 13, Int 16, Wis 11, Cha 11. Challenge Code C.

Equipment: Blaster pistol, skiff, comlink.

Skills: Appraise +10, Bluff +6, Climb +3, Diplomacy +5, Forgery +9, Gather Information +12, Hide +7, Intimidate +3, Knowledge (Corulag) +10, Knowledge (politics) +7, Knowledge (streetwise) +8, Move Silently +7, Pilot +5, Read/Write Basic, Sense Motive +3, Speak Basic, Spot +5.

Feats: Great Fortitude, Skill Emphasis (Gather Information), Toughness, Trustworthy, Weapon Group Proficiencies (blaster pistols, simple weapons).

Zafiel Snopps

Zafiel Snopps is a no-nonsense captain of industry far more concerned with keeping his powerful economy chugging along than in advancing New Order ideology. He is a warm but ruthless man, popular with the people but scorned by the bigwigs at the Imperial Academy. In the Rise of the Empire era and most of the Rebellion era, Snopps served as Corulag's senator. When that body was

dissolved, the Emperor appointed him Corulag's governor. Ever a survivor, he returned to the revived Senate when the New Republic took over.

Zafiel Snopps: Male Human Noble 15; Init +1; Defense 19 (+1 Dex, +8 class); Spd 10 m; VP/WP 76/11; Atk +12/+7/+2 melee (1d3+1, punch) or +12/+7/+2 ranged (3d6, blaster pistol); SQ bonus class skill (Gather Information), coordinate +3, favor +4, inspire confidence, inspire greatness, resource access; SV Fort +5, Ref +8, Will +11; SZ M; FP 0; DSP 0; Rep +9; Str 12, Dex 13, Con 11, Int 15, Wis 10, Cha 18. Challenge Code F.

Equipment: Uniform, blaster pistol, comlink, rank insignia, datapads.

Skills: Appraise +11, Climb +5, Computer Use +14, Diplomacy +26, Entertain (harp) +9, Gather Information +16, Intimidate +7, Knowledge (bureaucracy) +11, Knowledge (politics) +9, Listen +6, Pilot +6, Profession (Megacorp officer) +8, Read/Write Basic, Read/Write Herglese, Ride +6, Search +10, Sense Motive +14, Speak Basic, Speak Herglese, Spot +6, Swim +5.

Feats: Dodge, Fame, Influence, Iron Will, Point Blank Shot, Precise Shot, Sharp-Eyed, Skill Emphasis (Diplomacy), Trustworthy, Weapon Group Proficiencies (blaster pistols, simple weapons).

New Creature: Bulfus

The bulfus is a flying mammal, a bat-shaped wedge of sleek-furred muscle. It has the coloration and aspects of an otter—including oily, dark fur, double-lidded eyes, and pronounced whiskers—but a dissimilar shape. When it bears living young, its pups cling to the upper dorsals of the parent until they learn to fly at five months.

Bulfusi are nocturnal predators that live and breed at the water's edge in muddy burrows. They are equally adept at hunting in the water and in the air, in both cases sweeping low over the undergrowth seeking the small creatures that dwell within. Bulfusi can be domesticated, but tame bulfusi are rare, since their size and appetites make them poor pets. They also smell awful when wet (which is much of the time). Nonetheless, certain trainers employ them as entertainers or guard animals.

Wild bulfusi aren't terribly aggressive toward Human-sized beings if left alone, but they're fierce if disturbed—especially if they feel their young are threatened. They have a nasty bite. On the wing, a rampaging bulfus can knock a grown Wookiee off its feet in a devastating dive bomb attack.

Bulfus: Airborne predator 2; Init +4 (+2 Dex, +2 species); Defense 14 (+2 Dex, +2 natural); Spd 6 m, fly 20 m (poor), swim 10 m; VP/WP 12/10; Atk +3 melee (2d6+2, diving ram) or +3 melee (2d4+1, bite) or +4 ranged; SQ +2 species bonus on initiative checks; SV Fort +3, Ref +5, Will −1; SZ M; Face/Reach 2 m by 2 m/2 m; Rep +0; Str 12, Dex 14, Con 10, Int 6, Wis 8, Cha 7. Challenge Code B.

Skills: Listen +6, Spot +4, Swim +3.

Feats: Flyby Attack.

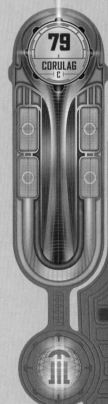

Drall

Planet Type: Terrestrial
Climate: Temperate to tropical
Terrain: Hills, meadows, forests
Atmosphere: Breathable
Gravity: Standard
Diameter: 13,220 km
Length of Day: 21 standard hours
Length of Year: 392 standard days
Sentient Species: Drall
Languages: Drallish, Basic
Population: 8 million
Species Mix: 96% Drall, 3% Human, 1% other
Government: Clan
Major Exports: Jewelry, medical products, some foodstuffs
Major Imports: Textiles, ore, tourism
System/Star: Corellia/Corell

Planets	Type	Moons
Corellia	Terrestrial	0
Drall	Terrestrial	0
Talus	Terrestrial	0
Tralus	Terrestrial	0
Centerpoint	Artificial	0
Selonia	Terrestrial	0
Crollia	Barren rock	0
Soronia	Frozen rock	0

Description

Drall is a temperate world with several large landmasses separated by deep oceans. A polar ice cap is present at each pole. The landmasses are covered with rolling hills, meadows, and scattered forests crisscrossed by numerous rivers and small, land-locked seas. Vegetation tends to be short, stocky trees and woody briar shrubs. Settlements congregate along the coasts and rivers or are underground.

Below the surface are extensive subterranean passages and caverns, some natural and some carved by the ancient Drall that dwelled there. These underground warrens are still used by the Drall, and entrances are located in their cities. However, many are still unexplored and uninhabited.

Drall's atmosphere allows more light and ultraviolet radiation to reach the surface than on other Corellian planets. Hence, the Drall dwell underground or in domed structures, where they are protected from the sun's harmful rays. Even Humans and other species that are not sensitive to light welcome the consistent climate that the domes provide, and partly for that reason Drall has become a popular tourist location.

History

Drall contains a secret subterranean planetary repulsor that was used to move the planet to its current location. There are no records of when this move occurred or where the planet's system of origin is located, despite the Drall's meticulous recording of their history.

The Drall are descended from burrowing mammals and originally lived in the cool, extensive underground cave system that riddles the planet. As traders and aliens began to visit their homeworld, the Drall established surface dwellings in the form of domed cities. These structures shield the furred Drall from the hot rays of the sun and allow them to interact with interstellar traders.

Approximately fourteen years after the Battle of Endor, Chewbacca and the Solo children traveled to Drall, escorted by their Drallish tutor, Ebrihim. While there, they discovered the planetary repulsor system and used it to disable Centerpoint Station, a powerful weapon commandeered by anti-Rebellion extremists.

People

The Drall are small in stature but carry themselves with utmost dignity and poise. They are intelligent and diligent record-keepers and are rumored to have recorded every trivial event since the dawn of intelligence. The Drall are famous scholars, researchers, and local historians. Their extensive libraries are their chief form of entertainment, as are verbal story-telling sessions called Ta'sharr. Drall delight in family gossip and often offend offworlders by prying into familial affairs.

Their planet is hot most of the year, and the Drall are covered with thick fur. Therefore, they rarely wear clothes except for a harness or belt to carry items. They are fond of trinkets and jewelry composed of common ores and gems, which they design into works of art.

Drall society is clan-based, and powerful family groups hold positions of power in a loose form of government. The head of each family is usually the eldest female, who holds the title of Duchess. The Duchess is consulted on all family matters and leads a daily Ta'sharr with all the children of the extended family. Drall family members work as trinketsmiths, scholars, or agricultural processors, or they support tourism to locations such as the Boiling Sea.

The Drall are a peaceful, quiet species. They lack an organized army and rarely carry weapons. Drall police officers are identified by the medallions worn around their necks and the flashsticks they carry to disable unruly Drall. The Wingriders are a division of the police that use great ibbot mounts to patrol the skies, facilitating trade between cities and serving as a mode of communication.

Locations

The following is a list of locations that might interest the heroes.

The Boiling Sea

The Boiling Sea is a large body of water located southeast of the city Mastigophorous. During the hot summer months, the water temperature increases, and the entire sea seems to churn and boil. However, this phenomenon is not due to the extreme temperatures. The summer months cause a massive algal bloom. The algae release gas bubbles when they die, making the water appear to boil. The algal bloom also attracts migratory ibbots to feed on the delicate plant masses.

The banks of the Boiling Sea have recently become host to a myriad of Drall dwellings and hotels. The former are winter retreats for wealthy Drall and in turn are rented out to tourists during the hot season. The latter are designed to accommodate the aggressive tourist industry that has bloomed in recent years. The Boiling Sea has become a popular site for the social elite of the galaxy. Exclusive resorts, health spas, and tour options are ready to separate tourists from their credits.

The Luminous Gardens

Situated on a hilltop overlooking the Boiling Sea is a health spa called the Luminous Gardens. Operated by a young female Drall named Drusa, the spa features hot spring baths, mineral baths, mud soaks, and aromatherapy. The Luminous Gardens employs some of the finest alien masseuses in the galaxy. Drusa hosts an extensive clientele and maintains a private business of gathering local (and sometimes galactic) rumors. For a price (usually paid in credits or information), these tidbits are available to others.

Meccha

Meccha is a mid-sized Drall town, made up of several domed buildings connected by skywalks. The domes' temperature is kept at about 17° C, comfortable for the furred Drall but chilly to most other species. The population consists mainly of farmers who toil in the fields at night outside the domes and rest inside during the harsh days. In addition to food, some of the agricultural products are used for medicinal purposes, such as the Vitapill.

To the north of Meccha is an artificial plateau used by the Drallish Wingriders. The plateau serves as a landing area and roost for great ibbots. The Wingriders maintain barracks, storage facilities, and other support services for their mounts.

The Caverns of Drall

Below the surface of Drall, a myriad of caverns and passageways twist through the planet. The worker class of Drall uses the upper caves as living quarters and storage facilities. The deeper caverns are unused, typically uninhabited and their original purpose forgotten. A few deep caves are used to grow fields of fungus that supplement Drall diets and are exported as an exotic delicacy to other planets.

Caverns near the Boiling Sea provide access to an all but forgotten planetary repulsor, which was once used to move the planet to its current location. Although it needs an overhaul, it can still function. However, the Drall would certainly be opposed to its use.

Flashstick

This device is a small metal baton with a crystal mounted on one end. When the user delivers a successful touch attack, the stick discharges a bright flash, blinding the opponent for 2d4 rounds. (See the character condition summary in Chapter Twelve of the *Star Wars Roleplaying Game*.) The flashstick is the main weapon employed by the Drallish police.

Flashstick
Cost: 100 credits
Damage: 1d2 (plus blindness)
Critical: 20
Weight: 1 kg
Type: Bludgeoning
Size: Small
Group: Simple

Dim Goggles

These goggles fit over a user's eyes and are secured with a comfortable strap. The goggles appear to be opaque, but the user can still see through them, although the surroundings appear shady. If a light-sensitive species uses these goggles, any penalties it incurs in bright sunlight are negated. When Drall need to be outdoors during the day, they usually wear these for comfort.

Dim Goggles
Cost: 50 credits
Weight: 0.2 kg

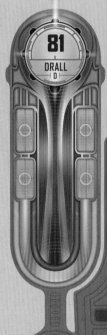

Meloria's Island Sanctuary

Sea Cliffs
(Ibbot Roosts)

Meloria's
Cave

Hidden
Airspeeder

Hidden
Path

Sensor
Dampening
Projector

Footpath

Beach

One Square = 2 Meters

Cryogenic
Unit

Dais

Living
Quarters

Generator

Malfunctioning
Blast Door

Fake
Living Quarters

Holoprojector
Unit

Holowall

Meloria's Cave

Vitapill

This small pill, made of a mixture of organic herbs and bacta emulsion, boosts a character's vitality. When a vitapill is consumed, the character gains 2d4 vitality points in the next round. A character can benefit from these stimulants only if he has vitality point damage. Any gain that puts a character over his maximum vitality point total is wasted.

Taking multiple pills in a 21-hour period is only partially effective. Each vitapill consumed after the first causes a cumulative –2 penalty to the number of vitality points regained: 2d4–2 for the second pill, 2d4–4 for the third pill, and 2d4–6 for the fourth pill. (There's no point in taking a fifth pill, because 2d4–8 will always be 0.) This penalty is not removed until 21 hours have passed since the most recent dosage.

Vitapill

Cost: 25 credits
Weight: n/a

For the GM

The adventure hooks and supporting characters described in this section are meant for GMs only. If you're a player, stop reading now.

Adventures

Feel free to use or adapt the following adventure hooks for your home campaign.

Locating Meloria

It's rumored that Meloria, a Jedi Knight who fell into dishonor, entered a self-imposed exile on the planet Drall. The Jedi Council, a lone Jedi, or the Rebel Alliance (depending on the era of play) sends the heroes to Drall to locate Meloria. Is she still alive? Has she slipped to the dark side?

Locating Meloria's hidden cave, situated on an island in the Boiling Sea, is difficult enough, but the heroes have competition. A Dark Jedi or the Imperials also have an interest in the fallen Jedi and any Jedi artifacts she might possess. Can the heroes locate her first? Perhaps the aid of Duchess Sarella and her Wingrider affiliations can shift the odds in their favor.

Information Gathering

The heroes need to gain several tidbits of information from a renowned and wealthy individual. This person could be an Imperial officer, a bounty hunter, or a wealthy merchant, depending on the era of play and the heroes' affiliation. The individual is fond of visiting the Luminous Gardens, a health spa on Drall.

First, the heroes need to make an appointment at the spa. Getting in on short notice could require several bribes, unless the heroes are able to arrange a favor from Duchess Sarella (see below). Then the heroes need to confront the target. He is certain to have guards disguised nearby, not to mention that the Luminous Gardens security force frowns on disturbances involving its clients. Finally, will the individual divulge the information?

Allies and Antagonists

The following characters are just a few of the interesting personalities the heroes might encounter on Drall.

Duchess Sarella

Duchess Sarella is a heavyset Drall with graying fur. Her ears are pierced and sport several intricate dangling ornaments. She keeps all four of her claws painted in bright colors. Her husky, commanding voice, unusual for a Drall, is capable of several accents and inflections during storytelling. The duchess has a dominating, mothering personality but is frequently confident and arrogant.

Sarella has been the head of her family for over thirty years. As such, she is respected in many circles among the other clans. She has ties within the government as well as within the traders. In addition, Duchess Sarella knows the advantage of alliances with other species and often has dealings with offworlders, including occasionally sending members of her family to serve corporations as research scientists. However, her greatest resource is a Drall named Drusa, owner of the Luminous Gardens health spa. Through this alliance, Drusa feeds Sarella local and galactic information.

Duchess Sarella: Female Drall Noble 4; Init –1; Defense 13 (–1 Dex, +1 size, +3 class); Spd 6 m; VP/WP 18/11; Atk +3 melee (1d2–1, punch) or +3 ranged; SQ bonus class skill (Gather Information), coordinate +1, favor +2, inspire confidence, resource access; SV Fort +1, Ref +1, Will +7; SZ S; FP 1; DSP 0; Rep +2; Str 8, Dex 8, Con 11, Int 19, Wis 17, Cha 17. Challenge Code B.

Equipment: Ceremonial necklace, credit chip (500 credits), 4 datapads.

Skills: Appraise +10, Diplomacy +15, Entertain (ballad) +9, Entertain (storytelling) +9, Gather Information +10, Hide +3, Intimidate +5, Knowledge (bureaucracy) +10, Knowledge (Drall) +10, Knowledge (politics) +10, Listen +6, Read/Write Drallish, Sense Motive +9, Speak Basic, Speak Drallish, Spot +6.

Feats: Skill Emphasis (Diplomacy), Trustworthy, Weapon Group Proficiencies (blaster pistols, simple weapons).

Wingrider Elamm

Elamm is short (even for a Drall) and slight of build, perfect stature for a Wingrider. His fur is tan and longer than normal, allowing beads to be braided into it around his head. He lacks customary trinkets and is otherwise adorned only with a bandoleer containing easily accessed pouches.

Elamm is a Wingrider, part of the Drallish police force that also serves as messengers and couriers. He has served his post for over a decade and rides a great ibbot nicknamed "Sha'lott" ("graywing" in Drallish). Unlike most Drall, Elamm enjoys being outside, especially when flying at high altitude, where the breezes keep him cool even in the hottest summer months. Although a member of Duchess Sarella's clan, Elamm is a free spirit and follows no one. He is uncommonly quiet for a Drall, almost reticent, and rarely attends Ta'sharr sessions. He prefers to be on the move, although he spends most of his time in the vicinity of Meccha.

Wingrider Elamm: Male Drall Scout 9; Init +3; Defense 20 (+3 Dex, +1 size, +6 class); Spd 6 m; VP/WP 36/9; Atk +8/+3 melee (1d4+1 plus blindness, flashstick) or +8/+3 melee (1d2+1, punch) or +6/+1 ranged (1d4, sling); SQ evasion, extreme effort, heart +1, skill mastery (Handle Animal), trailblazing, uncanny dodge (can't be flanked, Dex bonus to Defense); SV Fort +4, Ref +7, Will +5; SZ S; FP 0; DSP 0; Rep +2; Str 12, Dex 16, Con 9, Int 15, Wis 13, Cha 18. Challenge Code D.

Equipment: Great ibbot mount (with harness and saddle), cloak with hood, sling with 20 bullets, flashstick.

Skills: Balance +7, Handle Animal +13, Hide +11, Jump +5, Listen +3, Move Silently +15, Read/Write Basic, Read/Write Drallish, Ride +17, Speak Basic, Speak Drallish, Speak Selonian, Spot +15, Survival +15, Treat Injury +7, Tumble +9.

Feats: Alertness, Animal Affinity, Rugged, Skill Emphasis (Handle Animal), Track, Weapon Group Proficiencies (blaster pistols, blaster rifles, simple weapons).

Meloria

Meloria is a female Human in her mid-thirties. She wears a form-fitting black jumpsuit with a lightsaber holstered at her side. Her long brown hair is pulled back into a ponytail. Her skin is tan, her muscles well toned, and her expression grim.

Meloria grew up on Corellia and was identified as a potential Jedi shortly after birth. She never embraced her training completely and became bitter at having a "predestined fate." She enjoyed the physical prowess the Force gave her and focused her training on martial disciplines. Despite her lack of dedication to the mental aspects of Jedi training, her combat skills and unnatural reflexes impressed even her Jedi Master.

Shortly after she became a Jedi Knight, her quick reflexes betrayed her. While attempting to apprehend a bounty hunter, she killed an innocent who wandered into the action. Distraught and unable to cope mentally with her mistake, she disavowed her Jedi status and swore never to use the Force again. She traveled to Drall and settled on a small island in the Boiling Sea. There she farmed the land to support herself and lived in a small cave until she fell into total obscurity. Despite the isolation, or perhaps because of it, she never recovered from her error. She used the last of her savings to purchase a cryogenic unit and cryogenically preserved herself inside

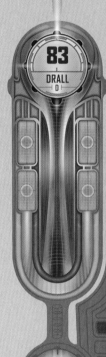

her cave. She decided that if the Force deemed it necessary, she would be freed. Until then, she would be frozen in time.

Meloria: Female Human Jedi Guardian 7/Scout 7; Init +7 (+3 Dex, +4 Improved Initiative); Defense 22 (+3 Dex, +9 class); Spd 10 m; VP/WP 111/16; Atk +16/+11/+6 melee (3d8+2/19–20, lightsaber) or +14/+9/+4 melee (1d3+2, punch) or +15/+10/+5 ranged; SQ deflect (attack –4, defense +1, extend defense and attack), evasion, extreme effort, heart +1, increase lightsaber damage +1d8, skill mastery (Computer Use), trailblazing, uncanny dodge (can't be flanked, Dex bonus to Defense); SV Fort +12, Ref +14, Will +8; SZ M; FP 0; Rep +4; Str 14, Dex 16, Con 16, Int 12, Wis 11, Cha 14. Challenge Code F.

   Equipment: Lightsaber, all-temperature cloak, outdoor clothes, medpac, electrobinoculars, field kit, sensor pack.

   Skills: Astrogate +8, Climb +6, Computer Use +14, Pilot +10, Read/Write Basic, Repair +8, Speak Basic, Speak Drallish, Tumble +12.

   Force Skills: Empathy +10, Enhance Ability +14, Force Defense +14, Force Stealth +14, Heal Self +13.

   Feats: Combat Reflexes, Dodge, Exotic Weapon Proficiency (lightsaber), Force-Sensitive, Improved Initiative, Lightning Reflexes, Starship Operation (space transport), Weapon Finesse (lightsaber), Weapon Focus (lightsaber), Weapon Group Proficiencies (blaster pistols, blaster rifles, simple weapons).

   Force Feats: Alter, Burst of Speed, Control, Lightsaber Defense, Sense.

New Creature: Ibbot

Drall is home to an impressive host of colorful avians called ibbots. Sixty-eight varieties of ibbots exist, each specialized to fit a particular niche of Drall's ecology. They come in a wide range of sizes, from the blue-breasted hover ibbot (wingspan 7 centimeters) to the great ibbot (wingspan 10 meters). Most are herbivores, feeding on algae that grows along the banks of the seas, but a few, such as the yellowtail ibbot hawk and the crested arrow ibbot, are true predators.

The Drall raise a domestic variety, the common (or brown) ibbot, to supplement their diet. It has a mild, slightly salty taste and can be prepared in numerous ways. Indeed, when Drall sample offworld cuisine, they often comment, "It tastes like ibbot."

Two sample ibbots appear below. Great ibbots are used as steeds by the Drall Wingriders. Flame ibbots scrape algae off rocks along the shore of the Boiling Sea and are capable of squirting a jet of scalding water at predators and nosy tourists alike.

MELORIA

Great Ibbot: Airborne herd animal 7; Init +4 (+2 Dex, +2 species); Defense 18 (+2 Dex, –2 size, +8 natural); Spd 20 m, fly 40 m (poor); VP/WP 52/40; Atk +7 melee (1d8+6, bite); SQ +2 species bonus on initiative checks; SV Fort +10, Ref +4, Will +0; SZ H (wingspan 10 m); Face/Reach 10 m by 4 m/4 m; Str 22, Dex 14, Con 20, Int 6, Wis 6, Cha 10. Challenge Code D.

   Skills: Listen +4, Search +4, Spot +8.

   Feats: Alertness, Flyby Attack.

Flame Ibbot: Airborne herd animal 1; Init +5 (+3 Dex, +2 species); Defense 16 (+3 Dex, +1 size, +2 natural); Spd 10 m, fly 60 m (average); VP/WP 6/14; Atk –1 melee (1d2–2, bite) or +4 ranged (2d4, scalding water jet); SQ scalding water jet, +2 species bonus on initiative checks; SV Fort +4, Ref +3, Will –1; SZ S (wingspan 4 m); Face/Reach 2 m by 2 m/2 m; Str 6, Dex 16, Con 14, Int 2, Wis 9, Cha 10. Challenge Code B.

   Skills: Listen +4, Search –1, Spot +3.

   Special Qualities: *Scalding Water Jet*—A flame ibbot can squirt a jet of scalding water every 1d4 rounds, to a maximum range of 20 meters. The attack deals 2d4 points of damage.

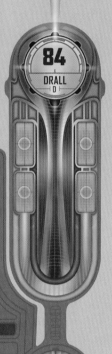

Duro

Planet Type: Terrestrial
Climate: Temperate
Terrain: Automated agri-plants, barren wasteland
Atmosphere: Toxic
Gravity: Standard
Diameter: 12,765 km
Length of Day: 33 standard hours
Length of Year: 420 standard days
Sentient Species: Duros
Languages: Durese
Population: 12,000 (on world), 1.6 billion (orbital cities)
Species Mix: 53% Duros, 36% Human, 11% other (on world); 91% Duros, 9% other (orbital cities)
Government: Corporate
Major Exports: Starships, starship parts, high-tech goods
Major Imports: Foodstuffs, ore, labor
System/Star: Duro/Duro

Planets	Type	Moons
Lors	Searing rock	1
Duro	Terrestrial	0
Koli	Frozen rock	2

Description

Polluted by centuries of heavy industry and indifferent leadership, the Duro homeworld is a stench-laden, moonless world barely fit for habitation. Automated food processing plants on the planet's surface generate the foodstuffs that feed the inhabitants of twenty orbital Duro cities. Almost every other facility or structure on the surface is long-abandoned or obsolete.

Orbital cities house Duros who haven't taken to the stars. The rest of the Duro system contains hundreds of smaller stations, depots, and shipbuilding facilities. Bburru, largest of the major orbital cities, serves as the system's capital. During the time of the New Republic, Duro also harbors one of the most important shipyards in the galaxy.

Prior to Duro's overpollution and development, the world was an unremarkable planet with rolling plains, few mountains, and little tectonic activity. Some cynical historians muse that the Duros developed space travel early in their history because their world was so boring. Mutant fefze beetles are the only species to have survived the subsequent pollution. Even the notoriously tenacious cannibal arachnids of Duro legend are gone. During the Yuuzhan Vong campaign against the New Republic, refugees living on Duro began agricultural and land/water reclamation projects in earnest, but only with limited success.

History

The cradle of one of the greatest species of space explorers, the Duro system is strategically located—not just within the Core, but also along the crucial Corellian Trade Spine. Populated by thousands of orbital cities, space platforms, shipyard facilities, and research stations, the Duro system is a tribute to one of the galaxy's oldest and greatest spacefaring folk.

Thousands of years before the Battle of Yavin, Duros scientists developed interstellar flight during the reign of Queen Rana. Their explorations took them throughout their sector, and they used their new technology to build space stations, catalogue new worlds, and establish a colony on Neimoidia. With progress came pollution, overdevelopment, and hypermechanization. Over the centuries, nearly all Duros sought refuge in the orbital cities above their world. Some spread farther, traveling into every corner of the galaxy.

With the dispersal of the Duro population, the political infrastructure of the homeworld weakened. Massive corporate interests had little trouble deposing the final reigning sovereign, Duchess Geneer. Corporate interests did little to prevent further pollution of the world, instead promoting the establishment and habitation of the orbital cities that were built over the centuries.

When the Empire came into power and seized the shipyards and planet, it stripped what was left of Duro's remaining natural resources. The planet was simply left for dead. In a move to stir agitation between the Corellians and the Duros, the boundaries of the respective sectors were redrawn so that Duro became part of the Corellian sector. (The New Republic later reversed this decision, putting the system back into the Duro sector.) The corporations in power tried to remain neutral at first, but their executives knew that failure to yield to the Empire would be their end. Although few outside the circles of power knew it, the Empire soon established a Reprogramming Institute on Duro's surface for the "reeducation" of dissidents.

After the Rebel victory at Endor, the Empire fled Duro within a few months. Immediately, the mega-corporations reassumed their positions in conducting the system's affairs. Some ten years after the Battle of Yavin, the Empire reoccupied Duro, but New Republic forces eventually repelled Imperial incursions.

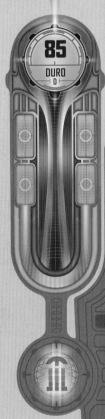

The Yuuzhan Vong's drive into the New Republic caused an already beleaguered world further grief. The machinations and infighting of corrupt shipping magnates allowed for a fairly easy Yuuzhan Vong victory. Using their feared dovin basal biotechnology, the Yuuzhan Vong pulled all but one of the orbiting cities out of space and crashed them into Duro. The Yuuzhan Vong plan was to heal the heinous damage that "vile" technology had inflicted on the world, then use the system as a staging point for deeper incursions into the Core Worlds.

People

Sometimes called "star pioneers," Duros are one of the most commonly encountered species in the galaxy. Arguably the greatest spacefaring people known, they are comparable to the Corellians for their wanderlust and uncanny capability in handling spacecraft. Duros are even credited by some as having invented the hyperdrive, though the claim is impossible to verify. Most find work in fields pertaining to either building, maintaining, or piloting starships. The species' general temperament makes Duros especially easy to get along with in almost any crowd. They are quiet, peaceful, and very dependable, both as friends and workers. Many have an uncanny gift for storytelling. Duro travelers and explorers have been known to hush a room with one of their many epic tales.

Locations

Descriptions of several important locations follow.

Bburru Station

The largest of Duro's orbital cities, Bburru is also the system's capital, housing the offices of many administrators. Crowded with migrant workers, pilots, and adventurers, the station boasts an expansive series of docking facilities. For many off-duty pilots bringing freight into the area, it is typically the first stop insystem. The huge station is well appointed, with an open central plaza of such size it seems as though it should belong on a pleasant world far removed from the acrid "Duro-stink" so near.

Some twenty-six years after the Battle of Yavin, the Yuuzhan Vong attacked Duro in its attempt to gain a foothold in the Core. The resulting conflict, the Battle of Duro, resulted in the destruction of nineteen of the twenty orbital cities. Only Urrdorf City, which did not have hyperspace capability, survived the initial Yuuzhan Vong incursion.

Event Horizon

A seedy cantina even by the underworld's standards, Event Horizon is a dangerous, smoke-filled dive in which the walls carry placards warning Neimoidians, droids, and repo agents to stay out. Frequented by smugglers, gunrunners, outlaw techs, and sundry other unsavories that ply the Corellian Trade Spine, the bar is owned by a surly Quarren known locally as Clawfish. A retired outlaw tech, Clawfish has forgotten more illegal contacts than most infochants make in a lifetime.

Event Horizon is located deep within the infrastructure of Rrudobar, one of the smaller of the Duro orbital cities. One side of the cantina is intended for typical terrestrial patrons. The other consists of a series of wading pools and hydro-spas for aquatic species. As a result, the bar is extremely popular with fellow Quarren, Mon Calamari, Priapulin, and other species more comfortable in aquatic environs. Patrons are free to mix between the two zones. If a patron can handle the humidity, Event Horizon is one of the best places in the Duro system for a cheap, stiff drink, learning the latest word on the street, or starting a nasty brawl.

Duro Starshipwright Shipyards

Though not fitted with warship docks—such as facilities on Kuat, Corellia, or Mon Calamari—the Duro Starshipwright Shipyards (DSS) are a bustling center of starship productivity. The shipyards can accommodate vessels ranging from massive cargo carriers (such as those the local starshipwrights were forced to build during the Empire) to the small one-pilot starfighters used by military and pirate groups.

Devoted primarily to light freighter design and construction, DSS also receives many requests for weapons upgrades and "refitting" assignments. In other words, the shipyards contract a lot of less than legal modifications for smugglers, bounty hunters, and other

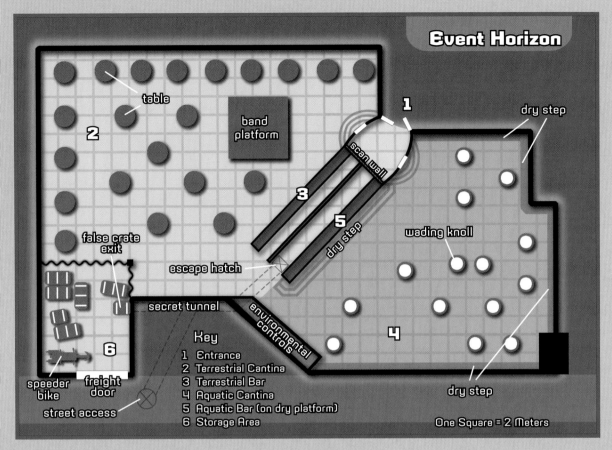

dry step

1

scan wall

3

5

dry step

wading knoll

2

table

band platform

false crate exit

escape hatch

secret tunnel

environmental controls

4

dry step

6

speeder bike

freight door

street access

Key
1   Entrance
2   Terrestrial Cantina
3   Terrestrial Bar
4   Aquatic Cantina
5   Aquatic Bar (on dry platform)
6   Storage Area

One Square = 2 Meters

unsavories. DSS hosts a fairly extensive black market. Dozens of outlaw techs not only sell illegal drives but also install them.

Duro Delta Twelve Orbital Shipyard

Duro Delta Twelve is an aging orbital shipyard in the Duro system. During the days of the Old Republic, DD 12 was a bustling construction yard constantly building new sections and powering down older ones in need of repairs or updating. DD 12 fell to less than half capacity once the Empire rose to prominence, and many of its semi-independent sections were powered down and abandoned. Its remaining main sections, however, continue to see regular traffic during the Rebellion era, as merchants drop off freighters for repair, deliver much-needed starship construction material, and temporarily house shipments awaiting new vessels for transport. This combination of high traffic and abandoned areas makes DD 12 a popular location for clandestine meetings of all sorts—the Rebellion frequently uses it to contact Duro sympathizers. In fact, the meeting that convinced the Duro Shipwrights' Guild to support the Rebel Alliance occurred in a forgotten section of DD 12.

A typical abandoned section of DD 12, pictured in the accompanying map, contains several airlocks designed for small shuttles and transports. A few crates may be found in hallways and dark rooms, either forgotten supplies or contraband shipments hidden by smugglers. Broken loader droids sit in quiet hallways, and refuse piles up along the walls. Many sections include power generators that provide light and heat for secret meetings and smuggler's dens. Various groups might use a single section at the same time, each claiming a small part of the area. Broken corridors have been protected with transparisteel domes, so air and heat don't escape into the vacuum of space.

New Creature: Mutant Fefze Beetle

The only creature known to inhabit Duro during the Rebellion era is a nonsentient, mutated species of fefze beetle. Thought to be descended from Fefze, a Human-sized insect species recruited to work on Duro in the last decades of the Republic, these mutants have lost all connection with their hive mind. They have since grown into vicious, chattering beasts that attack any moving thing at the first opportunity.

Mutant Fefze Beetle: Vermin 2; Init +3; Defense 23 (+3 Dex, +10 natural); DR 7; Spd 12 m; VP/WP 9/11; Atk +1 melee (1d6, claw); SQ darkvision 20 m, scent; SV Fort +3, Ref +6, Will –4; SZ M; Face/Reach 2 m by 2 m/ 2 m; Str 10, Dex 16, Con 11, Int 3, Wis 3, Cha 3. Challenge Code B.

   Skills: Climb +5, Hide +4, Search +1, Survival +1.

For the GM

The adventure hooks and supporting characters described in this section are meant for GMs only. If you're a player, stop reading now.

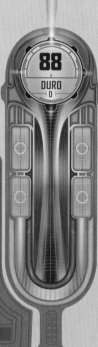

Adventures

From the depths of its underworld to its orbiting cities, adventure survives on Duro, even during times of rampant pollution and devastation.

All the Admiral's Men

Admiral Cov, a grizzled veteran of several Rebel battles, recruits the heroes to find the Kadlo Talisman, an ancient hand-sized idol from the reign of King Kadlo. Cov boldly states that Kadlo is one of his greatest ancestors. He relates that in recent months, the Talisman was taken from a tomb raided by looters, but the thieves were found killed on Bburru only days later—without the Kadlo figurine. A trusted informant has recently contacted the admiral with news that the Talisman was spotted insystem. Now the hunt begins in earnest.

When the characters finally locate the idol deep in an orbital city's underworld, the individuals holding the Talisman are crewmen from the cruiser *Resolve*, Admiral Cov's flagship! Further investigation reveals that the crewmen are mutineers against Cov who have been bought out by DurAble, a powerful Duro distributor with interests opposed to the admiral's. Can the characters stem the mutiny against the good admiral?

Murder, Imported

Before the Yuuzhan Vong invade the system, Duro's stale surface is used by SELCORE (the New Republic Senate Select Committee for Refugees) to house millions of refugees displaced by the larger conflict against the aliens. Expansive sealed synthplas domes, filled by three wedges of mud-brick hut groups, dot the world. Each dome ideally houses one thousand refugees, but more are crammed into the areas. With various species rivalries comes deadly conflict.

When a young Rodian tough is accused of killing a fellow refugee—an old acquaintance of one of the characters—chaos ensues. The characters are pulled into the middle of a potentially explosive situation. The Rodian punk maintains his innocence. Several possible eyewitnesses, his fellow thugs included, won't speak to anyone investigating. But one refugee insists the characters' friend was dead when the ship landed. Can the characters get to the truth and live?

Allies and Antagonists

The following supporting characters are designed for use in your campaign.

Formmn Badees

An up-and-coming Duros pilot during the Rebellion era, Formmn Badees dreams of flying against the Empire, but he's been relegated to helping at his older brother's small chop-shop on the outskirts of the Duro system. Aching for some action, young Formmn lives vicariously through holovids he watches in the loud, oily shop he and his brother manage. An idealist hoping for a brighter future, Formmn consorts with some rather rough smugglers and

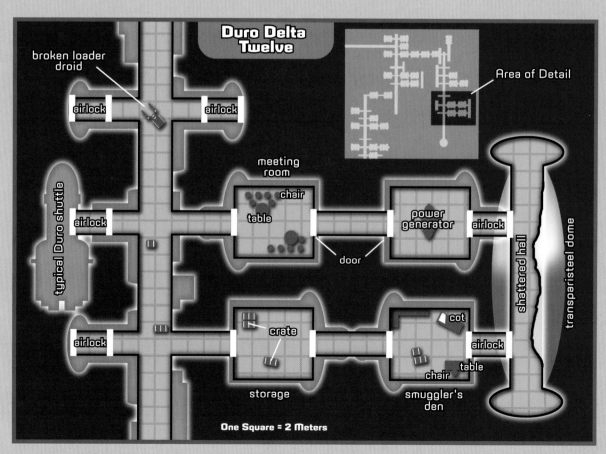

Duro Delta Twelve

broken loader droid

airlock

airlock

Area of Detail

typical Duro shuttle

airlock

meeting room

chair

table

door

power generator

airlock

shattered hall

transparisteel dome

airlock

crate

cot

airlock

storage

table

chair

smuggler's den

One Square = 2 Meters

pirates in different watering holes throughout the system. For all his skill and promise, Formmn has never been beyond New Plympto, where he once delivered some alluvial dampers to a customer stranded on the outskirts of the system.

Formm Badees: Male Duros Fringer 4; Init +3; Defense 17 (+3 Dex, +4 class); Spd 10 m; VP/WP 19/10; Atk +3 melee (1d3, punch) or +2 (3d6, blaster pistol); SQ barter, bonus class skill (Appraise, Computer Use), jury-rig +2; SV Fort +4, Ref +5, Will +1; SZ M; FP 1; DSP 0; Rep +0; Str 10, Dex 17, Con 10, Int 13, Wis 11, Cha 11. Challenge Code B.

Equipment: Blaster pistol, comlink, tools.

Skills: Appraise +6, Astrogate +5, Computer Use +8, Knowledge (spacer lore) +6, Knowledge (streetwise) +6, Listen +4, Pilot +8, Read/Write Basic, Read/Write Durese, Repair +6, Sense Motive +3, Speak Basic, Speak Durese, Spot +6, Survival +4.

Feats: Alertness, Ambidexterity, Gearhead, Spacer, Weapon Group Proficiencies (primitive weapons, simple weapons).

Clawfish

The brutal owner and proprietor of the Event Horizon cantina on Rrudobar, Clawfish is a nasty-tempered Quarren male with only one remaining facial tentacle. Inquiries as to how he lost the other usually result in serious trouble. A former outlaw tech who ran with some of the wildest groups in the Core and the Corporate Sector, Clawfish retired some years ago to establish Event Horizon. Bitter, callous, and downright ornery, Clawfish is actually a fairly good being once someone pierces his rough exterior and gets to know him. At least, that's the rumor—nobody's actually gotten to know him that well.

Clawfish: Male Quarren Scoundrel 8; Init +0; Defense 15 (+5 class); Spd 10 m; VP/WP 33/17; Atk +8/+3 melee (1d3+2, punch) or +8/+3 melee (2d6+2, vibroblade) or +6/+1 ranged (3d6, blaster pistol); SQ breathe underwater, illicit barter, low-light vision, lucky 2/day, precise attack +1; SV Fort +5, Ref +6, Will +4; SZ M; FP 0; DSP 0; Rep +2; Str 14, Dex 11, Con 17, Int 13, Wis 13, Cha 10.

Equipment: Vibroblade, blaster pistol, old tools.

Skills: Appraise +6, Astrogate +4, Computer Use +9, Demolitions +4, Forgery +5, Gather Information +6, Intimidate +7, Knowledge (Corporate Sector) +11, Knowledge (Duro) +8, Pilot +6, Profession (bartender) +4, Profession (outlaw tech) +15, Read/Write Basic, Read/Write Calamarian, Read/Write Durese, Read/Write Quarrenese, Repair +17, Search +4, Speak Basic, Speak Mon Calamarian, Speak Durese, Speak Quarrenese, Spot +4, Swim +6.

Feats: Gearhead, Headstrong, Heroic Surge, Skill Emphasis (Profession [outlaw tech], Repair), Weapon Group Proficiencies (blaster pistols, simple weapons, vibro weapons).

Til

A spy in the grand tradition of his extended creche-mate Garindan of Tatooine, Til is a compact Kubaz male who prowls the underworld regions of the smaller orbital cities.

CLAWFISH

Most beings involved in the local underworld know Til as "Crunch," a hacker and information gatherer of considerable skill. Beings who deal with him frequently are often repulsed by his disturbing appetite for organs from the mutated (nonsentient) fefze beetles of Duro. He munches on viscera from the vile bugs while encrypting, hacking, or deciphering some of the most difficult software, usually to the revulsion of his employers. The only beings who make consistent use of Crunch's skills and aren't put off by his eating habits are the three or four Hutt lords who occasionally take residence insystem to oversee various "business endeavors."

Til's true occupation is as an informant for Clan Desilijic, one of the most powerful Hutt clans. The lively underworld in the Duro system is well monitored by the Desilijic clan, and most of that information comes from Til.

Til (a.k.a. Crunch): Male Kubaz Diplomat 4; Init +1; Defense 12 (+1 Dex, +1 class); Spd 10 m; VP/WP 0/15; Atk +3 melee (1d3+1, punch) or +3 ranged (3d8, heavy blaster pistol); SQ light sensitive; SV Fort +3, Ref +2, Will +5; SZ M; FP 1; DSP 2; Rep +1; Str 13, Dex 12, Con 15, Int 14, Wis 12, Cha 13. Challenge Code A.

Equipment: Heavy blaster pistol, comlink, forged IDs.

Skills: Computer Use +9, Diplomacy +5, Gather Information +11, Hide +6, Knowledge (streetwise) +7, Move Silently +6, Read/Write Basic, Read/Write Durese, Read/Write Huttese, Read/Write Kubazi, Search +7, Sense

Motive +3, Speak Basic, Speak Durese, Speak Huttese, Speak Kubazi.

Feats: Sharp-Eyed, Stealthy, Trustworthy, Weapon Group Proficiency (blaster pistols).

DDF E-Wing

Designed by FreiTek, Inc., the same team who designed and built the exceptionally popular X-wing, the E-wing was the first starfighter developed and built specifically for New Republic forces. Faster than the X-wing or A-wing, the E-wing is a powerful defensive interceptor. It is easily the strongest component of the Duro Defense Force. Hyperspace-capable, the fighter is also employed by the New Republic's mutual aid organizations that contribute to the defense of other Core Worlds. Depending on the era, a number of the Duros fighter pilots who lead the DDF fighter groups have seen action at Naboo, Endor, Sluis Van, or any number of Republic, Rebel Alliance, or New Republic battles.

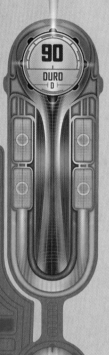

Duro Defense Force E-wing

Class: Starfighter
Size: Tiny (11.2 m long)
Hyperdrive: ×2
Passengers: 0
Cargo Capacity: 110 kg
Consumables: 1 week
Cost: 185,000
Crew: 1 (Skilled +4)
Initiative: +6 (+2 size, +4 crew)
Maneuver: +6 (+2 size, +4 crew)
Defense: 22 (+2 size, +10 armor)
Shield Points: 30
Hull Points: 150 (DR 10)
Maximum Speed in Space: Ramming (12 squares/action)
Atmospheric Speed: 1,440 km/h (24 squares/action)
   Weapon: Triple heavy blaster cannon (fire-linked); **Fire Arc:** Front; **Attack Bonus:** +12 (+2 crew, +4 size, +6 fire control); **Damage:** 6d10×2; **Range Modifiers:** PB +0, S −2, M −4, L −6.
   Weapon: Proton torpedo launcher (3 torpedoes); **Fire Arc:** Front; **Attack Bonus:** +10 (+2 size, +4 crew, +4 fire control); **Damage:** 9d10×2; **Range Modifiers:** PB +0, S −2, M −4, L −6.

DDF Dagger-D

An intrasystem fighter designed by the Duro System Shipwrights' Guild in conjunction with FreiTek, the Dagger-D is a sleek but rugged craft that patrols the space and skies of the Duro system. Blade-shaped with a massive arced Novaldex BlasterDrive nacelle, the Dagger-D is an effective and fairly inexpensive intercept and pursuit craft. While not designed to withstand significant punishment, the compact fighter holds its own against average space scum. For larger firefights, the DDF E-wings are quick to respond.

Duro Defense Force Dagger-D Police Fighter

Class: Starfighter
Size: Tiny (11.8 m long)
Hyperdrive: None
Passengers: 2
Cargo Capacity: 85 kg
Consumables: 2 days
Cost: 27,500
Crew: 1 (Skilled +4)
Initiative: +6 (+2 size, +4 crew)
Maneuver: +6 (+2 size, +4 crew)
Defense: 22 (+2 size, +10 armor)
Shield Points: 30
Hull Points: 60 (DR 10)
Maximum Speed in Space: Ramming (10 squares/action)
Atmospheric Speed: 1,200 km/h (20 squares/action)
   Weapon: Triple blasters (2 fire-linked); **Fire Arc:** Front; **Attack Bonus:** +8 (+2 size, +4 crew, +2 fire control); **Damage:** 3d10×2; **Range Modifiers:** PB +0, S −2, M −4, L −6.

Esseles

Planet Type: Terrestrial
Climate: Temperate
Terrain: Urban, ocean
Atmosphere: Breathable
Gravity: Standard
Diameter: 14,783 km
Length of Day: 22 standard hours
Length of Year: 405 standard days
Sentient Species: Human
Languages: Basic
Population: 1.5 billion
Species Mix: 86% Human, 8% Herglic, 2% Bothan, 4% other
Government: Representative democracy
Major Exports: Foodstuffs, raw materials
Major Imports: High tech, starships
System/Star: Essesia/Essess

Planets	Type	Moons
Shella	Searing rock	0
Danzer	Gas giant	2
Esseles	Terrestrial	1
Pocia	Gas giant	19
Ithona	Gas giant	5
Talleles	Gas giant	2
Kodasta	Ice ball	2
Permeles	Ice ball	0

Description

Esseles is the dominant world in Darpa sector, the area of the Core that borders the Colonies along the Perlemian Trade Route. It was a highly volcanic world in its recent geological past—perhaps ten million years ago—and its surface is now densely covered in imposing, young mountain chains that have not yet been worn down into gentle slopes by storms and ice ages.

The atmosphere is fairly thick, and the resulting greenhouse effect produces a climate that is warm and damp within the heavily populated regions throughout most of the year—except for a short dry season in midsummer. The large population centers are nestled into the narrow valleys and few plains that can be found on the five rugged continents.

History

In the time before the Clone Wars, Esseles was the seat of a regional empire that controlled most of Darpa sector. The Esselian empire was relatively benign, concerned primarily with trade and regional security. It maintained cordial relations with its neighbors, and sent nineteen senators to Coruscant—one for each of its worlds. The Esselian empire collapsed soon after the Clone Wars, not so much as a direct result of the conflict, but due to the economic downturn that accompanied it. The pocket empire, unable to meet its financial obligations, turned governorship of its client worlds over to their respective citizens and dissolved.

In the Rebellion era, Esseles's few remaining offworld holdings were "liberated" by the Empire, and the once mighty empire found itself reduced to a single world. Even so, the pride of Esseles was very much alive, and the planet remained the head of most of Darpa sector's worlds in a variety of informal and unofficial ways.

While friendly enough with the Empire, Esseles held itself somewhat aloof from the ideologies and programs emanating from Coruscant. Most Esselians considered themselves loyal to Esseles first, the Empire second. This situation began to change slowly with the rise of a local New Order party, which devoted years to the task of transforming culture and taking over Esseles's parliament.

Such efforts met with limited success, but with the fall of the Empire, Esseles transitioned smoothly back into the revived New Republic. Happily for its citizens, the world suffered little during the retreat of the Imperial Navy. The one battle fought between Imperial and New Republic forces occurred in the outer system, and the Imperials retreated with little incident. Its economy remained strong, and it emerged from the Galactic Civil War as a major high-tech industrial center.

People

Esselians are by nature an independent and proud people, much taken with festivals and pageantry that celebrate their culture and way of life. There seems to be a patron hero for every day of the year, and not a week goes by that holovids aren't commemorating some ancient battle or triumph of the faded Esselian empire.

As enamored with their past as they are, Esselians are neither morose nor decadent. They firmly believe their best years are before them—even as the Republic Senate fell into corruption and bickering, was disbanded by Emperor Palpatine, and finally arose anew out of the ashes of his fallen empire. Esselians are eternal optimists.

They also put a great deal of stock in tradition and are very much creatures of habit. Once a task has been done long enough to establish a pattern, it is likely to be done that way indefinitely. This tendency makes Esselian culture resilient, but also somewhat intractable.

Locations

Here are some of the locations heroes might have occasion to visit while on Esseles.

Calamar

Esseles's rich history and mild climate have made Calamar, the capital city, something of a center of high culture. Its suburbs are given over to vast parks, art centers, colleges and universities. Theater, newsnet, and holoproduction entertainment are major industries on Esseles—especially in sunny Calamar—and productions are widely disseminated in a wide range of Core and Colonies systems.

One of the Core's most effective Rebel cells in the Rebellion era was based in Calamar's entertainment industry. In addition to producing a number of subtly subversive works that slipped past the Imperial censors undetected, the cell also took a more martial role in opposing the Empire.

Terril Naval Base

New Calamar on the southern continent is home to Terril Naval Base, one of the largest planetside military installations in the sector. Once the seat of Esselian military power, Terril in the Rebellion era is home to the sector command—the support staffs and families of those crewing no fewer than ten Star Destroyers are stationed here.

Terril was home to a prominent Jedi chapter house in the time of the Old Republic, which served as a staging point for Jedi activities in Darpa sector. This site was disbanded with the rise of Palpatine, but vague rumors

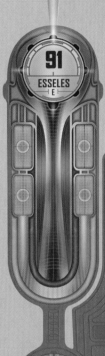

Esseles: Imperial Conference Center

one square = 10 meters

Key

1 Entrance Foyer
2 Auditorium
3 Holovid Room
4 Small Conference Suite
5 Banquet Hall
6 Kitchens
7 Seminar and Meeting Hall

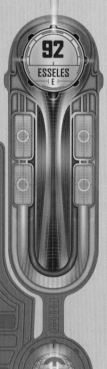

long persisted that the Jedi left a cache of holocrons secreted somewhere on the base.

Esprix Estate

The Esprix Estate is the official residence of the Republic Senator of Esseles. A palatial estate built in an ornate style reminiscent of the Naboo school of architecture, it is endowed with many of the attributes one expects of a high-ranking official's residence—office suites, ballrooms, salons, and the like.

It is also the base of Esseles's spynet. From within basement command centers and fortified interior bunkers, Esseles's spymasters direct an extended network of operatives gathering information in the military and economic spheres. The presence of this organization is not widely known among the general population, but Coruscant is aware of it, which is why, in the Rebellion era, Esprix is the moff's residence and its assets are in the hands of the feared Imperial Security Bureau.

Togatto Speedway

While the sport of Podracing never really caught on throughout the Core, it has taken root with a vengeance on Esseles. Togatto Speedway, located in the tropical city of Nurrale, is home to one of the Core's top Podracing courses. Its hairpin turns and tortured loops and spirals through the core of the imposing but dormant Togatto volcano makes it a popular spectacle.

Togatto Speedway is owned and controlled by one of Esseles's major criminal syndicates, the Ferlani family. The group has its fingers in the speedway and other sports events and infrequently clashes with its chief rival, the Calamar-based Largo family. The speedway is a great place to look for action.

Fort Cravus

On the coast near Nurrale is an ancient fortress erected by Lord Cravus, a cruel warlord who carved out a planetary empire predating even the Esselian empire by centuries. This imposing stone structure, its walls studded with bas-relief sculptures of Cravus's early conquests and triumphs, has survived the centuries and is now a museum displaying artifacts from this and other empires from the region's past.

Unbeknownst to all, several dozen of Cravus's grim assassin droids lie slumbering in a sealed vault hundreds of meters below the fortress, awaiting the electronic signal that will awaken them to lay waste to the planet.

New Feats

Esselian culture imparts a number of benefits to its citizens. Here are a few new feats that reflect these benefits.

Bureaucratic Flair

You have a talent for divining the workings and intricacies of bureaucracy in all its forms. Whether you're attempting to free your impounded starship or pass a trade bill, you are adept at manipulating a bureaucracy's institutions and members to your benefit.

Benefit: You gain a +2 aptitude bonus on all Diplomacy checks and a +2 aptitude bonus on all Knowledge (bureaucracy) checks.

Headstrong

The stubbornness and hidebound traditions of your people are known throughout the galaxy. You are exceptionally strong-willed and difficult to sway from your intended course.

Benefit: You receive a +1 bonus on Will saves and a +2 aptitude bonus on Intimidate checks.

High Culture

You are steeped in the refined pursuits of life, from genteel sports and the theater to music and literature. You are schooled from an early age to not only appreciate such things but also participate in them.

Benefit: You receive a +2 aptitude bonus on all Entertain checks and a +2 aptitude bonus on all Tumble checks.

Living History

The past, far from being an irrelevant collection of moldering facts, is a living resource you draw from in all walks of life.

Benefit: You receive a +2 aptitude bonus on all Knowledge checks.

For the GM

The adventure hooks and supporting characters described in this section are meant for GMs only. If you're a player, stop reading now.

Adventures

The following adventure ideas might draw the heroes into Esselian intrigues.

Going Gangbusters

Esseles's underworld is on the verge of erupting. The Largo family recently made new allies in the political realm, and rival syndicate families have begun falling in police or Imperial raids. Largo chieftains insist they have nothing to do with the raids.

With Ferlani's Togatto Speedway threatened, Luthus Ferlani hires the heroes to discover who is collaborating with the politicians. Dodging police and gangsters alike, they delve into their investigation—skulking around various dives, underground gambling halls, corporate offices, and possibly the Esprix Estate. Gradually, they learn the crackdowns are a plot conceived by a clique of young criminals from all the families who are determined to displace their elders and forge a new alliance with Esseles's political masters. They plan to assassinate what leaders remain at the upcoming Annual Jatzday Race at Togatto Speedway, setting the stage for a climactic encounter at the speedway.

A Taxing Party

Emperor Palpatine has issued a secret order to raise taxes in the Core by instigating alien "riots" the Empire can blame for new "security taxes." Moff Graffe plans to convene a secret conference of government officials and pro-Imperial journalists to decide how this might be accomplished on Esseles.

Intent on exposing this plot, local Rebel spy Deena Mipps brings the heroes in to secretly film the conference. They succeed after some close calls with security and Graffe's two Chiba protocol droids. With holovids in hand of officials conspiring to harm Esselian alien citizens, the Rebels decide how best to embarrass the moff as he decries atrocities among the alien population. Broadcasting the conference on the holovid is one solution, but this must be done from the holovid uplink station at a south pole installation to override Imperial efforts to jam the beam from orbit.

The Esseles Bombers

Sympathy for the Rebel Alliance is growing among the people. Moff Graffe brings in Garthus Hal and his gang to commit a series of public atrocities in the name of the Rebel Alliance, hoping to turn public opinion against the Alliance.

Garthus Hal goes to work with gusto, bombing a monorail station in the name of alien power and a concert hall in the name of Alderaan. He also kills a number of popular Podracers at the Togatto Speedway in the name of the Rebel Alliance. The people cry out to the Empire to protect them—and Luthus Ferlani sends for bounty hunters.

The bombers are moving at random with cover provided by Graffe, making them hard to pin down. Watching Graffe instead of looking for the bombers yields better results—the moff soon meets with Garthus in New Calamar. Once identified, the pirates can be taken down in small groups if the heroes are cautious. On the other hand, the heroes might be forced to act quickly before the pirates commit a particularly horrifying atrocity. Meanwhile, Ferlani's bounty hunters are looking for Rebels to roast. . . .

Allies and Antagonists

The heroes might encounter some of the following movers and shakers on Esseles as friends or foes.

Garthus Hal

Garthus is a slight, pasty-faced man with a shock of black hair, jug-handle ears, and sunken eyes. He has been in turn a soldier, a pirate, and a gambler, but what he's best known for is his work as a bomber for hire. Garthus and his lads are known in the Outer Rim as "go-to guys" when someone wants a building to burn or explode. He and Graffe got to know each other on a dreary backwater world where Graffe was stationed, because they were the only two skilled sabbac players within parsecs.

Garthus Hal: Male Human Scoundrel 5/Soldier 4; Init +2; Defense 18 (+2 Dex, +6 class); Spd 10 m; VP/WP 52/12; Atk +7/+2 melee (1d3, punch) or +7/+2 melee (2d6, vibroblade) or +9/+4 ranged (3d8, heavy blaster pistol) or +9/+4 ranged (8d6+6, thermal detonator); SQ illicit barter, lucky 1/day, precise attack +1; SV Fort +8, Ref +7, Will +1; SZ M; FP 0; DSP 0; Rep +2; Str 11, Dex 15, Con 12, Int 15, Wis 8, Cha 14. Challenge Code E.

  Equipment: Heavy blaster pistol, vibroblade, 10 thermal detonators, comlink, security kits, medpac, glow rod.

  Skills: Appraise +9, Astrogate +11, Bluff +10, Computer Use +13, Demolitions +14, Disable Device +10, Forgery +7, Gamble +7, Gather Information +10, Intimidate +11, Knowledge (Esseles) +6, Knowledge (spacer lore) +8, Move Silently +7, Pilot +14, Profession (gambler) +7, Read/Write Basic, Read/Write Rodese, Repair +5, Speak Basic, Speak Rodese.

  Feats: Combat Expertise, Combat Reflexes, Dodge, Great Fortitude, Heroic Surge, Mobility, Quickness, Skill Emphasis (Demolitions), Spacer, Spring Attack, Weapon Group Proficiencies (blaster pistols, simple weapons, vibro weapons).

Deena Mipps

Deena Mipps is a perky and immensely popular noblewoman turned newsnet reporter. She is hardly the sort one would expect to lead a Rebel cell, but indeed Mipps is ideally placed to pick up on news before the censors repress it. As a celebrity journalist, she's able to worm her way into a variety of conferences, Imperial bases, and sites that another agent would have difficulty penetrating.

Deena Mipps: Female Human Noble 4/Scout 1; Init +3; Defense 16 (+3 Dex, +3 class); Spd 10 m; VP/WP 20/12; Atk +3 melee (1d3, punch) or –1 melee (2d6, vibroblade)

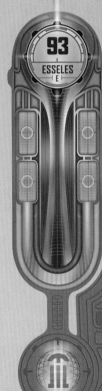

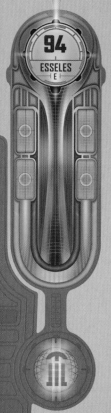

CHIBA DR-10

or +6 ranged (stun DC 15/12, stun grenade) or +6 ranged (3d4, sporting blaster); SQ coordinate +1, favor +2, inspire confidence, bonus class skill (Bluff), resource access; SV Fort +3, Ref +6, Will +5; SZ M; FP 0; DSP 0; Rep +2; Str 10, Dex 16, Con 12, Int 13, Wis 10, Cha 18. Challenge Code C.

Equipment: Sporting blaster, vibroblade, 2 stun grenades, datapads, medpac, comlink, holorecorder, holo-projector, recording rod.

Skills: Appraise +6, Bluff +9, Computer Use +6, Diplomacy +10, Disguise +9, Entertain (storytelling) +7, Hide +6, Intimidate +6, Knowledge (alien species) +6, Knowledge (streetwise) +3, Listen +1, Move Silently +9, Pilot +8, Profession (newsnet reporter) +5, Read/Write Basic, Search +3, Sense Motive +5, Speak Basic, Speak Ryl, Spot +1.

Feats: Persuasive, Starship Operation (space transport), Stealthy, Weapon Group Proficiencies (blaster pistols, blaster rifles, simple weapons).

Luthus Ferlani

Of all the crime bosses on Esseles, Luthus Ferlani is probably the most well traveled, having spent ten years of his youth representing his father's offworld interests in Hutt Space. This slight but intense man of sixty years brought Podracing back with him to Esseles and made it a centerpiece of his empire when he took over the family business in Nurrale. Luthus is a kindly-looking man who projects a fatherly de-meanor, but is truly terrifying when roused to anger.

Luthus Ferlani: Male Human Scoundrel 6/Noble 4/Crime Lord 2; Init +4 (+4 Improved Initiative); Defense 17 (+7 class); Spd 10 m; VP/WP 42/12; Atk +7/+2 melee (1d3–1, punch) or +7/+2 melee (2d6–1, vibroblade) or +8/+3 ranged (3d4, hold-out blaster); SQ bonus class skill (Gather Information), contact (1), coordinate +1, favor +2, illicit barter, inspire confidence, lucky 2/day, precise attack +1, resource access; SV Fort +4, Ref +9, Will +12; SZ M; FP 0; DSP 5; Rep +8; Str 9, Dex 11, Con 12, Int 15, Wis 14, Cha 17. Challenge Code F.

Equipment: Hold-out blaster, vibroblade.

Skills: Appraise +13, Bluff +14, Computer Use +12, Demolitions +11, Diplomacy +16, Entertain (storytelling) +12, Forgery +10, Gather Information +14, Intimidate +15, Knowledge (Esseles) +14, Knowledge (streetwise) +11, Move Silently +6, Pilot +7, Profession (crime lord) +14, Read/Write Basic, Read/Write Huttese, Sense Motive +13, Speak Basic, Speak Huttese, Speak Rodese, Spot +6.

Feats: Frightful Presence, Headstrong, Improved Initiative, Infamy, Quickness, Skill Emphasis (Bluff, Diplomacy), Weapon Group Proficiencies (blaster pistols, simple weapons, vibro weapons).

Chiba DR-10

The Chiba DR-10 is a floating, spherical protocol droid much favored by Imperial diplomats and officials who venture into hostile territory. The Chiba, sometimes referred to as the "Chiba Drio," is a capable protocol droid fully equipped to handle most translation and negotiating tasks. It can also advise its master on matters of Imperial law.

The Chiba is equipped with a pop-out blaster, which can come in handy when negotiations run short. Its sensor package and tracking capabilities make it a fine security droid; a Chiba can easily function as a patrol, guard, or probe droid.

Chibas do have one potential flaw. Because their beha-vorial inhibitors are programmed differently from those of other protocol droids, they tend to become aggressive, impatient, and sarcastic over time.

Chiba DR-10: Hovering protocol droid, Diplomat 1/Scout 2; Init +6 (+2 Dex, +4 Improved Initiative); Defense 12 (+2 Dex); Spd 10 m; VP/WP 6/9; Atk +3 ranged (3d6, blaster pistol); SQ trailblazing; SV Fort +1, Ref +4, Will +5; SZ M; Face/Reach 2 m by 2 m/2 m; Rep +0; Str 8, Dex 14, Con 9, Int 16, Wis 12, Cha 8. Challenge Code B.

Equipment: 360-degree vision, blaster, comlink, heuris-tic processor, improved sensor package, infrared vision, motion sensors, recording unit, repulsorlift unit, telescopic vision, vocabulator.

Skills: Appraise +7, Computer Use +7, Diplomacy +6, Gather Information +6, Knowledge (alien species) +8, Knowledge (bureaucracy) +7, Listen +7, Search +9, Sense Motive +5, Spot +2.

Unspent Skill Points: 0.

Feats: Improved Initiative, Point Blank Shot, Track, Trustworthy, Weapon Group Proficiencies (blaster pistols, simple weapons).

Cost: 12,000 credits.

Fresia

Planet Type: Terrestrial
Climate: Temperate
Terrain: Islands, oceans
Atmosphere: Breathable
Gravity: Standard
Diameter: 10,308 km
Length of Day: 528 standard hours
Length of Year: 132 standard days
Sentient Species: Human
Languages: Basic
Population: 2.3 million
Species Mix: 96% Human, 4% other
Government: Nationalized corporate/Imperial Military
Major Exports: Starship technology, repulsor technology
Major Imports: Various
System/Star: Fre'ji

Planets	Type	Moons
Frellor	Searing rock	1
Fresia	Terrestrial	7
Fretaria	Frigid rock	0
Frenoris	Frigid rock	2

Description

Among the least populated of the habitable Core Worlds, Fresia is a small planet of rocky islands and fractured archipelagoes. An extremely slow axial rotation provides for local days that last for several standard weeks. Several moons make for complex and severe tidal cycles.

Although Fresia has borne no native sentient life, indigenous wildlife is abundant. Perhaps most notable is the Coromon Headhunter, the creature after which the legendary Z-95 Headhunter starfighter was named. Hundreds of aquatic and land creatures abound, but reptiles and amphibians are rare, given the world's cool mean temperature and wildly varied climate. Violent storms are frequent, especially around dawn.

History

Fresia's history is tied directly to that of its primary resident, the Incom Corporation. Smaller than many moons, the rocky world has served for more than a dozen centuries as the base world of Incom, the manufacturer of the T-65 X-wing starfighter and T-16 Skyhopper. Two millennia before the Battle of Yavin, a group of investors purchased the uninhabited world. Fresia quickly grew to

be a system of note, as Incom's reputation for quality starship design gained the attention of prominent guilds and manufacturers from Kuat to Fondor and all points in between.

Incom Industries' first truly successful craft was the Z-95 Headhunter, a joint effort with Subpro (a non-Core corporation). Named for a vicious creature on the Coromon Islands, the starfighter pushed Incom into the forefront of starship manufacturers, and the design team won unparalleled acclaim. As contracts grew and business increased, Incom Industries became Incom Corporation. The firm's products enjoyed even greater success as the corporation grew.

Shortly after Incom completed the first few X-wing starfighter prototypes, the Empire occupied Fresia and "imperialized" Incom by direct order of the Emperor. All non-Navy starfighter production came to a halt. Many members of the X-wing design team, suspected of being sympathizers of the Rebellion, were arrested and hauled off to undisclosed locations by Imperial Security Bureau agents. Within a month, Rebel commandos staged an unbelievably daring operation in which they rescued the senior design team of the X-wing project, aiding their defection to the Alliance. The entire team not only escaped but also took every existing X-wing prototype with them. Rebel operatives seized the remaining plans and destroyed the assembly facilities in their wake. The commando raid was an unparalleled success and a huge blow to the Imperial Navy—the Alliance had seized the superior starfighter. Though the Empire did a respectable job in keeping the defection a secret, the fact remains that the Navy "settled" for the TIE series, a point that still irks some officers and pilots. When Imperial propaganda covered up the Rebel operation, loyal New Order representatives stressed the idea that overwhelming inexperienced Rebels with TIE attacks would quickly crush the Rebellion.

Following the Empire's seizure of Incom, Cloud City executives bought one of Incom's subsidiaries, Bespin Motors. This transaction effectively severed all the corporation's ties to the Imperial Military. Each of the Incom designers and technicians remaining on Fresia was either loyal to the Empire, indifferent, or cautious enough to keep his dissenting opinions to himself. By the time of the New Republic, the designers who defected from the Empire formed the Republic-aligned FreiTek firm and produced new variants of the X-wing, as well as newer fighters such as the E-wing.

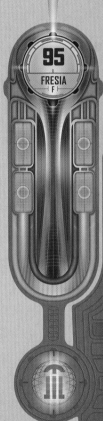

95
FRESIA
F

People

Exceptionally long days and nights affect the mood of Fresia's residents drastically. To counter those effects, all Incom facilities are "diatrolled," in that the facilities undergo morning, mid-day, evening, and dark cycles every standard day. Areas away from the main facilities, such as where the laborers are housed, do not benefit from diatrolled systems.

Throughout the Rebellion era, an Imperial presence makes this harsh world even more intolerable. Given Fresia's high concentration of aquatic environs, the Empire maintains a platoon of aquatic stormtroopers on the world to complement the standard stormtroopers and Army troopers. The constant presence of Imperial troopers at a corporation creates a "siege mentality" that affects the morale and motivation of Incom's designers and workers. By the time the Rebellion turned its attention to Incom, many key designers were already eager to betray their Imperial overlords.

Locations

Some of Fresia's key locations demonstrate the influence of Incom and the Empire on this dangerous world.

Coromon Islands

A roughly crescent-shaped chain of islands runs diagonally across the cold northern latitudes west of the ViGureni continent. The Coromon Islands are the most densely settled and developed landmasses on Fresia. Incom structures and manufacturing plants cover most of the land above the highest tide lines. Several of the tidal areas have been fitted for various amphibious or submersible projects, such as the pending AH-77 Twen-chok combat submersible. The original X-wing plants, long since refitted for the current Howlrunner development, are on the island known as Prime Coromon, while much of the administrative duties are handled on Northwest Coromon.

Barracks for the Human staffers and all designers (99 percent of whom are Human) are on Coromon Besh, a landscaped isle a short distance from most of the main manufacturing plant islands. The laborers (mostly enslaved Wookiees, Yuzzem, and B'trillans) are housed on the rugged Lower Coromon Chain, a series of windblown crags a good hour's transport from the manufacturing plants. The Lower Coromon Chain is situated in a particularly nasty stretch of gazarant feeding grounds, which helps prevent escape attempts by the workers. Colonel Garr, the Imperial officer in charge of the "reorganized" Incom, has mandated that Mon Calamari should not be used as workers in the Fresia manufacturing plants. Despite their technical aptitude, their aquatic origins would give them an undue advantage during any insurrection.

Cerise Fog Debris Field

The Cerise Fog Project, Incom's largest onplanet testing mishap, was a failed experiment conducted on Fresia by Incom's Bespin Motors subsidiary. Publicly, Incom representatives have claimed that the experiment involved a failed prototype for the design of components for Cloud City and similar mining operations. The remaining wreckage supports this claim, consisting primarily of mangled and twisted repulsor units, Tibanna gas-seals, and other material consistent with the development of Bespin's famed city among the clouds.

Yet some rumors suggest that Cerise Fog was a military project, one conducted by Incom during the Clone Wars. Allegedly, experimental vehicles used at the facility were designed specifically to counter crafts developed by MandalMotors, including speeders that had been pitted against Jedi and Republic forces. The significant amount of debris that Incom recovery teams removed from the site bears this theory out. Under the watchful eye of the Empire, such rumors will probably never be proven one way or another.

The wreckage is scattered along roughly 30 kilometers of the Buichol Isthmus, a razor-narrow strip of high crags that connects the Greater and Lesser Piq Islands. Due to Fresia's nasty tidal variations and pounding surf, most wreckage from the incident that landed in the cold seas was not retrieved. It was quickly dashed against the rocks and pulverized in the unrelenting surf—at least, according to Incom's official statements at the time.

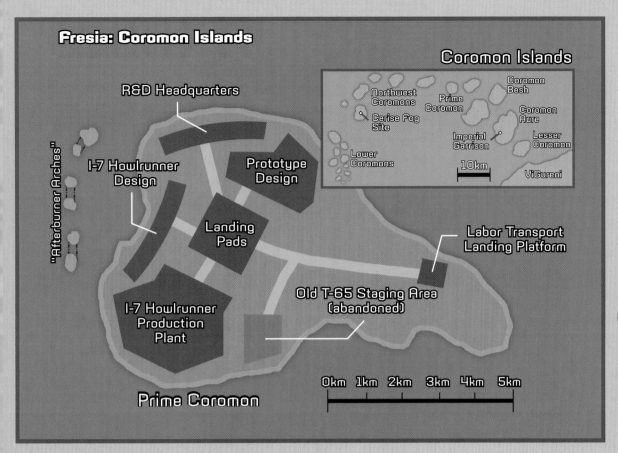

Fresia: Coromon Islands

- R&D Headquarters
- "Afterburner Arches"
- I-7 Howlrunner Design
- Prototype Design
- Landing Pads
- I-7 Howlrunner Production Plant
- Old T-65 Staging Area (abandoned)
- Labor Transport Landing Platform

Prime Coromon

Okm 1km 2km 3km 4km 5km

Coromon Islands

- Northwest Coromons
- Cerise Fog Site
- Prime Coromon
- Coromon Besh
- Coromon Aure
- Imperial Garrison
- Lesser Coromon
- Lower Coromons
- ViGureni

10km

Incom I-7 Howlrunner

Named for the fierce predator of the harsh desert-world Kamar, the Howlrunner was the first and perhaps best starfighter Incom produced after the company's "reorganization" by the Empire. A capable craft designed for use in both atmosphere and vacuum, the Howlrunner has a design that makes it ideal for wide distribution, since it was intended to patrol a multitude of different environments for the remaining Imperial forces.

The Howlrunner shares a few traits with its predecessors, the Z-95 and T-65, mostly are in its flight systems and weapons design. Aside from those small similarities, the I-7 is a marked change for Incom (likely a result of the Imperial management). While the trademark nose that the "old" Incom designers favored is easy to identify on the FreiTek E-wing that was developed for the New Republic, the Howlrunner is a sweep-wing fighter, more akin to a *Lambda*-class shuttle than to any previous Incom design.

One of the difficulties Incom faces in distributing the Howlrunner is Incom's legacy as the creator of the X-wing, easily the most recognizable of Rebel ships. While Incom is working tirelessly to erase its association with the Rebellion, it knows it is still hard-pressed to win over Imperial pilots and officers, especially since the TIE series has dominated the Navy fleets for so long. Howlrunners saw some use in the outlying regions of the Empire shortly after Thrawn's campaigns, but they were not pressed into heavy use until the reborn Emperor's strikes against Coruscant.

Incom Corporation I-7 Howlrunner

Class: Starfighter	**Crew:** 1 (Normal +2)
Size: Tiny (11.4 m long)	**Initiative:** +4 (+2 size, +2 crew)
Hyperdrive: None	**Maneuver:** +7 (+2 size, +2 crew, +3 engine quality)
Passengers: 0	**Defense:** 22 (+2 size, +10 armor)
Cargo Capacity: 80 kg	**Shield Points:** 40
Consumables: 2 days	**Hull Points:** 120 (DR 10)
Cost: 165,000	

Maximum Speed in Space: Ramming (10 squares/action)
Atmospheric Speed: 1,200 km/h (20 squares/action)

Weapon: Heavy laser cannons (2 fire-linked); **Fire Arc:** Front; **Attack Bonus:** +13 (+2 size, +2 crew, +6 fire control, +3 equipment); **Damage:** 6d10×2; **Range Modifiers:** PB +0, S –2, M –4, L –6.

For the GM

The adventure hooks and supporting characters described in this section are meant for GMs only. If you're a player, stop reading now.

Adventures

Feel free to use or adapt the following adventure hooks for your home campaign.

The X-Drone Dump

The X-Drone is a project so secret that even the Bothans haven't heard rumors about it—until recently. During the Incom defection, a Bothan tech specialist bought a salvaged astromech unit. Buried deep within its projector memory were the initial schematics from the Cerise Fog project. Fields of fog were created to test a droid-piloted Z-95 Headhunter fighter with capabilities and firepower beyond that of the traditional Headhunter. Alliance leaders scoff at the idea of deploying a capable craft without a pilot, but they also remember the effectiveness of waves of droid starfighters at the Battle of Naboo. Is it possible the Empire might change its tactics? The characters are hired (or assigned) to search the pounding waves of the debris field for further data.

Toe to Toe

The characters get word that a group of commandos is planning to raid the Incom facilities on Fresia. In what may prove to be a retread of the Rebel actions that garnered the X-wing, the commandos intend to "rescue" the senior design team of the Howlrunner project. There's a problem, however: The commandos in question are corporate spies, not Rebel rescuers. The characters are sent as a counterespionage team to foil the pending kidnapping and capture (or rescue) the Howlrunner designers before their adversaries can get to them. Depending on the characters' allegiances, their employers can be Rebel strategists, rogue investors, or even Incom and the Empire itself. Regardless of whether Riun Riev (see below) or the other Howlrunner designers are rescued, the Howlrunner project will continue nearly unhindered, thanks to the Empire's incredibly redundant bureaucracy and staffing. However, the designers could become useful allies of the Rebellion if they are rescued.

Allies and Antagonists

The following supporting characters are designed for use in your campaign.

Colonel Faltun Garr

Installed to oversee the "new" incarnation of Incom, Colonel Garr is a competent, if not overly charismatic, career officer. Garr was in his mid-sixties during the Galactic Civil War. He was a pure soldier until the last decade, when he rose steadily through the ranks stationed at Kuat Drive Yards and various Sienar plants. Some view his transfer to the bleak outcroppings of Fresia as a demotion, but Garr is eager to accept the position and enthusiastic about leading the development of a new, superior starfighter for the Emperor's glory.

Colonel Faltun Garr: Male Human Soldier 14; Init +1; Defense 22 (+1 Dex, +9 class, +2 Defensive Martial Arts); Spd 10 m; VP/WP 77/12; Atk +16/+11/+6 melee (1d4+2, punch) or +15/+10/+5 ranged (3d6, blaster pistol); SV Fort +10, Ref +5, Will +8; SZ M; FP 1; DSP 2; Rep +4; Str 14, Dex 13, Con 12, Int 16, Wis 15, Cha 10. Challenge Code F.

Equipment: Blaster pistol, code cylinder.

Skills: Astrogate +7, Bluff +2, Computer Use +9, Diplomacy +8, Gather Information +8, Intimidate +14, Knowledge (business) +15, Knowledge (tactics) +17, Listen +7, Pilot +8, Read/Write Basic, Read/Write Huttese,

Search +10, Sense Motive +8, Speak Basic, Speak Huttese, Speak Shyriiwook (understand only), Spot +6, Treat Injury +7.

Feats: Armor Proficiencies (heavy, light, medium), Combat Reflexes, Defensive Martial Arts, Dodge, Heroic Surge, Iron Will, Martial Arts, Persuasive, Point Blank Shot, Power Attack, Precise Shot, Quick Draw, Weapon Group Proficiencies (blaster pistols, blaster rifles, heavy weapons, simple weapons, vibro weapons).

Riun Riev

This pudgy Sullustan engineer currently works on Incom's Howlrunner project. Designer Riev is one of the few non-Humans who were allowed to stay with Incom after the Empire took control of the company. Riev has been assigned the unenviable and daunting task of "rekindling the integrity and security of the Incom brand"—or, in other words, "erasing the Rebel image." Why such an assignment was dumped on him and not given to some public relations firm is not for him to question. He works feverishly to perfect starfighters that can absorb even greater punishment than Incom's earlier X-wing. His recent decision against equipping Howlrunners with hyperdrives, though unpopular in some circles, has thus far met with Navy approval.

Riun Riev is no Imperial lackey—he works out of fear for his life. He knows failure in his current task could result in a short but exceptionally unpleasant stay on Kessel, Akrit'tar, or some other equally inhospitable place. Riev's office overlooks the Afterburner Arches just offshore from his office, and he can often be seen staring out into the tumultuous seas. Some Incom staffers suspect that Riev is a bit of a daydreamer. Others theorize that he finds inspiration for his genius in the intricate coral arches of his workspace. None realize that he secretly watches and hopes for a team of daring Rebel commandos to rise from beyond the Arches to whisk him and his Howlrunner project away from Fresia and Colonel Garr, just as they did with the X-wing team so long ago.

Riun Riev: Male Sullustan Expert 12; Init +1; Defense 15 (+1 Dex, +4 class); Spd 10 m; VP/WP 44/10; Atk +9/+4 melee (1d3, punch) or +10/+5 ranged (3d8/19–20, blaster carbine); SQ darkvision 20 m; SV Fort +4, Ref +5, Will +8; SZ M; FP 0; DSP 0; Rep +6; Str 11, Dex 13, Con 10, Int 16, Wis 10, Cha 9. Challenge Code D.

Equipment: Diagnostic computer, R5 astromech droid, datapad, tools, blaster carbine.

Skills: Astrogate +12, Climb +2, Computer Use +20, Craft (repulsorlift engines) +18, Craft (starfighters) +21, Craft (starship weapons) +21, Gather Information +8, Knowledge (business) +10, Listen +2, Profession (engineer) +15, Read/Write Basic, Read/Write Binary, Read/Write Sullustese, Repair +23, Speak Basic, Speak Durese, Speak Sullustese, Spot +3, Survival +8, Treat Injury +3.

Feats: Fame, Gearhead, Skill Emphasis (Craft [starfighters], Craft [starship weapons], Repair), Weapon Group Proficiencies (blaster pistols, blaster rifles).

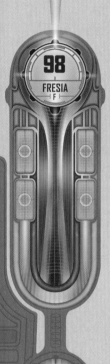

Scay Danson

One of the premier industrial saboteurs and commandos, Scay Danson is a heartless being whose only loyalties are to the highest bidder—and, even then, only for the duration of the job. Scay has been known to steal a prototype from a firm for one sum, and then accept the contract to retake those same files for a higher price. It is a life he loves, and one that has made him quite wealthy. Born to a respected Corulag family, Danson has the social status necessary to reach the higher echelons of various corporate firms. Though he takes work in nearly every field, from weapon plants to droid manufacturers and even fashion, his preferred tasks typically involve the prominent industry leaders personified by Sienar Fleet Systems, Industrial Automaton, and BlasTech.

None of his current employers are aware that Scay worked for years as an informant for Imperial Security Bureau agents in the Kuat system. During that tenure, he was able to acquire copies of files so highly classified that many of the Naval officers who contract him now have never been authorized to view their contents. He makes great use of the information he has garnered. Losing those files would cripple the ease with which he seems to gain access to supposedly secure installations.

Scay Danson cuts a dashing, confident image, one augmented by his considerable training in both combat and technical skills. He stands an even 2 meters tall and has piercing green eyes and perfect posture. He's a typical corporate officer and an ideal insertion agent.

COROMON HEADHUNTER

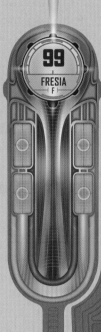

Scay Danson: Male Human Scoundrel 8; Init +7 (+3 Dex, +4 Improved Initiative); Defense 18 (+3 Dex, +5 class); Spd 10 m; VP/WP 28/10; Atk +6/+1 melee (1d3, punch) or +6/+1 melee (2d4, vibrodagger) or +9/+4 ranged (3d6/stun DC 15, ion pistol); SQ illicit barter, lucky 2/day, precise attack +1; SV Fort +2, Ref +9, Will +2; SZ M; FP 1; DSP 0; Rep +0; Str 10, Dex 17, Con 10, Int 13, Wis 11, Cha 17. Challenge Code D.

Equipment: Various disguises, vibrodagger, ion pistol, false IDs, security codes.

Skills: Bluff +8, Diplomacy +5, Disguise +10, Escape Artist +10, Forgery +5, Gather Information +11, Hide +13, Intimidate +8, Knowledge (business) +8, Listen +7, Move Silently +14, Pilot +8, Read/Write Basic, Search +7, Sense Motive +4, Speak Basic, Speak Bothese, Spot +7, Treat Injury +5.

Feats: Combat Reflexes, Improved Initiative, Low Profile, Skill Emphasis (Hide, Move Silently), Weapon Group Proficiencies (blaster pistols, simple weapons, vibro weapons).

New Creature: Coromon Headhunter

A tough and compactly built predator that prowls the main landmasses of the Coromon Islands, the Coromon headhunter is an agile rock-hopper. The creature hunts along the pounding surf and throughout the low scrub and timber of the islands' higher terrain. Its rather grue-some name is derived from its most common method of killing its prey. The headhunter uses razor-sharp double dew claws on its forelegs that are capable of decapitating most targets. The creature's fearsome notoriety is height-ened by its habit of eating every part of its kill—bones, fur, and all—except for the skull, which the headhunter stores in its den. Any hapless being who inadvertently encounters a (hopefully) abandoned headhunter lair is invariably stopped in his tracks by the sight of hundreds of skulls piled along the walls.

Coromon Headhunter: Predator 12; Init +8 (+4 Dex, +4 Improved Initiative); Defense 20 (+4 Dex, +6 natural); Spd 16 m; VP/WP 100/18; Atk +16/+11/+6 melee (1d6+4, foreclaw) or +16/+11/+6 melee (2d6+4, double dew claw) or +16/+11/+6 melee (1d8+4, bite) or +16/+11/+6 ranged; SV Fort +12, Ref +12, Will +5; SZ M; Face/Reach 2 m by 2 m/2 m; Str 18, Dex 19, Con 18, Int 4, Wis 12, Cha 10. Challenge Code D.

Skills: Hide +16, Jump +14, Move Silently +16, Spot +3.

Feats: Dodge, Improved Initiative, Mobility, Power Attack, Spring Attack.

Galantos

Planet Type: Terrestrial
Climate: Temperate
Terrain: Gelatinous pools
Atmosphere: Breathable
Gravity: Light (85% standard)
Diameter: 10,840 km
Length of Day: 31 standard hours
Length of Year: 299 standard days
Sentient Species: Fia
Languages: Fian
Population: 500,000
Species Mix: 91% Fia, 7% Human, 2% other
Government: Democracy
Major Exports: None
Major Imports: Chromite
System/Star: Utos

Planets	Type	Moons
Pomagra	Searing rock	0
Galantos	Terrestrial	0
Ducocon	Terrestrial	0
Sweep	Asteroid belt	—
Yetoros	Gas giant	8
Horticar	Gas giant	11
Camos	Gas giant	31
Nalzin	Captured comet	0

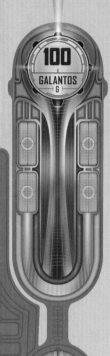

100
GALANTOS
G

Description

Thousands of viscous, organic lakes undulate in the pits of Galantos's rocky crust, glistening like puddles in a road after a fresh rainstorm. Each sinkhole filled with living, greenish gelatin acts as a biological catalyst for a world with no topsoil. All indigenous flora and fauna, including the native Fia, live in the gelatin seas, some of which are hundreds of kilometers in diameter. Meteor impacts occasionally blast out new craters, which are then filled with new gel oozing up from the strata below.

As Core worlds go, Galantos is a relative newcomer. Four thousand years ago, a map of the Core resembled a fat ring with a section missing—one that represented the murky swirls of the Unknown Regions. Sufficient sectors have since been cataloged to create an unbroken ring of Core Worlds hugging the blazing bulge of the Deep Core. However, even the most introspective and isolated mapmaker would be a fool to think of Galantos and other recently discovered planets as the peers of Coruscant and Corellia. Core Worlds only by virtue of geography, any true scholar knows they are as far removed from the sophistication of Core culture as the Denarii Nova is from the Black Hole of Quintas.

Travelers who frequent the Widek Bypass hyperlane while looping around the Koornacht Cluster from Orooturoo to Widek stop at such obscure Farlax sector planets as Wehttam, Thobek, and Galantos. The gelatinous geography of Galantos is unique among its planetary neighbors—some say without parallel in the whole of the explored galaxy.

History

Life on Galantos evolved on the rubbery skin of one of the green seas. The primitive ancestors of toli trees casually released their seed pods into the winds. This primordial pollen spread to nearly every gel-pool on the planet. Isolated by kilometers of lifeless rock, curious pockets of biodiversity sprang up in different ecosystems, distinguished by such factors as sunlight, temperature, acidity, and viscosity. Evolving animals learned to traverse the rubbery wasteland to reach new habitats and hunting grounds.

The bipedal Fia became the masters of Galantos, constructing crude communities atop the gel and twisting the resources of their world to their own purposes. In time, offworlders brought them galactic technology, and the Fia traveled to the stars. After opening trade with neighboring Wehttam, they welcomed the few Republic merchants who made the hard journey to the Farlax sector. The adventurers made soft landings in the thick gelatin of Galantos.

After Palpatine's rise to power, the Farlax sector came under Imperial rule. Star Destroyers bypassed enigmatic Galantos in favor of the stardocks located in the Koornacht Cluster. The Fia opened new lines of trade, including the importing of chromite from New Brigia, but a massive Imperial withdrawal from the region eight months after the Battle of Endor left the sector economically adrift. The Fia withdrew as well, casting suspicious and fearful eyes toward offworlders.

The rise of the Yevetha twelve years later confirmed the Fia's quivering anxieties. Within the Koornacht Cluster—a blazing array of stars the Fia had always called the Multitude—the Yevetha wiped out dozens of "foreign" settlements in a massacre known as the Great Purge. The Fia learned of the killings when a survivor from Polneye, Plat Mallar, attempted to reach their world. When faced with the possibility that they could be next, they panicked.

Jobath Knox, ranking councilor of the Fia, journeyed to Coruscant to petition Chief of State Leia Organa Solo for help. She ratified Galantos's emergency petition for membership in the New Republic and sent the warships *Gol Storm* and *Thackery* to patrol the space around

SKREE SKATER

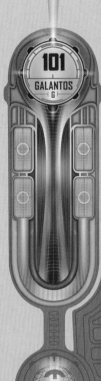

and-stone houses surrounded by rings of thorny arbu trees, which protect the inhabitants from skree-skaters and other predators. The largest cities, such as Gal'fian'deprisi, are modern constructions that incorporate ferrocrete and transparisteel. All Fian structures are engineered to move in concert with the rolling surface beneath them and can withstand all but the most violent "gelquakes." The Fia get much of their building material from mines in the outlying wastelands.

Fian culture is organized around seventeen Gods of Age, from Hus'yoyu (birth to age six) to Erio'anum (age ninety-seven to death). As a Fia ages, he or she worships a new god each time a life stage has expired. Often this change in worship results in significant behavioral changes. A Fia who was shy and studious may turn gregarious or seductive upon reaching a milestone birthday.

Locations

Descriptions of several important locations follow.

Gal'fian'deprisi

The largest city on Galantos is Gal'fian'deprisi, a community of barely a hundred thousand individuals. Half-sunk into the gelatin of the Gar'glum Sea, it resembles a giant clam crowned with needle-sharp steeples. Buried repulsorlift buoys help support its considerable bulk. Gal'fian'deprisi has no landing pads for starships, so all visitors must touch down in the rocky Chirk'pn Wastes—where limited starport facilities are available—and pay for

Jobath's world. Thankfully for the Fia, the Yevetha suffered a stunning defeat under the guns of the New Republic fleet before they could ever set foot on Galantos.

Now many Fia hope the same will hold true for the Yuuzhan Vong. So far, the Yuuzhan Vong have shown no interest in conquering territory as inaccessible as the Farlax sector. Many former residents of Coruscant, noticing the same geographical inconvenience, have fled to Galantos after the fall of their homeworld. This has led to a severe culture clash—and a strain on the surface of Galantos's delicate gelatin pools.

People

The Fia have evolved to move about on the glutinous, oscillating surface of their organic pools. They are a squat, bottom-heavy species with paddle-shaped feet. Fia have a keen sense of balance, and the species has evolved a vital immunity to motion sickness. Fia do not feel comfortable on solid ground; they associate a rigid, motionless surface, particularly the dead wastelands outside their gelatin seas, with death itself.

The habitable areas of Galantos are few, even for the Fia. The Fian population has remained sparse, so as not to overtax their environment. Half a million Fia live on the planet, with perhaps ten thousand found elsewhere in the Farlax sector. Almost no Fia live in the greater galaxy outside the Core.

Fia are generally friendly among their own kind. A Fian hermit would be a shocking sight to his fellows. For this reason, the number of communities on the planet is low, and many gelatin seas are uninhabited. The smallest villages are clusters of fiber-

Chirk'pn Wastes

Gar'glum Sea

Landing Pads

Black Hammer Pirate Base

Gal'fian'deprisi

Net'lseb Toli Park

Landing Pads

1km

Galantos: Gar'glum Sea

passage aboard a Vert'bo airship. Those who hike across the gel are welcome to do so, but the Fia take no responsibility for death by animal attack, exposure, or submersion.

Net'lseb Toli Park

Net'lseb Toli Park lies directly on the surface of the Gar'glum Sea, located in the vibrant landscape surrounding Gal'fian'deprisi. This kilometer-wide garden of toli trees, fragrant blossoms, and fragile wildlife is secured within an energy perimeter. Net'lseb Toli has its own security force to shoot any skree-skaters who glide too close to its borders. Such security measures have made the park one of the primary tourist attractions for Fia visiting from other parts of Galantos.

Black Hammer Pirate Base

The headquarters of the Black Hammer pirates sits in the Chirk'pn Wastes at the edge of the Gar'glum Sea. Similar settlements have a long history on Galantos. Many offworld traders operate depots on the flat rock beds at the edges of the gel pools. After raiding convoys bound for Gal'fian'deprisi, pirates bring their spoils to the Black Hammer base, a rusty assortment of supply silos and laser batteries. The Fia, never a warlike people, are now split between their distaste for fighting and the need to protect traffic in the system.

Vert'bo Airship

Most nonsentient lifeforms on Galantos get about either by skating across the smooth surface of the gel or taking to the sky, where they can catch jet streams. The Vert'bo airship does both. For short trips or simple taxiing maneuvers, it slides on four long runners, steered by twin aft propellers. For longer journeys, lighter-than-air gases are metabolized in its organic engine and fed into lift balloons, which can carry the ship to an altitude of 5 kilometers. The Vert'bo airship is a traditional Fian craft, incorporating no repulsorlift technology. The vessels are rarely armed, but recent raids by the Black Hammer pirates have convinced some Fia to equip their airships with mounted blaster cannons.

Vert'bo Airship

Class: Air/Ground	Crew: 2 (Expert +8)
Size: Colossal (22 m long)	Initiative: +0 (–8 size, +8 crew)
Passengers: 40	Maneuver: +0 (–8 size, +8 crew)
Cargo Capacity: 1 ton	Defense: 7 (–8 size, +5 armor)
Cost: 50,000 (new), 28,000 (used)	Shield Points: 0
	Hull Points: 80 (DR 5)
Availability: Prevalent	Speed: 10 m (ground)
Era: All	Atmospheric Speed: 60 km/h (1 square/action
	Altitude: 5 km

* *This vehicle provides full cover to its pilot and passengers.*

Weapon (optional): Deck-mounted blaster cannon; Fire Arc: Turret; Attack Bonus: +4 (–8 size, +8 crew, +4 fire control); Damage: 5d8; Range Increment: 300 m.

Weapon: Two swivel laser cannons; Fire Arc: Turret; Attack Bonus: +7 (–1 size, +4 crew, +4 fire control); Damage: 5d8; Range Increment: 200 m.

For the GM

The adventure hooks and supporting characters described in this section are meant for GMs only. If you're a player, stop reading now.

Adventures

The bizarre gelatin-enriched environment of Galantos serves as a catalyst for adventure. Three examples are showcased below.

Gelquake!

The heroes arrive at Galantos's capital of Gal'fian'deprisi to make a delivery. (In The New Jedi Order era, they might be bringing supplies to refugees fleeing the Yuuzhan Vong.) Shortly after they touch down, the Gar'glum Sea is rocked by a meteor strike more severe than any in centuries. Toli trees are uprooted, and Gal'fian'deprisi is fissured like a cracked egg. Exotic creatures wriggle out of the effluvia, engulfing victims in their path. As the entire gelatinous expanse heaves with violent shock waves, can the heroes save the victims of this natural disaster? Will they even be able to ensure their own survival?

Hammer into Anvil

The time has come to rid Galantos of the dreaded Black Hammer pirates. Councilor Jobath enlists the characters in this crusade. A victory could ensure the future gratitude of this powerful local ally. The Black Hammers' base in the Chirk'pn Wastes receives regular supply shipments from cowed merchants in Gal'fian'deprisi. A local airship operator, Brabe, may approach the heroes and offer his vessel to their cause, or he may simply follow them and make himself a nuisance. Either way, the heroes need all the help they can get. The leader of the pirates, Stima Ardella, commands a Corellian corvette, a dozen armed swoops, and a quartet of old Naboo starfighters.

Restoration

While Gal'fian'deprisi is being repaired from a recent gelquake, tens of thousands of Fia are relocated to a small, uninhabited gelatin pool 200 kilometers distant. The heroes are asked to help transport operations by carrying survivors aboard their own ship. For the hard-hearted, money can be a great motivator. As it happens, Councilor Jobath's selection of this pool as a safe haven was a spectacularly poor one. Deep in the virgin toli forest, a ravenous pack of skree-skaters lurks. If given free rein, they will kill the entire Fia encampment—far more food than they could ever eat. The heroes must gear up for the hunt and dig in.

Allies and Antagonists

The following supporting characters are designed for use in your campaign.

Jobath Knox

Jobath, chief councilor of the Fia, is the elected head of the people of Galantos. He has a security background with the Net'lseb force and knows how to handle a blaster, counting a skree-skater kill among his past triumphs. Upon ascending to the age of forty, he assigned his allegiance to the God of Age known as Gotagei. A reverent initiate, he assumed a more settled, grounded life that led him into politics. Jobath is an honest, pragmatic Fia, but he will go to extreme ends to meet the needs of his constituents.

Jobath Knox: Male Fia Soldier 1/Noble 4; Init +0; Defense 14 (+4 class); Spd 8 m; VP/WP 37/12; Atk +3 melee (1d3–1, punch) or +4 ranged; SQ bonus class skill (Treat Injury), coordinate +1, favor +2, inspire confidence, resource access, surefooted; SV Fort +4, Ref +2, Will +5; SZ M; FP 4; DSP 0; Rep +2; Str 8, Dex 10, Con 12, Int 14, Wis 13, Cha 14. Challenge Code C.

    Equipment: Comlink, datapad, holorecorder.

    Skills: Appraise +4, Balance +6, Computer Use +5, Diplomacy +10, Gather Information +4, Knowledge (Galantos) +10, Knowledge (politics) +9, Knowledge (spacer lore) +10, Profession (councilor) +9, Read/Write Basic, Read/Write Fian, Repair +4, Ride +2, Sense Motive +8, Speak Basic, Speak Fian, Speak Ryl, Treat Injury +4.

    Feats: Animal Affinity, Armor Proficiency (light), Trustworthy, Weapon Group Proficiencies (blaster pistols, blaster rifles, heavy weapons, simple weapons, vibro weapons).

Brabe

A Vert'bo airship operator from Gal'fian'deprisi, Brabe is one of the few Fia who isn't willing to knuckle under to Stima Ardella and her cutthroats. Though the Black Hammer gang has not menaced him directly, he believes the pirates are driving away the visitors he needs to make a living. He has armed his airship with blaster cannons and is looking for someone to help him kick the pirates off his planet. There's a limit to the risks he'll take, however. Brabe is a family man who peppers every conversation with irrelevant anecdotes about his eight children.

Brabe: Male Fia Fringer 4; Init +0; Defense 14 (+4 class); Spd 8 m; VP/WP 28/14; Atk +4 melee (1d3+1, punch) or +3 ranged (3d6, blaster pistol); SQ barter, bonus class skill (Balance, Tumble), jury-rig +2, surefooted; SV Fort +6, Ref +2, Will +2; SZ M; FP 0; DSP 0; Rep +0; Str 12, Dex 11, Con 14, Int 10, Wis 12, Cha 10. Challenge Code C.

    Equipment: Blaster pistol, Vert'bo airship (*Skreeee*).

    Skills: Balance +6, Bluff +3, Climb +3, Diplomacy +2, Gather Information +2, Handle Animal +3, Jump +5, Knowledge (Galantos) +7, Listen +4, Pilot +6, Profession (airship operator) +7, Read/Write Basic, Read/Write Fian, Speak Basic, Speak Fian, Spot +3, Survival +4.

    Feats: Acrobatic, Trustworthy, Weapon Group Proficiencies (blaster pistols, primitive weapons, simple weapons).

BRABE   VR

Stima Ardella

Head of the Black Hammer pirate band, Stima Ardella is a vicious Trandoshan. She wanders the sector exacting her rage on all who invite her displeasure. She has set up shop in the Chirk'pn Wastes. Her crew has raided traffic along the Widek Bypass and brought Galantos's imports and exports to a screeching halt. Stima can be found at her base in the Wastes or aboard her flagship *Smokeswimmer*. She is a dead shot with her twin disruptor pistols.

Stima Ardella: Female Trandoshan Scoundrel 14; Init +6 (+2 Dex, +4 Improved Initiative); Defense 21 (+2 Dex, +8 class, +1 natural); Spd 10 m; VP/WP 55/11; Atk +12/+7 melee (1d3+2, punch) or +12/+7 melee (2d6+2, vibro-blade) or +12/+7 ranged (3d8+6, custom disruptor pistol); SQ darkvision 20 m, illicit barter, lucky 3/day, precise attack +3; SV Fort +4, Ref +11, Will +4; SZ M; FP 2; DSP 8; Rep +3; Str 14, Dex 15, Con 11, Int 10, Wis 10, Cha 13. Challenge Code F.

    Equipment: Twin disruptor pistols, vibroblade, tooth filing kit, Corellian corvette (*Smokeswimmer*).

    Skills: Astrogate +10, Bluff +9, Computer Use +5, Demolitions +6, Disable Device +5, Disguise +4, Escape Artist +4, Gather Information +9, Hide +10, Intimidate +6, Knowledge (Galantos) +10, Knowledge (spacer lore) +12, Listen +8, Move Silently +7, Pilot +15, Read/Write Basic, Read/Write Dosh, Repair +8, Search +5, Sense Motive +1, Sleight of Hand +4, Speak Basic, Speak Dosh, Spot +8, Tumble +7.

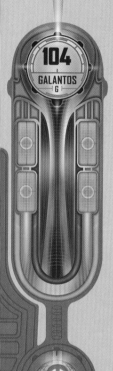

Feats: Exotic Weapon Proficiency (disruptor pistol), Heroic Surge, Improved Initiative, Point Blank Shot, Power Attack, Precise Shot, Skill Emphasis (Bluff, Gather Information, Pilot), Weapon Group Proficiencies (blaster pistols, simple weapons, vibro weapons).

New Species: Fia

Fia are a rare sight in the galaxy. Quick to run and slow to anger, they are friendly among their own kind but wary of outsiders. This squat, compact species enjoys a greater resistance to injury and disease than most. Fia encountered away from Galantos are more outgoing, but they long for the strange beauty of their rolling, gelatinous homepools.

Fia Commoner: Init +0; Defense 10; Spd 8 m; VP/WP 0/12; Atk –1 melee (1d3–1, punch) or +0 ranged; SQ surefooted; SV Fort +1, Ref +0, Will +1; SZ M; FP 0; DSP 0; Rep +0; Str 8, Dex 10, Con 12, Int 10, Wis 12, Cha 10. Challenge Code A.

  Equipment: Variety of personal belongings.

  Skills: Balance +6, Craft (any one) +2 or Knowledge (any one) +2, Profession (any one) +3, Read/Write Basic, Read/Write Fian, Speak Basic, Speak Fian.

  Feats: None.

  Special Qualities: *Surefooted*—Fia have a low center of gravity and are used to moving environments. They gain a +6 species bonus on Balance checks and are immune to motion sickness.

  Species Traits: –2 Str, +2 Con, +2 Wis.

  Automatic Languages: Basic, Fian.

New Creature: Skree-skater

The skree-skater is the dominant carnivore on Galantos. It glides across the surface of gelatin pools on runnerlike feet, chasing down terrified creatures and skewering them on the tip of its razor-edged beak. Skree-skaters are solitary hunters who rely on stealth to track their prey. Most have colored, quivering camouflage to help them hide in the pockets they burrow into gelatinous terrain. When the time is right, they explode from these submerged pockets to ambush unwary prey. The creatures get the first part of their name from their shrieking battle cry, which causes the gel around them to quiver momentarily.

Skree-skater: Gelatin Predator 10; Init +8 (+4 Dex, +4 Improved Initiative); Defense 24 (+4 Dex, +10 natural); Spd 10 m, burrow 4 m (through gelatin only); VP/WP 68/20; Atk +12/+7 melee (1d8+2, piercing beak) or +14/+9 ranged; SQ gelatin, low-light vision, scent; SV Fort +10, Ref +11, Will +4; SZ M; Face/Reach 2 m by 2 m/2 m; Rep +0; Str 15, Dex 19, Con 17, Int 5, Wis 12, Cha 7. Challenge Code C.

  Skills: Hide +14, Jump +6, Listen +12, Spot +6, Survival +5.

  Feats: Improved Initiative, Skill Emphasis (Survival), Toughness, Track.

  Special Qualities: *Gelatin*—Skree-skaters gain a +10 species bonus on Hide and Move Silently checks when moving on gelatinous terrain, along with the ability to burrow through the gel.

Kuat

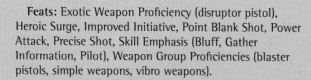

Planet Type: Terrestrial
Climate: Temperate
Terrain: Plains, forests
Atmosphere: Breathable
Gravity: Standard
Diameter: 10,000 km
Length of Day: 20 standard hours
Length of Year: 322 standard days
Sentient Species: Human
Languages: Basic, Kuat
Population: 3.6 billion
Species Mix: 80% Human, 20% other
Government: Aristocracy
Major Exports: Luxury goods, alcohol, art, food
Major Imports: Electronics, machinery, raw materials
System/Star: Kuat/Kuat

Planets	Type	Moons
Ristel	Searing rock	0
Goravas	Volcanic rock	1
Daver Kuat	Terrestrial	2
Kuat	Terrestrial	2
Gortis	Barren rock	3
Rasapan	Gas giant	22

Description

One would be hard pressed to find a more dramatic contrast of high-tech industry and natural beauty than the world of Kuat. Home of the massive Kuat Drive Yards, this small, green, terraformed planet has played—and continues to play—a significant role in galactic shipbuilding. The most prominent planetary feature is the colossal Kuat Drive Yards (also known as KDY). This series of shipyards and construction facilities encircles the planet like a large metal ring and employs billions of beings.

  Kuat is a designed world, terraformed by experts back in the days of the Old Republic. It has three continents and a scattering of islands. The climate is temperate, with a cool, wet winter and a warm, dry summer. Most of the planet is made up of carefully groomed gardens, lush forests, and rolling green plains. Hostile animals simply don't exist on Kuat. Terraformers stocked the rebuilt world with inoffensive herbivores, such as the drebin. Fortunately, the species chosen have short life spans (and many of them are lost to predators), so the planet hasn't been overrun with furry, plant-eating creatures.

  Kuat's two moons are named Bador and Ronay. Though not terraformed, they contain weapons and drive-testing facilities. Security is as tight on the moons as it is in the Yards.

History

Human aristocrats settled Kuat more than twenty-five thousand years before the Battle of Yavin. Ten wealthy merchant families banded together, determined to make the biggest, most influential shipbuilding concern in the galaxy. There was some initial unpleasantness when fledgling trade consortiums (ancient precursors of the greedy Trade Federation) tried to prevent the merchant families from realizing their goal. Several acts of sabotage, espionage, and skirmishes with supposed pirates made business difficult, but none of these occurrences could be traced back to the source.

The merchant families hired the finest terraformers, ecologists, and animal breeders in an effort to make Kuat into a paradise. It took two decades, but the effort paid off. What was once a barren, uninhabited world became a lush planet with its own custom-designed ecosystem. While the terraformers worked on the planet below, engineers and construction personnel began creating the first half-dozen shipyards of what would eventually become known as the Kuat Drive Yards.

KDY rapidly gained a reputation in the Republic for being a first-class shipbuilding company. It is hardly surprising that when the Empire took over, Kuat was one of the first worlds to be secured under Imperial control. During the Rebellion era, KDY became one of the Empire's most valuable assets. A healthy percentage of the Empire's mass-destruction technology came from KDY. The shipyards designed and built the Empire's infamous Star Destroyers. In fact, KDY constructed a second Super Star Destroyer, *Executor II*, which was later renamed *Lusankya* and buried on Coruscant to serve as the Emperor's secret getaway ship.

KDY is also known for inventing the *Firespray*-class patrol ship—the template for Boba Fett's ship, *Slave I*—and the Nebulon-B frigate, a ship favored (some would say stolen) by the Rebel Alliance. KDY also manufactures various planetary weapons, such as the v-150 Planet Defender ion cannon used by the Rebels at the Battle of Hoth.

After the Imperial defeat on Endor, Palpatine's successors realized they couldn't afford to let Kuat's shipyards fall into Rebel hands. Fifteen Star Destroyers were dispatched to guard the system. Spacetroopers rigged the yards with explosives in case it became necessary to scuttle them. Fortunately, the yards remained intact when the Empire fell.

Kuat joined the New Republic four years after the Battle of Endor. At the same time, the senior design engineers of KDY fled the planet and headed into the Deep Core to build the *Eclipse*-class Star Destroyers for the reborn Emperor.

During the Yuuzhan Vong crisis, KDY helps to defend the galaxy against extragalactic invaders. Kuat has even hosted briefings held by New Republic Defense Force commanders. Kuat, Mon Calamari, and Bilbringi have since gone to full alert with carrier groups deployed to defend their respective systems.

People

The Kuati are a proud, class-conscious people. It is a point of pride to trace one's ancestry back to the original ten families—sometimes known as The Ten—that built and settled the planet. Upper-class Kuati live on the planet in expansive estates. Kuati merchant houses are extremely insular. Most are made up of a single extended aristocratic family.

The merchant houses have adopted a system to prevent unwanted political alliances that result from interhouse marriages. Kuati patriarchs marry from within their own families, but do not sire their own children. Instead, when a Kuati house patriarch wants an heir, he buys a telbun, a young, middle-class male who has been raised from birth as a breeder. Telbuns are trained to excel in athletics and culture. Selected specimens are usually extremely attractive and mentally sharp. At the right age, they are ranked according to their scores in a series of genetic, mental, and other breeding-related tests. Patriarchs then select a telbun who possesses desired qualities. The family of a selected telbun is richly rewarded.

After a telbun sires a child, he stays on with the merchant family as a tutor and guardian. However, he is never considered a blood relative. In fact, telbuns are often treated like common laborers. A telbun dresses in heavy purple and red robes and signifies his loyalty with an elegant cylindrical hat. Each telbun is forced to obey his patriarch's every demand. Telbuns are given a modified version of their patriarch's name, indicating to whom they belong.

Locations

Although the Kuat Drive Yards dominate the world, other sites may interest heroes—although most of them are off limits.

Kuati Space Stations

Three huge space stations handle interstellar traffic in the system. One accommodates passengers, another manages freight, and a third focuses on planetary defense. During the Rebellion era, the third space station acquiesces to the demands of the Imperial Military. In the time of the New Republic, the station that once handled Imperial forces is adapted to suit New Republic forces.

In any era, the three stations control arrivals and departures insystem, as well as keep out undesirables. Each station maintains scheduled shuttles providing access to Kuat City. Kuati Security Forces vigilantly and ruthlessly patrol the three stations. The laws are stringently enforced, with a zero-tolerance policy toward gunfire. The last problem anyone wants is a crazed offworlder shooting a weapon inside a space station.

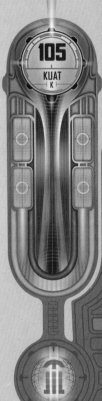

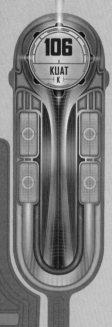

Kuat City

Accessed by shuttles from the space stations, Kuat City has no spaceport groundside. The city hosts numerous shops, hotels, restaurants, and places of general merchant business. A mercantile forum allows the various merchant houses to meet and discuss trade practices. After the fall of the Empire, the New Republic maintains a small embassy in the city, as well as a smaller subembassy up in the Yards. Unless a Kuati actually lives on the surface, the only way she can access the well-groomed lands of Kuat is via the city. Outsiders must secure numerous costly permits to visit the countryside. The Kuati police reserve the right to refuse anyone entry into the lands, regardless of the ability to pay the appropriate fees. If visitors some- how secure an interview or audience, they may get the chance to go "planetside," where they'll no doubt be impressed by Kuati displays of wealth and status.

Kuat Drive Yards

The heart and soul of Kuat reside in the Drive Yards. These massive shipyards encircle the planet, producing some of the most memorable ships and ship classes in the galaxy. Visitors can find bars, hotels, restaurants, shops, medical facilities, and entertainment. Most Kuati citizens live in apartment complexes built into the ring. Kuati Security Forces patrol all areas within the Yards. Many offworlders remain in the ring during their visit, never smelling fresh Kuati air during their entire stay. As one would expect, the Yards have weapons systems to

defend against raiders and other smaller ships, although they lack the ability to take on Star Destroyers or Nebulon-B cruisers.

For the GM

The adventure hooks and supporting characters described in this section are meant for GMs only. If you're a player, stop reading now.

Adventures

A busy place such as Kuat can be a source of intrigue, especially between merchant houses. During the Rebellion era, Kuat is heavily guarded and patrolled by both the Empire and the Kuati Security Forces, so heroes should be careful where they walk.

A Plague on Both Your Houses

While relaxing in a bar up in KDY, the heroes overhear someone muttering a few interesting words: "the yards," "sabotage," and "explosives." The man, named Trondor Pyn, is a shipwright at KDY. Recently, a few representa- tives from House Andrim, one of the Kuati merchant houses, approached him with an unusual request. The Andrim representative told him that the House wished to have someone spy on a rival house, House Purkis. In return, Trondor would be well compensated.

Trondor took the assignment, but he got caught. The House Purkis representatives let him go under the condition that he would spy for them instead. Trondor agreed—he would have done almost anything to avoid being turned over to the Kuati Security Forces. However, he didn't take into consideration the stress and extra risks of being a double agent. He's losing sleep, gaining weight, and drinking too much. All in all, Trondor's coming unhinged.

He has finally come up with what he thinks is a good plan to get both houses off his back: He intends to sabo- tage both houses' largest drydocks. Trondor has recruited eight of his most trusted friends, a motley band of work- ers who know how to take care of themselves. To bail himself out, he's paying them with the funds he's received from both houses. Trondor intends to blow up both drydock facilities, thereby giving both houses larger prob- lems to deal with, including mass casualties from collateral damage. He hopes the crisis will divert both houses' attention away from him, possibly giving him a chance to escape offworld or bolt for a hiding place during the confusion. Unless the heroes intervene, the atrocity will make every offworlder in the shipyards a suspect—including them.

X Marcus the Spot

In its effort to completely control the Kuati shipyards, the Empire has instituted a policy of cracking down on free- lance tech specialists and shipwrights. The most promising of these is young Marcus Sione. The Empire feels that grabbing a kid should be child's play—but with a kid such as Marcus, it isn't. His escapes are miraculous

Kuat Drive Yards Orbital Array

```
              4
    15  2  11
  14          14
 5              8
                  11
14                  10
12                    13
4  10                   11
11                        14
                            11
   Kuat
1                          3
11
12                        10
13                      12
 10                   9  11
   11 13 12         13
      7  12 4 11  6
```

Key

1	Supply Space Station	8	Deponn Shipyards
2	Residential Space Station	9	Kuat Main Spaceport
3	Military Space Station	10	Drydocks
4	Kuat Security Forces Headquarters	11	Warehouses
		12	Machine Shops
5	Kuat Drive Yards Offices	13	Factories
6	Maw Shipyards	14	Apartments
7	Andrim Shipyards	15	Commercial Zone

enough that some of his adversaries begin to suspect he may be a Force-user. As events progress, the Empire gets increasingly brazen about taking Marcus, calling in more and more help.

The heroes encounter Marcus just as a group of thugs hired by an agent of the Empire try to grab him in a semisecluded spot. After the heroes help drive off the thugs, Marcus tells them he has no idea why he's being hounded. He asks if he can stay with the heroes for a while—perhaps tuning up their ship for them—until he's certain his persecution is over. Unbeknownst to Marcus and the heroes, their trail is picked up by Lucius Rothingham, an Imperial lackey, who keeps track of their whereabouts while trying to avoid detection himself and reports back to his masters periodically.

Using the information provided by Rothingham, the Empire makes several more attempts to capture Marcus, employing bounty hunters and whatever other scum they can get to work for them. The heroes should have their hands full trying to keep a teenager on a short leash while evading Imperial forces, bounty hunters, and kidnappers.

Upper Echelons

A representative from House Andrim contacts the heroes during a routine stopover on Kuat. She has an errand of the utmost delicacy and would like the heroes to consider her offer. (This approach is quite plausible if the heroes played through "A Plague on Both Your Houses" and performed capably.) The representative, Jestra Andrim, explains that the assignment is a courier mission involving a round trip from Kuat to another remote Core World (such as Belgaroth) and back again. Jestra seeks an initial agreement to undertake the mission. If it's given, she invites the group to an evening party at House Andrim's manor down on the planet's surface.

The next morning, Jestra outlines the mission. House Andrim has created some new weapons systems for Imperial starships. The systems have already been delivered and have been fitted on a pair of Imperial Star Destroyers, *Burning Vengeance* and *Legacy*. Both vessels are currently undergoing closed weapons testing in the Belgaroth system. House Andrim has an agent on Belgaroth secretly monitoring the systems, since it fears that the Empire may attempt to downplay the system's effectiveness when dealing with the price. The agent has already made his report, but he can't get offplanet due to an Imperial interdiction on the system. The heroes must travel to the remote world, meet the agent, get the data, and bring it back to House Andrim on Kuat. There's a bonus if the heroes can get the spy off the planet as well.

What House Andrim and the heroes don't know is that the agent has been discovered and has been killed by an agent of a rival Kuati house, House Depon. Even worse, the rival Kuati successfully interrogated him before he died. An operative of House Depon has taken the agent's identity and wants to get home. He'll do his best to accompany the heroes back to Kuat. Then, if possible, the impersonator attempts to eliminate some of the heroes and possibly sabotage their equipment.

KUAT SHIPYARDS   DR

Allies and Antagonists

The following supporting characters are designed for use in your campaign.

Marcus Sione

It is only natural for a world dedicated to shipbuilding to spawn a few "freelance" tech specialists. Starship techies will gladly service a disabled freighter or do some modifications on a favorite scout ship. By the time of the Battle of Yavin, Marcus Sione is thirteen years old. He's known as "The Wizard" for his eerie, almost supernatural instincts when it comes to ship repair. Since he can't be found hanging around in bars, tracking him down is often difficult. When he's found, however, it's always worth the trouble.

Marcus has dirty blond hair and is quite solid for a boy his age. He has no problem telling people how smart and capable he is. Fortunately for him, he can back up his claims with results. Without people to mentor him, he's also slowly becoming amoral. In Marcus's mind, the worst kind of person is one who would willingly destroy machinery. In most cases, the destruction of a fine computer is more horrifying to him than the death of a random individual. Since this genius's brilliance has its origins in the Force—a possibility some have begun to suspect—Marcus could become a useful slave of the dark side.

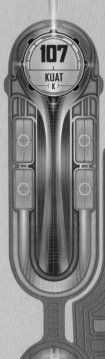

107

KUAT

K

Marcus Sione: Male Human Expert 10; Init +2; Defense 15 (+2 Dex, +3 class); Spd 10 m; VP/WP 0/12; Atk +7/+2 melee (1d3, punch) or +9/+4 ranged; SV Fort +4, Ref +5, Will +6; SZ M; FP 0; DSP 0; Rep +5; Str 10, Dex 15, Con 12, Int 18, Wis 9, Cha 10. Challenge Code C.

   Equipment: Datapad, glow rod, holorecorder, macrobinoculars, security kit, tool kit.

   Skills: Appraise +6, Astrogate +6, Climb +2, Computer Use +17, Craft (computers) +15, Craft (electronic devices) +18, Disable Device +5, Gather Information +2, Hide +4, Knowledge (engineering) +14, Knowledge (technology) +10, Listen +5, Pilot +7, Read/Write Basic, Read/Write Binary, Read/Write Durese, Repair +21, Search +10, Sense Motive +1, Speak Basic, Speak Durese, Speak Sullustese, Spot +5, Swim +6, Tumble +8.

   Feats: Fame, Force-Sensitive, Gearhead, Sharp-Eyed, Skill Emphasis (Craft [electronic devices], Repair), Starship Operation (space transport).

Beekly Grimlok

Some individuals consider killing other living beings a bit too pedestrian. A select group of amoral sentients call themselves "technological assassins," eschewing the more common term "saboteur." Beekly Grimlok is one such deviant, and he's one of the better ones. A disgruntled former employee of KDY, Grimlok uses his construction knowledge to disable, blow up, and otherwise destroy ship drives, droids, weapons systems, and even small bases and space stations. Collateral damage and the accompanying loss of life are incidental to him.

   Beekly didn't start out as a KDY employee. He left Rodia about a year before the Battle of Yavin and wandered the galaxy, improving his skills and hunting on wilderness planets. His money ran low, and a few Imperial encounters deprived him of most of his resources. He had no choice but to find a job. Since Beekly is technologically adept, KDY was a good choice. He was fired around the time of the Battle of Hoth for his inability to keep his mind on his work, and soon thereafter began plying his current trade.

   Beekly is a Rodian who stands 1.7 meters tall. He wears a long overcoat, with all his gadgets and killing machines stored in hidden (but easy to reach) pockets and pouches. Beekly is short-tempered and somewhat paranoid, but he refuses to let these shortcomings interfere with his professionalism.

   Beekly doesn't hate technology—far from it. He considers destroying machines and technological devices a bit more satisfying than hunting living prey. Or perhaps he just likes to break things. No one's had the nerve to ask.

Beekly Grimlok: Male Rodian Fringer 4/Expert 2; Init +4; Defense 16 (+4 Dex, +2 class); Spd 10 m; VP/WP 52/14; Atk +9 melee (1d3+5, punch) or +4 ranged (3d8/19–20, blaster carbine) or +8 ranged (3d8, heavy blaster pistol); SQ barter, bonus class skill (Demolitions, Disable Device), jury-rig +2; SV Fort +6, Ref +6, Will +4; SZ M; FP 0; DSP 1; Rep +0; Str 20, Dex 18, Con 14, Int 16, Wis 10, Cha 10.

   Equipment: Heavy blaster, blaster carbine, all-temperature cloak, comlink, credit chip (200 credits), datapad, electrobinoculars, 4 energy cells, field kit, glow rod, holorecorder, recording rod, sensor pack, mastercraft security kit, tool kit, 4 thermal detonators, 6 frag grenades.

   Skills: Astrogate +6, Bluff +4, Computer Use +6, Craft (space transports) +10, Demolitions +10, Disable Device +10, Gather Information +5, Intimidate +6, Listen +6, Read/Write Basic, Read/Write Huttese, Read/Write Rodese, Repair +12, Search +6, Sense Motive +9, Speak Basic, Speak Huttese, Speak Rodese, Spot +2, Survival +7.

   Feats: Cleave, Gearhead, Power Attack, Skill Emphasis (Intimidate, Sense Motive), Track, Weapon Group Proficiencies (blaster pistols, primitive weapons, simple weapons).

Lucius Rothingham

During the Empire's occupation of Kuat, a number of undercover spies help to make sure that the shipyards run smoothly. Lucius Rothingham is one of those operatives. He loves serving the Empire, which he sees as a means of keeping order. A former engineer, Rothingham feels that the galaxy should run like a finely tuned engine, and the Empire is a means of bringing this about. A born pragmatist, Lucius decides to throw in his lot with the Imperials and help bring order to the galaxy. Even after the Empire falls, he strives to maintain its ideals and works toward its eventual restoration. Rothingham's conscience is subordinated by his desire to serve well. Throughout his career, he spies, kidnaps, interrogates, and sometimes kills for the Empire. Lucius reports to Captain Anton Kale and gets along very well with him.

   Rothingham is a well-educated man with a broad knowledge base. He's adept at technical matters, which helps in his assignment on Kuat. He has an annoying and inhuman habit of using mechanical and technical metaphors in his speech (for example, "This idea's burnt a chip. Reset and restart."). A Human in his mid-thirties at the time of the Battle of Yavin, he stands 1.9 meters tall and has several tattoos on his arms and chest.

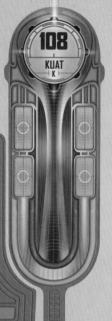

BEEKLY GRIMLOK

Lucius Rothingham: Male Human Expert 4/Scoundrel 4; Init +2; Defense 16 (+2 Dex, +4 class); Spd 10 m; VP/WP 35/18; Atk +8 melee (1d3+2, punch) or +8 ranged (3d6, blaster pistol); SQ illicit barter, lucky 1/day, precise attack +1; SV Fort +6, Ref +7, Will +6; SZ M; FP 5; DSP 0; Rep +2; Str 14, Dex 15, Con 18, Int 16, Wis 12, Cha 15. Challenge Code C.

Equipment: Blaster pistol, credit chip (1,000 credits), comlink, mastercraft security kit, tool kit.

Skills: Bluff +8, Computer Use +12, Diplomacy +5, Disable Device +10, Gather Information +9, Hide +8, Intimidate +5, Knowledge (streetwise) +10, Knowledge (tactics) +10, Listen +7, Move Silently +8, Profession (engineer) +11, Read/Write Basic, Repair +15, Sense Motive +4, Sleight of Hand +8, Speak Basic, Spot +8, Survival +8.

Feats: Blind-Fight, Gearhead, Quick Draw, Skill Emphasis (Profession [engineer], Repair), Track, Weapon Group Proficiencies (blaster pistols, simple weapons).

Captain Anton Kale

The Empire requires strong officers to keep their worlds in line. Anton Kale is the commander of Imperial forces on Kuat. He's a Rebel's nightmare: absolutely efficient, brutally loyal, and vigilantly insightful. After seeing how the Old Republic's Senate became corrupt and fractured, Kale was convinced of the moral certitude of the Empire. He approved of Palpatine's grab for power and saw order restored to the galaxy. Kale truly believes the Empire is best for everyone. Naturally, force must be exercised to maintain order, and Kale sees that as an effective tool. Kale and Lucius Rothingham get along splendidly.

Kale has an inquisitive, imaginative mind. He loves engineering and ship design, so he personally lobbied to be assigned to Kuat. There, he could be near where ideas and designs are turned into functioning space vessels. Kale's penchant for unconventional tactics makes him a formidable opponent—he is not bound by linear, by-the-book thinking. This complex man finds as much delight in the stress tests of a well-made starship as he does in torturing a Rebel spy to the point of unconsciousness.

Kale believes in the Force and thus knows that those who wield it are to be feared and respected. He does not underestimate his enemies or fail to appreciate the strengths of his allies. After the Emperor's death, Kale does his best to continue fighting for the Empire. As long as some form of the Empire still exists, he'll be dedicated to it and serve it the best he can. He is a refined, cultured man in his late fifties with a square jaw and distinguished gray hair. His steely eyes can either light up with delight or go icy cold with visions of torturing Rebels. He stands 1.7 meters tall and speaks with a deep baritone voice.

Captain Anton Kale: Male Human Soldier 4/Noble 1/Officer 3; Init +5 (+1 Dex, +4 Improved Initiative); Defense 17 (+1 Dex, +6 class); Spd 10 m; VP/WP 70/14; Atk +8/+3 melee (1d3+2, punch) or +7/+2 ranged (3d6, blaster pistol); SQ bonus class skill (Intimidate), favor +1, leadership, requisition supplies; SV Fort +8, Ref +5,

Will +9; SZ M; FP 0; DSP 0; Rep +4; Str 14, Dex 13, Con 14, Int 16, Wis 18, Cha 18. Challenge Code D.

Equipment: Blaster pistol, comlink, datapad, uniform, rank insignia.

Skills: Bluff +8, Computer Use +10, Diplomacy +12, Gather Information +12, Intimidate +10, Knowledge +10, Knowledge +5, Listen +7, Pilot +10, Read/Write Basic, Search +10, Sense Motive +13, Speak Basic, Spot +7, Treat Injury +7.

Feats: Armor Proficiencies (light, medium), Dodge, Gearhead, Improved Initiative, Mobility, Point Blank Shot, Shot on the Run, Weapon Group Proficiencies (blaster pistols, blaster rifles, heavy weapons, simple weapons, vibro weapons).

KDY-4 Series Tech Droid

About two centuries before the Battle of Yavin, the techs at KDY realized that they needed their own special droid line for constructing and repairing starships. Thus, they designed the KDY-4 line of second-degree droids. The KDY-4 unit is nicknamed "the builder's buddy" because of its extreme usefulness and easygoing manner. Standing a little over 1.5 meters high, each one has four appendages (including two that fully retract into the chassis) and a trio of standard magnetic-lock legs.

KDY-4s possess a library of data on ship construction and repair. In fact, it is said that their memory banks contain the blueprints, operating manuals, and troubleshooting diagnostic guides of common ship classes from around the time of the founding of the Trade Federation to the establishment of the New Republic. Some older models have truly massive ship databanks.

KDY-4s are constructed exclusively at KDY facilities and are not generally for sale to non-Kuati. It is possible for an offworlder to buy one—it's just not very common. KDY representatives happily boast that the droid combines "the versatility of an R2 unit, the eloquence of a 3PO, and the muscle power, skill, and experience of the strongest shipyard worker." There's been no word on what Industrial Automaton, Cybot Galactica, and the Shipwrights Union think of that particular slogan.

KDY-4 Series: Tracked repair/shipbuilding droid Expert 5; Init +3; Defense 14 (+3 Dex, +1 class); Spd 10 m; VP/WP 0/14; Atk +6 melee (1d6+3, claw) or +6 ranged; SV Fort +3, Ref +4, Will +5; SZ M; Face/Reach 2 m by 2 m/ 2 m; Rep +1; Str 16, Dex 16, Con 14, Int 19, Wis 13, Cha 12. Challenge Code B.

Equipment: Heuristic processor, improved sensor package, infrared vision, low-light vision, diagnostics package, vocabulator, comlink, translator unit, recording unit, two telescopic appendages, two tool mounts, internal storage (3 kg), environmental compensation (space), magnetic feet.

Skills: Computer Use +7, Craft (capital ships) +10, Craft (sublight drives) +12, Disable Device +5, Knowledge (engineering) +9, Knowledge (physics) +9, Knowledge (technology) +12, Repair +17, Search +8, Spot +8.

Unspent Skill Points: 25.

Feats: Gearhead, Skill Emphasis (Knowledge [technology], Repair, Spot).

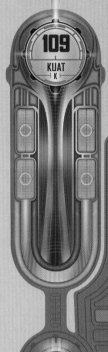

Metellos

Planet Type: Terrestrial
Climate: Temperate
Terrain: Urban
Atmosphere: Breathable
Gravity: Standard
Diameter: 12,600 km
Length of Day: 24 standard hours
Length of Year: 361 standard days
Sentient Species: Human
Languages: Basic
Population: 900 billion
Species Mix: 90% Human, 10% other
Government: Bureaucracy
Major Exports: Advanced tech, business services
Major Imports: Foodstuffs, office supplies
System/Star: Metellos

Planets	Type	Moons
Menias	Searing rock	0
Maedano	Barren rock	1
Majesticas	Toxic rock	0
Metellos	Terrestrial	3
Maddules	Gas giant	9
Mores	Gas giant	17
Militar	Gas giant	5

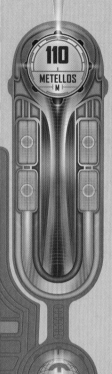

Description

Metellos—"the Coruscant that wasn't." For twenty-five hundred years, Metellos has labored in the shadow of its wealthier, flashier, and happier neighbor, hoping its efforts would pay off in glory. But like the drifting of the stars, the destiny of a planet is far beyond conscious control. Metellos might seem impressive to a hayseed from Tatooine, but its natives can't escape the feeling that their planet is an also-ran in the Core Worlds.

Overpopulation is Metellos's gravest problem. The planet has nearly as many people as Coruscant, but it packs them into a fraction of Coruscant's habitable area. To compensate, the wealthy executives of Metellos constructed floating cities that drift 1,200 meters above the housing precincts. More than a thousand such cities are currently in operation.

Metellos also shares Coruscant's habit of promoting urbanization, even if it's at the expense of environmentalism. However, the system lacks Coruscant's cultural relevance, and its history is one of smoke-stained industry instead of splendor and flourish. Conquerors and statesmen don't come from Metellos. They look upon the planet as a column on a balance sheet while they plan great things in their Coruscant palaces.

Metellos is urbanized from pole to pole, with only a few septic seas and desert wastelands still untouched by durasteel. Unlike Coruscant, Metellos has an architecture that tends toward the horizontal. Some regions of the planet—notably the seventeen immense stratablocks that dot its surface—are multilayered to as high as a kilometer above the ground, tapering off into single-story structures packed roof-to-roof all the way to the horizon. Many tracts, particularly those far from the stratablocks, are shabby, environmentally toxic, and inhabited by diseased squatters.

History

The story of Metellos dates back so far that its early history is as murky as Coruscant's. The planet was settled before the formation of the Republic, presumably by colonists from Coruscant prior to the development of the hyperdrive. Coruscant and Metellos share many similarities, not the least of which is their location within the same star sector.

As history moved on, it became clear that Coruscant was the favored child. Coruscanti explorers discovered five hyperspace lanes leading out from their planet, two of which—the Perlemian Trade Route and the Corellian Run—became vital arteries for the stellar confederacy that would become the Republic. As centuries passed and the Republic took shape, many merchants, dignitaries, and prospectors realized that setting up shop on Coruscant was easier than making the added hyperspace jump to Metellos. Natives of Metellos found themselves almost literally in Coruscant's shadow, stuck to the "galactic west" of the new hub when all the action was going on in the east.

For a time, Metellos hosted an eclectic community of hyperspace trailblazers. Each hoped to discover an analog to the Perlemian Route that would open up the galactic western quadrant, making Metellos the center of a new economic system. The so-called Metellos Trade Route proved disappointing. It never managed to expand through the gravitational anomalies that littered the fringes of the Unknown Regions.

Metellos persisted in its efforts long after hope had faded, leading to centuries of economic recession. Too proud to ask for help in the Republic Senate on Coruscant, the rulers of Metellos stripped their planet's resources in an effort to gain temporary capital. Because Metellos had never taken steps to ensure environmental balance (unlike, say, Chandrila or Alderaan), unchecked population growth led to poorly planned housing, exponential resource depletion, and a staggering gulf between the haves and the have-nots.

Seven centuries before the Battle of Yavin, the directors of Metellos's most powerful corporations created clean, floating communities for the rich and well connected. Designers used the herd cities of Ithor as their model, but these airborne metropolises would never be mistaken for any product of Ithorian artisans. Gridlike and unimaginative, their traylike white blocks look like ponderous, sharp-cornered clouds to those stuck on the surface.

Progress continued on the Metellos Trade Route in fits and starts. Eventually, the hyperlane stretched as far as Orooturoo in the Farlax sector, but few entrepreneurs were interested in territory sandwiched between the Unknown Regions and the Deep Core. Metellos nursed its stunted economy until the rise of the Empire, when Palpatine gave the planet's ruling executives a stake in the Outer Rim's Corporate Sector Authority. The influx of credits fattened the pocketbooks of the rich, but it did little to alleviate the suffering of "groundpounders." The New Republic's rule eventually led to the establishment of a representative democracy on Metellos, but even then, elected officials remained puppets of local corporate interests.

Six years after the Battle of Endor, forces loyal to the reborn Emperor swept across the Core. On Metellos, an Imperial armada under the command of Admiral Delvardus routed the New Republic defensive fleet and shelled the planet in a cruel and wholly unnecessary show of force, killing more than five billion people. Metellos's recovery took time, since the New Republic shifted its priorities to restoring damaged Coruscant.

During the Black Fleet Crisis, Metellos saw use as a supply point for the New Republic's fifth fleet as it struck at the Koornacht Cluster. The invasion of the Yuuzhan Vong—and the fall of neighboring Coruscant—has panicked many Metelleans, who believe the enemy won't ignore a world as urbanized as theirs for long.

People

More than nine hundred billion people call Metellos home, making it one of the most densely packed planets in the galaxy. The population is divided into two social classes: the gentry and the groundpounders. The gentry (a self-mocking name adopted by Metellos's decadent executives) rule the floating cities and the upper levels of the stratablocks. The groundpounders are the datapushers, plant laborers, con artists, thieves, and indigents who populate the vast sweep of low homes, warehouses, and factories that form the planet's undistinguished landscape. Most wealthy visitors to Metellos never set foot on the surface, conducting their business aboard airborne megalopolises or attending meetings within stratablock spires. By contrast, most of the groundpounders never leave. They live and die within a few hundred kilometers of their home tract, bumping shoulders with more people in a day than most citizens of the Outer Rim meet in a year.

Locations

Descriptions of several important locations follow.

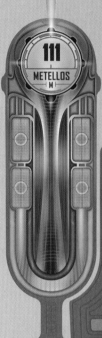

Moridebo District

From the air, the low-income Moridebo district appears as an unbroken floor of black, gray, and dirty green rooftops clumped in no discernible pattern. Moridebo has its own dialect and subculture. It even has its own favored cuisine: a combination of meat and lard shaped to resemble fruit (a confection some offworlders contemptuously refer to as "meatalos"). Factories, stadiums, and smoking ash-dumps occasionally make a break in the rooftops, but the architecture remains stunted until one approaches the outskirts of Stratablock 7.

Stratablock 7

Standing out against the Moridebo district like a mountain rising from a lumpy sea, Stratablock 7 is typical of Metellos's towering communities. It reaches for the sky as if a chunk of Coruscant had simply been dropped there. The wealthiest of the groundpounders live in the lowest levels, while junior executives among the gentry inhabit luxury dormitories within the high towers. Stratablock 7 is home to two rival corporations—CarsinShare and Nonsu—that deal in the gathering and selling of business information. Many of those in the Moridebo district work in some way for CarsinShare or Nonsu, producing the materials they need to operate the floating city of Ektra (usually visible in the skies above Stratablock 7).

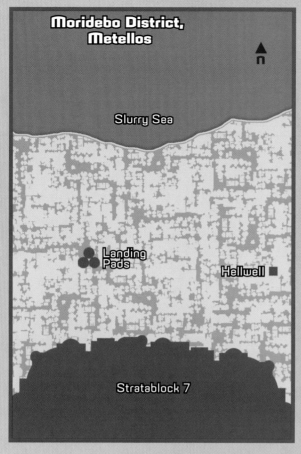

Moridebo District, Metellos

N

Slurry Sea

Landing Pads

Hellwell

Stratablock 7

Ciuray Sea and the Hellwell

Close by the Moridebo District, foolish travelers find the Ciuray Sea, known as the Slurry Sea by the locals. Inky and stagnant, its waters are processed for drinking by shoreline sterilization plants. The Ciuray Sea has long been a dumping place for sensitive items, including murdered bodies. Another repository for detritus is the Hellwell, a 20-meter-wide vertical shaft created centuries ago by a vanished mining company.

For the GM

The adventure hooks and supporting characters described in this section are meant for GMs only. If you're a player, stop reading now.

Adventures

Feel free to use or adapt the following adventure hooks for your home campaign.

Early Retirement

Hynla, the Chadra-Fan chief of the CarsinShare corporation, is eager to recover a lockbox that was lost by the rival Nonsu company. The lockbox's datacards contain critical information. Depending on the era, they could include evidence of the return of the Sith, Imperial fleet movements for the next six months, or clues to an insurrection mounting in the New Republic. Hynla is eager to hire the heroes for the job.

The Chadra-Fan also has a fanatic interest in the death matches between CarsinShare and Nonsu held in the bowels of the floating city of Ektra. Clearly, any operatives he hires for corporate espionage will need a plausible cover story. Heroes who look like good fighters may find themselves forced into jobs as CarsinShare gladiators. If they win, Hynla insists that they stay on the company payroll and search for the lockbox. If they lose, they're scheduled for "early retirement" from the corporation. The gladiatorial arena sits directly above the city's hanging repulsorlift spire. A hole in the floor goes all the way down the length of the spire and opens onto 1,200 meters of empty air above the rooftops of Metellos. Losers are kicked out the bottom of Ektra City.

Not all retired gladiators come to a fatal end. Unbeknownst to Hynla, the guerrilla leader Rinn Renado has been using repulsorlift vehicles to catch losing combatants in mid-fall. He enlists them in his fight against the corporations, offering to provide a new life, a new identity, and an opportunity for revenge. Those who refuse Renado's on-the-spot offer are dismissed as ingrates and dumped over the side of the vehicle. Heroes who fail to stay on Hynla's good side can be recruited by his opposition.

Race to the Prize

Rinn Renado and his followers in the Moridebo district want to inflict as much damage as they can on CarsinShare and Nonsu to end their regional domination. He's learned that an escaped protocol droid has financial data of interest to both corporations. On a planet such as Metellos, where could the quarry hide? The possibilities are endless. Rival search teams from CarsinShare and Nonsu will be searching through the chaos of the Moridebo district, traveling the labyrinthine levels of Stratablock 7, and even spelunking to the bottom of the Moridebo Hellwell. The heroes must outrace their rivals if they hope to steal the data first. Steeps aren't the only creatures standing in their way. A bruiser named Lowal Pulse lends his muscle to an enemy team—and takes special pleasure in killing anyone who may have survived the gladiatorial contests.

Allies and Antagonists

The following supporting characters are designed for use in your campaign.

Hynla

Head of the CarsinShare corporation, Hynla is an elderly Chadra-Fan who has taken an interest in gladiatorial contests as a sporting way for his company to demonstrate its superiority over Nonsu. He can be found in his transparisteel-prismed office aboard Ektra City or in the huge wood-paneled CarsinShare boardroom deep within Stratablock 7. A connoisseur of smells, Hynla has recently developed a keen appreciation for the subtle scent of blood.

Hynla: Male Chadra-Fan Diplomat 7; Init +2; Defense 15 (+2 Dex, +1 size, +2 class); Spd 6 m; VP/WP 0/10; Atk +3 melee (1d2–1, punch) or +6 ranged (3d6, blaster pistol); SQ darkvision 20 m, isolation aversion, low-light vision;

SV Fort +2, Ref +4, Will +5; SZ S; FP 1; DSP 1; Rep +2; Str 9, Dex 14, Con 10, Int 14, Wis 10, Cha 12. Challenge Code B.

Equipment: Datapad, code cylinder, blaster pistol, 500 credits.

Skills: Appraise +5, Bluff +11, Computer Use +9, Diplomacy +11, Gather Information +9, Hide +6, Intimidate +3, Knowledge (business) +10, Knowledge (Metellos) +10, Read/Write Chandra-Fan, Repair +5, Sense Motive +10, Speak Basic, Speak Chandra-Fan.

Feats: Dodge, Mobility, Persuasive, Trustworthy, Weapon Group Proficiency (blaster pistols).

Lowal Pulse

Lowal Pulse is a ringer for the Nonsu corporation in the gladiatorial contests held aboard the floating city of Ektra. He cuts a notch in the edge of his ear after every victory. Both ears are now fringed with dozens of incisions. When he's not competing, Pulse works in the Moridebo district, spying on his fellow laborers and breaking the arms of those who call him a sellout.

Lowal Pulse: Male Human Scoundrel 6/Thug 7; Init +4 (+4 Improved Initiative); Defense 14 (+4 class); Spd 10 m; VP/WP 40/15; Atk +13/+8/+3 melee (1d3+2, punch) or +13/+8/+3 melee (2d6+2, vibroblade) or +11/+6/+1 ranged (3d8, heavy blaster pistol); SQ illicit barter, lucky 2/day, precise attack +1; SV Fort +8, Ref +7, Will +3; SZ M; FP 0; DSP 2; Rep +2; Str 15, Dex 11, Con 12, Int 10, Wis 9, Cha 10. Challenge Code E.

Equipment: CarsinShare ID, concealed vibroblade, heavy blaster pistol.

Skills: Bluff +6, Computer Use +2, Escape Artist +6, Hide +6, Intimidate +4, Jump +7, Knowledge (Metellos) +12, Listen +7, Move Silently +8, Pilot +4, Read/Write Basic, Repair +8, Search +8, Speak Basic, Spot +8, Tumble +7.

Feats: Armor Proficiency (light), Combat Reflexes, Improved Initiative, Point Blank Shot, Precise Shot, Quick Draw, Run, Skill Emphasis (Knowledge [Metellos]), Toughness, Weapon Group Proficiencies (blaster pistols, blaster rifles, simple weapons, vibro weapons).

Rinn Renado

Known simply as "Boss" to many in the Moridebo district, Rinn Renado leads a resistance movement opposed to the domination of CarsinShare and Nonsu. Despite his expertise in guerrilla tactics, he has little understanding of reform politics. Consequently, he has no real short-term goal

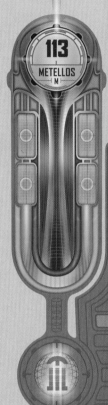

STEEP

beyond anarchy. Renado is known to almost everyone in Moridebo, but few will tell an offworlder where to find him.

Rinn Renado: Male Human Scoundrel 17; Init +6 (+2 Dex, +4 Improved Initiative); Defense 22 (+2 Dex, +10 class); Spd 10 m; VP/WP 68/10; Atk +14/+9/+4 melee (1d3+2, punch) or +14/+9/+4 melee (2d4+2, vibrodagger) or +14/+9/+4 ranged (3d8/19–20, blaster carbine); SQ illicit barter, lucky 3/day, precise attack +3; SV Fort +5, Ref +12, Will +6; SZ M; FP 0; DSP 3; Rep +4; Str 14, Dex 14, Con 10, Int 12, Wis 11, Cha 15. Challenge Code G.

Equipment: Comlink, vibrodagger, blaster carbine, datapad with detailed intelligence on Moridebo district.

Skills: Appraise +5, Bluff +13, Computer Use +8, Demolitions +8, Diplomacy +7, Disable Device +8, Disguise +9, Escape Artist +9, Forgery +8, Gather Information +8, Hide +13, Intimidate +9, Jump +5, Knowledge (business) +14, Knowledge (Metellos) +17, Listen +11, Move Silently +10, Pilot +8, Read/Write Basic, Repair +8, Search +10, Sense Motive +5, Sleight of Hand +7, Speak Basic, Speak Shyriiwook (understand only), Spot +9, Survival +4, Tumble +12.

Feats: Cleave, Combat Reflexes, Headstrong, Heroic Surge, Improved Initiative, Point Blank Shot, Power Attack, Skill Emphasis (Bluff, Hide, Knowledge [Metellos], Listen), Weapon Group Proficiencies (blaster pistols, blaster rifles, simple weapons, vibro weapons).

New Creature: Steep

Named for their habit of soaking themselves in the sewage of the Metellean seas, steeps are carnivorous amphibians with white, rubbery skin more than 10 centimeters thick. They are often seen bobbing on the surface of the black water. At night, they sometimes stalk down alleyways on their four webbed feet looking for children to swallow. Steeps have the dangerous combination of tough hides and small brains. They usually won't stop attacking until they are dead.

Steep: Predator 8; Init +3 (–1 Dex, +4 Improved Initiative); Defense 18 (–1 Dex, –1 size, +10 natural); DR 10; Spd 8 m, swim 16 m; VP/WP 52/14; Atk +12/+7 melee (2d6+5, bite) or +6/+1 ranged; SQ amphibious, low-light vision; SV Fort +8, Ref +5, Will +3; SZ L; Face/Reach 2 m by 4 m/2 m; Rep +0; Str 20, Dex 8, Con 14, Int 2, Wis 12, Cha 6. Challenge Code C.

Skills: Intimidate +8, Listen +2, Spot +10, Survival +7.

Feats: Improved Initiative, Skill Emphasis (Survival), Track.

New Plympto

Planet Type: Terrestrial
Climate: Temperate to tropical (none in The New Jedi Order era)
Terrain: Forests, mountains, swamps (barren wasteland in The New Jedi Order era)
Atmosphere: Breathable
Gravity: Standard
Diameter: 10,125 km
Length of Day: 18 standard hours
Length of Year: 244 standard days
Sentient Species: Nosaurians (none in The New Jedi Order era)
Languages: Nosaurian (none in The New Jedi Order era)
Population: 14 million (7 million during the Rebellion era, unpopulated in The New Jedi Order era)
Species Mix: 95% Nosaurian, 4% Human, 1% other (unpopulated in The New Jedi Order era)
Government: City-states (none in The New Jedi Order era)
Major Exports: Ji rikknit (illegal after the Rebellion era), simple trade goods (none in The New Jedi Order era)
Major Imports: Weapons, high-tech goods (none in The New Jedi Order era)
System/Star: New Plympto

Planets	Type	Moons
Ranste	Searing rock	0
Sasan	Terrestrial	2
New Plympto	Terrestrial	1
Bilagen	Frozen rock	0

Description

A lush little world among the outlying systems of the Corellian sector, New Plympto features forests of hiakk trees with silvery 200-meter-tall trunks. The treetops are the home of multilegged crustaceans known as rikknit. Near New Plympto's coasts, forests give way to tangled thickets, then meadows and swamps carpeted in mats of algae. These are the domains of the Nosaurians, a sapient species of reptilians.

History

Corellian traders first contacted the Nosaurians some ten thousand years before the rise of the Empire. Plympto proper is a minor star system on the Corellian Trade Spine. The Corellians treated the Nosaurians as a client species (much like the Frozians and Altawar's Corragut). Corellian cartels later made considerable profits exporting ji rikknit, an addictive substance made from rikknit ovum sacs. The Nosaurian clans and city-states that cooperated prospered as well. In time, many Nosaurians left to migrate along the Corellian trade routes.

By the time the Old Republic began to crumble, trouble was brewing on New Plympto. Efforts to breed rikknit in captivity failed, and overhunting left the creatures close to extinction. Supreme Chancellor Valorum banned exports of ji rikknit and declared the rikknit a protected species. The decree turned many Nosaurians into poachers and plunged the planet into an economic depression. After Palpatine rose to power, the Imperial Procurator classified New Plympto and eleven other alien-inhabited Core Worlds as "expendable," allowing bureaucrats free rein in using their resources. The Nosaurians found themselves near-slaves, with the sole remaining law that of the blaster.

Shortly before the Battle of Yavin, the Nosaurians organized a guerrilla movement under the one-eyed General Fefar Blackeye. The rebellion fell apart when Blackeye was captured, and its spirit died when rebels learned he had died in a cage on Coruscant. Since then, many Nosaurians have blamed Humans for their troubles. New Plympto briefly seceded from the New Republic during the Corellian insurrection, becoming an ideal breeding ground for anti-Human Diversity Alliance terrorists.

In The New Jedi Order era, the Yuuzhan Vong seized New Plympto but had to contend with Nosaurian commandos. Angered, the Yuuzhan Vong released a bioengineered plague that wiped the planet clean of life. New Plympto became a poisoned, quarantined world. The Nosaurians are now homeless.

People

Standing between 1.2 and 1.5 meters tall, Nosaurians have delicate limbs, three-toed feet, and four fingers on each hand. Because of their high, piping voices, a discussion between two Nosaurians is a symphony of trills and swoops. When agitated or angry, Nosaurians turn to a deeper register of brays and barks.

One quirk of the species is "singing down the sun." When New Plympto's pale yellow sun drops below the horizon, Nosaurians bray at the top of their lungs. This compulsion is almost impossible for them to suppress. Those living offworld sometimes bray at inopportune times, victims of internal clocks gone haywire. Popular legend has it that Fefar Blackeye was captured by a clever Imperial commander who pinned him down in a hiakk copse and waited for sundown.

A few affiliated clans dominate the Nosaurian city-states. Nosaurians shed their downy birth feathers at age 13, then spend several years proving their worth as apprentices to masters of affiliated clans. During this time, the clans argue over the proper arranged matings for each class of youths. These debates are often public. Male Nosaurians battle rivals throughout their adolescence, sometimes trying to settle issues by (literally) locking horns. Once the matings have been determined, the former rivals are expected to work together for the clans. Female Nosaurians aren't pushed into rivalries but are otherwise treated as equals.

Locations

After the Yuuzhan Vong invasion, the New Republic decontamination teams who visited New Plympto found its cities empty and its once-proud forests reduced to broken sticks. The landscape had been scarred by Yuuzhan Vong biohatcheries and Shaper *damuteks*. The plague had literally liquefied the planet's life, leaving behind an ankle-deep, stinking jelly. Visitors before this time, on the other hand, should encounter a beautiful world filled with breathtaking locales.

Phemiss

Most visitors' first port of call is Phemiss, the capital city that sprawls for kilometers between the Pharine River and the Tsilor Sea. Nosaurian buildings, such as those found in Phemiss, are lumps of adobe with round doorways that sprout turrets studded with windows. They huddle together in circular blocks that open onto a central courtyard. These courtyards are used for raising young and holding clan meals. Phemiss's mesh of circular blocks is a navigational nightmare for offworlders, most of whom wisely leave the driving to Nosaurians.

In the city's newer districts, Nosaurian blocks give way to square blocks of more typical construction. The liveliest part of town is the drifters' district, a ramshackle collection of Nosaurian and offworlder blocks around Phemiss Low Port, the best of the planet's three spaceports. Clanless Nosaurians live here. The drifters' district is not only home to Phemiss's rogues and criminals but also to its free thinkers and adventure-seekers. If one wants to cut a deal on New Plympto, the juke joints and eateries of the drifters' district are the place to go.

During the rise of the Empire, Imperials razed parts of the drifters' district to build squat black factories for processing ji rikknit. Imperial engineers slashed a grid of avenues across the rest of the city, mutilating or destroying dozens of clan blocks. In the Rebellion era, stormtroopers patrol the district.

The Hajial Chase

Adventurers who want to see the primeval New Plympto should explore the Hajial Chase, some 400 kilometers inland from Phemiss. The Chase is a particularly old stretch of forest atop a soaring escarpment that rises out of the hiakk woodlands. The forest floor is home to herds of feathered "foragers" who use their chin-tusks to dig for grubs and fungi, as well as the speedy two-legged "striders" who strike at the periphery of the herds, taking the sick, old, or young. High above is the domain of the rikknit. Molted exoskeletons or improperly secured food

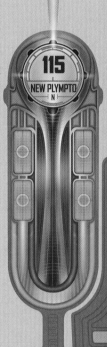

caches sometimes plunge out of the skies, scattering startled foragers and striders alike.

The Karsten Moon

New Plympto's lone satellite houses the spaceport known as Karsten High Port and the consular offices of the galactic government. The Karsten Moon's atmosphere domes also shelter illegal ji rikknit processing plants, ship-repair facilities, and a fair number of dives and flophouses. These duracrete blockhouses are dug into the yellow soil and connected by long, dingy tubes that radiate out from the spaceport like spokes.

The Rikknit Harvest

During the time of the rikknit harvest, Nosaurian scouts and soldiers use crampons called tree-claws to make their way into the treetops. A few meters below the rikknit nests, they spread nets between the trees, clamp their tree-clawed feet to either side of a hiakk trunk, and unfold their harvest blades. These blades are used to sever the silken bonds holding food caches aloft and slash ovum sacs from the bodies of unwary females.

The best way to survive a battle with a rikknit is to strike by surprise and then quickly climb down out of danger. Nonetheless, all hunters become adept at fighting while holding on only with their feet. Truly skilled tree-fighters can move through the forest canopy by swinging from branch to branch, allowing them to harvest nest after nest without climbing up and down each tree.

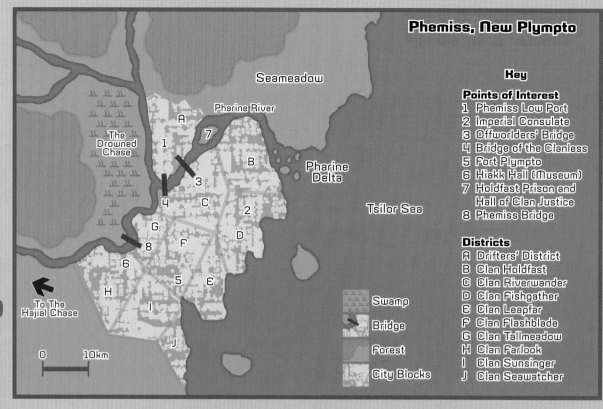

Phemiss, New Plympto

Key

Points of Interest
1 Phemiss Low Port
2 Imperial Consulate
3 Offworlders' Bridge
4 Bridge of the Clanless
5 Port Plympto
6 Hiakk Hall (Museum)
7 Holdfast Prison and
    Hall of Clan Justice
8 Phemiss Bridge

Districts
A Drifters' District
B Clan Holdfast
C Clan Riverwander
D Clan Fishgather
E Clan Leapfar
F Clan Flashblade
G Clan Tallmeadow
H Clan Farlook
I Clan Sunsinger
J Clan Seawatcher

Swamp

Bridge

Forest

City Blocks

Tree-claws confer on their wearer a +4 equipment bonus on Climb checks.

A harvest blade is a type of pole ax that can be folded up for ease of carrying. Folded, it is just half a meter long; unfolded, it has a reach of 4 meters.

Tree-Claw
Cost: 100 credits (pair)
Weight: 0.5 kg (pair)

Harvest Blade
Cost: 125 credits
Damage: 1d4
Critical: 20
Range Increment: —
Weight: 1.5 kg
Type: Slashing
Size: Large
Group: Exotic

New Feat: Brachiation

You can move through the trees like a skilled Nosaurian tree-fighter.

Prerequisites: Climb 6 ranks, Jump 6 ranks, Str 13.

Benefit: You move through trees at your normal land speed by using your arms to swing from one branch to the other. To allow brachiation, the area through which you are moving must be at least lightly wooded, with trees no farther apart than 5 meters. You may not use this ability while holding an item in either hand, or while wearing armor heavier than medium.

For the GM

The adventure hooks and supporting characters described in this section are meant for GMs only. If you're a player, stop reading now.

Adventures

Feel free to use or adapt the following adventure hooks for your home campaign.

High above the Hajial

The heroes are hired to put the poacher Glarc Leapfar out of business. In Phemiss, they have the chance to meet Xant Flashheel, a clanless Nosaurian with a taste for adventure. Before they can take out a legend such as Leapfar, they'll have to find him. Their best source for gathering information will be the drifters' district, but eventually, they'll run afoul of those who want poaching to continue. Corellian toughs and Nosaurian thugs ambush anyone asking too many questions about their profitable and illegal businesses in the forests.

The quest for Leapfar leads them to the Hajial Chase, where they must survive the forest and apprehend Leapfar amid the dangers of the treetops. In doing so, the heroes learn that impoverished Nosaurians are poachers out of desperation. They may be surprised to find that New Plympto's politics aren't as black-and-white as they believed. Will they try to kill Leapfar for credits, or warn him of enemies who want him killed?

Showdown on the Karsten Moon

A radical Ho'Din environmentalist named Maki Salak plans to poison a shipment of ji rikknit before it leaves Karsten High Port. The heroes' mission team must defeat Salak and his gang, find the tainted shipment, and destroy it. The heroes don't know that another group—perhaps Imperial Intelligence or a cabal within the Republic or the New Republic—wants the tainted shipment to get to its destination. This ensures some deadly consequences for the group's targets. To resolve their mission, the heroes must not only defeat Salak's thugs but also outwit intelligence operatives.

Allies and Antagonists

The following supporting characters are designed for use in your campaign.

Xant Flashheel

This young Nosaurian outcast loves the excitement of the drifters' district in Phemiss. He burns with a desire to see the rest of the galaxy. His hair-trigger temper is evidenced by the fact that he has broken two horns, despite being barely out of adolescence. Xant haunts the area around Phemiss Low Port, offering his services as a guide and a swoopshaw driver. (A swoopshaw is a modified speeder bike that holds four passengers and lacks weapons or armor.) To the annoyance of his passengers, he insists on playing music at ear-splitting volumes. Given the slightest opening, he discusses underground Corellian music at great length.

Xant Flashheel: Male Nosaurian Fringer 3; Init +2; Defense 16 (+2 Dex, +4 class); Spd 10 m; VP/WP 17/11; Atk +2 melee (1d3, punch) or +2 melee (1d6, horns) or +4 ranged (3d6, blaster pistol); SQ barter, bonus class skill (Escape Artist), jury-rig +2; SV Fort +3, Ref +4, Will +0; SZ M; FP 0; DSP 0; Rep +0; Str 10, Dex 15, Con 11, Int 12, Wis 8, Cha 11. Challenge Code B.

Equipment: Swoopshaw, blaster pistol, Corellian pop-music datacards, datapad/personal music player.

Skills: Bluff +3, Climb +3, Escape Artist +7, Hide +5, Knowledge (New Plympto) +7, Listen +1, Pilot +11, Read/Write Nosaurian, Search +7, Speak Basic, Speak Nosaurian, Spot +7, Survival +4.

Feats: Alertness, Skill Emphasis (Pilot), Weapon Group Proficiencies (blaster pistols, primitive weapons, simple weapons).

Maki Salak

The Ho'Din are renowned for their healing abilities and love for the environment—not just that of their native Moltok, but those of worlds across the galaxy. Some have been enraged by the ecological devastation that seems to accompany exploration and colonization. Maki Salak is one of these radicals. Salak was once a country doctor on Sacorria, but the spice addicts and ji rikknit tipplers he had to treat disgusted him. He left Sacorria and formed a cell of environmental extremists. Their hope is that poisoning ji rikknit shipments will eliminate the market for the substance and save the rikknit.

Maki Salak: Male Ho'din Expert 11/Noble 2; Init +2; Defense 15 (+2 Dex, −1 size, +4 class); Spd 12 m; VP/WP 8/11; Atk +8/+3 melee (1d4, punch) or +8/+3 melee (1d6, staff) or +10/+5 ranged (3d4, hold-out blaster); SQ +4 species bonus on Knowledge (wilderness lore) checks, +4 species bonus on Survival checks in heavy vegetation environments, bonus class skill (Intimidate), cold-blooded, favor +1, inspire confidence; SV Fort +3, Ref +7, Will +10; SZ L; FP 0; DSP 0; Rep +3; Str 11, Dex 14, Con 11, Int 15, Wis 11, Cha 14. Challenge Code C.

Equipment: Staff, poisoner's kit, datapad with extensive collection of scientific datacards, comlink, holoprojector (with sound), medpac, hold-out blaster.

Skills: Bluff +4, Climb +6, Computer Use +10, Craft (poisons) +19, Gather Information +12, Hide −2, Intimidate +16, Knowledge (biology) +19, Knowledge (bureaucracy) +10, Knowledge (New Plympto) +16, Knowledge (Sacorria) +10, Profession (doctor) +15, Read/Write Ho'din, Sense Motive +7, Speak Basic, Speak Frozian, Speak Ho'din, Speak Nosaurian, Treat Injury +9.

Feats: Persuasive, Skill Emphasis (Craft [poisons], Knowledge [biology], Profession [doctor], Treat Injury), Surgery, Weapon Group Proficiencies (blaster pistols, simple weapons).

Glarc Leapfar

A legendary tree-fighter, Glarc Leapfar is the leader of a poaching gang that harvests ovum sacs from the rikknit of Hajial Chase. His arboreal strength ensures that few locals would dare contest him for dominance. Roaming the treetops of New Plympto in magnificent displays of brachiation, his trained warriors can harvest a fortune in rikknit ova each day. Confederates smuggle the sacs into Phemiss, where they're processed in the drifter's district and taken to the Karsten Moon. Operatives within the High Port hide the ji rikknit among legitimate cargos for pickup and sale by drug lords across the galaxy.

Since Glarc understands the forest ecosystem, he tries to ensure that his harvesting won't destroy the remnant population of rikknit. However, as demand for addictive ova increases through the galaxy, Glarc may have trouble ensuring a steady supply. Soon, he suspects, desperate amateurs from offworld will muscle in on his territory. Glarc will have to show that his martial skills are worthy of the arboreal legends he has inspired.

Glarc Leapfar: Male Nosaurian Scout 10; Init +2; Defense 18 (+2 Dex, +6 class); Spd 10 m; VP/WP 45/12; Atk +10/+5 melee (1d4+2, harvest blade) or +9/+4 melee (1d3+2, punch) or +9/+4 melee (1d6+2, horns) or +9/+4 ranged (3d6, blaster pistol); SQ evasion, extreme effort, heart +1, skill mastery (Move Silently, Survival), trailblazing, uncanny dodge (can't be flanked, Dex bonus to Defense); SV Fort +6, Ref +7, Will +6; SZ M; FP 0; DSP 0; Rep +2; Str 15, Dex 15, Con 12, Int 10, Wis 12, Cha 12. Challenge Code E.

Equipment: Tree-claws, harvest blade, net, electrobinoculars, field kit, blaster pistol.

Skills: Climb +14, Escape Artist +8, Hide +10, Jump +14, Knowledge (New Plympto) +8, Listen +9,

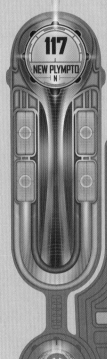

Move Silently +12, Read/Write Nosaurian, Speak Basic, Speak Nosaurian, Spot +6, Survival +10, Tumble +7.

Feats: Acrobatic, Brachiation, Skill Emphasis (Move Silently, Survival), Track, Weapon Finesse (harvest blade), Weapon Focus (harvest blade), Weapon Group Proficiencies (blaster pistols, blaster rifles, simple weapons).

New Species: Nosaurian

Nosaurians are even-tempered by nature, but the perceived injustices inflicted upon the species by Humans in power have left many angry. They are slightly shorter than Humans and have thick skin ranging from light green to black. Nosaurians can be of any class, though soldiers and fringers are most common in The New Jedi Order era.

Nosaurian Commoner: Init +1; Defense 11 (+1 Dex); Spd 10 m; VP/WP 0/10; Atk +0 melee (1d3, unarmed) or +0 melee (1d6, horns); SV Fort +0, Ref +1, Will +0; SZ M; FP 0; DSP 0; Rep +0; Str 10; Dex 12; Con 10; Int 10; Wis 10; Cha 8. Challenge Code A.

Skills: Climb +2, Knowledge (any one) +2, Profession (any one) +2, Read/Write Nosaurian, Speak Basic, Speak Nosaurian, Survival +2.

Feats: None.

Species Traits: +2 Dex, –2 Cha; +2 species bonus on Climb and Survival checks.

Automatic Languages: Nosaurian, Basic.

New Creature: Rikknit

Rikknit are crustaceans that dwell in the tops of hiakk trees. Various varieties have eight, ten, or twelve legs. In the upper forest canopy, rikknit hunt insects, birds, and other rikknit. They spin webs, which are used for storage and nests, not for catching prey. Females attach ovum sacs to their abdomens with a thick cord of connective tissue. Nosaurian hunters try to sever these cords with their harvest blades.

An ovum-sac cord has a Defense of 14, 1d8+4 wound points, and hardness 4. A rikknit can grow her ovum sac back in 4 to 6 weeks.

Rikknit: Forest vermin 4; Init +2; Defense 14 (+2 Dex, +2 natural); DR 2; Spd 12 m, climb 12 m; VP/WP 18/11; Atk +3 melee (1d6, bite), +1 melee (2d4, 2 claws); SQ darkvision 20 m; SV Fort +4, Ref +6, Will +0; SZ M; Face/Reach 2 m by 2 m/2 m; Rep +0; Str 11, Dex 14, Con 11, Int 3, Wis 9, Cha 1. Challenge Code B.

Skills: Climb +17, Jump +4, Listen +4, Spot +1.

Feats: Multiattack.

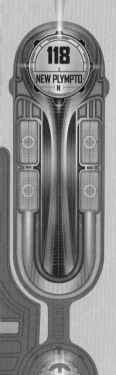

Nubia

Planet Type: Terrestrial
Climate: Arid
Terrain: Plains, mountains, urban
Atmosphere: Breathable
Gravity: Standard
Diameter: 10,490 km
Length of Day: 29 standard hours
Length of Year: 289 standard days
Sentient Species: Human
Languages: Basic
Population: 1.2 billion
Species Mix: 92% Human, 8% other
Government: Democracy
Major Exports: Starship parts, foodstuffs, ore
Major Imports: Low-tech items
System/Star: Nubus

Planets	Type	Moons
Traxal 1	Searing rock	0
Traxal 2	Searing rock	0
Nubia	Terrestrial	1
Nimbia	Gas giant	8
Nothar	Frozen rock	2

Description

Nubia is a small, temperate planet. Shallow oceans separate its two main landmasses. The terrain consists of rolling fields bisected by immense mountain ranges. The fields are dry, but huge underground aquifers provide a ready water source for irrigation.

Nubia's surface is used efficiently by its inhabitants. Temperate fields have been converted to massive agricultural farms that take advantage of the planet's warm temperatures and long growing season. Particularly dry areas exist, and these have been utilized for urban sprawl. Mountains are riddled with small mining cities. The mountains are rich in ore deposits, including lodes of bronzium that have attracted numerous businesses.

Nubia boasts headquarters for several large corporations. Industrial Automaton is based on Nubia, but the largest corporation is PharmCorp, an agricultural research and pharmaceutical company. Nubia Star Drives, Inc., is a large starship manufacturer known for its powerful ion engines and nonmilitary vessels. The company manufactures the Nubian cloudbus—widely used for planetary mass transit—and a line of bulk transports. TradeCo, Inc., is an upstart sectorwide shipping company with custom-designed cruisers. TradeCo ships Nubian grain products to markets across the sector.

History

Twenty-two thousand years ago, Humans settled Nubia after discovering immense subterranean aquifers there. Massive pumps installed across the planet provided a method to bring water to the surface, which encouraged colonists to settle. In a few decades, Nubia established itself as an agricultural power. A hastily organized democracy soon ruled the planet. Few citizens care to admit that the democracy is corrupt, with puppet officials appointed after rigged elections. The real power is secretly the head of PharmCorp, a Hutt named Prall. Over time, many galactic powers have coveted Nubia's resources, but they have had to contest with the shadow government that rules the planet.

During the Rebellion era, the Empire coveted the planet's massive grain production and envisioned it fueling their war efforts. They also feared that the Rebels might utilize Nubia Star Drives, Inc., to manufacture ships. As such, the Empire stationed a Star Destroyer in orbit over Nubia and instituted martial law on the surface. An Imperial governor assumed authority, and within hours, stormtroopers patrolled the streets.

When the Empire fell, the New Republic returned the world to its original government and granted it a council seat in the Senate. However, the New Republic felt it necessary to take an active role in removing the Imperials in the system, which stirred resentment in some of the populace. Some believe the New Republic to be even worse than the Empire.

People

It's been said that Nubians are among the hardest-working sentients in the sector, but they also play hard. To relieve the stress of working long hours, the population has developed several entertainment outlets. To supplement the usual gambling parlors, cantinas, and holovid theatres, Nubia's Humans have created two new sports: ronto racing and grav-ball. Ronto racing involves brash jockeys riding massive saurian beasts through an array of obstacles on an oval track. Nubia boasts eight such tracks scattered about the planet. Race days are social events, and wagers add yet more spice to the contests.

Grav-ball is played in small, indoor courts. Teams of six players equipped with remotely powered hover boots bounce around the three-dimensional court in an attempt to score goals. The ball is held on the end of a repulsor baton and can be passed from player to player. Grav-ball games are held on informal levels in health clubs and on a planetwide level with professional leagues. The one hundred twenty-eight professional teams compete for a bid to the Annual SecBowl, the sector championship.

Locations

Descriptions of several important locations follow.

Nuba City

Nuba City, the capital city of Nubia, is located on the western side of a mountain range. Skyscrapers arranged in a chaotic jumble dominate the landscape. Cloudbuses, speeders, and other aircraft fill the smog-laden sky. An underground monorail provides mass transit in and around the city.

A full-service starport, including repair and refueling facilities, is situated to the west of the city. The monorail has a station here, providing inexpensive transport to Nuba City and its popular nightlife. The most famous night spot is an expensive cantina called The Dark Side of the Planet. It is owned and operated by a Twi'lek named Tul Bulba. Tul's establishment features skilled Twi'lek dancers and exotic offworld cuisine.

Tallera Downs

Located to the south of Nuba City are the spectacular Tallera Downs, the most famous ronto racetrack on Nubia. The 2.5-kilometer track has seating for one hundred twenty thousand screaming fans, and several thousand more in hovering luxury suites. The track features rocky slopes, mud pits, and water hazards. Tallera Downs hosts the annual Tallera Open, the most prestigious race on the circuit. The monorail has a station here, and the center of the track hosts a huge bazaar on race day.

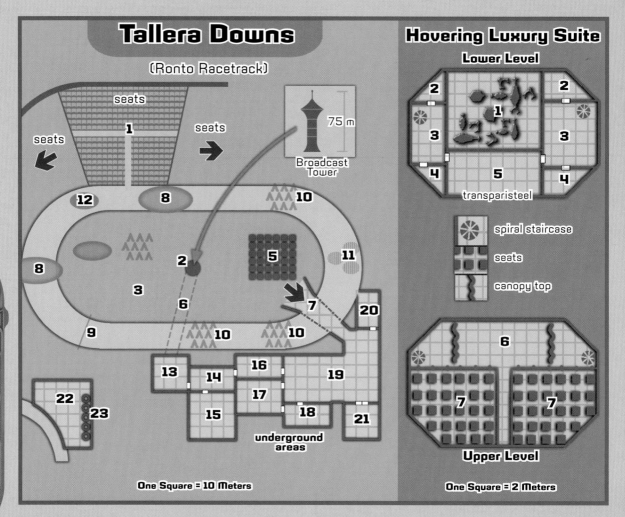

Tallera Downs

(Ronto Racetrack)

seats

seats

seats

1

2

3

8

9

12

8

10

11

5

6

7

20

13

14

16

17

15

18

19

21

22

23

10

10

10

Broadcast Tower

75 m

underground areas

One Square = 10 Meters

Hovering Luxury Suite

Lower Level

1

2

2

3

3

4

4

5

transparisteel

spiral staircase

seats

canopy top

6

7

7

Upper Level

One Square = 2 Meters

The Nubian Palace

The Nubian Palace is an orbiting luxury resort catering to the upper crust of Nubia. Visitors can sample any of a dozen casinos (each with a different theme), the Solar Garden, four holovid suites, a pair of cantinas, and a virtual reality suite. On the half-hour, cloudbuses carry tourists to and from the resort.

Unknown to most, Prall, the head of PharmCorp, owns and operates the Nubian Palace. The palace is a cover for the transfer of illicit contraband to and from Prall's operatives. Since it also generates significant income as an entertainment facility, it's an ideal base of operations for the crime lord. Prall is vigilant, all the more because some of the substances he personally samples have induced an intense sense of paranoia that no amount of surveillance and security can alleviate.

The Solar Gardens

Situated in the Nubian Palace, the Solar Gardens are a large interior park nestled between two restaurants. A huge transparisteel wall oriented toward the sun grants a spectacular view of Nubia's surface and allows an extended growing season. The gardens contain many exotic species of flora, including floating archidias. The gardens are a popular tourist attraction, providing locations for meeting places or picnics.

Hover Boots

The engineers at Nubia Star Drives, Inc., developed hover boots to facilitate the construction of Nuba City's skyscrapers. While worn, the boots are energized by tiny repulsor engines manipulated with the wearer's toes. The boots have no internal power supply, however. The user must remain within 60 meters of a hover transformer, a device about the size of a speeder that casts an energy field around a selected construction site. Up to ten pairs of boots can be powered by the same transformer.

Hover boots have a flight ceiling of 60 meters and can ascend at 15 meters per round or descend at 30 meters per round. The boots don't produce lateral movement—they can only move the wearer up or down.

Workers later converted the boots for use in the Nubian sport of grav-ball. Each team has four players, and the game requires two referees, so a single transformer can power everyone's boots. In grav-ball, players push off walls and floors (and occasionally each other) for movement. The chairman of the largest Grav-ball Federation is a feisty Toydarian named Zen Lotto, who judges some of the largest matches personally while flitting around the energy fields of famous Nubian arenas.

Nubian Cloudbus

Nubia has a great need to move large numbers of people quickly. A fast, high-altitude means of mass transit was needed to carry people between isolated mining towns, expansive farms, and numerous orbital stations. The Nubian B4 Cloudbus fills this role admirably. Similar to a cloud car, the cloudbus is an unarmed light vehicle used to transport several dozen passengers. The elongated oval vehicle is fitted with three large Nubian Star Drives ion engines. Each blue-and-gray cloudbus is maintained by the Nubian government.

Nubian B4 Cloudbus

Class: Airspeeder	Crew: 2 (Normal +2)
Size: Gargantuan (10.5 m long)	Initiative: -2 (-4 size, +2 crew)
Passengers: 36	Maneuver: -2 (-4 size, +2 crew)
Cargo Capacity: 200 kg	Defense: 12 (-4 size, +6 armor)
Cost: 88,000 (new),	Shield Points: 0
37,500 (used)	Hull Points: 60 (DR 5)
Availability: Prevalent	Atmospheric Speed: 11
	squares/action (700 km/h)
Era: Rise of the Empire	Altitude: 75 km

* This vehicle provides full cover to its pilots and passengers.

For the GM

The adventure hooks and supporting characters described in this section are meant for GMs only. If you're a player, stop reading now.

Adventures

Feel free to use or adapt the following adventure hooks for your home campaign.

Crop Circles

The heroes are hired by a PharmCorp public relations manager to investigate the appearance of crop circles. Investigating the crop circles reveals that several rogue harvester droids are responsible. Further investigation reveals that the droids are controlled by remote commands transmitted by a crime lord's goons stationed in a nearby cave. Their boss works at the Nubian Palace, an orbiting casino from which the heroes can clearly see the crop circle shapes. It's a secret code, but who's decoding it? And what does it say?

While the heroes contemplate the code, they're attacked by Barabel thugs. Who do they work for? Why did they attack? If the code can be deciphered, it could lead to further adventures on Nubia.

A Day at the Races

The heroes are hired by the Nubian government to foil an assassination attempt at the Tallera Open, a prestigious ronto race. The government provides a transmitted code to its operatives conveying a date, time, a luxury suite number, and the victim's name. (The heroes could receive this transmission personally, or they may have recovered the code in the previous adventure.)

First, the heroes must find a way to attend the race—the hottest ticket in the sector. They then need to locate the suite. The luxury suites at Tallera Downs hover over the racetrack, so the heroes must solve the problem of getting to the suite before they can hope to foil the assassination attempt. They may be able to commandeer a nearby medical speeder or disguise themselves as vendors and use a repulsor platform; in any event, getting to the suite should be relatively easy (if time-consuming).

To succeed, the heroes need to find out how the assassination is going to take place. Will it be a precise blaster shot from a sniper? Or will someone disable the suite's hover engines, sending it careening into the crowd?

Allies and Antagonists

The following supporting characters are designed for use in your campaign.

Prall the Hutt

Prall is a young, slender Hutt with mottled, tan-gray skin. His left eye is yellow, and his right is blue; both twitch at irregular intervals. He lulls opponents into thinking that he abhors personal contact, yet he has attached a metal spike to his tail and is proficient in attacking opponents with it.

Prall is the head of PharmCorp, Nubia's largest agricultural company. Although it appears that Prall is a legitimate business owner, the company is merely a profitable front. He is a powerful crime lord who has bribed the local government with money, favors, and protection. He specializes in illegal armaments, biological weapons, black market pharmaceuticals, and information. He also owns the Nubian Palace, an orbiting resort over Nubia that serves as a convenient cover for his operations. His sluggish reactions are the result of massive amounts of chemicals that he "tests" personally. Years of methodical abuse have unhinged his mind—he frantically pursues endless paranoid speculations about the rival who's going to kill him and take his place.

Prall the Hutt: Hutt Scoundrel 8/Noble 1/Crime Lord 7; Init -3; Defense 15 (-3 Dex, -1 size, +9 class); Spd 2 m; VP/WP 128/20; Atk +11/+6 melee (stun DC 12, stun baton) or +11/+6 melee (1d8+3, tail spike) or +11/+6 melee (1d4+3, punch) or +5/+0 ranged; SQ can't be knocked prone, contacts (3), favor +1, Force resistance (gains +6 species bonus on Will saves against Force skills and Force feats), illicit barter, inspire fear -4, lucky 2/day, minions, precise attack +1, resource access; SV Fort +9, Ref +8, Will +12; SZ L; FP 0; DSP 6; Rep +14; Str 16, Dex 5, Con 20, Int 17, Wis 13, Cha 16. Challenge Code G.

Equipment: Metal tail spike, repulsor sled, several datapads, stun baton, Nubian amphibians (snacks).

Skills: Appraise +19, Bluff +25, Computer Use +14, Diplomacy +22, Forgery +22, Gather Information +22, Hide -7, Intimidate +21, Knowledge (business) +20, Knowledge (streetwise) +19, Listen +14, Read/Write Basic, Read/Write Huttese, Search +5, Sense Motive +19, Speak Basic, Speak Huttese, Speak Nikto, Speak Rodese, Spot +6.

Feats: Alertness, Fame, Frightful Presence, Heroic Surge, Infamy, Iron Will, Sharp-Eyed, Skill Emphasis

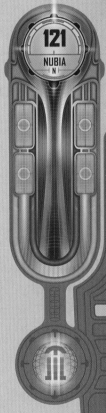

(Bluff, Intimidate, Knowledge [business]), Weapon Group Proficiencies (blaster pistols, simple weapons).

Dace Wilder

Dace is a small, wiry male Human with spiky blond hair, blue eyes, and a charming smile. Dace is the current ronto racing champion and has won two of the last three Tallera Opens. Although he has more money than he can spend, retirement never enters his mind—he lives for the thrill of the race. He owns a trio of carefully bred rontos, maintains a private suite in Nuba City, and frequents another suite on the Nubian Palace. He makes many public appearances and can be found at the most upscale of social gatherings.

Dace's wealth and social status allow him to entertain political beliefs some would consider eccentric. He is opposed to any form of government, including the Empire and the New Republic. If forced to choose between the two, Dace favors the New Republic, but only because he fears that the Empire would eliminate ronto racing completely. If convinced that Nubia was in danger of being taken over by the Empire (or the New Republic), Dace would carefully use his wealth and status to prevent it.

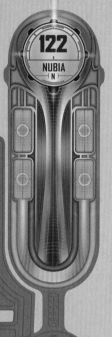

ARMADID

Dace Wilder: Male Human Fringer 5; Init +4; Defense 19 (+4 Dex, +5 class); Spd 10 m; VP/WP 28/12; Atk +5 melee (1d3+2, punch) or +1 melee (2d4+2, vibrodagger) or +7 ranged (3d6, blaster pistol); SQ barter, bonus class skill (Bluff, Swim), jury-rig +2, survival +2; SV Fort +5, Ref +7, Will +1; SZ M; FP 0; DSP 0; Rep +1; Str 14, Dex 18, Con 12, Int 10, Wis 10, Cha 16. Challenge Code C.

Equipment: Blaster pistol, vibrodagger, riding outfit, grooming kit, leather ronto harness.

Skills: Bluff +11, Climb +12, Handle Animal +11, Read/Write Basic, Ride +12, Speak Basic, Spot +8, Survival +8, Swim +12.

Feats: Athletic, Endurance, Weapon Group Proficiencies (blaster pistols, primitive weapons, simple weapons).

Deja

Deja is an adventurous Jawa who is a long way from home. Most Nubians keep their distance from this short, foul-smelling alien in a dirty robe. Deja attempts to converse with others using Basic, but he doesn't fully understand the concept of verb tense, and complex sentences are hard for him. He especially enjoys naps, taking several each day.

During his naps, Deja has elaborate dreams. His first great vision caused him to be exiled from his tribe. His revelation showed a sandcrawler being attacked by white-armored "skeletal" warriors. When he informed his shaman of the vision, he was ridiculed and punished. Two days later, his tribe discovered the remains of a destroyed sandcrawler. Frightened, his tribe banished Deja, and he became an outcast.

Deja traveled to Mos Eisley and offered his services as a mechanic. He has skill at fixing and jury-rigging anything, including droids, vehicles, and starships. During one of his naps in the engine room of a space transport, the ship took off because of a malfunction in the hyperdrive. Deja found himself stranded on board. After Deja fixed and improved the hyperdrive motivator, the crew accepted the diminutive Jawa. Then, once they had tired of his curses, his stench, and the temporary nature of most of his repairs, they dropped him off at the nearest starport. For years, Deja has wandered the galaxy, serving as a free-lance mechanic. He currently resides on Nubia.

Deja: Male Jawa Fringer 7/ Force Adept 2; Init +4; Defense 23 (+4 Dex, +1 size, +8 class); Spd 6 m; VP/WP 47/10; Atk +6/+1 melee (1d2–1, punch) or +6/+1 melee (1d6–1, heavy spanner) or +11/+6 ranged (3d8/19–20, ion rifle); SQ barter, bonus class skill (Computer Use, Disable Device), dark-vision 20 m, jury-rig +4, primitive, survival +2; SV Fort +8, Ref +10, Will +7; SZ S; FP 0; DSP 0; Rep +1; Str 8, Dex 18, Con 10, Int 17, Wis 14, Cha 8. Challenge Code E.

Equipment: Heavy spanner (used as a club), ion rifle, tool kit, robes, power pack, security kit, glow rod, credit chip (400 credits).

Skills: Computer Use +11, Craft (droids) +18, Disable Device +10, Hide +20, Listen +14, Move Silently +8, Pilot +11, Read/Write Jawa, Read/Write Jawa Trade Language, Repair +6, Search +10, Sense Motive +10, Speak Jawa, Speak Jawa Trade Language, Spot +9, Survival +14.

Force Skills: Enhance Senses +8, Farseeing +7.

Feats: Force-Sensitive, Gearhead, Rugged, Skill Emphasis (Craft [droids], Farseeing), Weapon Group

Proficiencies (blaster pistols, blaster rifles, primitive weapons, simple weapons).

Force Feats: Alter, Sense.

Floating Archidia

The floating archidia is a flower species native to Nubia that has a unique method of seed dispersal. The flower, typically a brilliant purple, pale blue, or crimson, detaches from the plant during pollination. Several tiny gas sacs filled with hydrogen give the flower buoyancy. Breezes then carry the floating flower as far as several kilometers before the hydrogen sacs slowly shrink and the seeds are dispersed. The fragrance emitted by the flowers is rumored to have a euphoric effect on most species. Secretly, PharmCorp scientists have developed a way to concentrate the archidia's pollen into an inhalable poison.

Archidia Fragrance

Type: Inhaled DC 15
Initial Damage: 1 Wis
Secondary Damage: 1 Wis

Concentrated Archidia Poison

Type: Inhaled DC 22
Initial Damage: 2d4 Wis
Secondary Damage: 3d4 Wis

New Creature: Armadid

The armadid is a large, Force-using predator that stalks the mountains of Nubia. The creature is about 3 meters long, with bony, armored plates on its domed back. It sports a short, stocky tail with a crablike pincer at its end. Its short legs can be retracted under protective armor. Its head is triangular, with a tooth-filled maw and a pair of curved horns used to gore prey. When hunting, it lies in wait, using its gray armor for camouflage in rocky terrain. With a short burst of speed, it can overtake unsuspecting prey.

Armadid: Mountain predator 3; Init +6 (+2 Dex, +4 Improved Initiative); Defense 21 (+2 Dex, –1 size, +10 natural); Spd 10 m; VP/WP 32/20; Atk +5 melee (1d6+3, tail) or +5 melee (2d4+3, horns) or +4 ranged; SQ camouflage, low-light vision; SV Fort +8, Ref +5, Will +0; SZ L; Face/Reach 2 m by 4 m/2 m; Rep +0; Str 17, Dex 14, Con 20, Int 4, Wis 9, Cha 9. Challenge Code B.

Skills: Climb +11, Hide +4, Listen +3.
Feats: Force-Sensitive, Improved Initiative.
Force Feats: Burst of Speed.

N'zoth

Planet Type: Terrestrial
Climate: Arid
Terrain: Dry plains, deserts
Atmosphere: Breathable
Gravity: Standard
Diameter: 9,500 km
Length of Day: 28 standard hours
Length of Year: 354 standard days
Sentient Species: Yevethans
Languages: Yevethan
Population: 700 million
Species Mix: 100% Yevethan
Government: Caste
Major Exports: None
Major Imports: None
System/Star: N'zoth/C'Rel

Planets	Type	Moons
K'Zar	Searing rock	0
T'Grel	Searing rock	0
V'Rof	Volcanic rock	1
G'Hol	Terrestrial	1
N'zoth	Terrestrial	3
M'Buh	Barren rock	4
—	Asteroid belt	—
D'Pur	Gas giant	14
F'Tang	Frozen rock	0

Description

N'zoth is the homeworld of the Yevethans, a species known for its extreme xenophobia. The Yevethans aren't just the dominant species on the planet—they're the only species. Exclusionary attitudes preclude other species from ever settling there. The N'zoth system is in the Koornacht Cluster, a fact the ancient Yevethans never suspected. The suns burn so brightly in the N'zoth sky that all other stars are blotted out. This astronomical anomaly encouraged the Yevethans to believe throughout their ancient history that they were alone in the galaxy.

From space, N'zoth appears as a gray-green planet with yellow clouds. Seasons on N'zoth are unremarkable and boring, thanks to a smaller than normal axial tilt. A dry world orbiting a yellow sun, N'zoth has three moons: Pa'aal, Pa'rak, and Pa'red. Summers are hot and dry, while winters are warm and dry. The siringana, a vicious predator native to N'zoth, is a perfect example of how even nature is harsh and inhospitable on the world.

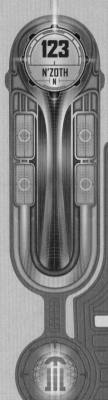

History

Thanks to the obscuring power of the Koornacht Cluster's bright suns, the ancient Yevethans never knew there were other stars in the galaxy. Consequently, they thought they were the only intelligent species in the universe. The Yevethans perfected space travel and eventually colonized eleven nearby planets. On all these planets, the most intelligent lifeforms Yevethan explorers found were animals, thus preserving the idea that the N'zoth indeed were the only significant species in the universe.

This belief went unchallenged for millennia until Imperial forces invaded N'zoth in the early years of the Empire. Yevethan arrogance was no match for Imperial firepower, and the world quickly fell. The Empire built a shipyard code-named Black 15 and established a garrison on the planet. An Imperial government enslaved the Yevethans, putting them to work in the shipyards as maintenance and technical personnel.

With amazing speed, the Yevethans mastered shipbuilding and weapons technology. Eight months after Imperial forces were defeated in the Battle of Endor, the Empire decided to withdraw from several systems and consolidate their forces. N'zoth was one of those systems. During the early stages of the withdrawal, a charismatic Yevethan named Nil Spaar launched an attack to liberate the world using highly trained Yevethan commandos. Since the Empire was already cutting its losses, reinforcements

never arrived to defend the targets of this ambush. Swiftly, the Yevethans seized control of the yards and all nine Star Destroyers, including the Super Star Destroyer *Intimidator*. Spaar then trained *Intimidator*'s turbolasers on Imperial citizens, killing twenty thousand of them.

Once the Black Fleet and the Black 15 shipyard were claimed for the Yevetha Protectorate, Nil Spaar took over as viceroy after the death of the former viceroy, Kiv Truun. The Black 15 yards were moved out of N'zoth orbit to a secret location. The surface yards took up the slack, churning out new spherical thrustships built by the Nazfar Metalworkers' Guild.

Twelve years after the Battle of Endor, Nil Spaar launched the Great Purge, a campaign of extermination aimed at all foreign settlements in the Koornacht Cluster. With typical Yevethan cruelty, the attacks were launched while Nil Spaar went through the motions of negotiations with Leia Organa Solo on Coruscant. At the end of the campaign, Nil Spaar, in his flagship *Aramadia*, returned to N'zoth to a hero's welcome. It seemed that the Yevethans were unstoppable.

Finally, a New Republic fleet met the Black Fleet and Yevethan thrustships in the Battle of N'zoth. During this furious action, Imperial slaves forced to crew the captured Star Destroyers rebelled. By activating a series of hidden slave circuits, the Imperial citizens hijacked all nine ships of the Black Fleet and leaped into Deep Core space, taking Nil Spaar with them. With the guns of the Black Fleet gone, the New Republic fleet easily defeated the Yevethan thrustships, and the day was won.

Nil Spaar's flagship *Aramadia* was eventually recovered in the Deep Core, but no trace of Nil Spaar himself has ever been found.

Even during The New Jedi Order era, the New Republic keeps a watchful eye on N'zoth in case the Yevethans are tempted to cause more trouble.

People

The skeletal, crested Yevethans are one of the most xenophobic species in the galaxy. Female Yevethan are called *marasi* and males are called *nitakka*. Their young are birthed in separate chambers—birth-casks called *mara-nas*.

Their society is stratified into castes. A Yevethan can never advance to a higher caste. In some rare situations, a member of a higher caste may be downgraded to a lower caste. The only fate worse than being a lower-caste member on N'zoth is being an alien. A lower-caste member is part of society, albeit in the dregs of it. Non-Yevethans are treated as the scum beneath Yevethan feet.

Yevethans consider a killing to be murder only if the killer was a lower-caste member and the victim of a higher caste. Naturally, killing low-castes or aliens is not murder.

"Dominance killing" is a common occurrence among the higher castes. Lower-caste *nitakka* are often slain so that their blood can nourish the birth-casks of the higher caste's children.

Although Yevethans are extremely arrogant, narrow-minded and harsh, they do possess an uncanny knack for learning new technology. Naturally, this fact isn't lost on them, since it gives the Yevethans yet another reason to think highly of themselves. Yevethans are so xenophobic that even learning Basic is a repulsive concept. As a rule, lower-caste members are forced by their superiors to learn Basic so they can serve as translators. A cadre of extremely high-caste Yevethans has deigned to learn Basic simply because they believe that some things should not be heard by lower-caste ears.

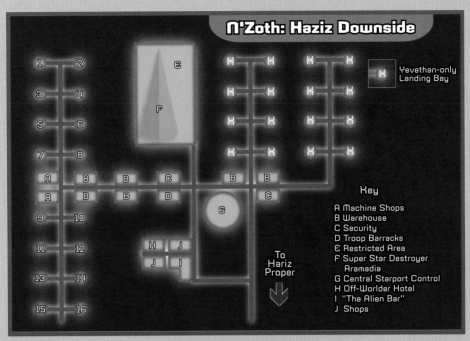

Yevethan-only Landing Bay

Key

A Machine Shops
B Warehouse
C Security
D Troop Barracks
E Restricted Area
F Super Star Destroyer
  Aramadia
G Central Starport Control
H Off-Worlder Hotel
I "The Alien Bar"
J Shops

To Hariz Proper

Locations

To the average Yevethan, even the humblest part of N'zoth is better than the best location on an alien world. Here are some of the more prominent locales.

Giat Nor

N'zoth's capital city, Giat Nor, is home to one million of the planet's seven hundred million Yevethans. Giat Nor hosts the royal palace, the caste meeting halls, and an elaborate monument to Nil Spaar. Outsiders are forbidden to enter Giat Nor; even so, some daring souls have managed to disguise themselves (often using a kit as described below) and enter. Any aliens discovered in Giat Nor are summarily slaughtered. The royal palace is still much as Nil Spaar left it. It boasts a private breedery with sixteen alcoves for birth-casks, as well as a grated floor for blood sacrifices. There is currently no viceroy or royal ruler. Many Yevethans hold on to the hope that some day Nil Spaar will return.

Hariz

Hariz is located 150 kilometers southeast of Giat Nor. This smaller city boasts a spaceport called Hariz Downside. A section of the spaceport has been cordoned off for Nil Spaar's flagship, *Aramadia*. The Super Star Destroyer is preserved there as an inspiration for generations of Yevethans to come. Aliens are allowed in Hariz, but they are watched closely and treated with sullen hostility. Yevethans want little to do with aliens or their goods. "Tougher than importing to N'zoth" is a common traders' saying to indicate the impossibility of a task.

Hariz is connected to Giat Nor by a hover-train system. Any aliens who attempt to board the train are harshly rebuffed. A second attempt at boarding usually results in the shooting of the offender. Hariz's open-air marketplace is quite well stocked, but the only goods anyone is interested in buying or selling are those of Yevethan manufacture.

The Valley of Rejection

This desolate valley 300 kilometers west of Giat Nor is a gash in the earth some 220 kilometers long. There is very little shade here, and the formations trap heat. Disgraced Yevethans are often exiled here, as are aliens on whom the Yevethans wish to bestow an especially dire punishment. The valley has a settlement of particularly sturdy and clever offworlders, who manage to eke out an existence despite the unforgiving land. When a Yevethan is exiled to the valley, the banishment is done with much ceremony and ritual. When an offworlder is sent here, the landspeeder barely slows down before the victim is unceremoniously tossed out.

Disguise Kit

Used by spies all over the galaxy, this disguise kit adds a +2 circumstance bonus on Disguise checks. It includes an easily hidden voice-distorter, prosthetics, pigments, and contact lenses. With this kit, a humanoid character can pass for a member of some other humanoid species of similar size. Anyone caught with such a kit is bound to raise suspicion among authority figures.

Disguise Kit
Cost: 500 credits
Weight: 1 kg

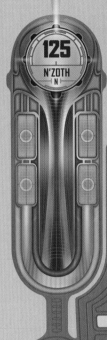

For the GM

The adventure hooks and supporting characters described in this section are meant for GMs only. If you're a player, stop reading now.

Adventures

How many adventures can heroes possibly have on a world where aliens are despised, distrusted, and forbidden from accessing selected parts of the planet? Plenty, if the heroes have the guts!

Extreme Breaking and Entering

When Nil Spaar embarked on his Great Purge in his flagship, he took a few trophies from his victims. Those trophies were put on display when *Aramadia* was decommissioned and turned into a museum. One of the ship's cargo bays was remodeled and turned into the trophy room. The more remarkable trophies include a pair of Jedi lightsabers and a large green gem known as the Eye of Deth. Although some legends in Basic hint that the proper name of the artifact is the "Eye of Death," it is actually named for Deth Korakill, a mercantile warlord slain by Nil Spaar during the Purge.

The heroes hear about the contents of *Aramadia's* trophy room courtesy of an old soldier in a bar, who swears he survived the Purge and saw those items loaded onto the flagship. (Force-using heroes may have reason to recover the lightsabers, while mercenary types would suspect the value of the Eye of Deth.) Breaking into and entering *Aramadia* is no easy task. Aside from the usual alarms and sensors, attack droids and sensor probes patrol the ship's corridors. Several squads of elite Yevethan guards are stationed in barracks a mere 5 minutes from the ship's permanent berth.

Painful Rejection

Possibly as a result of breaking the law or violating a taboo—such as entering *Aramadia* to loot the trophy room—the heroes are dumped into the middle of the Valley of Rejection and left to die. In the valley, the heroes encounter extreme heat, no water, and vicious siringana. All hope is not lost, however. As obscure legends suggest, there is an alien settlement in the valley. Consisting of twenty-three Humans, five Rodians, five Sullustans, and a Twi'lek, the settlement is called Werstilhere ("We're Still Here"). It's a testament to the exiles' guts and ingenuity.

Naturally, the heroes won't be content to spend the rest of their lives in Werstilhere. After gaining the acceptance of the settlers, the heroes can attempt to salvage some old wrecks and arrange some sort of transportation that will get them back to Hariz. Once there, the heroes must get their ship back from the impounding forces and leave N'zoth with all due haste.

Of course, no Yevethans live in the settlement. Even an exiled Yevethan would rather die in the hot, barren wastes than become an ally of some alien refuse. On the aliens' side, they'd just as soon kill a Yevethan exile as look at one. Adversity has made for strange alliances—and allowed an Imperial spy in the settlement to keep his political loyalties secret.

Habbala Brupt, a particularly traitorous Sullustan, was captured and exiled by the Yevethans for breaking a minor taboo. Fortunately for the Sullustan, the natives never discovered his true nature. The spy will do everything he can to get out of the settlement. If he manages to get free, he will report the heroes to the Empire (or Imperial Remnant) and arrange for them to be hunted down.

Claws of N'zoth

The New Republic learns that the Yevethan government has captured a Yuuzhan Vong spy on N'zoth. In an unusual show of diplomacy, the Yevethans have agreed to hand over the spy to New Republic agents once they have concluded their own interrogation.

Minister Zorbazat Xong meets the heroes as they arrive on N'zoth and escorts them to a nearby detention center, where Yevethan security coldly demonstrates how the Yuuzhan Vong should be dealt with. While the heroes look on, Xong oversees a brutal interrogation that ends with the spy's death. He then gives the heroes the corpse "to take back to your vile masters." A successful Diplomacy check (DC 35) convinces Xong not to kill the spy. The Yevethans attack and imprison heroes who try to bully them.

Allies and Antagonists

The following supporting characters are designed for use in your campaign.

Minister Zorbazat Xong

Heroes coming to N'zoth won't have a friend in the world. The one Yevethan heroes consistently encounter is the Minister of Homeworld Security, Zorbazat Xong. He's the perfect mix of an exasperating bureaucrat and overly zealous security guard. To his eternal shame, Zorbazat learned Basic to make his job easier. This poor career move has only intensified his hatred of the species that speak that language. A true Yevethan, Zorbazat doesn't approve of aliens on his precious world. If hard-pressed, he may concede the economic benefits of allowing travelers on N'zoth, if only for brief periods of time. This opinion could bring his loyalty into question, so it is a view he does not express openly.

Zorbazat is cold, efficient, and unfriendly. He cannot be bribed, since he sees anything that aliens have to offer as pure rubbish. However, he can be fooled or tricked into revealing important information from time to time. Zorbazat is living proof that one need not be bright to be arrogant. He wears a perpetual sneer that's extreme even by Yevethan standards.

Zorbazat can rapidly become the heroes' worst nightmare when they visit N'zoth. He can demand spot checks of the heroes' ship at his whim. He can tear up the heroes' customs sheets and make them fill them out all over again. Worst of all, he can follow the heroes around

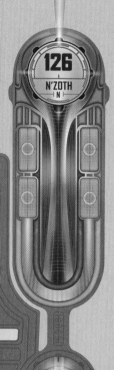

or arrange to have them followed, potentially foiling any schemes they may have. If necessary, Zorbazat can call security personnel for backup.

Zorbazat Xong: Male Yevethan Expert 3/Soldier 3; Init +1; Defense 14 (+1 Dex, +3 class); DR 3; Spd 10 m; VP/WP 40/12; Atk +8 melee (1d3+3, claw) or +6 ranged (3d6, blaster pistol); SQ xenophobia; SV Fort +5, Ref +3, Will +6; SZ M; FP 2; DSP 0; Rep +1; Str 16, Dex 12, Con 12, Int 9, Wis 10, Cha 14. Challenge Code C.

  Equipment: Combat jumpsuit, blaster pistol, comlink, datapad.

  Skills: Appraise +4, Balance –2, Bluff +5, Climb +0, Computer Use +6, Escape Artist –2, Gather Information +4, Hide –2, Intimidate +5, Jump +0, Knowledge (N'zoth) +6, Move Silently –2, Pilot +5, Read/Write Yevethan, Search +1, Speak Yevethan, Spot +3, Survival +1, Swim +0, Treat Injury +3.

  Feats: Armor Proficiencies (light, medium), Iron Will, Point Blank Shot, Skill Emphasis (Spot, Treat Injury), Weapon Group Proficiencies (blaster pistols, blaster rifles, vibro weapons).

Habbala Brupt

Sullustans are known for being pleasant and jovial, full of curiosity and a love of exploration. There are exceptions, and Habbala is one of them. Embittered by a series of setbacks in his life, Habbala hit rock bottom on a journey to Corellia.

Habbala was fleeing his homeworld as a passenger on a transport when the ship was boarded by the Empire and subjected to a search. When the boarding party found Rebel sympathizers, the Imperial officer in charge ordered the extermination of everyone on board. Habbala begged for his life and offered to do anything in exchange for mercy. The shrewd officer considered the value of a spy from a species not known to indulge in such activities. The officer spared Habbala's life—and killed everyone else on board.

For the first few years, Habbala did a respectable job. His last assignment was to N'zoth. Although Habbala is a decent spy, he wasn't good enough to evade the Yevethans. Ironically, he came to their attention because of an inadvertent breach of native custom. Although his cover remained intact, he was sent to the Valley of Rejection.

After wandering the valley for weeks, Habbala found Werstilhere, the rumored offworlder settlement. They embraced him as one of their own. Habbala now bides his time, seething with shame and resentment, waiting for a means to get off the planet and back to the Empire. Once there, he intends to see that the Empire destroys the Yevethans.

Habbala Brupt: Male Sullustan Scoundrel 3/Scout 3; Init +9 (+5 Dex, +4 Improved Initiative); Defense 19 (+5 Dex, +4 class); Spd 10 m; VP/WP 33/10; Atk +5 melee (1d3+1, punch) or +9 (3d6, blaster pistol); SQ darkvision 20 m, heart +1, illicit barter, lucky 1/day, precise attack +1, trailblazing; SV Fort +3, Ref +10,

Will +3; SZ M; FP 3; DSP 0; Rep +2; Str 12, Dex 20, Con 10, Int 11, Wis 10, Cha 9. Challenge Code D.

  Equipment: Comlink, datapad, blaster pistol, security kit, recording rod, disguise kit. (If Habbala is encountered at Werstilhere, the N'zoth authorities have confiscated all his gear.)

  Skills: Bluff +5, Climb +3, Computer Use +5, Demolitions +3, Disable Device +5, Forgery +4, Gather Information +5, Knowledge (alien species) +9, Knowledge (streetwise) +9, Listen +5, Read/Write Sullustese, Repair +4, Search +5, Speak Basic, Speak Sullustese, Spot +7.

  Feats: Dodge, Improved Initiative, Track, Weapon Group Proficiencies (blaster pistols, blaster rifles, simple weapons).

New Creature: Siringana

If any creature epitomizes the harsh world of N'zoth, it's the siringana. A vicious predator of the deserts and wastelands, it kills not only for food but also for the pleasure of killing.

Siringana are reptilian quadrupeds with a pair of scythelike "arms" and a spiked tail. Their tough, leathery skin is a brownish color, the better to blend in with their desert surroundings. Siringana average about 4 meters from snout to tip of tail. Fortunately for those it preys on, siringana are never found in groups of more than three, since they inevitably turn on each other when they try to travel together in larger numbers.

The Yevethan actually revere the siringana with an almost holy awe. They see the creatures as perfect killing machines for their perfect world. Some high-caste members keep siringana pits on their grounds. Victims of special sacrifices are tossed into the pit. Although it's scarce consolation for the victims, such sacrifices are rare and highly celebrated.

Like most reptiles, siringana lay eggs. As much as the Yevethans revere the beasts, it doesn't stop them from devouring siringana eggs, which are a delicacy through-out the Koornacht Cluster. Fortunately for the species, the females lay eggs often.

When attacking, siringana actually seem to relish causing fear in their victims before moving in for the kill. They enjoy filling their victims with dread and paralyzing the unfortunates by their mere presence. It seems that, like the Yevethans who admire them, the siringana have an overdeveloped sense of ego.

Siringana: Predator 10; Init +5 (+1 Dex, +4 Improved Initiative); Defense 20 (+1 Dex, –1 size, +10 natural); Spd 30 m; VP/WP 60/15; Atk +14 melee (1d8+5/19–20, spiked tail), +9 melee (2d6+5, bite); SQ darkvision 20 m, scent, terrifying presence; SV Fort +9, Ref +8, Will +4; SZ L; Face/Reach 2 m by 4 m/2 m; Str 20, Dex 12, Con 15, Int 6, Wis 12, Cha 5. Challenge Code D.

  Skills: Hide +10, Intimidate +5, Move Silently +3, Spot +2, Survival +4.

  Feats: Cleave, Improved Critical (tail), Improved Initiative, Power Attack.

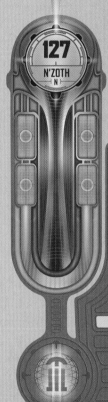

Ralltiir

Planet Type: Terrestrial
Climate: Temperate
Terrain: Urban, mountains, marsh
Atmosphere: Breathable
Gravity: Standard
Diameter: 13,449 km
Length of Day: 19 standard hours
Length of Year: 255 standard days
Sentient Species: Human
Languages: Basic
Population: 10 billion
Species Mix: 96% Human, 4% other
Government: Imperial governor
Major Exports: Financial services, marble
Major Imports: All
System/Star: Ralltiir/Rallt

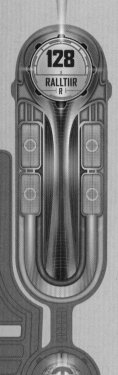
Planets	Type	Moons
Ockbur	Searing rock	0
Ralltiir	Terrestrial	28
Pauc'on	Barren rock	2
Clascvoria	Barren rock	1
Inwil	Frozen rock	3

Description

One of the great financial centers of the galaxy, Ralltiir is located in the Darpa sector along the Perlemian Trade Route. Though the planet is largely metropolitan, the undeveloped areas of its coastal regions consist of expansive marshes and wetlands. High mountain ranges dominate the spines of its three main continents. The topography and climate of the mountain ranges vary. The extreme latitudes are dotted with glaciers, while the central equatorial mountain range—called the High Ontis—is an arid expanse of desert scrub. Surrounded by more than two dozen moons, Ralltiir also benefits from what could be best described as "balanced" tidal forces. The moons' pulls largely counteract one another, sparing Ralltiir from extreme tides.

The sentient inhabitants of Ralltiir are overwhelmingly Human, but the planet's indigenous life is quite diverse. The dangerous Ralltiir tiger prowls the mountainous interior. The elusive but no less dangerous casting hawk, a hunting bird that thrives in both the rural and urban environs of the world, can be found on every continent.

History

Long a key financial world of the Republic, Ralltiir was a stable economic center for centuries but was shaken up during Palpatine's New Order. In the waning days of the

Republic and early years of the Empire, Ralltiir enjoyed a well-earned reputation as a safe haven for investment. Most financial institutions on Ralltiir maintained a political neutrality that buffered finances from the innumerable political machinations and uprisings upon which many markets depend for stability. Ralltiir's economy was a sentinel of security, one to which investors flocked in uncertain times. Rebel activity eventually grew in and around the world, but the markets were thought to be safe from harm.

Supporters of Emperor Palpatine ultimately undermined that stability by sabotaging the Ralltiir-based banking and account records of non-Humans and suspected Rebel supporters. Despite highly publicized efforts by the Ralltiir High Council to counter the infiltration (led primarily by secret Rebel sympathizers), the Emperor dispatched Lord Tion to stamp out all seditious activity on Ralltiir.

Tion's forces subjugated Ralltiir with brutal efficiency, securing the world and arresting suspected dissidents in short order. Imperial forces raised a blockade in the system, allowing only one ship to land: *Tantive IV*, a Corellian corvette under the command of Captain Antilles and Princess Leia Organa. While taking advantage of the chaos, Rebel agents were able to deliver information to Princess Leia about an Imperial project code-named "Death Star."

After the planet's initial subjugation, the blockade was lifted, but the Imperial forces remained. Ralltiir's economy faltered and fell into depression. Conglomerates and corporate interests moved their headquarters to other worlds. Lord Tion exploited this trend by installing a military tribunal with puppet leader Dennix Graeber as governor. Rebels were publicly executed, and the world was placed under harsh restrictions, to set an example and make the Empire's policies perfectly clear: Any world that did not swear total fealty to Palpatine would suffer the same consequences.

Through all this, the Emperor remained unaware that Governor Graeber was not his puppet. The governor was secretly (and anonymously) selling arms to various Rebel cells on Ralltiir. Ironically, while the assistance boosted the Rebels' strength, the resulting increase in Rebel activity on Ralltiir gave Palpatine the political and military support to continue the brutal subjugation of the planet.

Years later, Ralltiir began to rebuild its shattered economy. Progress was rapid until ten years after the Battle of Yavin, during the Imperial armada's recapture of the Core Worlds, when nearly all of Ralltiir was evacuated, and again the markets fell into recession. Within a year, heroes vanquished the reborn Emperor, and the markets rebounded with vigor.

During the Yuuzhan Vong invasion, the specter of economic instability still pervades much of Ralltiiri politics. The Ralltiiri Secretariat vetoed a proposal that would have allowed Ralltiir to accept refugees from the conflict. Such sentiments are typical of Ralltiir's self-preservation politics.

People

The citizens of Ralltiir are a cultured lot, largely dedicated to the financial industry. Beneath the facade of investments, profits, and progress, two opposing factions contest for power. One supports the Emperor and his New Order, while the other backs the Rebellion. Rebel cells abound throughout Ralltiir, making it a hotbed of Rebel activity in the Core.

Nearly all of Ralltiir's professionals are involved in finance. The rest either scheme as professional criminals or struggle as artisans and laborers for the planet's marble-mining companies. Because Humans dominate the world, most of the more affluent Ralltiiri adopt Coruscanti dress and culture, particularly during the Emperor's reign.

Locations

Descriptions of several important locations follow.

Grallia Spaceport

Ralltiir's primary landing facility is situated just offshore of beautiful Lake Grallia, directly across the lake from the main financial districts of the region. Grallia Spaceport is a bustling but orderly entry and departure port. Patrolled during the Emperor's reign by countless stormtroopers, it is a place where crime is rare, loiterers are nearly nonexistent, and order is the norm. But when the calm is broken, it is broken loudly. Vicious blaster fights, explosions, and kidnappings of prominent prefects (or local Imperial officers) all shatter the relative calm. The Rebel presence on Ralltiir is considerable. Denizens of the world are constantly on edge, awaiting the next outbreak of Rebel strikes or retaliatory Imperial raids.

Black Sun Fortress

During the rise of the Empire, Black Sun Master Alexi Garyn maintains a fortress on Ralltiir, built atop a granite outcropping in the Tas Sea. One primary tower and three smaller towers command breathtaking views of the turbulent Tas waters and the moon-filled Ralltiir skies. From the exterior, the fortress is similar to hundreds of other such extravagant retreats throughout Ralltiir. Many investors, shipping moguls, and other affluent residents of the world maintain similar bases in various remote locales.

Guarded by dozens of Black Sun's best trained guards and killers, what sets Master Garyn's facility aside is the massive subterranean structures under the fortress. Deep within the granite bedrock beneath the shallow seas, the Black Sun base expands to include nearly three square kilometers of catwalks, causeways, and warehouses.

The lowest depths of the fortress open into a large underground lake, several meters below the surface of the sea. Garyn maintains his personal landing bays underwater, along with several of his preferred craft. Staircases and paths carved from the eerie caverns lead to several platforms and other recesses, including a number of natural mineral springs in which the Black Sun Master occasionally relaxes.

Approximately six months before the Trade Federation blockade of Naboo, Garyn, his Dathomiri assassin Mighella, and all his Vigos were killed by the Sith assassin Darth Maul. It would be years before Black Sun would recover fully under the leadership of Prince Xizor.

Jumper Quarries

The old "jumper quarries" first got their name because their ownership was contested for centuries. These marble quarries in the remote canyons of the High Ontis are a dangerous region of tapped-out mines and chasms, some stripped to the verge of collapse. A few criminal groups (including Rebel cells) use the intricate networks of subterranean passages as hideouts.

One Rebel group, led by the Rodian Zeelo Fas, has fashioned a tunnel network that leads all the way from Docking Slip 120-54 in the spaceport to an old staging area some 40 kilometers away. The tunnel is fitted with numerous traps and sentry droids, but once those defenses have been circumvented, authorized visitors can board a small repulsor payloader that spirits them to a Rebel hideout. While the tunnel network is nowhere near as elaborate as that of the Black Sun fortress several hundred kilometers to the northwest, it is an impressive example of the ingenuity and adaptability with which the Rebels fight the tyrannical Empire.

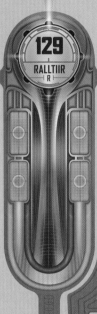

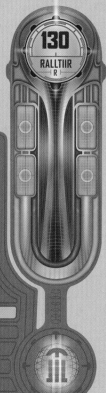

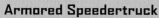

Below the Black Sun Fortress

Tunnel Leads out to Sea →

← Tunnel to Underground lake

Dry Tunnel to Underground Lake

Tunnels to Surface

1   Lift to Fortress
2   Warehouse (locked)
3   Swoop Storage
4   Bridge
5   Machine Shop
6   Shuttle Pad
7   Warehouse Caves

Armored Speedertruck

A stout repulsor truck fitted for the transport of tangible valuables, the RS armored speeder is a common sight throughout Ralltiir's financial sectors. It is common in other banking areas throughout the galaxy.

Ralltiir Securities Armored Speeder

Class: Speeder [Ground]	Crew: 2 (Skilled +4)
Size: Huge (7 m long)	Initiative: +2 (–2 size, +4 crew)
Passengers: 3	Maneuver: +2 (–2 size, +4 crew)
Cargo Capacity: 120 tons	Defense: 13 (–2 size, +5 armor)
Cost: 30,000 (new),	Shield Points: 0
22,500 (used)	Hull Points: 60 (DR 10)
Availability: Military	Speed: 70 m
Era: All	Altitude: 20 m

* This vehicle provides three-quarters cover to its crew and passengers.

    Weapon: Defense blaster; Fire Arc: Any; Attack Bonus: +2 (–2 size, +4 fire control); Damage: 3d8; Range Increment: 20 m.

For the GM

The adventure hooks and supporting characters described in this section are meant for GMs only. If you're a player, stop reading now.

Adventures

Feel free to use or adapt the following adventure hooks for your home campaign.

Black Sun Rising

The characters are sucked into a power struggle between organized crime factions of Ralltiir's vicious underworld. A local syndicate that owes the characters for a recent job has taken up residence in Garyn's old fortress.

    But while Black Sun has been weakened, it has not yet been destroyed. Fanatically loyal to Black Sun, the Kian'thar operative Shal'mak has come to Ralltiir to reclaim the fortress Garyn once commanded. (During the Rebellion era, her son Vigo Kreet'ah attempts the same task.) The characters must help defend the fortress from Black Sun agents long enough to collect their due, or they can cut a deal with Shal'mak herself—which might prove even more dangerous than facing her in combat.

Doctor's Orders

At the University Faculty Medical Center on the shores of Lake Grallia, Imperial stormtroopers have been posted outside the recovery room of Croy Winnis. The Imperial constabulary suspects Winnis may be a Rebel operative who provided information that allowed a recent Rebel raid in the system to kidnap a Cygnus Spaceworks design team. But Croy is more than a mere informant. He's a defector from Kuat Drive Yards attempting to deliver weapons technology to the Rebels.

    The characters are charged with the "retrieval" of Winnis, which is no small task. They must find a way into the Medical Center and rescue Winnis before the Imperials discover the true identity of the patient they're guarding.

Payload

The characters are called upon to investigate the theft of several shipments of Ralltiiri marble. Each missing payload is reportedly worth a cool five million credits. The corporation asking for the characters' help, XwiziMarble, is a small unit that works in the unforgiving eastern slopes of the High Ontis. The firm is well regarded in the galactic market, but since it is secretly sympathetic to the Rebellion, it would prefer not to get the Imperial authorities involved. The characters soon learn that the culprit is Ralltiir Consolidated Marble, an influential, Imperial-subsidized firm. Can the characters retrieve XwiziMarble's shipments without subjecting the company to Imperial reprisals?

Allies and Antagonists

The following supporting characters are designed for use in your campaign.

Bosrik Mak-Ageejay

A snobbish, condescending financial advisor for Regency Spires Imperial Trust, Bosrik Mak-Ageejay is one of the most despised—and effective—bankers on Ralltiir. Regency Spires was one of the few banks that weathered the Imperial subjugation fairly well, since most of its clientele at the time were Imperial officers and advisors.

Mak-Ageejay is a slender, impeccably groomed Human who sports the amber-tinted lenses common to Ralltiiri bankers. He is known for his considerable disdain for anything but the finest office amenities, most luxurious skylimos, and finest shimmersilk trousers. The officers of the Empire would be surprised if they learned that Bosrik has been using their "secure" funds to buy arms for the Rebellion from their own Governor Graeber. Mak-Ageejay savors that thought, the finest of ironies.

Bosrik Mak-Ageejay: Male Human Noble 8; Init +1; Defense 16 (+1 Dex, +5 class); Spd 10 m; VP/WP 28/10; Atk +6/+1 melee (1d3, punch) or +7/+2 ranged (3d4, sporting blaster); SQ bonus class skill (Gather Information), coordinate +2, favor +3, inspire confidence, resource access; SV Fort +2, Ref +5, Will +9; SZ M; FP 1; DSP 1; Rep +5; Str 11, Dex 13, Con 10, Int 16, Wis 16, Cha 15. Challenge Code D.

   Equipment: Datapad, sporting blaster (concealed).

   Skills: Appraise +11, Bluff +7, Computer Use +4, Diplomacy +11, Gamble +7, Gather Information +8, Intimidate +7, Knowledge (business) +11, Knowledge (streetwise) +11, Listen +10, Profession (banker) +11, Read/Write Basic, Read/Write Bothese, Search +8, Sense Motive +7, Speak Basic, Speak Bothese, Speak Huttese, Spot +10.

   Feats: Alertness, Cautious, Combat Expertise, Influence, Weapon Group Proficiencies (blaster pistols, simple weapons).

Stubble Trel

A grizzled marble miner and back-country character, Stubble is the "black nerf" of the influential Trel clan, a Coruscanti and Ralltiiri family of investors and well-to-do socialites. His net worth, by virtue of being a Trel, is something close to 20 million credits, but Stubble has no use for his wealth. He toils in the marble quarries in the most remote stretches of the High Ontis's alpine lakes, surviving off the land and living in a modest one-room shelter of cracked marble and weathered timber.

Stubble Trel is a compact Human who wears a leather jerkin, miner's dungarees, and Ralltiir tigerskin boots. His only contact is with other miners who work the XwiziMarble quarries. Though not engaged in galactic politics, Stubble has likely explored more of Ralltiir's underground networks—Rebel and criminal boltholes alike—than any other being.

Stubble Trel: Male Human Scout 4; Init +1; Defense 14 (+1 Dex, +3 class); Spd 10 m; VP/WP 26/19; Atk +6 melee (1d3+3, punch) or +4 ranged (3d8/19–20, blaster rifle); SQ heart +1, trailblazing, uncanny dodge (Dex bonus to Defense); SV Fort +5, Ref +3, Will +3; SZ M; FP 1; DSP 0; Rep –1; Str 16, Dex 13, Con 16, Int 12, Wis 13, Cha 14. Challenge Code C.

   Equipment: Mining tools, survival gear, medpac, blaster rifle.

   Skills: Climb +6, Craft (tools) +8, Demolitions +5, Disable Device +4, Knowledge (geography) +6, Knowledge (Ralltiir) +7, Read/Write Basic, Repair +4, Search +5, Speak Basic, Spot +4, Survival +10, Swim +6, Treat Injury +4.

   Feats: Low Profile, Skill Emphasis (Survival), Toughness, Weapon Group Proficiencies (blaster pistols, blaster rifles, simple weapons).

Shal'mak

Shal'mak is part of a long dynasty of crime lords on Shaum Hii, the Kian'thar homeworld. The aquatic, glassy-eyed criminal has long held a position with Black Sun's Core World interests while maintaining her work ethic as a derlac herder's wife. She actually inherited the position from her uncle, who in turn received his position from a second cousin.

A tempered, businesslike criminal, Shal'mak takes her work very seriously and does not indulge in the luxuries her wealth affords her. She is a dangerous foe and a capable leader. Her innate Kian'thar abilities often allow her to gain the upper hand in face-to-face dealings with friends and foes. Most of her endeavors on behalf of Black Sun deal with money laundering and financial matters.

Shal'mak: Female Kian'thar Scoundrel 5/Noble 2/Crime Lord 3; Init +1; Defense 19 (+1 Dex, +7 class, +1 natural); Spd 10 m; VP/WP 52/12; Atk +5 melee (1d3, punch) or +5 melee (2d6, vibroblade) or +6 ranged; SQ bonus class skill (Bluff), breathe underwater, contact (1), empath, favor +1, illicit barter, inspire confidence, inspire fear –2, low-light vision, lucky 1/day, precise attack +1, resource access, +2 species bonus on Swim checks; SV Fort +5, Ref +9, Will +9; SZ M; FP 3; DSP 4; Rep +10; Str 10, Dex 12, Con 12, Int 14, Wis 14, Cha 16. Challenge Code E.

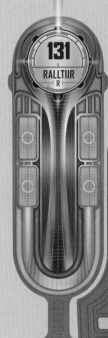

Equipment: Vibroblade.

Skills: Appraise +12, Bluff +16, Computer Use +9, Diplomacy +16, Forgery +7, Gather Information +16, Hide +6, Intimidate +13, Knowledge (streetwise) +13, Listen +8, Move Silently +4, Read/Write Basic, Read/Write Kian'thar, Search +4, Sense Motive +14, Speak Basic, Speak Huttese, Speak Kian'thar, Speak Rodese, Spot +4, Swim +7.

Feats: Alertness, Animal Empathy, Fame, Great Fortitude, Infamy, Skill Emphasis (Knowledge [streetwise]), Weapon Group Proficiencies (blaster pistols, simple weapons, vibro weapons).

Special Qualities: *Empath*—A Kian'thar gains a +4 insight bonus on Bluff and Sense Motive checks against living beings within 10 meters.

Skill Bonuses—Kian'thar gain a +2 bonus on Swim checks and a +2 bonus on Survival checks (aquatic and swamp environments only).

Bonus Feat—Kian'thar gain the bonus feat Animal Affinity.

New Creature: Casting Hawk

The casting hawk is a bird of prey that can be found almost everywhere on Ralltiir. The creature is a capable hunter and popular domesticated pet of some of Ralltiir's most affluent citizens. The hawk's wingspan is typically 1.5 to 1.8 meters. Males tend to be colored brown or rust red, with greenish-yellow mottling. Females and hatchlings are a light yellowish gray.

Not the strongest of hunters, the casting hawk makes up for its lack of power with a rather ingenious tactic. The creature's name is derived from one of the ways it hunts ground prey. The lone hawks typically establish aeries high atop the boughs of the liquid thoron tree, a thin-limbed conifer common throughout Ralltiir's wooded regions. The copious sap of the liquid thoron dries quickly, but it has a tensile strength comparable to syntherope, and it is extremely sticky.

Upon spotting prey below, the casting hawk breaks off several thin, green branches from the nearest liquid thoron tree and swoops over its prospective victim while carrying the branches in its talons. The dripping tree sap ensnares the creature, allowing the hawk to drag the hapless prey back to its aerie for a quick meal. A victim can avoid being ensnared by making a successful Escape Artist check or Strength check (DC 20 in either case). Many observers have likened this process to the use of tangle guns by Ralltiir's law enforcement agencies.

Casting Hawk: Airborne predator 2; Init +4 (+4 Improved Initiative); Defense 11 (+1 size); Spd 2 m, fly 16 m (good); VP/WP 14/12; Atk +3 melee (1d4, beak) or +3 melee (1d3, talon) or +3 ranged; SQ +2 species bonus on Spot checks; SV Fort +4, Ref +3, Will +1; SZ S; Face/Reach 2 m by 1 m/1 m; Rep +0; Str 11, Dex 11, Con 12, Int 4, Wis 12, Cha 10. Challenge Code A.

Skills: Listen +6, Move Silently +4, Spot +10.
Feats: Improved Initiative.

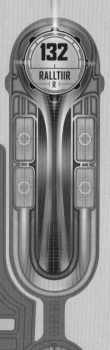

Recopia

Planet Type: Terrestrial
Climate: Temperate
Terrain: Islands, ocean
Atmosphere: Breathable
Gravity: Standard
Diameter: 14,463 km
Length of Day: 20 standard hours
Length of Year: 286 standard days
Sentient Species: Human
Languages: Basic
Population: 200 million
Species Mix: 74% Human, 4% Duros, 3% Bothan, 19% other
Government: Loose federation of city-states
Major Exports: Exotic animals
Major Imports: High-tech goods
System/Star: Recopi

Planets	Type	Moons
Inner Los	Searing rock	0
Penovia	Gas giant	14
Lacia	Gas giant	9
Recopia	Terrestrial	3
Outer Los	Ice ball	0

Description

Though Recopia is a Core World, it is not as heavily settled as most. Lacking valuable natural resources, it has remained a sparsely settled world with little to offer the rest of the galaxy—except, perhaps, anonymity in a region of space where that commodity is all too rare.

Geographically, Recopia is a world of sulfuric oceans over which poisonous clouds perpetually roil. The hostile seas are broken only by a series of plateau islands that rise high into the sky—sometimes a kilometer or more—before leveling off. Thousands of these plateaus exist on Recopia, some in tight clusters and others scattered hither and yon over vast tracts of ocean. Many of these plateaus rise above the poisonous levels of fog, making them habitable for those suitably motivated to live on them. Even on safe plateaus, the air reeks of unwholesome organic compounds, but these islands are lashed by frequent monsoons that help to cleanse the air. Only an eighth or so of the plateaus are populated.

Travel on Recopia is entirely by air. Even the crudest settlement has at least a rudimentary airfield for skyhoppers and transports.

History

Recopia was first settled thousands of years ago by Human colonists, in an age when hyperspace travel took much longer than it does in more recent times. At that time, any habitable planet—no matter how unpleasant—was deemed valuable real estate. These early settlements offered way station facilities for merchants traveling into the Core.

Many of these communities faltered when the development of faster hyperdrives reduced the need for traders to make layovers on Recopia. Others continued to slowly grow into city-states, as those seeking to escape the bustle of the Core arrived and put down roots. Religious pilgrims, pirates, refugees from war and disaster, and those seeking a new start settled on various islands shrouded in fog and rain.

Recopia lacked representation in the Republic Senate. Each city-state had its own government and law, each according to its nature. Some settlements featured Galactic-standard legal systems, while others enforced their edicts at the point of a vibroblade. Change came to Recopia in the Rebellion era, when an Imperial senator and a governor forced edicts upon its citizens. Those were chaotic times, as Imperial soldiers swept down on settlements without warning on the lookout for pirate enclaves, Rebel encampments, and the homes of renegade Jedi. Recopians grew less obsessed with isolation under such conditions. They soon drew together into a more cohesive federation, each city-state pledging to support the others in times of need. Recopia was among the first of the Core Worlds to abandon the beleaguered Empire and declare its allegiance to the New Republic.

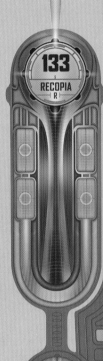

People

Recopians are hardy and taciturn folk who mind their own affairs. The average citizen shows little interest in traveling beyond the city-state where he was born. Although the Recopians' desire to be left alone is less pronounced in the larger city-states with spaceports, it is nonetheless a nearly univcersal trait among most people visitors are likely to meet. More aliens dwell on Recopia than on most other Core Worlds settled by Humans. Some city-states are entirely populated by one species. For instance, Duros and Bothans both maintain large local enclaves.

Locations

Descriptions of several important locations follow.

Scapio

Scapio is the closest thing to a capital city on Recopia, and it is the settlement where most offworlders gather. This is primarily because Thoren Spaceport is the only port on the planet to service passenger starliners. A chain of islands linked by a series

of bridges, Scapio is studded with structures built on and into the bedrock. A police force maintains order in most public areas, but visitors lingering in less savory areas risk attack by members of Scapio's many street gangs. In the Rebellion era, when the city is home to the planet's senator and military garrison, the streets are somewhat safer.

Hinder Market

Located on the island of the same name, the Hinder is a huge market where merchants who deal in shipping live animals to the Core meet to bargain with their peers. Beyond a compact freighter spaceport are blocks of pens, cages, low buildings filled with stalls, auction houses, and lending houses. It's a wild and chaotic place to outsiders, but a well-oiled machine to those familiar with its rituals.

Tuldok Ranch

Tuldok Ranch is a small, jagged plateau inhabited by the Tuldok clan. Everyone pretends that the Tuldoks are a band of roving traders, but most know them to be pirates who periodically roar off to plunder the Colonies. They never raise a hand to fellow Recopians, however. In fact, they eagerly rush to the aid of island communities in distress. The Tuldoks spent most of Palpatine's reign in the Colonies. Shortly before the Battle of Endor, they returned in triumph as Rebel privateers to menace the small Imperial garrison and prey on Imperial traffic. In the time of the New Republic, the Tuldoks assumed legitimate control of the planetary government.

DR

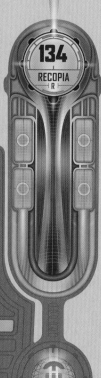

Seyugi Compound, Recopia

(Mallif Cove)

3

11
10
8
5
7
12

1
6
6 5 2
4
9 9

3
3

Big Vault
Door

One Square = 10 Meters

1 Lift Tube
2 Carbonite Freezing Chamber
3 Hibernation Vault
4 Power Turbine Room
5 Training Room
6 Barracks
7 Clinic
8 Meditation Chamber
9 Hydroponics Lab
10 Mess Hall
11 Galley
12 Armory

Mallif Cove

Mallif Cove is an island populated only by a village of religious recluses given to pondering the mysteries of the galaxy, muttering about surges in the universal field, and broadcasting eccentric religious programs on as many local holovid bands as they can pirate. The odd Mallif monks in their green cloaks are descendants of the Seyugi Dervishes, a terrible band of mysterious assassins who once menaced the Core. Today, not even the Mallifs are aware of their past. None suspect that beneath their humble cloister, the hidden fortress of the Seyugi holds a horrible secret.

New Prestige Class: Seyugi Dervish

The Seyugi Dervishes were once a fanatical cult of Core-based assassins. Acolytes honed their Force-augmented combat skills to sell their services as professional killers. The sight of the red-cloaked, white-masked figures struck terror in the hearts of Core elites for more than a century

before the Jedi moved to destroy their order. One Seyugi fortress hidden on Recopia escaped notice. Its Dervishes sleep in carbonite hibernation, awaiting the day they might awaken to terrorize the Core once more.

The Seyugi school neglects most Force theory in favor of developing deadlier, unarmed Force-augmented attacks. Practitioners of this style close quickly with opponents. Once an enemy is within reach of the Dervishes' smiting blows, the fight is as good as over. A Dervish master surrounded by a throng of equally skilled opponents is capable of slaying them all in seconds.

Requirements

To qualify to become a Seyugi Dervish, a character must fulfill the following criteria.

Base Attack Bonus: +4.

Skills: Hide 5 ranks, Move Silently 5 ranks, Tumble 5 ranks.

Feats: Alertness, Dodge, Force-Sensitive.

Special: Must apprentice under a Seyugi Dervish for one year before gaining the benefits of the class.

Game Rule Information

Vitality: Seyugi Dervishes gain 1d8 vitality points per level. The character's Constitution modifier applies.

Class Skills

The Seyugi Dervish's class skills, and the key ability for each skill, are as follows.

Climb (Str), Escape Artist (Dex), Hide (Dex), Intimidate (Cha), Jump (Str), Listen (Wis), Move Silently (Dex), Search (Int), Spot (Wis), Survival (Wis), Tumble (Dex).

Skill Points at Each Additional Level: 4 + Int modifier.

Class Features

Seyugi Dervishes gain the following class features.

Starting Feats

A Seyugi Dervish receives the following bonus feats.

Weapon Group Proficiency (simple weapons)

Weapon Group Proficiency (slugthrowers)

Weapon Group Proficiency (vibro weapons)

Martial Arts

At 1st level, a Seyugi Dervish gains Martial Arts as a bonus feat.

Smite

At 2nd level, a Seyugi Dervish gains a +1 bonus to damage with a successful Martial Arts attack and threat-

The Seyugi Dervish

Level	Base Attack Bonus	Fort Save	Ref Save	Will Save	Special	Defense Bonus	Reputation Bonus
1st	+1	+2	+1	+1	Martial arts	+1	+1
2nd	+2	+3	+2	+2	Smite +1	+2	+1
3rd	+3	+3	+2	+2	Improved alertness	+2	+0
4th	+4	+4	+2	+2	Smite +2	+2	+1
5th	+5	+4	+3	+3	Uncanny speed	+3	+1

ens a critical hit on a natural 19 or 20. At 4th level, the damage bonus increases to +2.

Improved Alertness
At 3rd level, a Seyugi Dervish gains a +4 aptitude bonus on Listen and Spot checks. This ability does not stack with the bonuses gained from the Alertness feat.

Uncanny Speed
Beginning at 5th level, a Seyugi Dervish can tap into the Force to move at lightning speed for a brief period of time (usually to close with an opponent). For 4 rounds, the Seyugi Dervish may multiply his speed by 5. This has the side effect of multiplying jump distances by 2. Using this ability requires a full-round action. At the end of the 4-round period, the Seyugi Dervish's speed drops to its normal value, and the character loses 5 vitality points. If the Seyugi Dervish has no vitality points remaining, he takes wound point damage instead.

For the GM

The adventure hooks and supporting characters described in this section are meant for GMs only. If you're a player, stop reading now.

Adventures
Feel free to use or adapt the following adventure hooks for your home campaign.

Pecoppi Hunt
The heroes uncover reports of Hinder Market merchants dealing in sentient alien species. They resolve to look into the rumors. The heroes arrive on Hinder Island as the annual Bandercamp Auctions are getting underway. The event is a five-week flurry of auctions in which merchants from all over the galaxy descend on Recopia to sell alien creatures to exotic pet dealers from the Core and the Colonies. An Arconan buyer points the heroes in the direction of the Guttersnipe, a smoky spice parlor and cantina by the north side cliffs said to be frequented by the slavers.

At the Guttersnipe, they encounter a gang of thugs drugging up some pecoppi parrots. Each cute, brightly colored bird is about the size of a Human head. It becomes clear that the pecoppi is barely sentient—enough to interact with simple, endearing language—and is sold when in a drugged stupor to avoid detection by inspectors. The trail leads to a walled manor near the north side cliffs. Within the walls, Tama Burr and her crew of thugs guard pecoppi in open pens. Clearing out the manor and defeating its defenders puts a stop to the trade.

Dervish Delights
A monk of Mallif Cove finds his way into the secret caves beneath the island and accidentally unleashes a troop of hibernating Seyugi Dervishes. Unable to gain entrance to the other chambers where a thousand of their brethren await revival, the Seyugi overwhelm the monks on the island. Led by Razi Khan, they fly to Scapio, seeking someone who can open their vault doors for them.

The Seyugi don't go in for for subtlety. They land in the middle of a street and fan out, threatening passersby and demanding—in an archaic accent—to be led to a "doorkeeper." They grow increasingly violent, overwhelming the local law enforcement. A cult of Seyugi should pose a serious challenge to the heroes.

Having seized a hapless slicer, Razi Khan heads back to the Cove. He abandons the group confronting the heroes. His trail leads to a hidden turbolift in the monks' compound, which descends into the bowels of the island. In a central room with three great vault doors, Razi Khan's slicer is at work opening the vaults. If the heroes don't stop him, Recopia will soon be overwhelmed by Dervish assassins.

Allies and Antagonists
The lawless, independent nature of Recopia, coupled with its resistance to nosy outsiders, makes it a prime gathering place for the Core's fringers, both those who traffic in the Core and those whose shady projects take them beyond its confines.

Tama Burr
In the Core is a large underground market for adorable, semisentient pets. Tama Burr knows where all the buyers and sellers are. She's a slight, raptorlike woman in her late forties with bulging green eyes and braided blonde hair. She favors colorful garb to complement the plumage of her pets and slaves. She is a confident woman who presents a brave front in the face of danger, but in her business dealings she is averse to taking risks. Burr specializes in avians, and she has a manor equipped to meet the needs of a variety of exotic species. She deals in nonsentient birds as well. In fact, she has provided numerous rare animals for the Abersaith Aviary on Corulag.

Tama Burr: Female Human Expert 3/Diplomat 2; Init +1; Defense 11 (+1 Dex, +1 class); Spd 10 m; VP/WP 0/10; Atk +2 melee (DC 15 stun, stun baton) or +2 melee (1d3–1, punch) or +4 ranged (3d4, sporting blaster); SV Fort +1, Ref +2, Will +8; SZ M; FP 0; DSP 0; Rep +1; Str 8, Dex 13, Con 10, Int 12, Wis 14, Cha 16. Challenge Code B.

  Equipment: Stun baton, sporting blaster, comlink, datapads, medpac.

  Skills: Appraise +9, Bluff +6, Computer Use +4, Diplomacy +7, Entertain (drama) +8, Forgery +6, Gather Information +10, Handle Animal +14, Knowledge (alien species) +7, Listen +4, Profession (animal dealer) +5, Read/Write Basic, Ride +3, Sense Motive +6, Speak Basic, Spot +6.

  Feats: Animal Affinity, Skill Emphasis (Appraise, Handle Animal), Trustworthy, Weapon Group Proficiencies (blaster pistols, simple weapons).

Razi Khan
Razi Khan, a warrior of the Seyugi cult, was frozen in carbonite for five hundred years. He is a tall man with

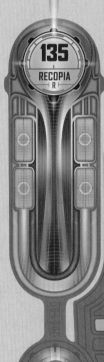

RAZI KHAN

dark eyes and no body hair whatsoever. He wears a red cloak at all times. When prepared for combat, he wears a white mask featuring a painted, stylized rancor maw. Seyugi Dervishes are trained to be patient and hide their emotions from their enemies, but Razi's long hibernation has left him jittery. He is likely to explode into a dark rage if his will is frustrated, attacking any who defy him. He is unaware of certain advances in technology, such as modern blasters and holovids.

Razi Khan: Male Human Scoundrel 6/Seyugi Dervish 4; Init +3; Defense +23 (+3 Dex, +9 class); Spd 10 m; VP/WP 58/14; Atk +8/+1 melee (1d6+3, punch) or +8/+3 ranged (2d6, slugthrower rifle); SQ illicit barter, improved alertness, lucky 2/day, smite +2, precise attack +1; SV Fort +6, Ref +9, Will +4; SZ M; FP 0; DSP 2; Rep +3; Str 12, Dex 16, Con 14, Int 10, Wis 9, Cha 13. Challenge Code E.

   Equipment: Slugthrower rifle, red cloak and white mask, comlink.

   Skills: Appraise +3, Bluff +7, Climb +8, Escape Artist +12, Gather Information +8, Hide +12, Intimidate +8, Jump +9, Knowledge (Seyugi lore) +7, Listen +11, Move Silently +16, Search +8, Sleight of Hand +10, Spot +12, Tumble +14.

   Feats: Alertness, Dodge, Force-Sensitive, Heroic Surge, Lightning Reflexes, Martial Arts, Nimble, Skill Emphasis (Move Silently), Weapon Group Proficiencies (blaster pistols, slugthrowers, simple weapons, vibro weapons).

Gull Tuldok

Gull is a large, booming man who leads one of the Tuldok clan's three raiding fleets. He has spent most of

his life in space, returning to Recopia only every five years or so to resupply, take on new crew members, and visit with his family. In the recent years of unrest, it has fallen to him to remain behind with his small fleet so he can protect the ranch and neighboring islands. Gull is finding this duty a trifle dull, so he spends a lot of his time in Scapio gambling with his shipmates and visiting merchants.

Gull Tuldok: Male Human Scoundrel 7/Soldier 3; Init +6 (+2 Dex, +4 Improved Initiative); Defense 19 (+2 Dex, +7 class); Spd 10 m; VP/WP 55/12; Atk +9/+4 melee (1d3+1, punch) or +9/+4 melee (2d6+1, vibroblade) or +10/+5 ranged (3d8, heavy blaster pistol); SQ illicit barter, lucky 2/day, precise attack +1; SV Fort +6, Ref +8, Will +3; SZ M; FP 0; DSP 0; Rep +3; Str 13, Dex 15, Con 12, Int 15, Wis 10, Cha 13. Challenge Code E.

   Equipment: Heavy blaster pistol, vibroblade, comlink.

   Skills: Appraise +15, Astrogate +12, Bluff +11, Demolitions +7, Disable Device +6, Escape Artist +7, Gather Information +17, Hide +8, Knowledge (spacer lore) +12, Listen +5, Move Silently +12, Pilot +13, Read/Write Basic, Read/Write Sullustese, Repair +7, Search +9, Speak Basic, Speak Sullustese, Spot +7.

   Feats: Armor Proficiencies (light, medium), Cleave, Combat Expertise, Great Cleave, Improved Initiative, Power Attack, Skill Emphasis (Gather Information), Starship Operation (space transport), Weapon Group Proficiencies (blaster pistols, simple weapons, vibro weapons).

New Creature: Krendel

The krendel is a large, amphibian lizardlike creature, a glossy yellow reptile with vibrant blue and green mottled spots running down its back. It has large, bulbous black eyes and rubbery, sticky pads on its feet that allow it to climb surfaces of sheer rock. Krendels are born and raised in Recopia's toxic seas but soon develop lungs and limbs. These biological advantages enable them to creep on land in search of their prey, usually seabirds nesting in the island cliffs. Since they can't see particularly well, they hunt primarily by scent and motion. Krendels hunt in mated pairs. Although they generally steer clear of settled areas, krendels occasionally blunder over the cliffs and into communities.

   The krendel has two attacks. Its gaping maw, filled with sharp, needled teeth, is bad enough, but even worse is the corrosive gas it can spew from a distended throat sac. The gas streams out in a 10-meter cone, dealing 4d6 points of damage, or half damage with a successful Reflex saving throw (DC 16).

Krendel: Aquatic predator 9; Init +1; Defense 15 (+1 Dex, −1 size, +5 natural); Spd 10 m, swim 20 m; VP/WP 32/14; Atk +11/+5 melee (3d6+3, bite); SQ breath weapon 4d6, amphibious, scent; SV Fort +8, Ref +7, Will +1; SZ L; Face/Reach 4 m by 4 m/4 m; Str 17, Dex 13, Con 14, Int 6, Wis 7, Cha 5.

   Skills: Climb +7, Search +4, Swim +13.

   Feats: Blind-Fight, Cleave, Improved Bantha Rush, Power Attack.

Rhinnal

Planet Type: Terrestrial
Climate: Temperate to arctic
Terrain: Mountains, rivers/lakes, urban
Atmosphere: Breathable
Gravity: Standard
Diameter: 12,900 km
Length of Day: 27 standard hours
Length of Year: 357 standard days
Sentient Species: Human
Languages: Basic
Population: 55 million
Species Mix: 92% Human, 8% other
Government: Imperial governorship or clan (depending on era)
Major Exports: Pharmaceuticals, medical personnel, textiles
Major Imports: Raw materials, foodstuffs
System/Star: Rhinnal

Planets	Type	Moons
Hern	Molten rock	0
Nensil	Barren rock	0
Seffi	Toxic oceanic	2
Rhinnal	Terrestrial	2
Basho	Ice ball	1
—	Asteroid field	—
Omeddyl	Gas giant	18
Ruby	Gas giant	21

Description

Travelers arriving on Rhinnal usually break out with satisfied grins after taking their first breath. The bracing air is invigorating after the controlled climate of Coruscant or the stale, recycled oxygen of a passenger liner.

Tens of thousands of years ago, Rhinnal awoke from a world-consuming ice age. The glaciers covering the landmasses slowly retreated, leaving behind a carved landscape of mountains, valleys, and crystal-clear lakes. Narrow fingers of ocean, surrounded by high cliffs on three sides, stab into the rocky continents and give the shorelines a fringed appearance when seen from the air.

Rhinnal has almost no axial tilt and exhibits insignificant seasonal variations. Huge stretches of the northern and southern hemispheres are smothered by glaciers, interspersed with frozen tundra and ice-choked rivers. The equatorial regions are distinguished by mossy slopes and evergreen forests. Every visitor to Rhinnal is advised to bring a heavy jacket. Snowfall is common at night, but in the equatorial regions, the powdery dustings usually melt with the light of dawn.

In recent decades, planetary engineers have used terraforming to increase Rhinnal's self-sufficiency, since crops have not taken hold in any corner of the planet. Part of the problem lies with the electromagnetic storms that sweep across the equatorial regions several times a year, often knocking out power to the starports and industrial districts for hours at a time.

History

Rhinnal is a proud member of the Darpa sector, a Core World territory located on the fringes of the Colonies region. It enjoys a position along the Perlemian Trade Route between its famous neighbors Esseles and Ralltiir, and it has been a stopover for Perlemian travelers since the early days of the Old Republic. At that time, Esseles held sway over the planets of the Darpa sector. Rhinnal was considered a colony, overseen by an Esselean governor.

As the centuries passed, Rhinnal earned a reputation as a center of healing. Jedi healers treated locals and offworlders alike at a chapter house near the Frieste River. In the capital city of Rhire, the State Medical Academy turned out some of the best physicians in the galaxy. The Jedi abandoned the chapter house at the start of the Clone Wars, but secular doctors continued to work at the historic facility.

After the rise of Palpatine, the Empire granted Rhinnal marginal independence. The Darpa sector's new Imperial ruler, Moff Jander Graffe, reined in Esseles's power and overturned Rhinnal's classification as a colony. Graffe also installed Imperial Governor Phadreas Kole to ensure Rhinnal's compliance with the precepts of the New Order. The locals barely noticed Kole's hands-off leadership. Opposition to Palpatine's regime remained muted, even among the Jedi sympathizers at the old chapter house. Six months after the Battle of Endor, the fall of nearby Brentaal to the New Republic rattled the citizens of Rhinnal. An organized resistance movement overthrew Governor Kole two and a half years later.

Rhinnal became a valued planet in the New Republic, sending its best doctors to combat numerous epidemics, including the Krytos virus and the Death Seed plague. When the Yuuzhan Vong invaded the galaxy, Rhinnal became a repository for refugees fleeing the military onslaught. Soon the planet reached its capacity, and Rhinnal officials turned down Leia Organa Solo's request to shelter further refugees. After the fall of Coruscant, Rhinnal turned itself into a fortress, fearing that it would be the next target of the Yuuzhan Vong invasion.

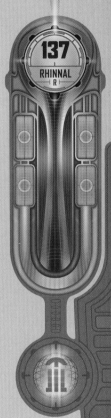

State Medical Academy

The State Medical Academy is right in the heart of Rhire. This immaculate campus covers many square kilometers, encompassing classrooms, laboratories, clinics, and three working hospitals. One specializes in treatment for Humans (mostly Rhinnal natives), one specializes in humanoid aliens, and one treats "exotic" aliens (such as methane breathers, shapeshifters, and silicon-based beings). During the Rebellion era, Moff Jander Graffe eliminated sector funding for the alien hospitals, but both institutions survived through private donations.

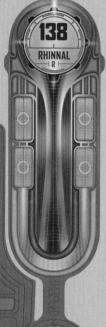

People

Before the refugee influx, Rhinnal supported a modest population of fifty-five million inhabitants, almost all of them Human. The residents of Rhinnal are distinct from most Core World stock, however. They are fiercely loyal to the ethnic clans into which they are born. Major governmental decisions are still made by clan heads. Such decisions can be vetoed by the planetary governor, but if a governor knows what's good for him, he will stand aside.

Native Rhinnalians are fond of elaborate ceremonies. Eighty-four days of the calendar are set aside for commemorations of some sort. Natives are known for their colorful, patterned clothing hand-woven from heavy gabal wool.

The local medical community is far more cosmopolitan. Most graduates of the elite State Medical Academy were born on other planets. As such, they bring outsiders' perspectives to life on Rhinnal. Celebrities, business tycoons, politicians, and all others who can afford the premiums visit the Rhinnal hospitals, often seeking a medical miracle after coming down with a terminal affliction.

Locations

Descriptions of several important locations follow.

Rhire

The capital city of Rhire is home to over seven million individuals. Located in the southern fringe of the inhabited equatorial band, Rhire sits just north of the mighty Frieste River. Blizzards blowing in from the south inspired Rhire architects to build all structures low to the ground, with a preponderance of sturdy cylindrical buildings capped with snow-shedding cupolas. Rhire sprawls far and wide to accommodate its many citizens. Street traffic is relatively light. Most residents travel via an underground shuttle system known as the Circulation Network (commonly called the Circ). Hydroelectric energy plants are stationed all along the Frieste River.

Jedi Chapter House

Near the gray banks of the Frieste lies the Jedi chapter house, built when Rhire was merely a supply outpost for hyperspace explorers. This simple, spired structure can accommodate almost a hundred patients. Following the Clone Wars, most Jedi chapter houses in the Core Worlds were demolished by COMPNOR fanatics, but Rhinnal's reputation was sufficient to spare this one from a similar fate.

Zirfan Glacier

North of Rhire, the Zirfan glacier butts up against the Sennes Mountains. In this frigid borderland, hunters shoot wild gabals and sell them for their wool. On the surface of the Zirfan glacier, hunters find schools of fireheads, ambulatory fish that burrow into the ice by raising their body temperature. Rhinnal's most spectacular lifeforms live in the oceans underneath the polar ice sheets, but few have made the journey to seek them out.

V-Fin Submersible Icebreaker

The crystal-clear waterways of Rhinnal are extensive. Submersibles are popular recreational vehicles for those who want to explore riverbeds and submerged caves. For a trip into the open sea or the polar climes, however, a sturdier craft is required. The V-Fin submersible icebreaker is built to withstand the battering of the ocean waves.

V-Fin Submersible Icebreaker

Class: Aquatic	Crew: 2 (Skilled +4)
Size: Huge (9.5 m long)	Initiative: +2 (–2 size, +4 crew)
Passengers: 10	Maneuver: +2 (–4 size, +4 crew)
Cargo Capacity: 20 tons	Defense: 13 (–2 size, +5 armor)
Cost: 26,000 (new), 11,000 (used)	Shield Points: 0
Availability: Licensed	Hull Points: 40 (DR 5)
Era: All	Speed: 40 m
	Maximum Depth: 2 km below water's surface

* This vehicle provides full cover to its crew and passengers.

Weapon: Sonic drill; Fire Arc: Front; Attack Bonus: +6 (–2 size, +4 crew, +4 fire control); Damage: 9d10; Range Increment: 20 m.

For the GM

The adventure hooks and supporting characters described in this section are meant for GMs only. If you're a player, stop reading now.

Adventures

Feel free to use or adapt the following adventure hooks for your home campaign.

Frozen in Time

If the sensor readings of a clan geologist are any guide, something has been discovered under the thick ice near Rhinnal's south pole. The geologist, Berra Sane, a territory scout for the Kieger clan, caught sensor readings of a starship hundreds of meters below the surface, trapped in ice. Some believe the craft is a pre-Republic Dellaltian warship more than twenty-five thousand years old. Depending on the era, any number of parties may want to get their hands on the rare find.

A V-Fin submersible icebreaker could make short work of the ship's frozen tomb, but tenticulons and fireheads are just two of the threats heroes may encounter as they pilot to the base of the iceberg. Rival groups are interested in claiming the prize for themselves, and drilling through the ice to the warship's resting place without accidentally shattering the craft will prove a delicate task. Also, Berra Sane—who may accompany the characters as a guide—wants to take sole credit for the discovery. She will betray anyone to achieve her evil ends.

Quarantine

While at the Rhinnal State Medical Academy, the heroes meet Dr. Garven Meccamitta. The doctor is concerned that the characters may have been exposed to an unknown pathogen during their adventure. He wants to quarantine them for at least a week. Arrogantly assuming that "those sort of people" won't respond to a polite request, Meccamitta tries to sedate the heroes with medical droids or knock them unconscious with a room-flooding knockout gas. Those who succumb awaken to find themselves weaponless within the locked-down isolation ward.

Escaping from this quarantine isn't a simple matter: The hospital is larger than a Star Destroyer. The heroes must also take pains not to harm innocent hospital employees—even Dr. Meccamitta is acting in what he feels are Rhinnal's best interests. Complicating the matter is Imono Durshana, a lunatic who is a member of the hospital staff. He believes the characters are cursed (possibly because of their actions in a previous adven-

ture). If he can get the drop on the "hexed" characters, he attempts to kill them.

Allies and Antagonists

The following supporting characters are designed for use in your campaign.

Berra Sane

Berra Sane is a lifelong resident of Austogie, a southern Rhinnal village falling within the region controlled by the Kieger clan. Trained as a geologist, she has been retained by the Kieger clan leader to scout out remote territories for future land grabs. Unscrupulous and money-hungry, Sane would betray her sister if it would bring her credits. So far, her skill at subterfuge has prevented others from divining her true nature.

Berra Sane: Female Human Fringer 4/Scoundrel 6; Init +6 (+2 Dex, +4 Improved Initiative); Defense 18 (+2 Dex, +6 class); Spd 10 m; VP/WP 36/12; Atk +7/+2 melee (1d3, punch) or +7/+2 melee (2d6, vibroblade) or +9/+4 ranged (3d6, blaster pistol); SQ barter, bonus class skill (Bluff, Treat Injury), illicit barter, jury-rig +2, lucky 2/day, precise attack +1; SV Fort +7, Ref +9, Will +4; SZ M; FP 1; DSP 3; Rep +1; Str 10, Dex 14, Con 12, Int 10, Wis 12, Cha 10. Challenge Code E.

   Equipment: Red and yellow patterned Kieger clan sash, medpac, vibroblade, blaster pistol.

   Skills: Bluff +12, Climb +9, Handle Animal +5, Jump +8, Knowledge (Rhinnal) +7, Listen +6, Move Silently +9, Read/Write Basic, Repair +7, Ride +8, Search +8, Sense Motive +7, Speak Basic, Spot +8, Survival +11, Swim +2.

   Feats: Athletic, Dodge, Improved Initiative, Mobility, Sharp-Eyed, Skill Emphasis (Bluff), Weapon Group Proficiencies (blaster pistols, blaster rifles, primitive weapons, simple weapons, vibro weapons).

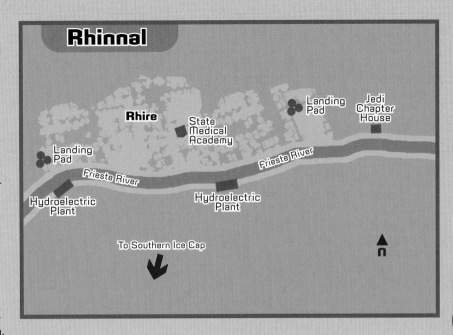

Rhinnal

Rhire · State Medical Academy · Landing Pad · Jedi Chapter House · Landing Pad · Frieste River · Landing Pad · Hydroelectric Plant · Frieste River · Hydroelectric Plant · To Southern Ice Cap · n

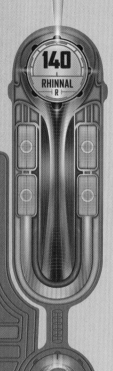

Dr. Garven Meccamitta

The dean and chief surgeon of the Rhinnal State Medical Academy, Dr. Meccamitta is one of the finest minds at a facility staffed with geniuses. Within the Rhinnal medical establishment, his word is law, and he can't quite understand why others don't automatically jump when he snaps his fingers. Meccamitta is a towering man dressed in a white surgeon's uniform. He has the annoying habit of rolling his eyes whenever anyone asks him a question.

Garven Meccamitta: Male Human Noble 2/Expert 14; Init +0; Defense 15 (+5 class); Spd 10 m; VP/WP 12/10; Atk +11/+6/+1 melee (1d3, punch) or +11/+6/+1 ranged; SQ bonus class skill (Bluff), favor +1, inspire confidence; SV Fort +4, Ref +6, Will +15; SZ M; FP 2; DSP 0; Rep +7; Str 10, Dex 10, Con 10, Int 18, Wis 12, Cha 14. Challenge Code C.

   Equipment: Medpac, datapad, comlink.

   Skills: Appraise +8, Bluff +14, Computer Use +15, Diplomacy +14, Gather Information +13, Intimidate +4, Knowledge (biology) +20, Knowledge (Coruscant) +19, Knowledge (forensics) +21, Knowledge (medicine) +24, Knowledge (Rhinnal) +14, Listen +5, Profession (administrator) +19, Profession (surgeon) +19, Read/Write Basic, Repair +8, Search +8, Sense Motive +3, Speak Basic, Spot +5, Survival +3, Treat Injury +23.

   Feats: Alertness, Fame, Iron Will, Persuasive, Sharp-Eyed, Skill Emphasis (Knowledge [medicine], Treat Injury), Surgery, Trustworthy, Weapon Group Proficiencies (blaster pistols, simple weapons).

Imono Durshana

Imono is a Force-sensitive Human who volunteered to work at the Jedi chapter house so that he could be part of something larger than himself. Since then, the idealist has become conspiracy-minded and delusional. He adopts an antagonistic attitude toward anyone who disagrees with him. Dressed in the understated green-and-blue chapter house uniform when on duty, Durshana has taken to wearing Jedi robes and carrying a nonfunctional lightsaber replica in his off hours.

Imono Durshana: Male Human Fringer 5; Init +2; Defense 17 (+2 Dex, +5 class); Spd 10 m; VP/WP 26/13; Atk +4 melee (1d3+1, punch) or +5 ranged (3d6, blaster pistol); SQ barter, bonus class skill (Computer Use, Disguise), jury-rig +2, survival +2; SV Fort +4, Ref +5, Will +1; SZ M; FP 0; DSP 0; Rep +1; Str 12, Dex 14, Con 10, Int 10, Wis 11, Cha 12. Challenge Code C.

   Equipment: Jedi medallion, datapad, false lightsaber, concealed blaster pistol.

   Skills: Disguise +8, Hide +8, Knowledge (Jedi lore) +6, Knowledge (Rhinnal) +8, Listen +4, Profession (medical orderly) +8, Read/Write Basic, Search +4, Sense Motive +3, Speak Basic, Spot +7.

   Feats: Force-Sensitive, Heroic Surge, Toughness, Weapon Group Proficiencies (blaster pistols, primitive weapons, simple weapons).

New Creature: Firehead

One of the strangest lifeforms on Rhinnal, fireheads are limbed fish that inhabit the polar seas. They tunnel through glaciers by using the heat that emanates from a knobby growth on their upper jaw, which smolders like a nubbin of molten lava. This same growth is used to kill prey. A school of fireheads hunts by ramming a larger creature, burning holes in its body, and then nibbles at the floating carcass.

Firehead: Aquatic herd animal 3; Init +4; Defense 16 (+4 Dex, +2 size); Spd 4 m, burrow 2 m (through ice only), swim 20 m; VP/WP 5/6; Atk −1 melee (2d6, heat attack) or +7 ranged; SQ amphibious, darkvision 20 m, heat attack, scent; SV Fort +4, Ref +5, Will +1; SZ T; Face/Reach 1 m by 1 m/2 m; Str 2, Dex 18, Con 12, Int 2, Wis 11, Cha 6.

   Skills: Survival +6, Swim +11.

   Feats: Skill Emphasis (Swim).

   Special Qualities: *Heat Attack*—A firehead can melt a tunnel through ice using a superheated growth near its mouth. This technique can also be used for attacking, dealing 2d6 points of damage to people or ships with a successful attack.

New Creature: Tenticulon

A natural predator of the firehead, the tenticulon lurks in the half-light beneath the polar ice sheets. Its enormous body is an amorphous blob towing dozens of ribbonlike arms, each with a specialized function. Some limbs blink to bewitch passing fish, others sting, and still others grasp and rend. The creature easily regrows lost appendages.

   Many residents of Rhinnal consider the tenticulon a myth; its existence remains (in their eyes) unproven. Others disagree, positing that the creature typically does not fight what it cannot kill.

Tenticulon: Aquatic predator 8; Init +2; Defense 4 (+2 Dex, −8 size); Spd swim 12 m; VP/WP 68/64; Atk +6 melee (1d6+6, 12 stinging tendrils), +4 melee (1d4+6, 12 grasping tentacles); SQ blindsight 80 m, breathe underwater, constrict 1d4+6, fast healing 1, immune to heat, swallow whole; SV Fort +5, Ref +8, Will +2; SZ C; Face/Reach 20 m by 20 m/50 m; Str 22, Dex 15, Con 8, Int 3, Wis 10, Cha 5. Challenge Code G.

   Skills: Move Silently +6, Spot +6, Survival +8, Swim +21.

   Feats: Multiattack, Power Attack, Skill Emphasis (Survival).

   Special Qualities: *Constrict*—The tenticulon can attempt to grapple with each grasping tentacle. If successful, the tentacle can constrict for 1d4+6 points of damage.

   Swallow Whole—If the tenticulon hits its target with at least five grasping tentacles, it can make a grapple check. If successful, a second successful grapple check will allow it to swallow its target whole, dealing 1d4 points of acid damage per round. The tenticulon's grapple check bonus is +30, and each additional grasping tentacle beyond the first five increases the bonus by 2.

Sacorria

Planet Type: Terrestrial
Climate: Temperate
Terrain: Forests, plains
Atmosphere: Breathable
Gravity: Standard
Diameter: 11,500 km
Length of Day: 23 standard hours
Length of Year: 343 standard days
Sentient Species: Human
Languages: Basic, Selonian, Drallish
Population: 600 million
Species Mix: 40% Human, 30% Selonian, 30% Drall
Government: Dictatorship
Major Exports: Wood, agricultural goods, alcohol
Major Imports: Weapons, electronics, luxury goods
System/Star: Sacorria/Sacorria

Planets	Type	Moons
Slag	Searing rock	0
Arcadia	Volcanic rock	1
Sacorria	Terrestrial	1
Noleria	Barren rock	2
Titanicus	Gas giant	14
Leviathan	Gas giant	16
Vo	Frozen rock	0

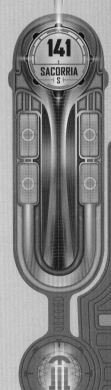

Description

Sacorria is a small, secretive world with tight laws, pleasant venues, and interesting plots. One of the outlying systems in the Corellian sector, it's considered a backward world when compared to the more powerful and influential Core Worlds. Nevertheless, native Sacorrians resent any implication that their world is any less important than Corellia.

Politics aside, this world of forests and fields is a wonderful place for vacationing, provided one doesn't mind the rules and regulations that go with it. Sacorria orbits a star of the same name, an orange giant also orbited by six other planets. Sacorria has one moon, called Sarcophagus, which serves as a graveyard for the planet's inhabitants. Native Sacorrians have no interest in intrasystem exploration and colonization, but they're accustomed to the arrival of offworld visitors.

History

Since history was first recorded on Sacorria, the mysterious Triad has always wielded power. The Triad is made up of three dictators, one from each of Sacorria's native species: Human, Drall, and Selonian. Each dictator has equal power, and two out of three need to agree before a policy can be carried out. Most decisions are unanimous.

In the days of the Old Republic, Sacorria kept to itself, although it had token representation in the Senate. During the Rebellion era, the Triad was merely a mouthpiece for the Diktat of Corellia. After the fall of the Empire, Sacorria actually stuck its neck out and became more active in galactic politics—ultimately, a foolish decision. When Palpatine died and the Diktat's influence waned, the Triad asserted itself and tried to become the rulers of a separate Corellian empire.

Triad agents had discovered that the five inhabited worlds in the Corellian system contained repulsors of ancient design. Apparently, the ancient machines were originally used to move the five planets into their present orbits. The same agents later discovered how to use Centerpoint Station as a means of inducing stars to go nova, making Sacorria a force to be reckoned with.

Fourteen years after the Battle of Endor, Triad-backed rebellions sprung up on the five Corellian planets. Revolutionaries established a jamming and interdiction field in the Corellian system, making New Republic intervention problematic. Lando Calrissian and his lady friend Tendra Risant responded to free the enslaved systems. Together, they set events in motion that enabled a New Republic fleet to intercept and destroy the Triad's fleet.

Despite its failure in this grab for power, the Triad remains unbowed and unmoved. To this day, the Triad system of government remains in place on Sacorria.

People

The planet's population consists of almost equal proportions of Humans, Drall, and Selonians. The three species get along well enough that their way of life continues without major incidents. Most are motivated by a love for their world and the desire to see it take its rightful place among the great powers of the galaxy. The Sacorrian people are fiercely proud of their world and the strict laws, rules, and regulations that control everyday life. Offworlders who complain about the excessive rules are considered rude and insulting.

The Triad creates Sacorrian law. Remarkably, Sacorrians have no qualms following laws set up by a trio of rulers who are so shrouded in secrecy that even their names are not known. In some ways, the Sacorrian mindset is perplexing and contradictory. On one hand, the Sacorrians are a secretive, insular lot. On the other, they are a proud people who want to see their influence spread over the galaxy. The Sacorrian people supported the Triad's attempts to carve out an empire. Although

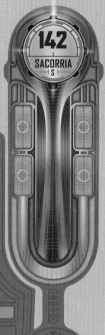

the plan was thwarted, the rulers still have the people's support.

Patriotic Sacorrians can rationalize even the most extreme laws. For instance, the Triad has not only instituted a ban on marriages to offworlders but also forbidden any woman to marry without the consent of her father or guardian. Sociologists and loyal Sacorrians see this as the Triad's way of trying to maintain the so-called purity of the Sacorrian people and their particular traditions of marriage.

During the Rebellion era, the Sacorrian people seethed under the Empire's dominance. Although many Sacorrians joined the Rebel Alliance and fought the Empire, their motives were less than pure. To many Sacorrians, the goal was to break away from the Empire and be self-governing again. Once that goal was achieved, loyal Sacorrians knew that they could then resume carving out their own empire.

Locations

Descriptions of several important locations follow.

Sarcophagus

Sacorria's single moon serves as a vast burial ground for the planet's population. Sacorrians began using their moon as a burial ground as soon as lunar space travel was perfected. Before serving as a worldwide cemetery, Sarcophagus was simply referred to as "the moon." Although offworlders can visit Sarcophagus, none are buried there. Sarcophagus has numerous tombs, mausoleums, and graves on the surface, as well as burial caves and catacombs underground. An orbital shuttle provides service from planet to moon, and a Central Databank gives accurate directions to the vast majority of plots.

Although most Sacorrians view Sarcophagus with pride, they still maintain some lingering superstitions about it.

After all, who at one point or another can look up in the Sacorrian night sky, see the full moon, and not think of the billions of bodies buried up there? Most superstitions associate the full moon with death or other calamities. By tradition, training a high-powered telescope on Sarcophagus is considered disrespectful and illegal.

Dorthus Tal Prison

It stands to reason that a world with many laws also has a notable prison. Dorthus Tal is Sacorria's most outstanding facility. Although some may take issue with the term "escapeproof," Dorthus Tal boasts an impressive array of sensors, guards, droids, and complicated locks. Located on Dorthus Tal Island and powered by geothermal energy from a nearby volcano, Dorthus Tal Prison is a self-contained unit that offers little hope of a quick and easy escape.

Dorthus Tal City

Located on the same island as the prison of the same name, this city of twenty-five thousand souls boasts many quaint shops and pleasant pedestrian sites. Cobblestone Square is one of the better-known places of interest. The square has a variety of specialty shops. Walking the square is a delightful experience, especially with the city's old-fashioned architecture and numerous water fountains. Visitors can access the city via an air shuttle from the mainland, where Sacorria's main commercial spaceport is located. Security on the air shuttle is tight, since the authorities don't want to see any prisoners leaving the island (in the unlikely event of an escape).

Watchtower Base

This tall, imposing structure oversees Dorthus Tal island security. The watchtower is full of sensors, listening devices, cameras, surveillance drones, and jamming equipment. A garrison of two hundred guards lives here, staffing the tower and providing extra security for the prison if needed. Although Watchtower Base was built to handle the prison, there are unconfirmed reports that Dorthus Tal City is also kept under close watch. For that reason, many offworlders don't stay long in the city.

Sacorria Central Spaceport

This huge, gleaming, efficient spaceport facility lies on Sacorria's main continent, 500 kilometers from Dorthus Tal Island. It has an impressive collection of hotels, bars, and shops for offworlders. While the spaceport is heavily patrolled and all laws are enforced to their fullest extent, most offworlders prefer lingering around the spaceport because of its many conveniences—as well as its location out of range of Watchtower Base. The spaceport is located on the outskirts of Saccorata, a large city.

For the GM

The adventure hooks and supporting characters described in this section are meant for GMs only. If you're a player, stop reading now.

Adventures

Sacorria may be a backwater world with secretive people and volumes of laws, but it offers adventure and intrigue to those smart and brave enough to find it.

All for Love

When the heroes are relaxing during leave on Sacorria, two young Selonians approach them and engage them in conversation. Eventually, when they sense that no one important is listening, they discreetly ask if they can purchase passage to Corellia. They can pay 2,000 credits. The Selonians try not to act suspicious, but it's difficult for them. The GM should set things up so that the young Selonians seem to want to leave the planet for a legally suspect reason, such as espionage or smuggling.

The couple doesn't show any public displays of affection, so it's not obvious that they're involved with each other romantically. In truth, the young Selonians are in love and wish to wed. However, the would-be bride's father has forbidden the union, because the prospective groom's family doesn't have sufficient social status. The Sacorrians are doing something their culture considers virtually unthinkable: They intend to defy Triad law, flee the system, and marry on Corellia.

Unfortunately for them, their sneakiness leaves a lot to be desired. The bride's family has caught wind of the scheme and has hired a secret assassin organization called the Doloria to terminate anyone who helps the couple to escape. The Doloria are a fanatic cult of Selonian assassins who revere Sacorrian customs almost as much as they revere credits. If the heroes can get the young couple to Corellia, the Doloria stop pursuing them. However, the couple needs to gather a few items for their wedding, objects of great sentimental value. They won't go offplanet without them. The valuable items are stashed across town in a locker, and the assassins lie in wait nearby.

Jailbreak!

Here's a chance to introduce a scoundrel into a hero's life. Marcus Korrin is a con artist, pure and simple. (Use the mid-level con artist archetype presented in Chapter Fourteen of the *Star Wars Roleplaying Game* for Marcus's statistics.) As a Human who has alternately claimed to be Corellian, Alderaanian, and Belgarian, Marcus considers the galaxy to be his personal hunting ground for credits. His luck ran out on Sacorria, where he was arrested for petty theft and thrown into Dorthus Tal Prison.

Never without a plan, Marcus has managed to smuggle a message out of jail. Counting on the idealism of Rebel sympathizers who may be visiting Sacorria at any given time, Marcus has crafted a message designed to touch the conscience of anyone with a heroic bent. Now all he has to do is wait until his contact finds the right group of people.

The GM should select one of the heroes and give him or her a message courtesy of a mysterious errand-runner. The message is meant to prod the heroes into a well-intentioned jailbreak—a dubious undertaking, certainly, but not terribly ill-advised, considering how shaky relations are between the Rebel Alliance and Sacorria.

What Marcus doesn't know is that the warden, a Human named Kedar Blackgate, has not only found out about the message but allowed it to be delivered. Marcus is unintentionally luring a group of would-be jailbreakers into the prison to help test the jail's security.

The guards are under orders to capture the heroes alive, if possible. If the heroes are taken, they will be jailed for six months in the same minimum-security wing as Marcus. No worries, though—Marcus has another plan for escape, and this one's foolproof!

Shoo Fly, Don't Bother Me

An Imperial shuttle has crashed into a wilderness area 500 kilometers north of Saccorata. The Sacorrian authorities want the contents of the shuttle very badly. On the other hand, they don't want to put any of their own troops at risk. The heroes are the lucky intermediaries who will solve their problems.

First, the heroes are pulled in and detained on a series of trumped-up customs violations. The authorities give them this deal: Salvage the Imperial wreckage, and we'll drop all charges. You'll be free to leave.

The GM can run the heroes through an overland trek to reach the crash site. Once there, they'll be in for a rude surprise. The shuttle crashed in the middle of a large grain field, right on top of a colony of Sacorrian grain flies.

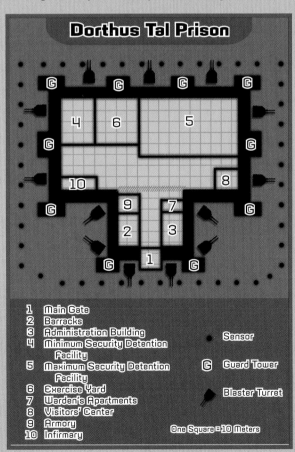

Dorthus Tal Prison

1. Main Gate
2. Barracks
3. Administration Building
4. Minimum Security Detention Facility
5. Maximum Security Detention Facility
6. Exercise Yard
7. Warden's Apartments
8. Visitors' Center
9. Armory
10. Infirmary

- Sensor
- G Guard Tower
- Blaster Turret

One Square = 10 Meters

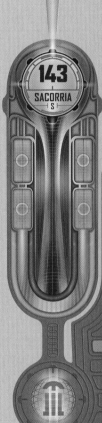

Making matters worse is the reason why the shuttle crashed in the first place. The Imperial couriers were transporting a pair of recently built assassin droids. While passing through a magnetic ion storm in the Sacorrian system, the droids activated and began killing everyone in sight. The shuttle crashed, but the droids survived and now lurk in the wreckage. The grain flies are too small for the droids to eliminate. The heroes, on the other hand, will be in considerable danger.

Aside from the assassin droids—or whatever's left of them when and if the heroes defeat them—there's little of value in the shuttle. The wreckage itself could possibly yield some salvageable parts. A question that all right-thinking heroes should be asking is, "Does anyone really want to turn over salvaged assassin droid technology to the Triad?" Sharp-thinking heroes may attempt to collect the remains of the Sacorrian grain flies (assuming they manage to kill some) and show the dead bugs to the Sacorrian authorities, claiming that they've done a service to Sacorria in eliminating a major nest. If the heroes can successfully convince the Sacorrians of the value of this service, the Sacorrians will give them a token bounty of 500 credits—and, more important, their freedom.

A Grave Errand
A bereaved widow approaches the heroes and asks a favor. She wishes to visit the grave of her husband on Sarcophagus, but she doesn't have enough credits to make the trip. Could these nice people be so kind as to give her a lift there? The trip takes less than an hour each way. Everything is at is seems, except for the people following the widow. It seems that her husband incurred the wrath of a crime lord by failing to deliver a smuggled shipment of Sacorrian grain whiskey. Now, his minions are tailing the woman to find out where it is. They believe the shipment was buried with her husband. If the heroes find out about the missing shipment, they'll have to break the law to recover it.

New Creature: Sacorrian Grain Fly
The Sacorrian grain fly is the worst bane of Sacorrian farmers. Swarms of these pests devour grain stockpiles unless preventative measures are taken. Even then, there's no guarantee that the grain is safe. To make matters worse, the grain fly delivers an extremely painful bite that makes farm workers reluctant to confront the pests. The flies are truly an expendable species. They have no use whatsoever, and if they were somehow removed from the planet's ecology, no other species would suffer.

Found in swarms, the grain fly is about the length of an adult Human's thumb. Its thorax is covered in fuzzy black hair, and its abdomen is a sickly blue-green. The fly's distinguishing characteristic is a set of small but nasty mandibles. Scientists say that the fly's mandibles secrete an enzyme that inflames a creature's nerve endings, producing a painful wound. The grain flies are actually herbivores, and their bite is purely a defensive mechanism. Bite victims rendered unconscious are not killed or eaten.

Sacorrian Grain Fly: Vermin 1; Init +5; Defense 23 (+5 Dex, +8 size); Spd 2 m, fly 12 m (good); VP/WP 2/1; Atk +3 melee (poison bite); SQ darkvision 20 m, poison; SV Fort –2, Ref +7, Will +0; SZ F; Face/Reach 0 m by 0 m/0 m; Str 1, Dex 20, Con 2, Int 1, Wis 10, Cha 1. Challenge Code A.

Skills: Listen +7, Search –1, Spot +4, Survival +4.

Feats: Flyby Attack.

Special Qualities: *Poison*—When a Sacorrian grain fly successfully bites, it injects a weak poison. A character who makes her Fortitude save (DC 10) feels a brief stinging sensation but suffers no debilitating effects. If a character is bitten and fails a saving throw, she is considered fatigued for 1 hour (–2 penalty to Strength and Dexterity, can't run). The effects of multiple bites are cumulative.

Allies and Antagonists
The following supporting characters are suitable for use in your campaign.

Colonel Kedar Blackgate
During the Rebellion era and for several years after the Battle of Endor, the warden of Dorthus Tal Prison is an imperious Human named Colonel Kedar Blackgate. Born on Sacorria and raised in a privileged family, Kedar joined the Sacorrian military at a young age and became the youngest man to attain the rank of colonel.

A fierce upholder of Sacorrian law, the arrogant Kedar seemed the perfect choice to command the Dorthus Tal Prison following a prison riot that was mishandled by the facility's previous warden. Kedar has assumed command of the prison with zeal, installing various innovative programs to prevent further riots. Although his methods are far more benevolent than those of his predessessors, most prisoners live in constant fear of him. He treats them and disciplines them like they were his own children, caring for their basic needs while enforcing a strict regimen of diet and exercise. He does not tolerate prisoner abuse and can put even the most hardcore criminal in his place with his icy glare.

Kedar has short black hair, a trimmed beard and goatee, and a pair of loyal massiff pets named Emperor and Merciless. He wears a Sacorrian military uniform or a black military jumpsuit that accentuates his trim, fit figure. A security gauntlet on his left hand allows him to control and override the prison's electronic defense systems.

Colonel Kedar Blackgate: Male Human Soldier 12/ Officer 6; Init +0; Defense 21 (+11 class); Spd 10 m; VP/WP 100/15; Atk +20/+15/+10/+5 melee (3d4+3/18–20, punch) or +16/+11/+6/+1 ranged (3d6+3, mastercraft blaster pistol); SQ leadership, requisition supplies, tactics; SV Fort +13, Ref +7, Will +10; SZ M; FP 7; DSP 2; Rep +11; Str 18, Dex 10, Con 15, Int 14, Wis 12, Cha 17. Challenge Code H.

Equipment: Military uniform, comlink, security gauntlet (requires a Computer Use check against DC 30 to operate), mastercraft blaster pistol (+3 bonus on damage), heavy battle armor (DR 7) (in private quarters).

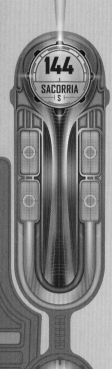

Skills: Bluff +11, Computer Use +23, Demolitions +5, Diplomacy +17, Gather Information +11, Intimidate +29, Knowledge (bureaucracy) +8, Knowledge (politics) +23, Knowledge (tactics) +23, Pilot +8, Profession (prison warden) +8, Read/Write Basic, Search +4, Sense Motive +9, Speak Basic, Treat Injury +16.

Feats: Advanced Martial Arts, Armor Proficiencies (light, medium, heavy), Frightful Presence, Improved Martial Arts, Infamy, Influence, Iron Will, Martial Arts, Persuasive, Point Blank Shot, Precise Shot, Quick Draw, Sharp-Eyed, Skill Emphasis (Intimidate), Trustworthy, Weapon Group Proficiencies (blaster pistols, blaster rifles, heavy weapons, simple weapons, vibro weapons).

Major Astar Vanqor

Major Astar Vanqor serves as Warden Blackgate's "right hand" and the commander of the Dorthus Tal Prison garrison. She has served Colonel Blackgate for years and trusts his judgment implicitly. She brooks no dissent, and she knows the names and history of every prisoner who has ever served time during her years of service at the prison.

Major Vanqor has a dark complexion, brown eyes, and an inscrutably stony gaze. Her well-toned physique, short hair, and impeccable military attire add to her formidable presence. A native Sacorrian, she regards all visitors to her world with suspicion.

Major Astar Vanqor: Female Human Soldier 6/Noble 1/ Officer 2; Init +3; Defense 20 (+3 Dex, +7 class); DR 5; Spd 8 m; VP/WP 51/10; Atk +10/+5 melee (2d4+3/19–20, punch) or +10/+5 ranged (3d8/19–20, blaster carbine); SQ bonus class skill (Spot), favor +1, leadership; SV Fort +7, Ref +10, Will +6; SZ M; FP 3; DSP 0; Rep +4; Str 16, Dex 16, Con 10, Int 12, Wis 11, Cha 14. Challenge Code E.

Equipment: Medium battle armor (DR 5), blaster carbine, comlink.

Skills: Computer Use +6, Demolitions +7, Diplomacy +11, Gather Information +8, Intimidate +8, Knowledge (tactics) +7, Listen +2, Read/Write Basic, Search +9, Sense Motive +11, Speak Basic, Speak Selonian, Spot +4, Treat Injury +3.

Feats: Armor Proficiencies (light, medium), Dodge, Far Shot, Improved Martial Arts, Lightning Reflexes, Martial Arts, Mobility, Point Blank Shot, Sharp-Eyed, Weapon Group Proficiencies (blaster pistols, blaster rifles, heavy weapons, simple weapons, vibro weapons).

Selonia

Planet Type: Terrestrial
Climate: Temperate
Terrain: Oceans, islands
Atmosphere: Breathable
Gravity: Standard
Diameter: 14,033 km
Length of Day: 26 standard hours
Length of Year: 355 standard days
Sentient Species: Selonian
Languages: Selonian, Basic
Population: 16 million
Species Mix: 99% Selonian, 1% other
Government: Imperial governorship or New Republic governorship, Selonian dens
Major Exports: Foodstuffs, minerals
Major Imports: High-tech goods
System/Star: Corellia/Corell

Planets	Type	Moons
Corellia	Terrestrial	0
Drall	Terrestrial	0
Talus	Terrestrial	0
Tralus	Terrestrial	0
Centerpoint	Artificial	0
Selonia	Terrestrial	0
Crollia	Barren rock	0
Soronia	Frozen rock	0

Description

A moist world of nearly equal land and oceans, Selonia is a mineral-rich planet. Its extensive network of subterranean passageways and warrens are home to an estimated sixteen million Selonians. Hundreds of islands are separated by an equal number of small seas, inlets, and straits, making surface navigation via the waterways a fairly complicated matter. It is often said that no point on land anywhere on Selonia is more than 150 kilometers from open water, and that no point on the water is more than 200 kilometers from the nearest shoreline.

Dominated in the extreme northern latitudes by the volcanic Cloudland Peaks, Selonia is lightly developed on the surface, giving it the appearance of being nearly uninhabited. The native Selonians reside almost exclusively in their subterranean dens. With few exceptions, very little of their civilization extends to the outside world.

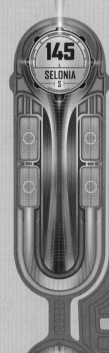

History

The true origin of Selonia is poorly understood. During the Corellian Crisis, some fourteen years after the Battle of Endor, it was discovered that a massive planetary repulsor lies beneath the world's surface. The artifact was used millennia ago to bring the world from an unknown system to its current position in the Corellian system. The other planets of the system were likely brought insystem by these means as well. (See the entries on Talus and Tralus, Corellia, and Drall for additional information.)

Prior to the Corellian Crisis, Selonia's history was one of relative isolation. One of three sentient species indigenous to the system, the Selonians are the most reclusive and nowhere near as well known or researched as their Human and Drall neighbors. Except for adventurers bound for the Cloudland Peaks, the world is seldom visited. Even residents of the same system know very little of the world or its inhabitants. That said, the Selonians do maintain a handful of buildings fitted with accommodations ideal for Humans and other non-Selonians.

While a number of notable Selonians have become embroiled in the politics of the Corellian system and larger galactic affairs, most are content to remain in their dens and undercities. The limited contacts Selonians have had with the outside galaxy have gone poorly. Some centuries ago, Selonia acted in concert along with Drall and Corellia to subjugate Talus and Tralus. The resulting victory for the Double Worlds gave the Selonians yet another reason to avoid mingling with or meddling in

"outside" affairs. Selonians are still reluctant to allow outsiders to meddle with Selonia's concerns. (See the entry on Talus and Tralus for further information regarding the conspiracy against the Double Worlds.)

Selonia's role in the Corellian Crisis was key, since its planetary repulsor was the first one discovered in the system. The struggle between two Selonian factions—the Republicists and the Absolutists—nearly resulted in a civil war. The Republicists, spearheaded by the Hunchuzuc Den on Corellia, wished to turn Selonia's repulsor over to the New Republic. In return, they wanted a guarantee of Selonia's sovereignty inside the New Republic and the Corellian sector government. The Absolutists sought the repulsor's destructive capabilities to ensure absolute Selonian independence by more direct means.

The Absolutists were later vilified for their complicity with the Triad, the three-member leadership of Sacorria, which included an outcast Selonian. Their further association with those who used trickery and deception— unacceptable conduct to Selonians—ultimately doomed the Absolutists, and the Republicists won the power struggle. The Republicists know the peace with the Sacorrian Selonians will take a long time to finalize, but as the old Selonian saying goes, "The agreed-upon we do at once. The inevitable can take a little while."

People

Honor, consensus, and the den are the three things that drive Selonians. Their social and family structure is anchored around the den, a genetically related group that consists of a single fertile female, a few fertile males, and hundreds of sterile females. Sterile females with a common father are genetically identical with one another and belong to the same "sept."

Thought to be descended from fierce riverbank predators, the native Selonians are easily one of the most isolationist species indigenous to the Core Worlds. Averaging 1.8 to 2.2 meters in height (sterile females being the largest and strongest), they are vicious in combat, with needle-sharp fangs, strong and retractable digging claws, and powerful tails.

Most Selonians suffer from a mild to marked form of agoraphobia (a fear of open spaces). Selonians spend their entire lives beneath their world's surface. A few are groomed for interaction with other species, trained to speak and read Basic, and instructed in the intricacies of Human and other cultures.

Dishonor and deception are unforgivable crimes in core Selonian society; Selonians are ferociously and relentlessly honest. They have often been likened to Wookiees in terms of trustworthiness. Even Selonians who have been outcast or live away from the Corellian sector adhere to the codes of honor, with very few exceptions. A dishonorable Selonian is virtually unheard of, though some outcast dens (not necessarily dishonored ones) do exist.

A small number of Selonians on other worlds throughout the Corellian sector and the larger galaxy have adapted well to the common galactic culture. They now serve as emissaries to the other cultures. The largest offworld population is centered around the Corellian capital regions, where Selonians maintain ancient tunnel networks extending for thousands of kilometers under the capital city. Although they dwell away from their home dens, their codes of honesty and consensus do not waver. The all-female Selonian Enclave in Bela Vistal on Corellia, where the Corellian Crisis began in earnest, is an example of Selonians who fare well within the galaxy's society.

A handful of Selonian dens reside on both Talus and Tralus. Outcasts from their own species, they are integral citizens of the Double Worlds. They do not recognize Selonia's Overden as having any authority over their society or statutes. Outcasts also reside on Sacorria.

Locations

Descriptions of several important locations follow.

Cloudland Peaks

A group of five volcanic islands in the northernmost latitudes of the world, the Cloudland Peaks are a series of towering mountain ranges piercing the upper atmosphere of the world. Depending on one's point of view, they either present grave danger or extreme adventure. Cloud and mist enshroud the higher elevations of the Cloudland Peaks, where the mean temperature hovers at approximately –10° C during the day and –45° C at night.

Shevo Banks

Exposed slopes of rock made smooth by centuries of water erosion, the Shevo Banks are a popular attraction for Selonians, who use the formations as slides. The Banks are situated under a series of ancient sea caves, now far removed from the water thanks to tectonic activity. The Shevo Banks are always jammed with frolicking adolescent Selonians.

Selonian Cone Ship

Selonian cone ships are short-haul craft incapable of interstellar flight. Shaped like roughly flattened cones about 20 meters high and 20 meters across, cone ships are uncommon in that they are forward-flight vertical craft—they launch much like archaic rocketcraft. The forward viewports are at the apex of the cone, with the entrance/exit hatch 1.5 meters from the base of the ship.

The cone ships are shoddily built and were decades old when the Selonians called them into service during the Corellian Crisis. Poorly maintained (if at all), they carry no weapons, are slow, and have poor maneuverability compared to standard galactic craft—especially those constructed by the nearby Corellian shipyards. Their sensors are so poor (–4 equipment penalty on Computer Use checks) that it is often easy to approach one from its stern. Even if a pilot wished to modify the craft to allow it better sensors or minimal armament, there would not be enough reserve power to use such equipment.

Many spacers maintain that the cone ships are proof that Selonians have no business flying spacecraft. Most Selonians agree. Any Selonian interested in traveling to the stars would certainly not wish to do so in a cone ship

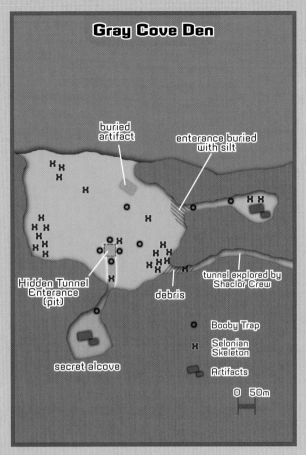

Gray Cove Den

buried artifact

enterance buried with silt

Hidden Tunnel Enterance (pit)

debris

tunnel explored by Shaclor Crew

○   Booby Trap

х   Selonian Skeleton

◢   Artifacts

0   50m

secret alcove

designed by his own kind. During the Corellian Crisis, the Corellian Han Solo and a pair of Selonians endured a perilous flight aboard such a ship.

Selonian Cone Ship

Class: Space transport	Crew: 1 (Untrained –4)
Size: Small (20 m long)	Initiative: –3 (+1 size, –4 crew)
Hyperdrive: None	Maneuver: –7 (+1 size, –4 crew, –4 construction)
Passengers: 4	Defense: 13 (+1 size, +2 armor)
Cargo Capacity: 50 tons	Shield Points: 0
Consumables: 1 month	Hull Points: 60 (DR 10)
Cost: Not available for sale	
Maximum Speed in Space: Cruising (4 squares/action)	
Atmospheric Speed: 480 km/h (8 squares/action)	

Weapons: None.

For the GM

The adventure hooks and supporting characters described in this section are meant for GMs only. If you're a player, stop reading now.

Adventures

Feel free to use or adapt the following adventure hooks for your home campaign.

Skip and a Jump

The life of a smuggler is never an easy one, especially when you don't even know you're a smuggler.

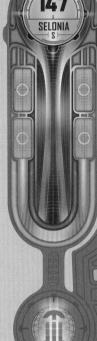

Contraband is found aboard the heroes' ship. While their ship is intended for impound, the characters are able to learn that the contraband in question is the "rightful" property of one Neic Norim, a Sullustan smuggler of some repute, who stashed the cargo aboard the heroes' ship while it was docked.

Neic narrowly escaped an "entanglement" involving a representative of Intra-Corellian Collections (InCorCol)—a private investigation service. However, his ship suffered enough damage that InCorCol is certain he is still in the Corellian system. Given that the characters have been caught with Neic's cargo, it is up to them to find the wily smuggler and clear the matter with both the Corellian Defense Force and the InCorCol agents. (For InCorCol agents, use the mercenary archetype statistics in Chapter Fourteen of the *Star Wars Roleplaying Game*; for more information on the CDF, refer to the entry on Corellia earlier in this book.)

Den Bones, Den Bones

An ancient den has been discovered in a remote stretch of islands on Selonia. Excavated by a group of Selonian archaeospelunkers, the den is believed to contain relics that once belonged to extended ancestors of a Den now residing on Sacorria. The Sacorria-based Selonians have learned of the find and are pressing the Selonian dens to turn over the relics. The dens of Selonia cannot agree on the best course of action. Because consensus is critical to the Selonian mindset, decisions have been slow in coming. The Sacorrian dens have no such compunctions. They are assembling a team to retrieve remains and artifacts they feel are rightly theirs.

What neither the characters nor the Selonians know is that this newly discovered den is the legendary Kas'as Chen'ru Den, or "Gray Cove" Den. Hundreds of Selonians were buried alive by the silt and suffocating fill of a fierce tidal storm millennia ago. The Gray Cove was among those dens scheduled to be "transported" (that is, deported) to Sacorria for minor infractions against the ancient central dens. When the forces of the Sacorrian dens arrived to collect the members of the Gray Cove, they were nowhere to be found. They had hidden in a secret place, only to fall prey to nature's whims.

The Selonian dens have managed to agree on a course of action. They want to hire the characters to impede the Sacorrian contingent until a firm decision can be reached. The heroes can start on Sacorria and prevent the expedition from ever lifting for Selonia. However, the characters must confront the lead Sacorrian crew deep in the tunnels and warrens of the abandoned isles on Selonia, where the tunnel-adapted aliens have a distinct advantage.

Allies and Antagonists

The following supporting characters are designed for use in your campaign.

Shaclor

Selonian society is not generally known to produce genuinely adventurous individuals, but if ever it did,

Shaclor would be one of them. A digger for Chanzari Den, Shaclor and her crew of eight are charged with the exploration of outlying Chanzari land, both on the surface and in the subsurface. Their territory includes an extensive strip of islands that once belonged to a forgotten clan, the descendants of which now reside on Sacorria. Curious, fearless, and trustworthy, Shaclor could be a valued ally to those who can gain her confidence.

Shaclor: Female Selonian Scout 4; Init +3; Defense 16 (+3 Dex, +3 class); Spd 10 m, swim 12 m; VP/WP 30/17; Atk +5 melee (1d3+2, claw) or +6; SQ agoraphobia, heart +1, trailblazing, uncanny dodge (Dex bonus to Defense); SV Fort +4, Ref +5, Will +2; SZ M; FP 0; DSP 0; Rep +1; Str 15, Dex 17, Con 14, Int 11, Wis 10, Cha 12. Challenge Code B.

   Equipment: Rescue beacon, maps.

   Skills: Climb +7, Diplomacy +3, Gather Information +3, Knowledge (Selonia) +6, Listen +4, Profession (bartender) +4, Read/Write Selonian, Search +5, Speak Basic, Speak Selonian, Survival +10, Swim +7, Treat Injury +3.

   Feats: Skill Emphasis (Survival), Toughness, Trustworthy, Weapon Group Proficiencies (blaster pistols, blaster rifles, simple weapons).

Neic Norim

An old Sullustan smuggler, Neic Norim was once a test pilot for SoroSuub before a grievous accident cost him his arm. One of Norim's favorite ploys is stowing contraband aboard some hapless pilot's craft bound for wherever the Sullustan intends the cargo to be delivered. Norim maintains a huge network of paid informants and operatives at customs offices in dozens of the most prominent spaceports throughout the Corellian system. His operatives see the contraband during its impound and confiscation and deliver it to their customers.

Neic Norim recently ran afoul of a loan shark looking to collect on some old debts. Though victorious, Neic escaped the fray with serious damage to his ship. He has taken refuge on Selonia, hiding his crew and craft among some abandoned tunnels. The tunnels suit him and his largely Sullustan crew just fine, since they remind the group of their native tunnels back home.

Thin to the point of being emaciated, Neic wears a traditional Sullustan combat jumpsuit, similar to those worn by Sullustan Rebels (such as Nien Nunb) during the Rebellion era. The sleeve of his right arm has been removed, revealing a gray-blue, skeletal prosthetic arm. (Like most prosthetics, the device does not enhance his abilities; instead, it replicates the functions of his lost limb.)

Neic Norim: Male Sullustan Scoundrel 4; Init +3; Defense 16 (+3 Dex, +3 class); Spd 10 m; VP/WP 14/9; Atk +4 melee (1d3+1, punch) or +6 ranged (3d6, blaster pistol); SQ darkvision 20 m, illicit barter, lucky 1/day, precise attack +1; SV Fort +0, Ref +7, Will +1; SZ M; FP 1; DSP 1; Rep +1; Str 13, Dex 16, Con 9, Int 14, Wis 10, Cha 9. Challenge Code C.

   Equipment: Blaster pistol.

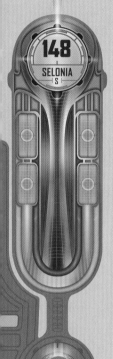

Skills: Appraise +3, Astrogate +6, Bluff +6, Climb +3, Computer Use +3, Diplomacy +2, Gather Information +5, Knowledge (business) +6, Knowledge (Corellia) +6, Knowledge (spacer lore) +7, Listen +7, Move Silently +7, Pilot +10, Profession (smuggler) +5, Read/Write Sullustese, Speak Basic, Speak Sullustese, Survival +3, Treat Injury +3.

Feats: Quick Draw, Skill Emphasis (Pilot), Starship Operation (space transport), Weapon Group Proficiencies (blaster pistols, simple weapons).

Fulin Gor

Once the New Republic had a (fairly) solid grasp on galactic affairs, it established the Observers, an experimental, quasiofficial part of the new government. Fulin Gor is one of the Observers, carefully chosen operatives who investigate potentially improper governmental activities. They do not typically announce their role, maintaining fronts as traders, tourists, or other commonly encountered beings. They reveal their identities only to their most trustworthy confidants.

A capable law enforcement agent, Fulin Gor now poses as a trader of rare woods. His assignment takes him throughout the Corellian sector, most recently to the seedy underworld of Coronet City. Currently, he's on Selonia, where he carefully watches the progress of the Hunchuzuc Den's rise to power and reports any violations of New Republic edicts to the High Council and the Senate.

During the Rise of the Empire and Rebellion eras, Gor works as an agent for the Iotran Police Force. He will pursue a lawbreaker anywhere in the galaxy and return him or her to Iotran Space for trial.

During the Yuuzhan Vong invasion, Fulin Gor throws in with any honorable group combating the alien menace. Observer Gor is a staunch supporter of the New Republic, and he will go to great ends to see the Yuuzhan Vong threat eliminated.

Fulin Gor: Male Human Soldier 12; Init +3 (–1 Dex, +4 Improved Initiative); Defense 17 (–1 Dex, +8 class); Spd 10 m; VP/WP 93/14; Atk +15/+10/+5 melee (DC 15 stun, stun baton) or +15/+10/+5 melee (1d4+3, punch) or +11/+6/+1 ranged (3d6, blaster pistol); SV Fort +10, Ref +3, Will +5; SZ M; FP 1; DSP 0; Rep +1; Str 16, Dex 8, Con 14, Int 14, Wis 13, Cha 12. Challenge Code E.

Equipment: Blaster pistol (concealed), stun baton (concealed), headset comlink, identification, 2,000 credits.

Skills: Astrogate +4, Climb +5, Computer Use +4, Diplomacy +3, Disguise +5, Gather Information +3, Intimidate +10, Knowledge (Selonia) +11, Knowledge (tactics) +10, Pilot +9, Profession (Iotran police) +15, Read/Write Basic, Search +8, Sense Motive +7, Speak Basic, Spot +7, Swim +5, Treat Injury +8.

Feats: Armor Proficiencies (heavy, light, medium), Athletic, Blind-Fight, Combat Reflexes, Heroic Surge, Improved Initiative, Low Profile, Martial Arts, Power Attack, Quick Draw, Track, Trustworthy, Weapon Group Proficiencies (blaster pistols, blaster rifles, heavy weapons, simple weapons, vibro weapons).

Talus

Planet Type: Terrestrial
Climate: Temperate
Terrain: Forests, mountains
Atmosphere: Breathable
Gravity: Standard
Diameter: 9,950 km
Length of Day: 24 standard hours
Length of Year: 392 standard days
Sentient Species: Human, Drall, Selonian
Languages: Basic, Drallish, Selonian
Population: 3.2 million
Species Mix: 64% Human, 21% Selonian, 11% Drall, 4% other
Government: Federation of the Double Worlds
Major Exports: Foodstuffs, metals, minerals
Major Imports: High-tech goods, medicinal goods

Tralus

Planet Type: Terrestrial
Climate: Temperate
Terrain: Forests, mountains
Atmosphere: Breathable
Gravity: Standard
Diameter: 9,710 km
Length of Day: 24 standard hours
Length of Year: 392 standard days
Sentient Species: Human, Drall, Selonian
Languages: Basic, Drallish, Selonian
Population: 2.4 million
Species Mix: 72% Human, 13% Selonian, 9% Drall, 6% other
Government: Federation of the Double Worlds
Major Exports: Foodstuffs, metals, minerals
Major Imports: High-tech goods, medicinal goods

Centerpoint Station

Planet Type: Artificial
Climate: Temperate
Terrain: Artificial
Atmosphere: Breathable
Gravity: Standard (none at poles)
Diameter: 100 km
Length of Day: 12 standard hours
Length of Year: 392 standard days
Sentient Species: Human, Drall, Selonian
Languages: Basic, Drallish, Selonian
Population: 540,000 at peak
Species Mix: 85% Human, 8% Drall, 5% Selonian, 2% other
Government: Executive Secretariat controlled by Fed-Dub
Major Exports: None
Major Imports: None
System/Star: Corellia/Corell

Planets	Type	Moons
Corellia	Terrestrial	0
Drall	Terrestrial	0
Talus	Terrestrial	0
Tralus	Terrestrial	0
Centerpoint	Artificial	0
Selonia	Terrestrial	0
Crollia	Barren rock	0
Soronia	Frozen rock	0

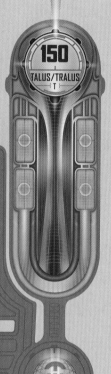

Description

The Double Worlds of Talus and Tralus orbit a common center of gravity as they revolve around the star Corell. At the center of mass between the two planets lies the ancient space station known as Centerpoint. Because of the two planets' proximity, Talus and Tralus are subject to greater than normal tidal forces. Savage windstorms and huge tidal surges are routine, and quakes are common.

Talus and Tralus revolve around Centerpoint every twenty-eight days (a local month) and around Corell every 392 days. The world closer to Corell at a given moment is "leading," while the other is "lagging." In the middle of a planet's fourteen-day lagging phase, it is eclipsed by the leader. Corell's light fades for a day, disappears almost entirely for another day, and slowly reappears over the next day. The severity of these eclipses varies—most are partial, but each world averages three total eclipses per year. Double Worlds astrology holds that those born on the lagging world during a total eclipse are favored by the heavens.

Centerpoint is a 100-kilometer-diameter sphere with twin cylinders extending from its equator. Thousands of years ago, explorers found its spherical core, which was illuminated by an artificial sun called the Glowpoint. Within a few generations, this core—dubbed Hollowtown—contained artificial lakes, farms, towns, and estates.

Centerpoint's secret is that it is a huge tractor-repulsor that can tow a planet across space through a hyperspace tunnel. This was the mechanism by which the Corellian system was assembled eons ago by an unknown species. The station can also be used to jam communications in a given area, interdict an entire star system, or even cause a star to explode in a supernova.

History

Talus and Tralus's ruling body, the Federation of the Double Worlds ("Fed-Dub"), was founded some five hundred years ago. It has long maintained standoffish relations with the rest of the system. In the Old Republic's final days, the Double Worlds saw an influx of Selonians, Drall, and Corellians tired of problems on their homeworlds. These immigrants fueled a boom in mining and agriculture.

That period ended during the Corellian Crisis, which came fourteen years after the destruction of the second Death Star. It began when the Sacorrian Triad discovered Centerpoint's secret. When the Triad activated the station, the Glowpoint—in effect, a pilot light—flared. Hollowtown was incinerated. Refugees fled to Talus and Tralus, where Triad-supported groups of immigrants began a series of bloody insurrections.

After the Corellian Crisis, Fed-Dub reclaimed Centerpoint, only to see it seized by the New Republic during the Yuuzhan Vong invasion. The New Republic intended to lure the Yuuzhan Vong fleet to Corellia and trap it with Centerpoint's interdiction field, setting up a showdown. Fed-Dub joined forces with other Corellian groups to oppose the plan, which fell apart after the Yuuzhan Vong attacked Fondor. With the help of Anakin Solo, Thrackan Sal-Solo fired Centerpoint at the Yuuzhan Vong and Hapan fleets, severely crippling both.

People

The Corellian system's inhabited worlds are nicknamed the Five Brothers. Double Worlders are sensitive about assertions that they come from the least important of the five worlds. After all, while Selonia has its Selonians, Drall its Drall, and Corellia its irrepressible Humans, Talus and Tralus have no intelligent native species. Since the Corellian Crisis, tensions have flared between "natives" of all three species and recent immigrants, who are often accused of being Triad agents. Corellia's Humans hold that the Double Worlds have become a dumping ground for prisoners and undesirables. No one is sure how Selonians reached Talus and Tralus, but the Double Worlds' dens refuse to bow to Selonia's dens, which in turn regard them as heretics. The Drall who reside on the Double Worlds maintain that they emigrated for the opportunity to study other species.

Locations

Descriptions of several important locations follow.

Qaestar Town

Located on Talus, the Double Worlds' largest city is dominated by its spaceport, a half-circle of duracrete platforms located on the Qaestar Ridge, 2 kilometers above town. These landing platforms connect to the city via 20-meter-wide promenades of stone called the Qaestar Steps.

Visitors must get a landing permit and change money at Qaestar Port Control, located at the bottom of the worn, treacherous steps. Spaceport services at Qaestar Town are provided only by violent and ruthless gangs who charge exorbitant amounts, won't take offworld money, and are willing to blast any spacer who doesn't go along with them. Most spacers resign themselves to walking down into town, battling the suspicious bureaucracy of Port Control, then walking back up the steps and handing over too much money to gangs that work too slowly. To make matters worse, ramshackle cantinas and flophouses clog the promenades, and beggars and thugs are thick there. Veteran spacers grumble that "getting into Qaestar's easier than getting out." Neophytes don't realize that the locals aren't just talking about the walk.

Sea of Jarad

This storm-tossed Tralus sea is far from the equator, where most major settlements are found. Life here is a throwback to an earlier age. Human clans and some Selonian dens (joined by the occasional offworlder who has proved her worth) form fleets of wide-hulled, oared ships called nagaks. Sea creatures known as styanax come to the Jarad to mate. They are pursued by hunters called stabmen, who harpoon them from nagaks. While few on Tralus have ever seen a live styanax, the lore of the hunt is a vital part of the planet's culture.

Hollowtown

Nestled at Centerpoint Station's heart is a 60-kilometer-diameter sphere warmed by the superhot Glowpoint. For millennia, farming communities and luxury estates huddled along the inner face of this sphere. The Glowpoint's activation turned Hollowtown into charred debris. Adventurers who visit the sphere after this disaster find ruins occupied only by Fed-Dub soldiers and scientists.

Hunting the Styanax

A styanax lance is a barbed spearhead trailing 100 meters of line, fired with a windlass-powered compressed-air launcher.

When the weapon's spearhead hits a styanax, the creature takes 3d4 points of damage, and a tug of war begins as the stabman tries to reel in the creature. On each succeeding round, the stabman and the styanax make opposed Strength checks, with the styanax taking a cumulative –1 penalty on its Strength check each round after the first that it's been lanced. The styanax takes 2d4 points of damage each round. If the stabman wins a Strength check, he draws the styanax 6d4 meters closer. A styanax is not reeled in if it wins an opposed Strength check; if it wins by 5 or more, it breaks free.

A styanax stops fighting when its vitality points drop to 0. It may then be reeled in at 24 meters per round.

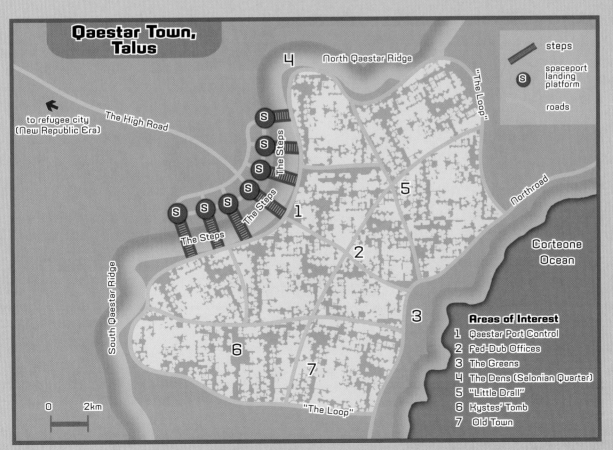

Qaestar Town, Talus

to refugee city
(New Republic Era)

The High Road

North Qaestar Ridge

"The Loop"

The Steps

The Steps

The Steps

South Qaestar Ridge

Northroad

Corteone Ocean

"The Loop"

steps

spaceport landing platform

roads

Areas of Interest
1 Qaestar Port Control
2 Fed-Dub Offices
3 The Greens
4 The Dens (Selonian Quarter)
5 "Little Drall"
6 Kystes' Tomb
7 Old Town

0   2km

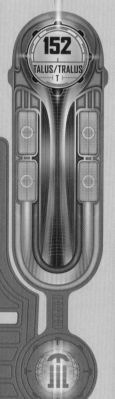

For the GM

The adventure hooks and supporting characters described in this section are meant for GMs only. If you're a player, stop reading now.

Adventures

Feel free to use or adapt the following adventure hooks for your home campaign.

Qaestar Missteps

The characters set down on the Qaestar Ridge on a mission to Talus but don't know about the spaceport's odd traditions. A young Selonian picks their pockets the moment their feet touch the duracrete, racing off on all fours down the promenade into Qaestar Town. If the characters give chase, it takes them hours to find the thief. When they return to their ship, they find that a service gang from the Qaestar Steps has locked them out of their vessel. The ruffians are engaged in a wild firefight with a rival gang. Untangling the mess could be a problem, particularly if Qaestar Town authorities arrive and decide to blame the whole thing on ignorant offworlders.

An Offer You'd Better Not Refuse

On Talus and Tralus, "What's your sign?" isn't just a cantina pick-up line. Astrology is a near religion, thanks to the Double Worlds' complex orbital interactions and frequent eclipses. For this adventure, one of the charac-

ters (or one of their associates from insystem) was born during a total eclipse on Talus—a very propitious time. Word gets to the superstitious gangleader Gentius Parl, who decides that his latest scheme can only succeed if the character with the lucky birthday plays a key role. The mission could be anything from a trip to recover lost treasure to a risky battle plan for eliminating a rival gang. Parl starts by trying to charm the characters into taking part, but he isn't inclined to take no for an answer, and he'll bring the "lucky" character along as a hostage if he must.

Beneath the Spine

A scout ship crashes in Kystes' Spine, a range of spikes and spires that marches from north to south across the continent of Aximia on Talus. The crashed ship bears a datacard with critical information. (Depending on the era, it could be the location of a Trade Federation battle droid factory, the plans for an Imperial battle-group deployment, or intercepted Yuuzhan Vong communications.) The heroes discover that a crew member took the datacard and fled into the tunnels beneath the Spine. Locating the missing datacard will be a challenge. Xenophobic Selonians dwell under the Spine, doing battle in the tunnels. The dens' champions are sometimes sent on revenge missions against intruders who profane the Spine with their presence—such as unwary heroes. To have any chance of finding the datacard in the winding tunnels, the heroes must win over or defeat a band of Selonian

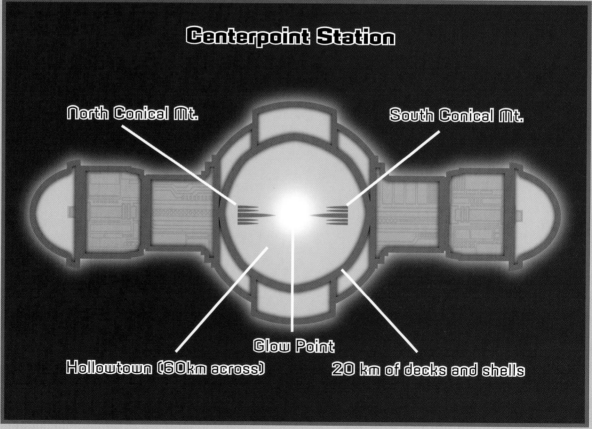

Centerpoint Station

North Conical Mt.   South Conical Mt.

Glow Point

Hollowtown (60km across)   20 km of decks and shells

champions and evade patrols of subterranean horrors called dimlurkers.

Killing a Legend
The heroes' quarry has sought refuge on Tralus among the styanax hunters of the Jarad. (Depending on the era, the heroes may be hunting a Dark Jedi, a Rebel agent, a fugitive smuggler, or a Yuuzhan Vong collaborator.) The heroes find a nagak captain who agrees to help them search for their quarry, but only if they prove their worth by recording a styanax kill under the eye of one of the Jarad's legendary stabmen. This won't be easy. First off, killing a styanax is no mean feat. What's more, stabmen are a competitive lot. Some apprentice stabmen must wait patiently for years before getting a chance to ride in a nagak prow and earning the privilege of firing the first shot at a styanax. The heroes must not only master a difficult trade but also survive the intrigues of their fellow crew members and become accepted as part of the crew.

Salvage Mission
One of Hollowtown's residents was Eben Kinahay, a Talusian collector of antiquities whose trove supposedly included a Sith holocron plucked from a derelict ship on Ziost centuries ago. He lived in a heavily guarded estate that dominated a wooded island on Sapphire Lake. The edifice had beautiful shadow-shields of gold that simulated day, night, and the seasons. The heroes are hired to find the wreckage of the estate in the seared interior of Centerpoint and recover the holocron. A gang of Selonian toughs led by Kinahay's son, Zyne, are after the same prize. Zyne Kinahay is no stranger to the holocron and its dark powers.

A Double Worlds Campaign
The Gamemaster can combine the above adventures into one long-running story. The heroes arrive at Qaestar and immediately run into trouble with spaceport gangs. They are rescued by Gentius Parl, who has been hired to find the Sith holocron but believes he can't succeed without an associate born during a total eclipse. Fortunately, one of the heroes (or an associate of the heroes) fits the bill.

After joining forces with Parl, the heroes go to Kinahay's Talus estate, where his effects are up for auction. The holocron isn't among the items for bid, but the heroes learn that a Kinahay retainer escaped in a scout ship with stolen goods, only to crash amid the peaks of Kystes' Spine. The heroes pursue the retainer beneath the mountains. Although they don't capture him, they do retrieve the datacard—only to find that it's encrypted, and the retainer has the only key to unlock it.

The retainer goes into hiding on Tralus, where the heroes must prove themselves as stabmen to get the styanax hunters of the Jarad to help track him down. Once they do so, they can find and enter Eben Kinahay's vaults in Hollowtown, setting the stage for a showdown with the evil Zyne Kinahay. Along the way, Gentius Parl may betray them—particularly if his "lucky" associate is incapacitated or killed.

Allies and Antagonists
The following supporting characters are designed for use in your campaign.

Gentius Parl
Parl is a tough brawler whose ferocity and brains mark him as an up-and-comer among the gangs of the Qaestar Steps. He wears his black hair long beneath an iridescent polycloth bandanna, a piratical style adopted by other members of his gang. Parl has a nose for business that on occasion can include the idea of making a completely legitimate deal. He also is a dedicated student of Double Worlds astrology and almost never makes a move without a detailed forecast to determine whether the heavens favor him or not. If confronted with an obviously competent party or approached by a group of adventurers with a good idea for making credits, Parl may serve as a partner or backer—particularly if one of the adventurers was born during a lucky time. Parl may even do his part honorably. But as the saying goes on Tralus, "Once of the Steps, always of the Steps." If things go against Parl or the heavenly portents turn malign, he won't hesitate to betray his partners.

Gentius Parl: Male Human Scoundrel 6/Noble 2; Init +5 (+1 Dex, +4 Improved Initiative); Defense 16 (+1 Dex, +5 class); Spd 10 m; VP/WP 34/11; Atk +7 melee (DC 15 stun, stun baton) or +7 melee (1d3+2, punch) or +6 ranged (3d6, blaster pistol); SQ bonus class skill (Intimidate), favor +1, illicit barter, inspire confidence, lucky 2/day, precise attack +1; SV Fort +2, Ref +8, Will +7; SZ M; FP 0; DSP 2; Rep +2; Str 14, Dex 12, Con 11, Int 15, Wis 14, Cha 14. Challenge Code D.

Equipment: Blaster pistol, stun baton, comlink, datapad, security kit.

Skills: Bluff +16, Diplomacy +15, Disable Device +11, Forgery +11, Gather Information +13, Intimidate +15, Knowledge (Talus and Tralus) +11, Read/Write Basic, Repair +9, Sense Motive +7, Sleight of Hand +7, Speak Basic, Spot +9, Treat Injury +6, Tumble +9.

Feats: Combat Expertise, Heroic Surge, Improved Initiative, Persuasive, Skill Emphasis (Bluff), Trustworthy, Weapon Group Proficiencies (blaster pistols, simple weapons).

Magalak
A champion of Kurtuln Den, Magalak is a deadly Selonian fighter who seems to know every meter of the tunnels beneath Kystes' Spine. She is regarded as odd by the rest of her den, for Magalak has never seemed comfortable within the tightly knit society. She seems happier in the company of her warrior band. She is happiest of all by herself beneath the mountains, waiting for combat.

Magalak will destroy anyone she sees as a threat to Kurtuln Den, but she is more curious than most Selonians and believes a wise warrior studies her adversaries before striking. In particular, she admires bravery. She may even approach a party on friendly terms if she sees that its members pose no threat to her den and have acquitted

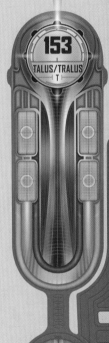

themselves well in the dark beneath the Spine. Her band consists of a dozen other sterile Selonian females, all 3rd- or 4th-level soldiers or scouts.

Magalak: Female Selonian Soldier 9/Scout 4; Init +7 (+3 Dex, +4 Improved Initiative); Defense 21 (+3 Dex, +8 class); Spd 10 m, swim 12 m; VP/WP 100/15; Atk +13/+8/+3 melee (1d4+1, claw) or +15/+10/+5 melee (1d8+1/1d6+1, Selonian glaive) or +15/+10/+5 ranged (3d6, blaster pistol); SQ agoraphobia, heart +1, trail-blazing, uncanny dodge (Dex bonus to Defense); SV Fort +10, Ref +8, Will +4; SZ M; FP 0; DSP 0; Rep +3; Str 12, Dex 17, Con 15, Int 10, Wis 9, Cha 11. Challenge Code F.

Equipment: Selonian glaive, blaster pistol, net, field kit.

Skills: Climb +14, Craft (simple and primitive weapons) +7, Hide +13, Intimidate +6, Jump +13, Knowledge (Talus and Tralus) +7, Listen +5, Move Silently +8, Read/Write Selonian, Speak Basic, Speak Selonian, Survival +5.

Feats: Ambidexterity, Armor Proficiencies (heavy, light, medium), Blind-Fight, Exotic Weapon Proficiency (Selonian glaive), Improved Initiative, Martial Arts, Skill Emphasis (Survival), Track, Two-Weapon Fighting, Weapon Finesse (Selonian glaive), Weapon Group Proficiencies (blaster pistols, blaster rifles, heavy weapons, simple weapons, vibro weapons).

New Weapon: Selonian Glaive

A Selonian glaive is made out of heavy wood and studded with razor-sharp obsidian blades and hooks. A young Selonian champion seeks out the materials for her glaive and crafts it in a formal ceremony (one that reminds some of a Padawan crafting her lightsaber). One end of the glaive is a club, while the other is a slashing weapon. The glaive is an exotic double weapon. Its bearer can fight with it as if with two weapons, but she incurs all the normal attack penalties as if using a one-handed weapon and a light weapon. When advancing in level, Selonian champions select feats to overcome these penalties. A character with the Advanced Martial Arts feat can also use the glaive's hooks to disarm opponents, gaining a +8 bonus on disarm attempts.

Selonian Glaive
Cost: 500 credits
Damage: 1d8/1d6
Critical: 20
Range Increment: –
Weight: 2 kg
Type: Slashing/Bludgeoning
Size: Medium-size
Group: Exotic

Van Jahan Surgoth

Most likely encountered on Tralus's Sea of Jarad, the stabman Surgoth barely merits a passing glance. He is small, laconic, and expressionless, disappearing among the other sinewy, sun-reddened men who crew nagaks. Only those who look closer see evidence of an extraordinary life, such as the white scars that cross his hands and arms. Surgoth is almost comically silent, preferring to teach his craft by showing and doing instead of talking. Given diligent students, he works for hours to instruct anyone willing to learn. Those who learn from him soon find, as countless Jaradmen before them have, the thrill of having earned an approving nod and grunt from a master of his craft.

Van Jahan Surgoth: Male Human Fringer 4/Scout 10; Init +3; Defense 21 (+3 Dex, +8 class); Spd 10 m; VP/WP 81/14; Atk +12/+7 melee (1d3+2, punch) or +8/+3 melee (2d6+2, vibroblade) or +13/+8 ranged (3d4, styanax lance); SQ barter, bonus class skill (Repair, Swim), evasion, extreme effort, heart +1, jury-rig +2, trailblazing, uncanny dodge (can't be flanked, Dex bonus to Defense); SV Fort +12, Ref +10, Will +7; SZ M; FP 0; DSP 0; Rep +2; Str 15, Dex 17, Con 14, Int 16, Wis 13, Cha 10. Challenge Code F.

Equipment: Styanax lance, vibroblade.

Skills: Balance +6, Bluff +3, Climb +9, Craft (space transports) +20, Gamble +6, Knowledge (Talus and Tralus) +20, Listen +20, Read/Write Basic, Repair +20, Sense Motive +4, Speak Basic, Spot +20, Survival +23, Treat Injury +9, Tumble +17.

Feats: Alertness, Blind-Fight, Exotic Weapon Proficiency (styanax lance), Far Shot, Point Blank Shot, Rapid Shot, Rugged, Skill Emphasis (Survival, Tumble), Weapon Group Proficiencies (blaster pistols, primitive weapons, simple weapons).

Zyne Kinahay

A tall, pale man clad in a black robe, Zyne Kinahay might be mistaken for a penitent from any of the galaxy's half-billion faiths. He is far more dangerous, however. Zyne's father, Eben Kinahay, always expected his son to follow in his footsteps as an antiquities dealer. He allowed the boy the run of his vast vaults, hoping that young Zyne would catch his father's fever for ancient art. Eben didn't know that Zyne was Force-sensitive, or that his talent would find inspiration in the Sith holocron that Eben had obtained decades before.

Zyne has not been seen or thought of much in the Corellian system for more than twenty years, but word of the Hollowtown disaster brings him back to the Double Worlds from the path he has been wandering—with a band of ruthless hirelings in tow.

Zyne Kinahay: Male Human Force Adept 5/Dark Side Devotee 9; Init +0; Defense 20 (+10 class); Spd 10 m; VP/WP 95/14; Atk +8/+3 melee (1d8–1/1d6–1 plus 3d8, Selonian glaive) or +8/+3 melee (1d6–1 plus 3d8, quarterstaff) or +8/+3 melee (3d4–1/18–20, punch) or +9/+4 ranged (3d6, blaster pistol); SQ Force weapon +3d8; SV Fort +9, Ref +7, Will +15; SZ M; FP 6; DSP 13; Rep +5;

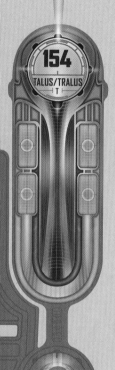

Str 9, Dex 11, Con 14, Int 14, Wis 16, Cha 14. Challenge Code F.

Equipment: Selonian glaive, quarterstaff, blaster pistol, dark side talisman, robes.

Skills: Intimidate +7, Read/Write Basic, Sense Motive +10, Speak Basic, Survival +10.

Force Skills: Affect Mind +20, Drain Energy +19, Farseeing +15, Fear +19, Force Defense +13, Force Grip +20, Force Lightning +15, Force Strike +6, Heal Another +7, Heal Self +10, Move Object +14, See Force +14.

Feats: Advanced Martial Arts, Exotic Weapon Proficiency (Selonian glaive), Force-Sensitive, Improved Martial Arts, Iron Will, Martial Arts, Skill Emphasis (Drain Energy, Fear, Force Grip), Weapon Group Proficiencies (blaster pistols, primitive weapons, simple weapons).

Force Feats: Alter, Burst of Speed, Control, Mind Trick, Sense.

New Creature: Dimlurker

The dimlurker is a horrid predator dwelling in the pitch-black caverns beneath the mountains on Talus known as Kystes' Spine. Eyeless and bone-white, dimlurkers eat most anything, from moss to insects to unwary Selonians. Dimlurkers bludgeon their prey with two flailing limbs that end in clubs of chitin, then hug the opponents to their bodies and constrict them. The dimlurker then opens its toothless mouth, swallows the prey whole, and dissolves it in its gizzard. Dimlurkers move silently and can hug walls or even ceilings with tiny suckers on their bodies. They can be located by the awful stench of rot that hangs around them.

Dimlurker: Subterranean predator 5; Init +1; Defense 15 (+1 Dex, −1 size, +5 natural); Spd 12 m, climb 12 m; VP/WP 29/12; Atk +7 melee (1d8+3, 2 claws) or +5 ranged; SQ crush 2d8+3, darkvision 20 m, terrifying presence; SV Fort +5, Ref +5, Will +2; SZ L; Face/Reach 2 m by 4 m/4 m; Str 16, Dex 13, Con 12, Int 2, Wis 13, Cha 7. Challenge Code C.

Skills: Climb +16, Hide +5, Jump +8, Listen +6, Move Silently +5.

Feats: Power Attack, Skill Emphasis (Move Silently).

Special Qualities: *Crush*—If a dimlurker hits a target with both claw attacks, it can make a free grapple check (+12 grapple check bonus) to grab the victim. The grapple attempt does not provoke an attack of opportunity and, if successful, allows the dimlurker to squeeze its prey in subsequent rounds for 2d8+3 points of damage (no attack roll required). A dimlurker cannot attack other opponents while grappling and crushing its prey, but it can move its full speed. The dimlurker can only attempt to crush creatures smaller than itself.

New Creature: Styanax

The styanax is a ferocious, snakelike, aquatic Tralusian predator with an armored head, fierce jaws, and a vicious

ZYNE KINAHAY

stinger on its whiplike tail. While not intelligent, styanax are crafty beasts. Veteran stabmen tell tales of Old Gloxix, a scarred, stingerless, 14-meter styanax. The creature's black hide trailed a beard of lances and torn lines when he was finally brought down by three nagaks 500 years before the Battle of Endor.

Styanax: Aquatic predator 6; Init +3; Defense 14 (+3 Dex, −4 size, +5 natural); Spd swim 16 m; VP/WP 34/88; Atk +8/+3 melee (1d8+6, bite) or +8/+3 melee (1d6+6, battering ram) or +8/+3 melee (1d10+6, tail whip); SQ breathe underwater, poison, low-light vision; SV Fort +11, Ref +8, Will +3; SZ G; Face/Reach 4 m by 10 m/2 m (4 m with tail whip); Str 23, Dex 16, Con 22, Int 3, Wis 13, Cha 9. Challenge Code D.

Skills: Listen +10, Move Silently +10, Spot +10, Swim +18.

Feats: Alertness, Power Attack, Skill Emphasis (Swim).

Special Qualities: *Poison*—Any creature stung by the styanax's tail must make a Fortitude save (DC 19) or take 2d6 points of temporary Strength damage; a second save must be made 1 minute later (same DC) to negate an additional 2d6 points of temporary Strength damage.

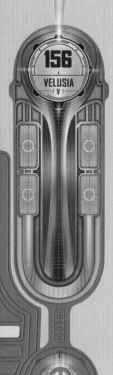

Velusia

Planet Type: Oceanic
Climate: Temperate
Terrain: Volcanic mountains, oceans
Atmosphere: Breathable
Gravity: Standard
Diameter: 9,650 km
Length of Day: 22 standard hours
Length of Year: 325 standard days
Sentient Species: Aquar
Languages: Basic
Population: 2.8 million
Species Mix: 68% Aquar, 32% other
Government: Corporate
Major Exports: Fish
Major Imports: Foodstuffs, high-tech goods
System/Star: Velus

Planets	Type	Moons
Sulphor	Searing rock	0
Velusia	Oceanic	2
Chronos Belt	Asteroid belt	–
Velumia	Gas giant	7
Vilimia	Gas giant	13
Iychtor	Frozen rock	1

Description

Velusia is a small planet almost entirely covered with salty oceans. The only landmasses are chains of volcanic islands congregated in the equatorial regions. Several volcanoes are still active. The rocky cliffs support hardy lichens and small, bushlike shrubs, but they lack large trees.

Velusia's greatest natural resource is its mineral-rich oceans. The oceans would yield a staggering amount of ore if filtered with microtechnology, but Velusia's population has not yet discovered this fact. The oceans teem with plankton, algae, and schooling fish, and immense aquatic predators complete the food chain. The shallow oceans (near the volcanic islands) contain numerous coral atolls inhabited by a dizzying array of invertebrates and fish. The north and south poles are ice-covered oceans.

History

Velusia is well known to travelers of the galaxy, but a cursory glance reveals little of interest to most space-faring cultures. The volcanic islands are unstable, wracked by eruptions and groundquakes, making them difficult to settle. The rocky surfaces can't support edible crops, so food must be imported. The volcanic islands have little ore. The oceans, although bountiful in aquatic life, are difficult to explore.

Thousands of years ago, a colony of Humans established a foothold on several of the islands. Over time, they eked out a subsistence living and developed traits suitable for their new environment, evolving into a near-Human species called the Aquar. While harvesting fish and plants from the sea, they raised hardy mountain herd animals to supplement their diet.

Decades ago, scouts from Nexcore Mining Corporation (NMC) discovered Velusia and purchased rights from the Aquar to explore it for ore deposits. The terms of the lease stated that any ore discovered in the next forty years would jointly belong to the Aquar and NMC. If nothing profitable were discovered, all the rights would shift to NMC's control. NMC established a starport and city called Mount Hollow in an extinct volcano shaft. The corporation hired many local Aquar as guides, scouts, and manual labor. Credits in hand, Aquar employees quickly learned about the benefits of modern conveniences.

About a decade ago, NMC discovered that the planet's ore was suspended in the ocean. The greedy corporation is attempting to hide the discovery for a few more years, when the lease expires and all profits thereafter would belong to NMC. To keep this knowledge secret, several Aquar researchers have been bought off, transferred to other planets, or swiftly eliminated.

To maintain an image of innocent ignorance, NMC has shifted its efforts to under-water exploration. NMC does not wish to waste a tremendous amount of money on its cover story. The corporation has allowed Mount Hollow to degenerate into a seedy starport inhabited by unemployed Aquar (who shunned the traditional ways), scoundrels, and petty thugs.

During the Rebellion era, the Empire established an aggressive oceanic harvesting program on Velusia. It employed massive floating harvester platforms to catch aquatic species with frightening efficiency. It's rumored that at least one Rebel cell was secretly located on one of Velusia's volcanic islands during this era.

People

The Aquar used to inhabit the volcanic islands in loose tribes, but now most live in Mount Hollow, employed by NMC or providing support services to the corporation. The recent generation of Aquar has been seduced by technology and shuns the simple customs of the species, much to the dismay of their elders. Aquar wear plain, form-fitting clothes and are dedicated workers skilled in aquatic pursuits. Although unfamiliar with modern technology, they are quick to adapt it to their use. NMC is ruthlessly recruiting the Aquar into its ranks as employees. If the trend continues, the Aquar's primitive culture could be forgotten in a few generations.

Locations

Among the many locations of interest on Velusia are its capital city, Mount Hollow, and the refuge of Khlor, a notorious bounty hunter.

Mount Hollow

Velusia's largest city and only starport is situated in the shaft of an extinct volcano called Mount Hollow. Established as a base of operations for NMC, the city is dirty and run-down. The city occupied the interior of the shaft at first and then and expanded into the mountainside for increased space (more living quarters, storage, and so on). Catwalks and platforms are everywhere. A main battery of six turbolifts provides access to different levels, although ladders and ropes suffice for minor trips.

Mount Hollow is divided into four strata. The topmost levels comprise a starport, complete with four durasteel landing pads at the rim of the volcano. A fully staffed service area is present for refueling and repairs. Nearby storage facilities and heavy equipment for cargo transfer are provided for merchants.

The first few levels beneath the starport contain hotels, cantinas, gambling halls, holovid theaters, and other amenities for travelers. A shopping promenade overlooking the shaft is a popular stop for visitors.

The mid levels contain living quarters and offices for NMC employees. These areas are mostly carved into the volcano walls and are inhabited by Humans and Aquar.

The lower levels were originally designed to house thousands of Aquar manual laborers and miners. However, NMC's financial woes have caused this area to become a seedy location used by unemployed Aquar, petty crime lords, thugs, and other scoundrels. This area is dirty, dimly lit, and wrought with crime and gang wars. The bottom of the shaft is a polluted pool of water that collects during rainfall. A massive filtration and purification refinery processes and pumps clean water to the upper levels for use.

Khlor's Hideout

The bounty hunter Khlor has established a permanent hideout on one of Velusia's volcanic islands. The island, 100 kilometers north of Mount Hollow, is about 7 kilometers in diameter and choked with thick vegetation. Several footpaths crisscross the island. To hone his skills, Khlor is fond of releasing sentient beings on the island and hunting them down over a few days until he becomes bored. Khlor has stocked the island with numerous poisonous creatures, from which he harvests poison for his use. When hiding on the island, he lands his ship, *Predator*, in a gully on the north end and covers it with camo netting. A prefab building serves as his lair; it also

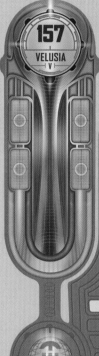

is covered with camo netting and vegetation to prevent it from being located from the sky. The island is riddled with snare trips, pitfalls, sensor trips, and stun mines.

Magna Bolas

This weapon is a trio of metallic, magnetic balls attached by a thin metallic cord. When thrown, it requires a successful ranged touch attack to hit. Although it deals little damage, the weapon is useful for entangling or stunning targets. The wielder decides whether to use the bolas to stun or entangle an opponent before the attack roll is made. On a successful hit, the target takes 1d3 points of damage and must make either a Fortitude save (DC 15) to resist the stun or a Reflex save (DC 15) to avoid entanglement; if the check fails, the victim is stunned or entangled.

See the Character Condition Summary in Chapter Twelve of the *Star Wars Roleplaying Game* for the effects of being stunned and entangled.

Magna Bolas
Cost: 500 credits
Damage: 1d3 plus special (see text)
Stun Fort DC: 15
Critical: 20
Range Increment: 5 m
Weight: 1 kg
Type: Bludgeoning
Size: Medium-size
Group: Exotic

For the GM

The adventure hooks and supporting characters described in this section are meant for GMs only. If you're a player, stop reading now.

Adventures

Feel free to use or adapt the following adventure hooks for your home campaign.

Missing Aquascout

The heroes are hired by Nexcore to locate a missing aquascout. The aquatic exploration vessel was surveying a deep oceanic trench for mineral deposits. Nexcore provides the heroes with another aquascout and basic underwater gear. En route, the heroes must contend with a giant bramblefish attracted to the shiny hull of the aquascout. Following a homing beacon, the heroes discover an AQX aquatic explorer droid assigned to the missing vehicle. After they retrieve the droid, it can give hints to the missing vehicle's whereabouts. Was the Empire responsible? Perhaps a rival corporation is also searching for a vein of ore. Or was it a mercenary vessel hired by a third party?

Escape from Khlor's Island

The heroes are trapped on the bounty hunter Khlor's private island sanctuary. Whether shipwrecked on the island or captured by Khlor as part of an old grudge, the heroes must escape. He releases the heroes and hunts them for sport. The overgrown island is riddled with traps such as pits, stun mines, and swinging logs. Numerous Imperial Mark IV hovering security droids track the heroes' whereabouts while Khlor hunts them down. Several maddened predators have been stocked on the island to give Khlor a little deadly competition.

Allies and Antagonists

The following supporting characters are designed for use in your campaign.

Khlor, Bounty Hunter

Khlor is a Human male adorned in dark clothes. He usually wears a voluminous black cloak to conceal his face. He has pale skin with short-cropped black hair and a matching goatee. A black Velusian fursnake named Sting is always curled around Khlor's neck and shoulders. Khlor is a highly skilled bounty hunter willing to offer his services to the highest bidder. He specializes in bringing bounties back alive and usually sets his weapons on stun. He also employs stun grenades, a stun glove, magna bolas, and electro-nets to achieve his captures. His modified scout ship is called *Predator*.

Khlor: Male Human Scoundrel 6/Soldier 4/Bounty Hunter 5; Init +5); Defense 24 (+5 Dex, +9 class); DR 4; Spd 10 m; VP/WP 140/16; Atk +18/+13/+8 melee (DC 12 stun, stun glove) or +16/+11/+6 melee (1d4+3,

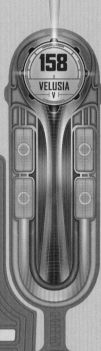

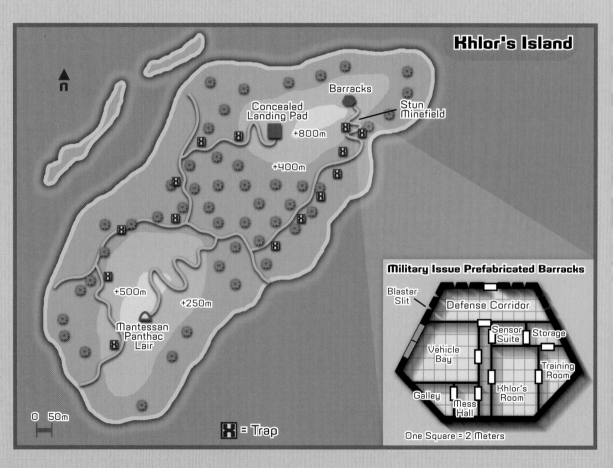

Khlor's Island

- Barracks
- Concealed Landing Pad
- Stun Minefield
- +800m
- +400m
- +500m
- +250m
- Mantessan Panthac Lair

0   50m

⊞ = Trap

Military Issue Prefabricated Barracks

- Blaster Slit
- Defense Corridor
- Sensor Suite
- Storage
- Vehicle Bay
- Training Room
- Galley
- Khlor's Room
- Mess Hall

One Square = 2 Meters

punch) or +14/+9/+4 ranged (3d8/19–20, blaster rifle) or +14/+9/+4 ranged (DC 12 stun, electro-net) or +18/+13/+8 ranged (3d8, heavy blaster pistol) or +18/+13/+8 ranged (DC 15/12, stun grenade) or +18/+13/+8 ranged touch (special, magna bolas) or +18/+13/+8 ranged (poison, blow gun); SQ illicit barter, lucky 2/day, precise attack +1, sneak attack +3d6, target bonus +3; SV Fort +12, Ref +14, Will +6; SZ M; FP 0; DSP 5; Rep +6; Str 16, Dex 20, Con 16, Int 14, Wis 11, Cha 14. Challenge Code G.

Equipment: Armored flightsuit (DR 4), heavy blaster, blaster rifle, magna bolas, stun glove, electro-net, comlink, Velusian fur snake, 6 stun grenades, 4 vials of Velusian fursnake poison, blowgun, binders, medpac.

Skills: Astrogate +13, Bluff +13, Computer Use +20, Disguise +14, Escape Artist +10, Forgery +12, Gather Information +14, Hide +13, Intimidate +14, Move Silently +13, Pilot +24, Read/Write Basic, Repair +14, Search +14, Sense Motive +11, Speak Basic.

Feats: Armor Proficiencies (light, medium), Exotic Weapon Proficiency (magna bolas), Far Shot, Heroic Surge, Martial Arts, Point Blank Shot, Quick Draw, Skill Emphasis (Pilot), Starship Operation (space transport), Track, Weapon Group Proficiencies (blaster pistols, simple weapons).

Vilhona

Vilhona is a slender Aquar with blue-green, fine-scaled skin and light green hair. Her hold-out blaster is concealed up her left sleeve, and her vibroblade has a retractable blade. She knows the lower levels of Mount Hollow like the back of her (webbed) hand. Vilhona was originally hired by NMC to be part of its security force. She completed the basic training program and was assigned to a research facility. Soon afterward, NMC laid her off, claiming budget cuts as a rationale.

Actually, Vilhona was let go due to her sensitive knowledge of NMC's research into Velusia's ocean-based ore deposits. She bounced from job to job until ending up in the seedy section of Mount Hollow. There, she formed her own band of vigilantes, the Sisters of the Crimson Mark. Although they pull off some random petty crimes, the group's sworn enemy is NMC. The Sisters stand opposed to the corporation's abuse of their people and its attempt to circumvent the terms of its planetary lease.

Vilhona: Female Aquar (Near-Human) Thug 8/Soldier 2; Init +5; Defense 18 (+5 Dex, +3 class); Spd 10 m, swim 10 m; VP/WP 25/14; Atk +12/+7 melee (1d3+2, punch) or +15/+10 melee (2d6+2, vibroblade) or +15/+10 ranged (3d4, hold-out blaster); SQ breathe underwater; SV Fort +11, Ref +7, Will +1; SZ M; FP 0; DSP 0; Rep +3; Str 14, Dex 20, Con 14, Int 11, Wis 8, Cha 16. Challenge Code C.

Equipment: Black leather jumpsuit, medpac, vibroblade (with retractable blade), hold-out blaster, comlink.

Skills: Bluff +7, Computer Use +5, Craft (blaster pistols and rifles) +3, Demolitions +1, Intimidate +9, Knowledge (streetwise) +6, Pilot +7, Read/Write Basic, Speak Basic, Swim +12.

Feats: Armor Proficiencies (light, medium), Dodge, Quick Draw, Quickness, Skill Emphasis (Craft [blaster pistols and rifles]), Weapon Finesse (vibroblade), Weapon Group Proficiencies (blaster pistols, blaster rifles, simple weapons, vibro weapons).

New Creature: Velusian Fursnake

Velusia's volcanic islands are host to many avians, and the Velusian fursnake is their main predator. The reptile averages 2 meters long. It has a thick coat of tan-brown fur to help maintain its internal temperature. The fursnake has a large triangular head with a tooth-laden mouth. Although painful, its bite is not venomous. Venom is stored in the fursnake's bony tail stinger.

Velusian Fursnake: Predator 1; Init +3; Defense 17 (+3 Dex, +1 size, +3 natural); Spd 8 m, climb 4 m; VP/WP 5/12; Atk +5 melee (1d3–1 plus poison, sting); SQ poison; SV Fort +3, Ref +5, Will –2; SZ S; Face/Reach 2 m by 2 m/2 m; Str 8, Dex 17, Con 12, Int 4, Wis 6, Cha 10. Challenge Code B.

Skills: Climb +3, Hide +7, Listen +4.

Feats: Weapon Finesse (sting).

Special Qualities: *Poison*—The fursnake's sting injects a poison that deals 1d6 points of temporary Dexterity damage unless the victim succeeds at a Fortitude save (DC 11). A second save must succeed 1 minute later to negate a similar amount of damage.

New Species: Aquar

The Aquar are an offshoot of Humans who have evolved to their current state after thousands of years on Velusia. An Aquar appears roughly Human, with the following exceptions: The skin is blue to green and, on close inspection, covered with fine scales. The fingers and toes are partially webbed, and hair color tends to be green. An Aquar's eyes are large. The nose is flat with three horizontal slits for nostrils, similar in appearance to gills.

Aquar (Near-Human) Commoner: Init +0; Defense 10; Spd 10 m, swim 10 m; VP/WP 0/10; Atk +0 melee (1d3, unarmed) or +0 ranged; SQ Species traits; SV Fort +0, Ref +0, Will +0; SZ M; FP 0; DSP 0; Rep +0; Str 10, Dex 10, Con 10, Int 10, Wis 10, Cha 10. Challenge Code A.

Equipment: Variety of personal belongings.

Skills: Craft (any one) +1, Knowledge (any one) +2, Read/Write Basic, Speak Basic, Swim +5.

Feats: Skill Emphasis (Craft) (bonus feat).

Species Traits: *Breathe Underwater*—Aquar can breathe underwater as normal and cannot drown in water. They receive a +4 species bonus on Swim checks.

Automatic Language: Basic.

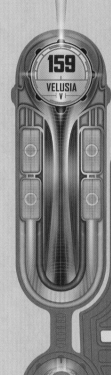

A Cast of Thousands
Starring You!

Join the Roleplaying Games Association, where thousands of members share an ongoing Star Wars RPG campaign, based on the rulebook you now hold in your hands! The Living Force campaign is playing at conventions, hobby stores, and even homes all over the world. Any RPGA member is welcome to play, and the RPGA Network can help you find games in your area, so you'll never have to face the enemy alone.

Anyone can watch the action. Here's your chance to live it. Join the RPGA today.

www.wizards.com/rpga